Emanuel Swedenborg, Elias De La Roche Rendell

The Word and Its Inspiration

with a narrative of the flood as set forth in the early portions of the Book of Genesis, critically examined - Vol. 1

Emanuel Swedenborg, Elias De La Roche Rendell

The Word and Its Inspiration
with a narrative of the flood as set forth in the early portions of the Book of Genesis, critically examined - Vol. 1

ISBN/EAN: 9783337180553

Printed in Europe, USA, Canada, Australia, Japan

Cover: Foto ©Lupo / pixelio.de

More available books at **www.hansebooks.com**

THE WORD

AND ITS

INSPIRATION

ORIGINALLY WRITTEN AND PUBLISHED IN ENGLAND IN THE YEAR 1850,
BY THE LATE

REV'D E. D. RENDELL,

UNDER THE TITLE OF "ANTEDILUVIAN HISTORY."

WITH A NARRATIVE OF THE FLOOD AS SET FORTH IN THE EARLY PORTIONS OF THE

BOOK OF GENESIS,

CRITICALLY EXAMINED AS TO ITS LITERAL SENSE AND EXPLAINED AS TO ITS SPIRITUAL TEACHING

BY THE

SCIENCE OF CORRESPONDENCE,

AS REVEALED BY EMANUEL SWEDENBORG IN HIS GREAT WORK, "THE ARCANA COELESTIA."

APPENDIX

FROM THE WRITINGS OF EMANUEL SWEDENBORG, AS TO THE ORIGIN OF THE SCIENCE OF CORRESPONDENCE.

And I saw in the right hand of him that sat on the throne a book written within and on the back side, sealed with seven seals.—REV. v, 1.

VOLUME I.

FROM THE SECOND ENGLISH EDITION.

PUBLISHED BY
CONNECTICUT NEW CHURCH ASSOCIATION,
NEW HAVEN, CONN.
1899.

WM. F. FELL & CO.,
ELECTROTYPERS AND PRINTERS,
1220-24 SANSOM STREET,
PHILADELPHIA.

CONTENTS.

	PAGE
PREFACE,	v
PREFACE TO THE SECOND EDITION,	xviii

CHAPTER I.
Introduction—General Structure of the Narrative, ... 1

CHAPTER II.
General Structure of the Narrative, continued, ... 19

CHAPTER III.
Original State of Man—The Successive Development of his Mental and Spiritual Powers—His Duty and Prerogative as an Image of God—The Excellency of Everything that was made 30

CHAPTER IV.
The Seventh Day, a Celestial State of Man, ... 54

CHAPTER V.
Adam a Religious Community—Eden, with its Garden and Eastern Situation—How to be kept, ... 61

CHAPTER VI.
The Trees of the Garden: specifically the Tree of Life, and the Tree of Knowledge of Good and Evil, ... 76

CHAPTER VII.
The River of Eden, and its being parted into Four Heads, ... 85

CHAPTER VIII.
Adam naming the Living Creatures, ... 97

CHAPTER IX.
Its not being good that Adam should be alone—His Deep Sleep—The taking of a Rib from him, and building it into a Woman, ... 108

CHAPTER X.
The Serpent and its Deception, ... 118

CHAPTER XI.

The Eating of the Forbidden Fruit, and Expulsion from Eden, ... 139

CHAPTER XII.

The Curse upon the Serpent—The Sorrows of the Woman—And the Curse upon the Ground for Man's Sake, ... 149

CHAPTER XIII.

Cain and Abel, with their Occupations, ... 162

CHAPTER XIV.

The Offerings of Cain and Abel: why the offering of Abel was respected, and that of Cain rejected, ... 179

CHAPTER XV.

The Death of Abel—The Curse on Cain; his Fugitive and Vagabond Condition, ... 190

CHAPTER XVI.

Cain's Complaint and Apprehensions—The Mark set upon him for his Preservation, ... 205

CHAPTER XVII.

The Land of Nod—Cain's Son—The Building of a City, and calling it after the Name of his Son Enoch, ... 219

CHAPTER XVIII.

The Birth of Seth—The Longevity of his Descendants—And the "Translation" of Enoch, ... 236

CHAPTER XIX.

The Corruptions of the Antediluvian World—The Sons of God taking to themselves Wives of the Daughters of Man, ... 253

CHAPTER XX.

The Giants that were in the Antediluvian World—And the Repentance of the Lord that he had made Man, ... 272

CHAPTER XXI.

The Ark—Noah and his Family entering into it—The Beasts preserved therein, ... 287

CHAPTER XXII.

The Deluge, and the Death of all Flesh but those who entered into the Ark, ... 313

PREFACE.

A satisfactory explanation of the early chapters of Genesis has become a desideratum in the Church; for there is no fact better established than that the Mosaic accounts of the Creation and the Deluge are no longer considered to express those sentiments which for many ages they have been supposed to do. What used to be regarded as "orthodox," upon those subjects, has been compelled to recede before the light of rational investigation and scientific discovery. This is admitted by men of eminence,—by minds stored with erudition and piety,—persons whose veneration for, and belief in, revelation are far above suspicion;—professors in our national universities, and other institutions for the dissemination of religion and learning. A decree, therefore, has gone forth against the old notions upon these subjects: the old vessels have been effectually broken; and all who carefully examine the fragments are convinced that it is impossible to repair them. It is true that several new systems have been formed on some modified ideas of the literal sense of those ancient writings; but an intelligent inspection of them has shown that they also are marred and full of flaws; so that there has ceased to be any authorized interpretation of those extraordinary documents.

In this dilemma, the old opinions continue to be taught to the rising generations; and so their minds are prejudiced in favour of a mistaken judgment. This, doubtless, produces no little uneasiness and alarm among those who know them to be untrue. The influences which have exposed the errors have not yet become sufficiently powerful to check their progress. This is to be lamented; but it is one of the consequences of objectors not offering such improved interpretations as can be safely adopted in the place of those which are discarded. The old errors may as well be taught as any new one, if teachings must be enforced on the subject before any more satisfactory views can be established. But why the teaching of demonstrated errors should be persisted in it is difficult to say. It is admitted that the work of him who would instruct society is not completed by pulling down the building which he has discovered to be dangerous: he is not to make a ruin, and then to leave it. In the case before us, the materials remain; and he is required to erect with them another building, which shall be more sound and useful in every particular. The distinguished men above alluded to have not neglected this duty, but they have not been successful in its performance. This is evident from the circumstance of their respective views not having satisfied each other or the public. The reason of this failure, it is believed, is traceable to a misunderstanding of the structure and purpose of those remarkable narratives; *i. e.*, to the supposition that they treat of mundane things.

The following work is constructed on an entirely different principle. It has no pretensions to originality, nor does it profess to offer a complete exposition of the subjects. The writer is sensible of many of its deficiencies, both in these and in other respects. His aim has been to indicate a course of thinking which, if pursued by abler minds, may lead to a more satisfactory treatment. A general outline of the meaning of those remarkable documents is all that he has intended to present; and this, of course, may be filled up with such light, shade, and colouring as the intelligence and experience of the reader are capable of supplying.

He holds that the real divinity of those extraordinary portions of revelation can be most satisfactorily maintained, without making any concessions to opinions which are offensive to religion, or to judicious and rational thinking. The adoption of new sentiments concerning them need not decrease piety or weaken faith: if they expel error and destroy superstition, their uses will be great. Those who, when some new truth is demonstrated to them, abandon a prejudice which they had thought to be an opinion, come thereby into greater liberty and purer light.

The interpretation which is presented in this work of the first seven chapters of Genesis is founded on the following general principle; namely, that the letter of the Word of God contains within it a spiritual sense, which is as its life and soul. This principle, it is believed, will commend itself to the soundest judgment and best feelings of religious and thinking men. Evidences of the existence of this principle can be produced from every page of the sacred volume; and it is rationally confirmed by the circumstance that, as a work of God, it must, to be in analogy with all His other works, contain within it something more than that which appears upon the surface, and something different therefrom.

It is plain that there must be a connection between the natural and the spiritual worlds; and that all things in the former derive their existence, more or less remotely, from some condition and activity in the latter. Now, as God's primary object in making a revelation to man is to furnish him with the means of knowing something concerning spiritual things, it is conceived that he has caused to be employed, in the writing of His Word, the visible objects of nature, to express the spiritual things to which they are related. Thus, that the earth in general, as the dwelling-place for man's body, is the appropriate symbol of that state in general which is the residence of his soul; and that all the various productions of the earth which the Scriptures mention, whether of the animal, the vegetable, or the mineral kingdoms, are the types of some corresponding principle of affection and thought belonging to such state, and, consequently, are significant of them.

Besides this law of correspondences, according to which it is believed the Scriptures are written, and from which their character as a revelation, and their quality as to inspiration, derive the most ample and satisfactory evidence, there are also employed, in their structure and composition, representatives, also significant. Among these representative objects, persons are very conspicuous; such, for example, as the sons of Jacob, the Priests, the Kings of Israel and Judah, the Pharaohs of Egypt, the Prophets, and others. All these are considered to be mentioned in the Scriptures, and to have their histories therein related, because they were designed to represent something pertaining to the Lord's Church and kingdom. This idea is, in some measure, acknowledged, in the circumstance of many of these persons being commonly spoken of as types. Every one, for instance, is aware that Joseph, who was sold into Egypt, was, in consequence of certain remarkable incidents in his life, representative of the Lord Jesus Christ during His manifestation in the world. The law under which those representatives were selected did not at all regard the quality of the person representing, but solely the thing to be represented; all the objects, therefore, which correspond to Divine and spiritual things are also representatives of them; and what is represented is likewise signified.

The distinction between correspondences and representatives is, that correspondence consists in the mutual relation which prevails between an efficient cause and its orderly effect. Thus, whatever exists and subsists in the natural world from the spiritual, is called correspondence. But representatives are all external things which are employed to give expression to internal things, and which may or may not correspond. Thus all correspondents are representatives; but all representatives do not correspond. For instance, when the expression and structure of the face act in unity with the affections and sentiments which exist in the mind, there is a correspondence between them; but when the face does not act in such unity, it then only represents. The kings, priests, and prophets, are said to represent Divine and holy things, not because they were Divine and holy, but because in their governmental, priestly, and prophetical offices, they were, to the natural minds of the Israelites, that which they conceived of things Divine and holy.

Such are the principles which are believed to have presided over the construction of the literal sense of God's most holy Word, and of which illustrative examples are presented in the following work. If the things mentioned in the Scriptures were not representative, and thence significative, of holy and spiritual subjects, it would not be easy to see how a rational idea of their Divine character could be formed; but with such a view of them, man may have some perception of their great sanctity and spiritual uses. Indeed, it seems difficult to see how Divine ideas could have been enunciated in any other way than by means of those human ideas, worldly objects and expressions, which are in correspondence with, or the representatives of, spiritual and heavenly things.

But while this is regarded as a feature peculiar to God's revelation, and, in our opinion, necessary to the ideas of its Divine origin and inspiration, it is to be observed that it is a principle which will admit of a diversity of literal structure; and, consequently, such a structure has always been employed as was in agreement with the characteristics of the people to whom it was originally vouchsafed. Hence has arisen that variety of style according to which different portions of the

Sacred Scriptures are written. This circumstance is more or less conspicuous in all the different books of the Word. There are, however, four great distinctions of style by which the Scriptures now in our possession are distinguished. These are—

First, that which is intended to express spiritual and celestial things *only*, through the instrumentality of an appropriate selection and arrangement of terrestrial and worldly objects. This we regard as the primitive Divine style, and consider it to have taken its rise with the perceptions of the aborigines of our race during the periods of their religious integrity. To them, at that time, it is believed that the objects of the visible world were as an open book, in which they could perceive Divine and holy things represented; and therefore, when treating of spiritual things, they would arrange their thoughts concerning them into a kind of historical series, in order to render them forcible and vivid. This we hold to be the style of the first eleven chapters of Genesis, or rather, up to the 14th verse of the eleventh chapter; and it is in consequence of men in later ages not having attended to this remarkable genius of that most ancient people, that those early portions of the book of Genesis have been considered so exceedingly difficult to understand.

The Second Style is historical, and treats, in the letter, of such facts and occurrences as, from the time of Abram, are recorded in those books commonly called historical. Nevertheless, this style, like the former, is replete with an internal or spiritual sense. Historical circumstances began to be employed for the purpose of representing spiritual things when mankind, and especially the descendants of Abram, to whom those documents, with the exception of the book of Job, were originally vouchsafed, had sunk into a merely sensual and selfish state. Job is evidently a more ancient book, produced, in all probability, upon the plan of the factitious history of the first style of revelation, though it does not appear to be so complete and regular in its structure.

THE THIRD STYLE is the prophetical. This also appears to have derived its condition from the factitious histories of the primitive people: not that it puts on an historical aspect, or that it is, like them, connected in an historical series; for it is well known to be much broken and interrupted, and likewise to contain many statements which, in the literal sense, are scarcely intelligible: still, in their internal sense throughout, there are expressed in an orderly series, sentiments of a purely spiritual character.

THE FOURTH STYLE is the Psalms. These, as may be easily seen, partake of an intermediate form between the prophetical and that of ordinary speech, and they treat of the internal states and religious experience of all those who are within the pale of the Lord's Church.

That these are just views of the style of the Psalms, with the prophetical and historical portions of the Holy Word, we think can hardly be disputed; and although what is stated to be the style of those parts which precede the time of Abram is equally true; yet, because that point may not be so readily perceived, it was deemed requisite to dwell a little thereon in the introductory chapter of the following work. To what is there stated we are desirous to add one or two other considerations.

It seems evident that the Lord, in causing a revelation to be made to man of spiritual and heavenly wisdom, has had respect to the genius and disposition of the people to whom it was vouchsafed. We gather this view from the facts which are apparent in what are emphatically called the Jewish Scriptures. From them it is plain that the letter of the revelations relating to that people, and of which they were made the depositories, was constructed, as we find it to be, in consequence of their remarkable condition. They were a most external and sensual people; and therefore the revelation, which in its external form is peculiarly theirs, partook of that historical and worldly character by which it is distinguished. This was all that they appreciated. Of spiritual things they had but little conception, and scarcely any care.

Now, if it be true that the literal structure of revelation has always been in conformity with the genius of the people to whom it has been made; if it be true that the most external style of revelation to be found in the Bible was adopted in consequence of the sensual condition of the Jewish people to whom it was committed; then it will follow that the revelation granted to a superior people could not have been of so external a character. If the genius of the people among whom the early portions of the book of Genesis were produced were eminently spiritual, and if the narratives be constructed in conformity with such character, then it is plain that the literal sense of that revelation must be different, and ought to be differently understood, from that which has been vouchsafed to the descendants of Abram. It seems contrary to all just criticism to suppose that the literal form of the revelation which was granted to a people who were acquainted with spiritual things is the same as that given to a community who were utterly ignorant of them. We therefore hold that their external structure must be differently understood, nor can we perceive the reasonableness of any contrary conclusion.

It is admitted that the first eleven chapters of Genesis were produced among a people who flourished long anterior to the time of Abram, and there is much reason to believe that they were originated in those periods of which poets and philosophers have spoken of as the *silver age*,—an age in which an Asiatic people were spiritually intelligent because they studied interior truths, and were also acquainted with those outer things in nature which were the symbols of them; an age, therefore, in which mankind would speak of spiritual subjects by means of those things they knew to be their representatives in the world.

Without extending these remarks, it is evident that the earliest narratives of antiquity were written in a style that was highly figurative; and this was a peculiarity belonging not to the history of one nation merely, but to all which have any pretensions to a record of their origin. Upon what principle, then, can this character be denied to that early history in the Bible which precedes the time of Abram? It cannot be because the literal sense of those documents is plain and easily to be comprehended! for when viewed as actual history, they are full of great and astounding difficulties, which no learning that has hitherto been exercised upon them has been capable of satisfactorily explaining. If the genius of the people who lived in remote antiquity were such as we have indicated, and if those narratives were produced among them, then they must have partaken of that genius; if they did not, they could not have been serviceable to them or instrumental in transmitting to posterity any just notions of that disposition and general turn of mind by which they were distinguished.

Most persons will admit that the minds of mankind during the purity of the Adamic periods were influenced by very interior and elevated sentiments; the affections of their wills were doubtless directed towards the Lord, and their understandings were enlightened by thoughts concerning Him. In such an intellectual condition nature must have been a sort of mirror reflecting internal and spiritual ideas. It is easy to conceive that such minds would regard the worldly things by which they were surrounded as the symbol of some internal state, spiritual experience, or heavenly ideas, belonging to the Lord and his kingdom. This, indeed, would enable them—

"To look through Nature up to Nature's God."

and behold, in all its objects, the expressive types of spiritual realities. To such minds creation must have been a rich display of objects, representing interior things pertaining to the Creator. When the people, distinguished by such a state, spoke of natural things, their ideas concerning them would, as it were, recede, and give place to spiritual conceptions. When they undertook to describe spiritual and holy subjects, they would select and arrange for that purpose such temporal and natural objects as they knew would accurately represent them. If these views be correct,—and we think they are admissive of satisfactory proof,—then it is evident that the literal sense of documents constructed upon those principles, was only a kind of vehicle for the signification of something else, and that its genuine meaning must have laid within, as a jewel within its casket.

If such a people undertook to record the moral and spiritual things which they experienced, according to the successive series in which they had transpired, it seems plain that they would do it by the arrangement of representative objects into an historical form. Such we conceive to have been the genius of the people among whom the first eleven chapters of Genesis were produced, and such the circumstances which influenced their construction; those documents, therefore, are not to be understood according to their literal sense, they being factitious history, intended to express, by correspondence and representation, only internal and spiritual things.

Distinguished authority for these views could be cited, and much corroborative evidence and reasonings proceeded with; but it is not convenient to lengthen these remarks. Enough may have been said to commend the subject to the careful consideration of those who may be interested in such an inquiry. It shows the principles on which the following work has been written, and to that the reader is respectfully referred for additional testimony and illustration. The religious connections of the writer will know the source whence these opinions have been suggested; to them, therefore, no explanation on this head is necessary: and it is presumed, that those who may be favourably impressed with them, after the perusal of the work, will find no difficulty in going directly to the same spring.

It may, perhaps, be necessary to offer some explanation of the circumstances which have led to this publication; and also to apologize for defects, which might not have occurred if it had been produced independently of them.

The materials for this work were, for the most part, originally collected and arranged in the form of lectures, which were delivered with some advantages to the church of which the writer is a member. These circumstances led to a request for re-delivering them elsewhere, and, subsequently, to the expression of earnest wishes for their publication. The author knew that they had been instrumental in rescuing from disbelief some who had long been doubting the truth of revelation; also, that they had afforded others more satisfactory evidence of the Divine origin and character of the early chapters of Genesis than they had previously possessed; and that they had assisted many in consolidating their faith in the holiness and sanctity of God's holy Word. As these advantages, under the Divine Providence, had arisen from their oral delivery, he was induced to hope that their publication might be followed by some farther usefulness, and therefore consented to the suggestion of his friends. He is not aware that there is any similar publication extant; and this led him to think that such a work might be generally acceptable to his own religious connections, as well as being, in some measure, serviceable to the public at large. Such are the circumstances which have led to the present publication, and it is hoped that it may supply, however feebly, something for an unoccupied niche in the edifice of true religious literature.

But as to the execution. It was felt that their character, as lectures, would not be so attractive or so generally acceptable as some other form that might be adopted. Hence it was determined to rearrange the matter into the shape in which it now appears. To do this was not unattended with difficulties. For the sake of the judgments of those at whose suggestion the publication was undertaken, the original features of the work could not be entirely sacrificed; and yet, with the view of providing something that might survive a mere temporary interest, some change was necessary. To accomplish both these objects, he has been compelled to admit some blemishes in arrangement, some peculiarities of treatment, and a few repetitions: for these the indulgence of the reader is requested. The notes are fresh matter, which it is hoped will add to the usefulness of the work.

For the general scope and design of this publication the author has no apology to offer, no indulgence to ask, no solicitude to express: feeling assured that a plain enunciation of spiritual truth has been aimed at, and sincerely believing in the religious soundness of the grounds which have been taken for it, he is content to leave the result in the hands of that wise Providence which, in superintending the greatest things of the universe, does not overlook the humblest efforts which are undertaken in the cause of Truth.

In conclusion, it may be observed that if this work had been written for his own religious connections merely, the author would, in many instances, have adopted another mode of treatment and expression; but as it was designed for more general use, he has considered it proper to avoid, so far as convenient, all the appearances of technicality, and to present the subjects in as popular a form as he thought their recondite character would permit.

The Postdiluvian History to the call of Abram is eminently interesting, and should this work prove acceptable, the author will feel encouraged to undertake its elucidation in a similar volume.*

PRESTON,
November 25, 1850.

* This has been done, and may be had of HODSON AND SON, 22, Portugal Street, Lincoln's Inn, London.

PREFACE TO THE SECOND EDITION.

The First Edition of this work, published in 1850, was sold in twelve months; it has since been reprinted in America, and translated into French. These circumstances have encouraged the author to suppose that his labours have been useful in suggesting expositions of the Mosaic narrative deserving of some thoughtful attention. A Second Edition is now issued, in consequence of repeated assurances that it has been desired by no inconsiderable number of the public, together with the expression of a belief that it may assist the cause of those Scripture studies which is now engaging the minds of so many earnest and thinking people in the Church.

It has occurred to the author that a few words referring to the unsettled condition into which the Church has drifted, in consequence of its not having any defined laws of Biblical interpretation, may not be out of place in the Preface to a work intended to illustrate a new principle of hermeneutics.

Much of the agitation which has disturbed the quiet of ancient orthodoxy during the last five-and-twenty years is traceable to the difficulties which science and criticism have discovered to mark the early portions of the Book of Genesis. The objections urged by the sceptics of the preceding century have had but little share in this result. They were coarse in their terms and vulgar in their spirit; and being put forth by the professed enemies of revelation, they did more to shock the piety of the Church than to disturb its faith. But a time came when some of the sons of the Church—men in high places—began to see some discrepancies between the physical condition of the earth and the commonly accepted interpretations of that narrative which was supposed to have been written as a description of its origin. Inquiry sprung up with great vigour within its own pale: it has been conducted with great perseverance, caution, and learning, and now no one doubts the necessity for a revised interpretation of the documents. Geology has entirely put aside those views of the Mosaic Creation and the Deluge which for ages have been accepted as solemn facts by the Universal Church. It is now generally acknowledged that those narratives could not have been written for the purpose of describing the origin of the world and its subsequent inundation. They do not agree with the testimony of the rocks. It is true that much learning and ingenuity has been exerted to show that those narratives may include the facts which science has unfolded; and that by extending the signification of some words and phrases beyond their usual import, diminishing the meaning of others, and viewing the whole as compendious and popular accounts rather than as exact histories, they may still be accepted by many as having a substratum of physical truth. These efforts, however, only show the lingerings of mistaken opinions, and the reluctance with which they are being abandoned. They do not prove that which they are made use of to maintain. Besides, they appear to us to aim a blow at the *inspiration* of those ancient writings, not intended but nevertheless real, and certainly fatal to that idea respecting them. Moreover, of what use are such documents as a *revelation* concerning physical occurrences, if the phenomena described do not agree with the facts discovered? It is said that Scripture is not given to teach us science. This is very true; but how can those who insist that Moses has given the literal history of the creation and a universal deluge escape the conclusion that statements are made to which science is opposed? Is not this, in effect, saying that the Scriptures reveal a science that is not true? But their inspiration implies that they are "God-breathed." How, then, can narratives, not accurate in the facts which it is supposed was their main object to communicate, be said to be *inspired?*—how can the words of such narratives be so distinguished if they have no settled significance? How can an individual be said to be inspired to write that which is inexact of physical processes, if such processes were the object of his writing, and to make use of terms which should be elastic or contracted in their meaning, simply to provide plausibility for that which is scientifically inaccurate? In such a view nothing is clear but its confusion. All the efforts which have been made by those reasonings to remove the discrepancies between the narrative adverted to and the discoveries of science, seem to overlook the idea of their inspiration. They appear to forget that those documents were really provided by Divine superintendence; and that this having been their origin, they must be accurate in the facts they are intended to reveal. This is not the case with the narratives before us, supposing them to treat of physical occurrences, and therefore we are compelled to seek for the facts referred to in some other phases of created existence. Where can they be found? We answer, in different states of the human mind; its relation to the Creator, and its separation from him. These, and not natural phenomena, seem to us to be the real purpose of a revelation from God to man; and those early narratives, like the parables of the Lord in later times, are figurative histories of spiritual events, true in their nature and exact in their expression. The most ancient form of thought is figurative language; it is well known to have prevailed throughout the East from the remotest times. God, however, did not adopt it as the vehicle for his revelation, because it was the style of those nations; but it became prevalent in those nations, because it was the original style which God mercifully employed to convey his instructions to the world.

Believing that, in the narratives to which we have adverted, there is given the history of the rise of humanity, its temptation, and fall; the increase of a peculiar condition of society, and its final overthrow; we also believe that the form in which all those particulars is described is that of symbol. For the adoption of this view, there are reasons respecting those histories, quite as cogent as those which suggest the necessity for it in reference to the Cosmogony and the Deluge. It is this view concerning those documents which the following work is intended to illustrate and explain. It recognizes and maintains throughout the Divine inspiration of the documents, and holds in the utmost veneration the literal forms through which its spiritual teachings are conveyed. The difficulties of those forms are noticed and occasionally dwelt upon, not because they trench upon the real significance of the histories, but chiefly to show the untenable nature of their literal interpretation: they are produced, simply to deal with what are considered to be mistaken explanations, in order to prepare the way for those expositions of the internal sense by which the letter can be satisfactorily reconciled with its spiritual purpose, and the whole triumphantly maintained as a Divine composition.

Since the publication of the first edition of this work, now fourteen years ago, many circumstances have transpired within the pale of the professing Church, which show very plainly that a mental revolution is progressing in reference to theological opinion and Scriptural interpretation. All parties seem to feel that much, which for many ages has been taken for granted, requires reconsideration. They are experiencing something of the growth of that spiritual liberty which is peculiar to our times, and they are influenced to inquire into and reason upon some of those theological sentiments which were originally forced into the Church by ancient controversies, and since then maintained more by ecclesiastical authority than by intellectual demonstration. Interpretations of Scripture are being revised; the "Articles of Religion" are discovered to have been loosely drawn; the utterances of the Church are distinguished from the testimony of Scripture. The history of the Creeds shows them to have been the outgrowth of subtlety and disputation: there is scarcely a subject in the whole field of theological inquiry that is not undergoing some scrutiny, with a view to bring it back to, and base it upon the simple evidence of Scripture. The whole mental fabric of the Church has been thoroughly disturbed, and there are few but the intellectually idle and indifferent who are not looking forward for something more perfect to come.

This state of things, which had been fermenting for a considerable period, at last found for itself a loud utterance in the "Essays and Reviews," and subsequently in the "Pentateuch," &c., of Bishop Colenso. These works represent a large party in the Church; not that the party endorse all the views which are stated, but that they sympathize with the dissatisfaction which is indicated, and the progress that is aimed at. The opinions suggested in those works, though sustained with much learning, and surrounded with an admirable spirit, are not such as we could implicitly accept: they appear to rest upon a principle which does not sufficiently acknowledge the Divine origin of the Scriptures, and which takes but little notice of their inspiration; and their tendency is rather to widen the boundaries of religious thinking than to build up a religious fabric. The opponents of those works, though strongly asserting the divinity and inspiration of the Word, do not seem to have any clear idea upon these points; certainly nothing that can be defined as a principle, and which can be appealed to as a proof. Hence, although there has been an abundance of replies, there has been a paucity of refutations. There have been arguments without reason, denunciations without caution, and persecution without mercy. Though the provocations were serious, the means taken for removing them have scarcely been efficient. The true materials for this purpose lie in a clear knowledge of those principles, in which the divinity and inspiration of the Word consist, and this neither party has possessed. The progressionists either forget or ignore those characteristics of the Word; their opponents insist upon their existence, but are not capable of defining their nature: and these, not satisfied with what argument could do, have called the law courts into requisition, and been worsted in the contest. The disputes have been tried, not as questions of truth or error, but as matters of ecclesiastical legality, and it has been declared, by the highest authority in the land, that the Liturgy does not express those stringent sentiments which the prosecutors had supposed. They have therefore failed in their effort to put a limit to religious utterance, and the party of progress have established the right to speak on such subjects with the freedom in which they have indulged. The Archbishop of Canterbury, in a recent charge delivered to the clergy on the miscarriage of this prosecution, expressly says, "I felt I was in nowise called upon to attempt a definition of inspiration, seeing that the Church has not thought fit to prescribe one." This is certainly the declaration of a dilemma. The matters in dispute remain precisely as they were, and what can settle those differences but arguments based upon a just appreciation of the divinity of the Scriptures, and a thorough definition of that in which their inspiration consists? Legal prosecution may pain the defendants, but it never will convince them; nor will any argument bring the disputation to an end which is not conducted on both sides from some well-defined principle concerning the divinity of the

Word. This is not merely the prior, but the grand question which the Church should endeavour to understand.

Amidst those controversies of the Establishment, Nonconformists have been advancing in liberality and learning; but the Roman Church, which never changes, has been looking on with rejoicing, and congratulating herself that she has the ability to settle all such matters by means of her authority,—that is, to silence inquiry without explanation, and punish doubt with the fears of anathema. Nevertheless, the troubles to which we have adverted have more or less infested every branch of the Church; nor are they yet allayed; quietude is not to be mistaken for peace: the fermentations are still going on; purification will follow. Those difficulties are in the hands of a wise Providence, and they may be viewed as storms which tend to clear the atmosphere, and open out a bluer sky and a brighter sunshine. We think there can be no doubt in the minds of those who can take note of the signs of the times, that there are some new and beneficent influences at work, designed to bring about some new perceptions concerning the WORD, and thus to enable the Church to ground its teachings upon a firmer and more intellectual basis than any it has previously enjoyed.

All the difficulties by which it has been assailed, all the perplexities by which it has been disturbed, have arisen out of some imperfect apprehension concerning the real nature of the Word. All parties, indeed, concede that it is a Divine composition; that is, they make use of the terms, but fail to define their significance. Evangelical learning is contributing no little information towards a better understanding of some of its literal contents. Travels and Archæology are bringing some of their valuable acquirements to assist in this desirable work; Natural History is rendering help of considerable importance; indeed, every department of knowledge is being brought into requisition to subserve this noble purpose. But all those efforts to aid us with a better understanding of the letter of the Scriptures have not yet added anything by which to comprehend the nature of its inspiration. To prove the truth of the letter, in cases of obscurity and doubt, is of great concern to all who believe in its Divine origination, but that of itself is no certainty of its inspiration: truth, indeed, is necessary to it, but it is no evidence of it. A great variety of books are true concerning the subjects on which they treat, but no one supposes that this is the result of anything beyond ordinary human ability and observation. It is also possible to write of truths in principle which may not be strictly accurate in form: of this the parables afford a beautiful example. To prove, then, that the subjects generally treated of in the Bible are true, does not explain to us anything upon the subject of its inspiration; that is a question which lies deeper than the teachings of the mere letter of the Word, and it is to be opened out by other considerations.

As before observed, the professing Church has no settled definition concerning the inspiration of the Scriptures. Differences of opinion prevail, both as to its nature and extent, and no party ventures to explain how they are inspired, otherwise than that they were written by men peculiarly illuminated for the purpose. According to this view, it was the writers who were inspired rather than their writings. No doubt the writers of the Divine Word were under some abnormal condition at the time they wrote. Many of them expressly say the Word of the Lord came unto them; and this must be true of all that is really divine in the Word. But where is the evidence of this fact? Surely there is something bequeathed to us in the writings of these persons by which to corroborate so grave a statement. The history, prophecy, doctrines, commands, promises, reproofs, and exhortations which they contain are all eminently serviceable to this purpose; but there are multitudes of things associated with all those particulars which go to weaken the force of the evidence with those critics who see nothing in the Scriptures besides that which is apparent in the letter. They say the letter, in numerous places, appears like an ordinary writing, neither so perspicuous in its style, so sublime in its subjects, nor so elegant in its diction, as that which distinguishes a variety of secular compositions: hence they say, "What can be the meaning of this passage?" "What can be the signification of that?" "Can this be Divine?" "Is it possible that God, who is infinitely wise, could have spoken in this manner?" and so on. But all those difficulties vanish when it is known that the supernatural influences exercised upon the writers must in some measure have been transferred to the writings which they were moved to prepare, and that the proof of their inspiration is to be sought for in the structure of that which they have written for the edification of the Church. As their spiritual mind was opened to receive a spiritual dictate from on high, it will follow that such a dictate must have been spiritual in its nature, and that, to bring down its significance for perpetuation in the world, it became requisite to clothe it with such natural imaginings as were suitable to this purpose. How can spiritual things be taught in a natural world by any other means? It was spiritual things which they were inspired to know; it was about those things that they were required to write; but these could only be represented to mankind by means of a literal sense peculiarly constructed, so that it might contain within it a spiritual significance. Hence the inspiration of the Word is to be sought for in its spiritual meaning. The literal structure, so numerous in its subjects and so varied in its style, is the medium which the inspired penmen had to make use of to express that which they were inspired to communicate; and as these inspirations induced a spiritual state, so what they have delivered from that state must be a spiritual sense. It could not have required the exercise of a miraculous influence upon their minds to have induced them to write events that were transpiring around them, or which might have been handed to them by tradition or by the observation of others; but it did require such an influence to induce them to select only such natural materials and events as should be the suitable vehicles for the things designed to be revealed. Thus it may be seen that the inspiration of the Word, as distinguished from the inspiration of the writers, consists in its possession of a spiritual sense; and, consequently, it is in that sense that its holiness pre-eminently resides. The letter, therefore, is adapted to this purpose, and though apparently rude in its style, it is more excellent than any other, because, being inspired, it contains something holy in every part of it, and is thus adapted to open heaven to the mind and to conjoin the obedient to the Lord. Hence, in the spiritual sense of the Word we possess the evidence both of the inspiration of the writing, and the inspiration of the writers. This internal sense is not that which a person may discover when he is studying the literal sense of the Word, with a view to explain some doctrine of his Church; that light is little else than an illustration of the letter; but the spiritual sense is, as it were, concealed within the letter, yet discoverable in it, like the soul within its body, or as the thought of the intellect is in the eye, or as the affection of love is in the countenance, which act together as cause and its effect. The literal things spoken of, and the spiritual things revealed, correspond to each other, and the writers have employed those natural images only which are adapted to convey spiritual truth. For this purpose, various forms of literature have been adopted. History, real and factitious, prophecy, poetry, geography, national peculiarities, individual characters, are all laid under contribution. Whatever literal truths there may be in any of those writings, they are all singularly representative, and the main design of their selection is, that they may be the continent of spiritual truths for the edification of the Church. No one supposes that the letter relates all that transpired in relation to the subjects on which it treats: only so much has been selected as was necessary, and this has been written in such a way as to subserve its chief purpose. Occasional difficulties exist in the letter, simply because the literal sense was not the main thing considered in its production; and also because the form in which the letter appears is best suited to convey those special sentiments of spiritual instruction which it contains. In the spiritual sense, the inspiration of the Word and of its writers becomes evident; the divinity of its character is unfolded in greater fullness, and before all this the occasional difficulties of the letter appear as nothing. The purpose of the letter was not to produce a complete narrative in any other sense than that it should be complete for its main design: thus, not for the sake of itself, but for the sake of its spiritual contents. We feel assured that this is the right view by which to meet the questions which have been raised concerning the Divine origination of the Word, and that no defences can be satisfactory which omit to take cognizance of those materials which the doctrine concerning its spiritual sense supplies. The Word has been approached with criticisms much in the same way as any other book having pretensions to antiquity and importance; its difficulties have been replied to much in the same spirit, and all parties seem to have overlooked the circumstance that it has been written according to a plan peculiarly its own; and because they have not gone sufficiently up to first principles, great perplexities have been created. Those first principles we believe to be the internal sense of the Holy Word,—a sense which pervades every part of it, and which, in our estimation, affords the most complete and perfect evidence of its sanctity, Divine origin, and heavenly purpose. The following work will afford some illustrations of the manner in which the recognition of this sense deals with the difficulties of the letter. It shows that such a form of it was requisite to represent the spiritual things intended to be revealed; and while explaining some of the main incidents related of the antediluvian world, it indicates the principle which underlies the form of all that it has pleased the most merciful Father of our spirits to reveal for the everlasting edification of mankind.

E. D. R.

PRESTON, *April*, 1864.

THE WORD AND ITS INSPIRATION.

CHAPTER I.

INTRODUCTION.—GENERAL STRUCTURE OF THE NARRATIVE.

"As to the particular form in which the descriptive narrative (of creation) is conveyed, we merely affirm that it *cannot* be *History*—it may be Poetry."—REV. BADEN POWELL, *M.A., F.R.S., F.L.S., F.G.S.*, *Savilian Professor of Geometry in the University of Oxford.* Art. *"Creation,"* in *Kitto's Biblical Cyclopædia.*

In order correctly to understand the written documents of antiquity, it is necessary to know something of the genius of the people among whom they were produced. Without this information, we are liable to great mistakes. Very different styles of writing have prevailed among the same nations at successive periods of their existence; and the deeper we penetrate into their mental history, the less literal and more poetical shall we find their methods of communication. This fact is not to be disregarded in prosecuting the inquiry we have now before us. It bears forcibly upon the point; and this leads us to ask, Whether Antediluvian History, as contained in the Bible, was written in accordance with that historical and grammatical criticism by which it has been common to interpret it in modern times? We think not. The record of creation has been found to give way before the discoveries and demands of science. The genius of a matter-of-fact people is not the precise thing by which to judge of the literary productions of a period essentially spiritual and poetical. Therefore we may again ask, Whether this peculiar condition of mind, which prevailed during the early periods of our race, when these remarkable documents were originally produced, may not have induced them to describe mental existences and moral processes in an historical form? May not the rise of the human mind out of inactivity and darkness, and its successive advancement into a state prolific with intelligence and virtue, have been described, by such a people, as the creation of a world? May not the intellectual sentiment and living affection, which are successively developed during such a process, have been considered by them as so many days of the Divine Work? We think it highly probable, and can even now perceive a certain general resemblance between the description and the process indicated. Every one is aware that it was usual, in after-times, to speak of the mind of man as a microcosm—a little world; while the Greek fabulists commonly represented man's various sentiments by numerous objects selected from animated nature.

This style did not originate with the Greeks; it prevailed long before they existed as a nation, and it can be historically traced among people of much higher antiquity; the Egyptians, for instance.

If, then, the early portions of Genesis should prove, as we believe they will, not to be a history of physical things, but the history of mental processes and phenomena, expressed in a peculiar way, it will follow that great and serious mistakes have been made concerning their signification, and that most of the valuable information they were written to convey to posterity has been entirely overlooked.

We are aware that there are those who have great hesitation in attaching any other meaning to the words of the Bible than that which they ordinarily bear. They seem to think that in giving up their grammatical sense, or natural application, they must relinquish their real and solid signification. But, as it is evident that there are multitudes of instances in the Bible, in which words are employed in a sense widely different from that in which they are commonly used, that hesitation cannot be well founded. The fact which it supposes cannot be maintained. Moreover, those who consider the words to be significant of spiritual things regard such things to be much more real, solid, and enduring than anything which the merely grammatical sense attached to them can express; and, therefore, the setting aside of their ordinary signification does not deprive them of a meaning that has relation to reality.

The "bending" of the language of God's Book to any other

than its obvious meaning is said to be an "impiety." * But is it not the circumstance of the meaning not being always obvious which necessitates the commentary? That which is plain needs no interpretation; the clear signification is brought out by the "bending," *i. e.*, the interpretation, since without it there are numerous instances in which there would be either no sense or something exceedingly ambiguous. There cannot be any impiety in the honest endeavour to render God's Book intelligible and instructive to its thinking readers. Impiety lies rather upon the other side,—in permitting ideas to be cherished, under the supposition that they are contained in God's Book, when in reality they are not to be found therein, but are crude inductions, arising from erroneous meanings being attached to its language. The very fact that it is God's Book implies that it contains more than immediately appears upon the surface, and thus, that the words are but the outer vehicle of some more interior thought, which interpretation is required to eliminate.

The narratives before us are conceded to be a Divine production; we believe that they, together with the whole Scriptures, contain within themselves much fuller evidence of this fact than any which merely verbal or historical criticism can ever reach. Our inquiries, then, do not involve anything touching their authenticity and genuineness as a revelation from God: that to which our investigation relates is the sense in which the Church should understand them. That they do require interpretation seems evident from the extensive commentaries which, from time to time, have been written for their elucidation. The design of those productions has been, for the most part, to uphold the literal sense of these documents: and yet how very unsatisfactory is much that has been written on this side of the subject, when compared with what a free and philosophical inquiry will demand. When such writers have reached points which have come into collision with the suggestions of reason, they have insisted on the necessity of faith, and pleaded the inexplicability of omnipotence. A becoming piety is always proper in such investigations, but it was never intended to

---

* E. B Pusey, Regius Professor of Hebrew in Oxford. Letter to Dr. Buckland, in his Bridgewater Treatise, Geology and Mineralogy, page 25.

divert us from the path of enlightened investigation. We freely admit the value of faith, and at once concede the incomprehensibility of the Divine Power. This admission and concession ought to induce us to approach Scripture investigation with humility and caution, but surely do not require us to relinquish the endeavour to rightly understand anything that has been delivered to us as a Revelation from God. Reason, considered as a faculty of our nature, is as much the production of God as is the revelation of the Scriptures. They are designed mutually to assist and illustrate each other: and whenever they are brought into collision, it is the result of some perversity on the part of man. When he is in order, the Scriptures will harmonize with his highest wants and perceptions.

Most persons are aware that there are many serious difficulties in the literal sense of the early portion of the Word which remain unsolved, and that bright minds and deep learning have been employed upon the inquiry without a successful issue.* There are large numbers in the Professing Christian world, who are not yet convinced that a right path has been chosen for this pursuit, and many will be glad to have the opportunity of freely considering some new views on the whole subject. These, in the course of this work, it will be our endeavour to provide; offering, as we proceed, such confirmation from revelation, evidence from history, and responses from the living sentiments of humanity, as our acquaintance with them will enable us to supply.

To doubt the truth of certain human interpretations of the Scriptures is one of the immunities of Protestant Christianity; and, notwithstanding religious differences have sprung out of

---

* "The difficulties, which have been usually brought forward in England, as affecting the historical character of the Pentateuch, are those which concern the Creation, the Fall, and the Deluge; and many, who feel these difficulties very strongly, are able to get over them, by supposing the two first to embody some kind of allegorical teaching, and the last to be a report of some dread catastrophe handed down in the form of legend from hoar antiquity."—*Dr. Colenso. The Pentateuch, and Book of Joshua, critically Examined. Preface,* p. xxii. It does not clearly appear whether the writer agrees with this supposition, but certainly it commends itself to thoughtful minds, and we trust that some evidence in support of it will appear as this work proceeds.

this freedom, very generous and enlightened views have been promoted by its exercise. We are about to employ this privilege in another department of biblical inquiry; but for no other purpose, so far as we know our own hearts, than to advance the interest of what we believe to be the general scope, rational meaning, and religious design of the early chapters of the Book of Genesis. We believe those documents to be descriptions of spiritual phenomena only, and think that men did not begin to attach a natural meaning to them until they had descended from an ancient state of intellectual eminence, and suffered their faith to pass into the obscurities of sensual apprehension. We hold that it could not have been the intention of the Sacred Writings to communicate to man instruction concerning physical truths. These were open to the scientific investigation and the common understanding of natural men: and the progress of science, in disclosing the monuments of the past ages of terrestrial existence, has established facts which are utterly repugnant to the popular interpretation of the first chapter of the Hebrew Scriptures. The evidences which geology has brought to light carry us back into an unutterable period of time. They prove a duration to the earth; demonstrate the existence of living structures, of great diversity and interest, belonging to both the vegetable and animal kingdoms; they proclaim the operation of phenomena, and certify to innumerable events, all of which are plainly inconsistent with the notion which regards the first chapter of Genesis to be a *circumstantial* account of primordial creation.

These facts are now very generally acknowledged by learned men of all parties; not that they have abandoned the idea of the Mosaic history giving an account of the creation, but that they have relinquished those long-standing opinions which it was supposed circumstantially to indicate.

The lapse of immense periods of time which geology proves to have taken place before the creation of man; also those evidences which show that, before that event, there had come into being successive orders of animal and vegetable life, differing from existing species, and all of which had as gradually become extinct, are discoveries which affect, in their consequences, the entire view to be taken of the whole subject. These facts, being inconsistent with what for centuries had been considered as the obvious meaning of the Mosaic cosmogony, demand, either that the narrative should no longer be considered as a description of physical creation, or that it should be so interpreted as to harmonize with the unquestionable discoveries of science. The former course was too serious a matter to be attempted. The notion of this record being a description of creation, in some sense, had become too venerable in the Church to be suddenly put aside; the latter, therefore, has been undertaken by learned men.

But after the display of much effort in that direction, it has been said that the object of Genesis "was not to state in what *manner*, but by *whom* the world was made."* This is cutting the difficulty shorter, but it does not explain it. A summary statement of this nature could not have been satisfactory to the authors of it; the details of the narration are too many to have permitted such a result. It certainly does state by *whom* the world was made; but is there not also a precise description of the order of the process, and are there not some indications of the *manner?* Every one knows that all things are distinctly said to have been *spoken* into existence; and there are few who have not noticed the *manner* in which the making of woman was begun. Into what palpable dilemmas will the adoption of erroneous premises conduct us! If it be once clearly perceived that an explanation of physical creation does not properly belong to a system of theology, then it will soon be acknowledged that the Mosaic description, considered as a revelation from God, must refer to other phenomena.

---

* Dr. Buckland's Bridgewater Treatise, p. 33. Art. Creation, Kitto's Cyclopædia of Biblical Literature. Eusebius also says, "It was not the intention of Moses to detail a philosophical account of the formation of the world, but to signify only that it did not exist of itself or by chance, but was the production of an all-wise and all powerful Creator."—*Oracles of Reason*, l. 4. p. 156. *Euseb. Præp. Ev.* 2. 7. "Scripture was not designed to teach us natural philosophy, and it is vain to attempt to make a cosmogony out of its statements. The Almighty declares himself the originator of all things: but he condescends not to describe the process or the laws by which he worked. All this he leaves for reason to decipher from the phenomena which his world displays."—*Scripture and Science not at Variance*. By *J. H. Pratt, M.A., Archdeacon of Calcutta, 1859*. Third Edition, p. 34.

The natural explanations which have been offered are too vague and general to be received as the true meaning of those ancient writings, neither have those views taken any hold upon the public mind. Expositors have not been agreed on any precise theory by which the earth came into existence; and, therefore, they have not succeeded in squaring up the narrative for popular acceptance. Hence, while the old ideas, which used to be regarded as the obvious sense of the history, are thoroughly exploded by scientific discovery, the new interpretations which have been attempted are received with distrust, so that popular Christianity is left in complete uncertainty as to the real meaning of the narrative.

It may not be unacceptable to notice what have been the principal views of the Mosaic record, which those scientific discoveries have led biblical students to adopt. At the very outset it is demanded that the literal interpreter of the Scriptures should make concessions—that he should give up much of the usual and ordinary signification attached to the language. The precise amount of yielding is not defined, but it is evident that it must be considerable.

It was long a customary thing to look upon the stratified condition of the earth as the result of the Noachic deluge. But it is now admitted upon all hands that this could not have been the cause. The vestiges of animals with which the strata abound, belonging to extinct genera and distinct periods, prove that they had lived at incalculable distances of time from each other; also that the strata in which they are found had been very gradually deposited. These, therefore, sufficiently prove that the few months' continuance of the deluge could not have been the cause by which those wrecks were produced.

Another hypothesis was that the earth's strata were formed at the bottom of the sea during the time which intervened between primordial creation and the flood, at which period it is supposed that the antediluvian continents were submerged, and the bottom of the sea raised to supply their place. This, however, is a mere conjecture, at which there is not the slightest hint in all the narrative, and against which there is this scientific fact—namely, the remains of land animals of distinct geological periods.

These two views, in which it has been attempted to maintain the literal sense of the Mosaic cosmogony, by referring geological phenomena to the catastrophe of the deluge, have now no weight with scientific men.

The next opinion which has been offered to the acceptance of the world is that the "days," in which Moses describes the creation to have been accomplished, are to be understood as great intervals of time; and this interpretation, it is asserted, will render his account consistent with the long successive periods which science demands. It is true that the term "day" is frequently mentioned in the Scriptures to denote, not twenty-four hours merely, but an undefined period; still, this fact does not meet all the conditions which the problem before us demands. Moses describes the vegetable kingdom to have been produced before the animal, whereas geology shows them to have been contemporaneous.* This, however, cannot well be urged against the view under consideration, because the mineral substances which enter into the composition of the osseous structure of the animal are less destructible than vegetable fibre. The points fatal to this view of the case are, that those periods of time are not only spoken of as days, but also as the alternation of evening and morning, to which the speculation attaches no significance. Moreover, those who take this view of the subject, when they come to the seventh day, abandon their own interpretation of that term, and insist upon the ordinary sense of it, on the ground of a statement made in the fourth commandment relating to the Sabbath. It is a view, therefore, which is not consistent with itself; neither does it reconcile the facts of animal deaths and vegetable ruin, which preceded the existence of man, with the narrative, which is plainly a description of the successive bringing into existence, and the merciful preservation, of various orders of life; and, at the same time, wisely keeping out of sight everything of a contrary nature. Surely, that can hardly be said to be a circumstantial account of the natural creation, during some periods of which, and long before the completion of the whole, extensive

* "The most ancient marine animals occur in the same division of the lowest transition strata with the earliest remains of vegetables."—*Dr. Buckland's Bridgewater Treatise*, p. 17.

destructions were effected, and concerning which not the least intimation has been given in the record, but all of them carefully concealed.

The force of such, and kindred objections, has been felt, and another conjecture has been ventured.

It has been argued that the first verse of Genesis, or the first and second, should be considered distinctly from what follows, and that all the physical phenomena of geology should be referred to the period indicated by the "*beginning*"; since it was in the beginning that God made the earth; that not being included in the work of the first day.* It is said that the Divine operations in the beginning, not being in any way connected with the history of our race, are passed over in silence, because the purpose of Moses is only to inform us of the progress of creation at the last great change which affected the surface of the earth, together with the production of its *present races* of animal and vegetable inhabitants.

Under this view of the case, the narrative of Moses is not considered to be the history of the *actual* beginning of the universe at all, but only as a statement of the origination of a certain epoch; it having been preceded by many others, each of immense duration, and all distinguished by a great abundance of organic life. This, certainly, is a very forced exposition of the subject; but if it be admitted to settle some of the difficulties which geology proposes to the more common view of the narration, it leaves others untouched which are equally formidable. Some of these it undertakes to deal with in general terms, and others more circumstantially, by *supposing* the existence of phenomena which *may* come within the meaning of the Mosaic history. For instance, it is there asserted that light prevailed three days before the sun, the moon, and stars.†

---

* See Dr. Buckland's Inaugural Lecture: Oxford edition, pp. 31, 32, and Dr. Chalmers' Evidences of the Christian Revelation, chap. vii.

† This objection has been frequently urged: the following is among the most accredited replies of theologians. "A difficulty has arisen in the minds of some critics and commentators, to account for the production of light before the creation of the sun, which has been considered as its source; and they have indulged in various conjectures on the subject. Some have supposed that it was caused by an imperfect sun, in which the elements of

When, then, it is asked,—if those luminaries were among the conditions of the "beginning," in the sense which is claimed for that term,—how it happens that they are described as first coming into being on the fourth day, in the narrative which is considered to relate, *not* to the "beginning," but only to an order of things which began myriads of years afterwards, the answer given is founded on a conjecture—namely, "that the darkness described on the evening of the first day was a temporary darkness, produced by the accumulation of dense vapours

light and fire were not yet collected in sufficient quantities to illuminate the earth. Others have imagined that, though the sun existed, his rays could not penetrate through the dense atmosphere so as to render the surface of the terraqueous globe visible. A third conjecture is that this first created light was only a lucid cloud, of the same nature as the Shechinah, which guided the Israelites by night in their journeyings through the wilderness. But this difficulty has arisen from adopting, with implicit confidence, a mere hypothesis of modern philosophy; an hypothesis which the recent improvements in science serve to render every day more questionable. Instead of the great elementary body of light emanating from the sun, there is reason to believe that light itself is an inconceivably subtle fluid, pervading all space, and wholly independent of the sun, which may be considered as its principal exciter, or the great agent in nature which gives it motion, and renders it the medium of vision. The late experiments in chemistry and galvanism have served to render such a fluid more familiar to us. Further, we know that there are many substances capable of emitting light independently of the sun. Among others may be mentioned, besides culinary fire, the different kinds of phosphori, the diamond, the glow-worm, the Bologna Stone, the fire-fly, ignis fatuus, putrescent fish, &c., and frequently the waters of the sea are seen to emit light."—*Commentaries and Annotations on the Holy Scriptures: By the Rev. John Hewlett, B. D.* We do not see how these statements meet the difficulty. The theories adverted to can have no weight before they are proved to be true: this they have not been; and, even if they had, may not the prior existence of the sun have contributed to the result? Moreover, the facts selected seem to tell against the argument they are intended to sustain. The light emitted by "culinary fire, the different kinds of phosphori," &c., are not displayed independently of the sources predicated: nor does philosophy know of any light—the light requisite to illuminate the universe—independently of the sun. Besides, how numerous are the animals which geologists have exhumed from the earth, and which were embedded in strata unnumbered years before the supposed creation of the sun on the fourth day. All those animals had eyes, and surely that may be taken as a proof of the existence of sunlight at a time immensely before that which the narrative contemplates for the existence of the sun.

upon the face of the deep"; and that "an incipient dispersion of these vapours may have readmitted light to the earth upon the first day, whilst the exciting cause of light was still obscured: and the further purification of the atmosphere, upon the fourth day, may have caused the sun and moon and stars to reappear in the firmament of heaven."* We can conceive some idea of the phenomena here indicated: but they are the mere hypotheses of science; and certainly they do not come within that fair meaning of the narration which they ought to do, if it is to be received as the description of natural creation. We hold that if it had been designed as a *revelation of the process by which the present or any other order of physical nature had its commencement*, it would have been written so as not to have presented the embarrassment which learning encounters and piety experiences from taking such a view of it.

Another opinion has been put forth, more recently than those which have been noticed. This, although somewhat similar to that which immediately precedes, regards the initial verses of Moses to be an announcement altogether independent of the descriptions which follow. They are considered to "express posteriority, without defining the separating interval"; and, during that interval, those vast changes are considered to have taken place in the structure and productions of the earth which science so abundantly demonstrates. This, of course, is urged to meet the conditions of geological facts.† It is next contended

---

* Dr. Buckland's Bridgewater Treatise. Second edition, pp. 29, 30.

† Another theory was set forth in 1857 by Hugh Miller, a geologist whose authority is of great weight. He says: "The conclusion to which I have been compelled to arrive is, that for many long ages, ere man was ushered into being, not a few of his humbler contemporaries of the fields and woods enjoyed life in their present haunts ; and that, for thousands of years anterior to even their appearance, many of the existing mollusks lived in our seas. That *day* during which the present creation came into being, and in which God, when he had made 'the beast of the earth after his kind, and the cattle after their kind,' at length terminated the work by moulding a creature in his own image, to whom he gave dominion over them all, was not *a brief period of a few hours' duration, but extended over, mayhap, millenniums of centuries*. No blank chaotic gap of death and darkness separated the creation to which man belongs from that of the old, extinct elephant, hippopotamus, and hyena ; for familiar animals—such as the red deer, the roe, the fox, the wild cat, and the badger—lived throughout the period which connected their

that the term *earth*, employed subsequently to the first verse, and throughout the whole description of the six days' work, means only a limited portion of the earth's surface, that was to be adapted for the residence of man and the animals connected with him. This portion is fixed in a certain geographical locality of Asia; which, having been brought into general ruin and disorder by geological causes, was also overspread with darkness, similar to that which has been known to accompany the disasters of an earthquake. This was the chaos, and that was its locality.* These speculations being premised, the creation of the existing species of things, the reintroduction of light by the removal of the local darkness, and thereby the manifestation of the heavenly bodies, together with all the other particulars of the description, are said to have taken place literally, according to the Mosaic language, in six natural days. These opinions are elaborately set forth, and their critical defence ably undertaken.† Nevertheless, to us, the argument has failed to be convincing.

It would be foreign to our purpose to discuss any of the details. It is sufficient, for the general design we have in noticing these views, to observe that they suggest physical senses to the terms, and ideas to the sentiments which they express, that never could have sprung out of the narrative itself;

time with our own; and so I have been compelled to hold, that the *days of creation were not natural but prophetic days, and stretched far back into bygone eternity.*"—*Testimony of the Rocks*, p. 10. It is enough to say on this, that it completely abandons the literal sense of the record; and, consequently, it cannot be that history of the physical creation which has been commonly supposed. If God, by the narrative, had intended to teach us concerning the order in which the universe was created, we may rest assured that he would have done it in such a way as to have prevented the necessity for the above speculations, and that it would have been in harmony with the phenomena discovered. What is written is plainly at variance with facts; and Miller's arguments prove the untenability of the theories of Chalmers and Buckland.

* "There are no traces of any such catastrophe as must be supposed, even over a limited portion of the earth's surface, subsequent to the latest tertiary formation."—Rev. B. POWELL, *M. A.*, &c. Art. '*Creation*,' *Kitto's Biblical Cyclopædia*.

† The Relation between the Holy Scriptures, and some Parts of Geological Science. By John Pye Smith, D.D., F.R.S., and F.G.S. Second edition, p. 268, onward.

also, that those senses and sentiments owe their origin to scientific conclusions, and not to the unbiased study and general tenor of the record. We put it to the fair judgment of the reader, and ask whether it is not so; whether it is rational to suppose that the Mosaic description of creation refers merely to certain local phenomena which were occurrent in Asia, and that the command for the appearance of light, with the declaration of making the sun, the moon, and stars, meant only the causing of those luminaries to reappear upon that locality, by removing the darkness which aqueous vapour, an earthquake, or some other geological causes, might have produced. We think not.

We do not understand the authors of the several schemes of interpretation adverted to as designing to make Moses speak the sentiments of modern philosophy; of which, indeed, he could have known nothing. This it would be impossible to do, to say nothing of the irreverence of such an attempt. Their principal aim seems to have been to show that his narrative of the creation is admissive of an explanation not inconsistent with such new discoveries; and so to maintain its position as a portion of the Word of God, which it most certainly is. We highly appreciate and most sincerely value this excellent motive, though we think the means which have been adopted are unsatisfactory and erroneous. We believe that the whole difficulty which these several interpretations have been invented to remove lies entirely in mistaking the real design of the early chapters of Genesis; and, specially, in supposing the initial portion of them to treat of the physical creation at all.

The old, and what used to be received as the pure and simple sense of this portion of the Divine Word, has been entirely uprooted, so that the great mass of the professing Christian Church is, as we have before remarked, actually without any settled or authoritative opinion upon the subject: and enlarged minds have well perceived that nothing satisfactory can be offered to its intelligent acceptance, so long as it is considered to speak of mundane things.

These circumstances have originated the opinion within that Church, and which is making favourable advancement among its people, that "it cannot be history—it may be poetry." The facts to which, as "poetry," it may be considered to relate, have yet to be unfolded. We concur with the sentiment that "it cannot be history":—that is, it cannot be the history of the origination of the outer world with its physical inhabitants: nevertheless we think that it is history;—the history of certain processes of the human mind (as intimated at the outset), by which it has successively risen from darkness into light,—by which its feeble beginnings of intellectual life were developed into more vigorous activity and greater excellence—by which a numerous and diversified series of living affections were brought into active existence; and that, finally, the whole process resulted in the production of that spiritual structure which is described as having been in the image of God.

It is, we most sincerely believe, the particulars of this general process of which the first chapter of Genesis is the history:—a history of the rise and progress of those spiritual things connected with the development of man into the Divine Image, but written in a symbolical style, agreeably to the method prevalent among the ancients—a style founded in the relationship which a high state of human excellence perceived to exist between spiritual and natural things, and which general style has been adopted by God as the true vehicle for all his revelations.

The communication of spiritual intelligence is the chief end of God's Word. Although the disclosure of certain information concerning the beginning of mundane things may be considered as coming within the province of revelation, because without it no absolute knowledge of such things can be attained; yet the main purpose of the revelation vouchsafed to us is, not to teach God's arrangements in the laws and productions of outer nature, but to announce to us the order and operation of an inner life, —to furnish information concerning spiritual things,—to point out the wisdom, show the benignity, and exhibit the love of God for the souls of men. The Bible contains the moral and spiritual history of our race,—that is, the history of the interior and undying things of man, and it speaks of other things in subordination to this object, and uses them solely for that purpose. The natural cosmogony of the universe is not given therein. Although this idea may be reluctantly received, science and criticism leave no choice in the matter.

How, then, it may be asked, are we to understand the reasons which are given for the ordination and keeping of the sabbath; namely, "In six days the LORD made heaven and earth; the sea, and all that in them is, and rested the seventh day; wherefore the Lord blessed the sabbath day, and hallowed it"?* This point deserves a moment's attention.

The Israelitish people, at the time the commandments were given, had sunk very deeply into a gross and sensual condition. They had scarcely any conception of religious truth, and they were withheld from the ignorance and wickedness of open idolatry more from the fear of consequences than from any real knowledge or love of God. The interior truths, expressed under the symbols of six days' creation, had even then long been mistaken for a matter-of-fact history; and, therefore, a reference to it (for some writing, or memorial declaring it, was evidently known to them) as an apparent and not as a genuine truth, became serviceable and useful to a people circumstanced as they were; and who clung with such pertinacity, as all their subsequent history proves them to have done, to documentary and traditional sentiments, however erroneous, provided they had some association with their own history. †

---

* Exodus xx : 11.

"Is it not a harsh and forced interpretation to suppose that the six days in verse 9 do not mean the same as the six days in verse 11, but that, in this last place, they mean six periods? In reading through the 11th verse, it is extremely difficult to believe that the seventh day is a long period, and the sabbath day an ordinary day; that is, that the same word 'day' should be used in two such totally different senses in the same short sentence, and without any explanation."—*Scripture and Science not at Variance. By J. H. Pratt, M.A., Archdeacon of Calcutta*, 1859. Third edition, p. 41, note.

† That the Scriptures contain a great variety of statements which are mere adaptations to the prevailing ideas of the times in which they were produced is well known. That this is the case in the matter referred to seems evident, because it will hardly be pretended that God had so to work during the six days of creation as to experience fatigue and require repose upon the seventh. Moreover, in the repetition of the commandment, given in Deuteronomy v., the above reason for the institution of the sabbath is altogether omitted, and, instead thereof, the sons of Israel were told that it was to be kept in remembrance of their having been delivered from servitude in Egypt; which reason, historically, is a pure accommodation to the ideas of the Israelites in respect to that event.

Besides the reason for alluding to the six days' work in the commandment, founded on an apparent truth, and adopted in accommodation to the prejudices of the people, there is another cause founded on genuine truth, and suited to the intellectual discernment of studious minds.

The sabbath was instituted for a sacred purpose; it was to be a day in which spiritual things were to receive special and distinguished attention on the part of man, because (as all the institutions essentially Israelitish were representative) it represented the peace and holiness of the Lord in having accomplished the work to which the first of Genesis relates, considered in its internal, which is its genuine, sense. When we see, what by and by we shall endeavour to prove, that that work was a spiritual process, by which, through six successive stages, humanity was developed into the image of God; and when we further remember that such development must have been the Lord's own merciful work, then we shall be able to see the force and reasonableness of the argument which the commandment asserts. It refers to a process through which it had pleased the Lord to raise man into a state of spiritual excellence, and at the same time regards this process as essential to the security of all the privileges which the sabbath not only represented, but which, as a selected portion of time, it was to be employed as a means for upholding. The literal structure, then, of the reason for observing the sabbath is in conformity with the literal structure of the first of Genesis, because they both relate to the same spiritual fact, and conduce to the internal rest, peace, and sanctity of man. The people, at the time of the Exodus, had long mistaken the outer sense of this latter document for its actual meaning; but the reason adverted to was not written to confirm them in that error; its true object was to recognize its spiritual design, and, therefore, it is referred to in a similar style of expression,—a style which Inspiration,—considered as the utterance of those living sentiments which were to have responses in perpetuated humanity,—preferred to adopt.

These considerations show very satisfactorily that the Mosaic description is not to be received as a circumstantial history of physical creation. The best minds have been compelled, by irresistible evidence, to abandon as erroneous the popular and long-standing view which has been cherished concerning it: and although great efforts have been made to sustain the idea of its cosmogonal character in some sense, yet it is evident, from the specimens of those efforts which have been adduced, that such senses are not those which Moses intended. But the giving up of such an interpretation of the narrative by no means involves any impeachment of its Divine authenticity: that fact concerning it stands upon other grounds, and it is indicated, rather by the intellectual experiences of mankind, than by any agreement of its statements with mundane phenomena.

However, rational investigation and the appliances of science have not only disturbed the erroneous interpretations which have so long weighed upon this portion of God's Word; they also bring considerations which extensively affect the supposed historical character of several succeeding chapters.

For instance, how difficult is it to conceive that Eve was really made from a rib taken from Adam during a deep sleep induced upon him for the purpose;—that a tree could produce the knowledge of good and evil;—that a serpent was capable of speech, and reasoned so successfully with the woman as to induce her to violate the command of God!

Moreover, in the fourth chapter there is an indication of the existence of another race of men besides those described as the descendants of Adam. When Cain went forth from the face of the Lord, it is said that a mark was set upon him, lest any finding him might slay him. At that period Cain was the only surviving descendant of Adam, who, with his mother, Eve, made only three in existence. Why, then, set a mark upon him to prevent others from slaying him, if there were no other persons than his father and mother to perpetrate the deed? Surely, the circumstance of imposing a mark for such a purpose plainly indicates to historical criticism the existence of another race besides that of Adam. There is also another fact, leading to the same conclusion, related in the same chapter. Cain is described to have possessed a wife; but there is no intimation of her origin: he also had a son, and built a city in the land of Nod; which circumstances plainly indicate that a number of persons must have been there collected, that some of them must have been acquainted with the arts, and many of them industriously employed in erecting required habitations. Farther on it is related that the sons of God, who are commonly understood to have been angels, or at least beings superior to mankind, fell in love with the daughters of men, and thereby originated a progeny that was mighty and valiant. We are also informed that the ordinary period of human life extended over several hundred years, and that the Lord repented that he had made man upon the earth. These, and many other statements which could be easily selected, forbid both science and criticism to approach them, if they are to be received as real and credible history.

This, however, was not their purpose. The meaning of these relations will be discussed in its proper place; we can here only generally observe that they, with all the other peculiarities recorded in the first eleven chapters of Genesis, were never intended to convey to mankind any information respecting the natural world or the early history of its inhabitants.

We believe that their true intention was to describe the moral and spiritual states which distinguished the people of primeval times; and that they are related in an historical form, because that was the method of speaking of such things common to those early periods of civilized life.

CHAPTER II.

GENERAL STRUCTURE OF THE NARRATIVE (Continued).

" All who have treated of divine subjects, whether Greeks or Barbarians, industriously involved the beginning of things, and delivered the truth in enigmas, signs, and symbols, in allegories and metaphors, and other such figures."— CLEMENT *of Alexandria. Strom.* l. v., p. 658. Ox. Ed.

There are few facts better established by learned criticism than that the histories pretending to describe the commencement of the Eastern and Western nations of antiquity are of a singularly allegorical kind, partaking more of the spirit of mythology than history, and leaning rather to the character of poetic imagery than historic truth. The first written intimations which we have of the beginning of society in India, Persia, and Egypt are all of a mythological kind. If we examine the documents which have come down to our own time relating to the commencement of the Scythian, Celtic, and Scandinavian nations, the same fact is observable. And every one is aware how peculiarly applicable these remarks are to what is said of the origin of the more recent nations of Greece and Rome. The city of Bœotia, in the former, is related to have been built by men grown from dragon's teeth, which Cadmus had sown for the purpose; and Rome is said to have been founded by Romulus, who, with his brother Remus, were rescued, in infancy, from the Tiber, and subsequently suckled by a wolf. Nor are the statements made in connection with the beginning of our own country entirely freed from mythos; but no one regards them, and the others referred to, as being historically true, and yet every one must admit that they had a significance well understood at the time they were originally conceived. It was evidently the genius of the people in those times to express some facts in fable. The fables, however, have remained, from their having acquired a permanency in writing; but their significance has perished, because this was not recorded, and also because the genus to which it was perceptible has passed away.

These facts are incontestable, and we are led from them to conclude that the documents of Genesis, popularly regarded as a description of the origin of the world, the beginning of humanity, and the first constitution and progress of society, are somewhat of a similar character, and that they describe the moral sentiments and religious conditions of men through their corresponding images in nature.

The peculiar genus of the people by whom the mythological history of nations was constructed and understood was but the remains of a very superior condition of human character. *Their* mythic narratives were, for the most part, expressed through the fanciful selection of arbitrary and conventional images. But in a more remote antiquity—nearer those times which the poets have described to be the golden age—men lived under the influence of more enlightened perceptions and sounder views. Their superior states must have enabled them to see in natural objects the actual symbols of those divine and spiritual sentiments out of which they had originated; and, under the influence of such a fact, it is easy to imagine that they would be led to express their own thoughts and sensations by means of appropriate images drawn from the theatre of nature. And we conceive that it was in such times, and by men of this genus, by whom, under the Divine auspices, the early chapters of Genesis were produced. Even Josephus, Pharisee as he was, informs us that Moses "spoke some things wisely, but enigmatically, and under a decent allegory"; and in another place he asserts that, after the description of the seventh day, "he began to talk philosophically";* that is, to write his history in some symbolical manner.

The more deeply we look into ancient history, the more certainly shall we be convinced that the style of writing which then prevailed was of an allegorical character, and that the outer things narrated can only be considered as the vehicles employed for the expression of some inward sentiment and thought. Concerning this, many authorities could be produced, from the "Fathers" and others, if it were needful for so clear a truth.

* See "Antiquity of the Jews," Preface, sec. 4, chap. 1, sec. 1.

Origen, however, plainly asserts that the narratives describing the making of woman and the conversation of the serpent were allegories expressive of some other facts than those which appear.*

The period of actual history, apart from that contained in the Bible, cannot be traced with any certainty far beyond the period of the first Olympiad.† The narratives produced before that time, whatever might have been their precise meaning, are found to be pregnant with marvellous relations. Subsequently this method of expression fell into disuse. The genus of the people in after ages became less poetic and more matter-of-fact; and every one now perceives that the wonders indicated in those fragmental writings of antiquity which have come down to our time are not to be received in their literal sense.

This has been the fate of those profane documents, because, not having been hallowed by the sentiments of religious respect, they have been subjected to freer thought. Yet the statements which are contained in the Bible narratives before the time of Abraham are not less amazing; and mankind would long ago have acknowledged their mythic character but for the powerful influence of a traditional opinion to the contrary. This, however, can have but little real weight when it is remembered that such traditions were originated by ecclesiastical authority, at a time when the true signification of those writings had long been overlooked.

It is well known that there is a remarkable resemblance in points between several events mentioned in acknowledged mythology and some of the circumstances related in the early portions of Genesis; ‡ as, for instance, between the flood of Deucalion and that of Noah, and between the Gigantes and Titanes of the Greeks and the giants and mighty men spoken of in Genesis vi: 4. It has been usual to regard those points of Attic and Oriental mythology which resemble the Scripture nar-

---

* Cont. Cels. l. iv., p. 187, Ed. Sp. Referred to by the Rev. S. Noble, "Plenary Inspiration," p. 559.

† That is, 775 years before the birth of Christ, and 22 years before the foundation of Rome.

‡ See "Analysis of Ancient Mythology," by Jacob Bryant. And the Dissertations of Sir William Jones in the "Asiatic Researches."

ratives, to have been derived therefrom, and to consider that the other descriptions with which we find them associated are the legendary embellishments of the respective nations in which they were produced. This might have been the case. But if so, it may be considered as offering some proof that the people esteemed such narratives (whether communicated to them from traditional or documentary sources matters not) as embodying some other idea than what is literally expressed. They would hardly have chosen what they believed to have been the actual facts pertaining to a more ancient people, to express the mythological history of themselves. They must have seen, in some measure, the esoteric meaning of what they so selected, and thence its suitability for being incorporated into their own mystic relations. The extravagances of those relations, of course, render them incredible as facts; nevertheless, they must have been designed to express some ideas and sentiments readily understood at the time of their origination. The adoption of points to be found in Scripture narratives into the fabulous relation of later times, evidently suggests that they were considered of a figurative character.

It is readily admitted that mythological and traditional intimations of the deluge are to be found among all nations. Sculptures among the Egyptian antiquities, and pictures among the more recent nations of Mexico and Peru, have been discovered, which are interpreted to be the memorials of that catastrophe. It is also said that ceremonies and sacrificial rites were instituted for its commemoration among the Egyptians, Chaldeans, Phœnicians, Greeks, Celts, and Scythians.* Inscriptions are collected, and even an ancient medal and a vase have been produced, having upon them objects alluding to the deluge.† These circumstances are commonly referred to as affording the most triumphant proofs that the Noachic deluge was a flood of waters, in agreement with the literal sense of the narration. But we

* Dr. Pye Smith, on "Scripture and Geology." Second edition, p. 101. See also "Records of Creation." By John Bird Sumner, M.A. Second edition, p. 39.

† Dr. Wiseman's "Lectures on the Connection between Science and Revealed Religion." Second edition, pp. 321, 336, where engravings are inserted.

contend that all these facts may be granted, and yet that conclusion be consistently denied.

It is evident that the narrative of the flood points to a very awful circumstance brought about by the wickedness of man. The language, however, in which it was originally described may still be figurative, and the evidences referred to nothing more than the traditional indications of the event so related. All those legends and historical notices must have sprung from one locality and the same description; they, therefore, do not prove that the literal sense of such description is to be received as credible history; they only *preserve* some general reminiscences of the *mode* in which the circumstance was originally related, and do not exhibit its signification. That stands upon other ground, and has to be deciphered by other means.

There cannot be any reasonable doubt that the early portions of Genesis were the productions of a period in which it was customary for mankind to express their religious states and sentiments in the form of allegory. If, then, those documents really did belong to such a period, and were the performances of such a genus, it is evident that they must have partaken of such a style;* and, therefore, they are not to be understood in the sense which the letter conveys; that would be a certain distortion of their true meaning.

In referring the production of those remarkable documents

---

* This argument is very beautifully stated in the following passage :— "Let it for a moment be supposed that it had pleased the Divine Majesty to grant an immediate revelation of his authority and his grace to the Athenians, in the age of Socrates, Plato, and Aristotle, and for their use ; we may reverentially believe that, in such a case, the communication would have been expressed in the terms and phrases to which they had habituated themselves, and moulded upon a system of references to the natural scenery around them, to their modes of action in social life, and to their current notions upon all other subjects. Not only would the diction have been pure Greek, but the figures, the allusions, and the illustrations, of whatever kind, would also have been Attic. The Hebraized style which was adapted to the people of Israel, would have failed to convey just sentiments to the men of Greece ; for, though it would not have been absolutely unintelligible, the collateral ideas would have been misapprehended, false bye-notions would have insinuated themselves, and the principal sentiments, to inculcate which was the object of the whole process, would have been grievously distorted."
—Dr. Pye Smith, "*Scripture and Geology,*" p. 239.

to the period in which that peculiar genus prevailed, we do not mean to insinuate that they are the mere fanciful results of that genus. We regard them as containing the inspiration of the Almighty, and venerate them as portions of the pure Word of God. What we intend by this reference is, that God was pleased to adopt, as the vehicle for his communications, the mode and style then prevalent with men, yet so regulating the expressions and marshalling the narrative that it should contain no word, indicate no sentiment, declare no story, but what was the exact counterpart of some spiritual things.

This characteristic, indeed, must be acknowledged to pervade the whole Word of God, though the representations that were selected in those remote times appear to have been more recondite than those which were adopted at a later period, in consequence of mankind having begun to mistake their sense or falsify their meaning.

The Scriptures peculiarly Israelitish commence with the history of the house of Abram: that history, indeed, contains general facts, as they are described; nevertheless, these facts are to be considered as the mediums for containing, and representatively expressing, those interior sentiments and spiritual ideas which are proper to them as a *Revelation.* The mere literal facts and history can hardly, in themselves, be viewed as revelations: it would not be satisfactory to suppose that any other divine interference with their writings took place than was requisite to determine the particular points which were to be stated as the true representations of spiritual realities, the disclosure of which must have been their main object, considered as revelations from God.

But the character of the Bible narratives anterior to the time of Abram, though equally divine, is observed to be very different in their literal structure; and some critics, from an apparent irregularity in the arrangement, have considered them fragmentary selections, while others pronounce them to be distinct compositions.* However this may be, they are plainly the productions of another hand than that which has written the history of the house of Abram; and there is some reason to

* See Vater's "Fragment Hypothesis;" Eichhorn's "Document Hypothesis;" and Dr. P. Smith's "Geology and Scripture," note, p. 202.

believe that they formed a portion of a more ancient revelation from God than that which is now extant. Moses himself has intimated that there were books of divine authority among mankind antecedent to his time. He has referred to them by name, cited passages from them, and embodied them in his own Pentateuch. Thus, after describing the several journeyings of the sons of Israel, and particularly their removal from Zared to the other side of Arnon, he writes, "Wherefore it is said in the Book of the Wars of Jehovah, What he did in the Red sea, and in the brooks of Arnon, and the streams of the brook that goeth down to the dwelling of Ar, and lieth upon the border of Moab." * Again, after announcing the conquest of the Israelites over the Ammonites and the villages of Heshbon, he writes, "Wherefore say the Enunciations" (*Hammoshelim*, *i. e.*, the books of the Enunciations,—as we say Prophets, for the books of the Prophets; which idea is obscured by the common translation, "They that speak in proverbs"), "Come unto Heshbon, let the city of Sihon be built and prepared: for there is a fire gone out of Heshbon, and a flame from the city of Sihon: it hath consumed Ar of Moab, and the lords of the high places of Arnon."† These passages announce the existence of two books, one of which was distinguished by an historical, and the other by a prophetical, character. In other portions of the Word we find citations from another work, called the "Book of Jasher," and the writers apply what they quoted from it to events which were then in the course of being accomplished.‡

That those ancient books were produced under divine superintendence, and designed for the spiritual guidance of the people to whom they were originally vouchsafed, seems evident, from the formal manner in which they are referred to, and the authority conceded to them. That one of them was constructed on the principle of expressing mental things in an historical

---

* Numb. xxi. 14. As a fact bearing upon the great antiquity of the Book here cited from, Dr. Lamb, Master of Corpus Christi College, Cambridge, has remarked, "that in this short passage we find a verb (*raheb*) which occurs nowhere else in the Bible."—"*Hebrew Hieroglyphics*," p. 9. It is considered to have been a word obsolete in the time of Moses, and thus that the book in which it occurs must have been a production long anterior to his time.

† Numb. xxi. 27, 28.   ‡ Josh. x. 12, 13 ; 2 Sam. i. 17, 18.

manner, plainly appears from the passage that is quoted from it. As, then, it is certain that the early portions of Genesis are distinguished by a peculiarity of composition, proving them to be documents of an entirely different character from those to which they are prefixed, there can be little doubt of their having originally formed a part of those more ancient divine records, the existence of which, in some remote period, is certain from the fragments which remain.*

This conclusion does not rest merely upon the probabilities of rational inference: there is some scriptural attestation of the fact. The fifth chapter of Genesis commences with the declaration, "This is the Book of the generations of Adam," and thereupon follows, in a style agreeable to those times, a record of all his descendants down to Noah and his sons. Doubtless this *Book of Generations* was a written document, containing the circumstances which the author of the Pentateuch has cited, and acknowledged in this instance, as we have seen he did in others.†

As, then, there is testimony sufficient to show that the Antediluvian History in the Bible was produced among a people whose genius led them to express their perceptions of interior and spiritual truth by means of external and natural symbols, occasionally arranged in the form of historic narrative, we think we may most fairly and reasonably arrive at the general conclusion that those documents were never intended to record the origin of mundane things, to express the phenomena of matter, or to deliver the social, civil, or political history of the first men. Their true purpose is of a much more sacred and religious character, which we shall endeavour to show. We shall also, in addition to the general remarks which have now been made, venture to adduce, in their proper places, such other particular reasons for the conclusion arrived at concerning the figurative structure of the Antediluvian History as the

---

* "We have no slight reasons for supposing that Moses compiled the chief parts of the Book of Genesis, by arranging and connecting ancient memoranda, under the Divine direction."—Dr. PYE SMITH, "*Scripture and Geology.*" Second edition, p. 202.

† "It means," says Dr. A. Clarke, "the account or register of the generation of Adam or his descendants."

specific points may seem to require. It is, however, always to be borne in mind that those reasons are designed to weigh only against the common apprehension of its literal sense; and, also, that in no case are they to be considered as questioning the divine origination of the documents, or suggesting doubts as to their spiritual value and purpose. We have deemed it requisite to make these statements, because there are some who suppose that the rejection of a long-standing interpretation is the same thing as throwing discredit upon the documents. Against this we solemnly protest. We renounce nothing respecting those narratives but that common opinion concerning them, which every sincere student has found it difficult to hold. We receive them as a genuine portion of the veritable Word of God, and, therefore, we regard them as a Divine Revelation concerning celestial and spiritual things; and look upon every single expression they contain to be significant of some interior affection and thought proper to man in the process of his religious development, or attendant upon him during the calamity of his transgression.

The style in which these documents is composed is the first of which we have any account, and perhaps it is the best adapted for the embodiment of divine communication; because it appears to have been a method of expression which prevailed among an orderly and illuminated people, who enjoyed the advantages of interior perception, and displayed an activity of intellectual principle very superior to any who have lived in subsequent ages. This was plainly referred to by Hannah, when she said, "Speak ye what is high, let what is ancient come forth from your mouth, for the Lord is a God of knowledge";* and also by the Psalmist, when he said, "Incline your ears to the words of my mouth. I will open my mouth in a parable: I will utter dark sayings of old: which we have heard and known, and our fathers have told us." †

There are two modes of speaking of the Scriptures, frequently adopted, to which, in concluding these remarks, it will be useful to refer.

The first is, that the statements of the Scriptures must be implicitly and reverentially received, whether we understand

---

* 1 Sam. ii. 3: Improved Translation.   † Psa. lxxviii. 1-3.

them or not; and that it is mere presumption for man, with his carnal mind and puny intellect, to attempt to comprehend those wonderful things which it has pleased God to deliver, rather for his faith than his knowledge! This may be a pious submission to divine authority, taking its rise in religious feeling; but it is certainly mistaken in its application. We have no doubt that such obedience is very becoming, provided it be accompanied with intelligence; but in the case before us it wants the ingredient necessary to enlighten and give it value. Those who can satisfy themselves with such notions are, therefore, beyond our reasonings. We can render them little service. They have faith for anything but that free and sensible enquiry into the legitimate meaning of God's Word which we regard to be the duty and prerogative of man.

The second mode is that which asserts that the Scriptures are "very simple in their structure," and describes them as being for "simple minds," "plain readers," "the common people," "the unlearned," and so forth: thereby insinuating that those explanations are to be suspected which require labour, research, and intellectual culture for their discovery and comprehension. It is readily granted that the Scriptures are so written as to be serviceable even to the lowest state of human apprehension, but we do not believe that such a state comprehends the whole truth contained in any one passage that may be presented to it. * There is just so much seen as the intellectual condition will admit of, and no more. The highest disclosures of Divine wisdom are not to be discerned by the lowest states of the human mind. The simple may receive the Word in simplicity, but the wise man understands it in wisdom, and the latter makes the nearest approaches to its true meaning. The Apostle declared the rule when he said, "When I was a child, I spake as a child, I understood as a child, I thought as a child: but when I became a man, I put away childish things." † The Word is rightly viewed when it is regarded not only as capable of improving the heart, but also of enlightening the under-

---

* "Of those who actually read the Scriptures, multitudes are very imperfectly able to understand most of what they read."—*Timothy Dwight, LL.D.* Sermon 152.

† 1 Cor. xiii. 11.

standing; and, therefore, its wisdom must be adapted to all the advancing conditions of the human mind. It is the wise and friendly character of revelation, not only to assist man in his intellectual elevation, but likewise to accompany him in his progress, and urge him onwards by calling attention to superior heights not yet attained. If we do not regard the Word in this light, we overlook much that is solemn and interesting in its objects: in such a case, its reality vanishes like a meteor, and its spirituality perishes like a dream.

CHAPTER III.

ORIGINAL STATE OF MAN.—THE SUCCESSIVE DEVELOPMENT OF HIS MENTAL AND SPIRITUAL POWERS.—HIS DUTY AND PREROGATIVE AS AN IMAGE OF GOD.—THE EXCELLENCY OF EVERYTHING THAT WAS MADE.

"The foundations of religion and virtue being laid in the mind and heart, the secret dispositions and genuine acts of which are invisible, and known only to a man's self; therefore, the powers and operations of the mind can only be expressed in *figurative terms and external symbols.*"—DR. JOHN CLARK. *Folio Collection of Boyle's Lectures.* Vol. iii., p. 229.

From the facts and principles which have been laid down, we are somewhat prepared to consider the evidence for regarding the early portions of Genesis as treating, *first*, of the original state of the most ancient people; *next*, of that progressive development by which they became spiritual, and at length celestial men, when they constituted the most ancient Church; *afterwards*, of their declining state and absolute fall; *then*, of the religious condition of succeeding generations; and *finally*, of the state of wickedness which prevailed among the posterity coeval with the flood, by which catastrophe the celestial dispensation perished.

Viewed in this light, assisted by the corroborations of other parts of the Scriptures, and the facts of spiritual experience, we shall be enabled to recognize in those portions of the Word a meaning beautifully consistent with itself, and in perfect harmony with all the demands of a true mental philosophy; and, at the same time, disclosing principles whereby may be answered every requirement which the most enlarged idea of revelation can suggest.

THE BEGINNING.

The narrative opens with this beautifully simple declaration : " In the beginning God created the heaven and the earth." The *beginning* certainly denotes the remotest time connected with the history of the human race; then was the period for commencing the operations subsequently described. But what phenomenon was about to be produced? We answer, that it was to be a condition of humanity, in the highest development of which the Creator was about to make the image and likeness of Himself. It was necessary, in the first place, to provide the plans through which this development could be accomplished in an orderly way. These are called "the heaven and the earth": the *heaven* being that internal constitution of man which connects him with a spiritual destiny; and the *earth*, that external condition by which he is related to a *natural* world. Hence, heaven, considered as the kingdom of God, is said to be within;* and the earth, regarded as man's outer nature, is frequently called upon to hear the Word of the Lord. † Of the existence of the internal and external man popular theology is sufficiently cognizant. The Apostle speaks of them as the inner and outer man. ‡ From this we learn that revelation opens with the information that man, by original creation, was distinguished by an internal and an external nature; that the former might be taken as an indication that he had been endowed with immortality, and the latter as the announcement of his responsibility.

But what were his mental and moral possessions? Of these, at first, we think he must have been obviously destitute. We can hardly conceive the idea of man being created with the *experience* and *information* which mental exertions and moral qualities would seem to imply. Therefore, his original condition, in these respects, could have differed but little from those states into which he has since been born. Thus he must have been ignorant, but innocent, still possessing all the capabilities for having developed the highest perceptions of wisdom and the holiest principles of virtue. The state, which has attended the beginning of man in all ages of his existence, may have been designed to inform us what was his condition when first originated. Of the process by which this was accomplished we have no revelation, but we are told something of the mental characteristics

---

* Luke xvii. 21.

† See Isa. xxxiv. 1; Jer. vi. 19; xxii. 29, &c., &c.

‡ Ephes. iii. 16 ; 2 Cor. iv. 16.

that first belonged to him. "The earth" is said to have been "without form, and void," to denote that, as to his external nature, he was destitute of the *order* which arises from enlightened teaching, and *void* of that living excellence which springs out of active goodness. To show the accuracy of this view of the subject, we find that a corresponding state is spoken of in precisely similar language. When the Jewish Church had become a desolation, the Lord thus describes its aspect: "I beheld the earth, and, lo, *it was* without form, and void; and the heavens, and they *had* no light":* nor was there any "man."† "Darkness," also, is said to have been "upon the face of the deep," for the purpose of declaring the ignorance which then prevailed in the perceptive capabilities of the mind. Perception is the "face," because, as is well known, all its ideas shine forth therein, and are indicated thereby: the mind is the "deep," and hence recondite thinking is sometimes so expressed.

This seems to inform us very plainly that man, by original creation, did not possess either the knowledge or the love of divine things. This destitution, however, did not arise from the voluntary rejection of those excellencies, as has been the case with men in after ages, but because, as yet, they had not been communicated. His original state, therefore, must have been one of passive innocence and docility. He was gifted with capacities merely, that were afterwards to be developed, and by which it was designed that he should love his God above all things, and his neighbour as himself. He was created perfect in the degree of his primeval existence, but not with the possession of those high things in which his capabilities could result. The degree was a faculty to become great, but not greatness itself. It is this which distinguishes humanity from the beasts. They were at once endowed with all that they were capable of, to the end that they might obtain no more, and so be beasts; but man was created with capacities only to the end that, by their use, he might knowingly progress in all things that are wise and good, and so be man. The perfection of the former, therefore, is their imperfection; while the deficiencies of the latter are the groundwork of his eminence.

* Jer. iv. 23. † Jer. iv. 25.

How long man continued in this primeval state there is no historical information. It is not necessary to suppose that it was any considerable time. Indeed, it is reasonable to imagine that it was only of short duration. The orderly condition in which his capacities were created, would qualify him to observe instructively the objects and circumstances by which he was surrounded, and thence he could acquire certain knowledges and moral impressions, which would constitute the intellectual materials on which the divine influences were afterwards to operate. The divine operation implies the possession of something on which to operate, and from which the higher excellences should be evolved. These had been mercifully provided in the human capacities, and the impressions, ideas, and sentiments that would be made upon them, during their original and orderly existence.

This, then, we conceive to have been the state of man up to the period when it is said that "the Spirit of God moved upon the face of the waters." By the Spirit of God moving, is meant the divine influences acting; and the "waters," on which it is described to have operated, are significant of those knowledges which had been previously acquired.* These, by innumerable acts of the divine mercy, were stored up in the mind, and therein preserved, until that favourable time should arrive when the divine influences might, as it were, brood over them, and so endow them with spiritual life. Those knowledges are here called "the face of the waters," to distinguish them from that ignorance and obscurity of mind which had been previously denominated "darkness upon the face of the deep."

The ideas here suggested are admissive of some degree of illustration, which may come home to the religious experience of many. When a man remembers the innocence of his childhood with delight; when he feels gratitude attending his reflections on the anxiety and care which his rearing and education must have cost his parents, and when he experiences pleasures arising in his bosom with the recollection of those

---

* That waters, in the Word, are employed to signify knowledges will abundantly appear in subsequent parts of this work. Baptism with water signifies introduction into the knowledges of the Church.

knowledges and attentions which friends and others have bestowed upon him;—when he experiences such gratifying sensations accompanying the common knowledges of his nature, then it is that the Spirit of God is moving upon the face of the waters: it is brooding* over those knowledges, and indicating the presence of spiritual life therein by the orderly sensations of *delight, gratitude,* and *pleasure* that are felt.

It is interesting to observe that there is a remarkable analogy between the process here described as attending the creation of man, and that which, under the Christian dispensation, is spoken of as belonging to his regeneration. They are both treated of as the result of the divine influence and operation. In the one case, God is said to move "upon the face of the waters"; in the other it is written, "Ye must be born of water and the Spirit."† It is true that the regeneration insisted on by Christianity implies the presence of evil, which in the first creation of man could not have existed. Nevertheless, there is a great similarity in the two processes, for the end contemplated by both is the implantation of the Divine image in man. In the one case, it was to be done before his fall; in the other, after it. In this latter case it may be more difficult to accomplish, because man, as a co-worker with God, has now to contend against his evils; and these throw obstacles in the way, and so retard his progress. With this exception, regeneration, considered as a divine work, is very similar to that which is described as his creation. The end in both cases is the same; so, also, are the means, viewed in their first principles, those being the divine influences. The intermediates are somewhat different. Man is *now* regenerated by the Lord through the *external* teachings of his Word; *then* he was regenerated by the Lord through

---

* The Hebrew verb, *merachepheth*, rendered *moved*, also signifies the act of incubation, of gently cherishing, of brooding over so as to evolve a something that may live. . . . This harmonizes very beautifully with the fact declared by the Lord when he said, "How often would I have gathered you together, as a hen gathereth her chickens under her wings!" (Matt. xxiii. 37). In both instances there is included the idea of bringing its subject into a condition of superior life: in the former case its evolution out of the unfallen capacities of man; in the latter the disentanglement of it from the influences of iniquity.

† John iii. 5.

the *internal* dictates of his wisdom. This flowed into him by an interior way, there being nothing to oppose its entrance; and, therefore, it successively brought forth those excellencies of character which terminated in the development of the Divine image. But now divine wisdom enters into man by an external way, because now there are evils to be removed, which must be seen and acknowledged in the external mind, before that "image" can be restored which the fall obliterated. When this is effected he is regenerated, being "a new creature"; for regeneration consists in the implantation of new thoughts, affections, and intentions, and thus in the actual creation, in man, of new principles of spiritual life and action. Hence it is sometimes called a creation, as in the case of the Psalmist, when he prayed, "Create in me a clean heart, O God; and renew a right spirit within me."* It is, therefore, a term declaratory of the actual creation of the orderly principles and development of religious life. It brings into existence, in the state of him who is its subject, a new intellectual and moral activity, which are not experienced and cannot be imagined by the merely natural man, for he, says the Apostle,† "knoweth not the things of God." It is, then, the creation and successive unfolding of states conducive to this elevated condition of humanity before the fall, which we believe to be treated of in the first chapter of Genesis.‡

The general similarity between creation and regeneration is evident; therefore, we may sometimes fairly appeal to the experience of the one, for an occasional illustration of the phenomena indicated in the other.

It was observed that the Spirit of God moving upon the face of the waters meant the divine influences operating upon those general knowledges which man had been enabled to accumulate during the early stages of his primeval existence. This was the preparatory state to that in which the Lord said, "Let there be

---

* Psalm li. 10.   † 1 Cor. ii. 14.

‡ "That the literal meaning is, *primâ facie*, one wholly adverse to the present astronomical and geological views of the universe is evident enough."—*The Mosaic Cosmogony. By C. W. Goodwin, M.A.,* p. 251. The whole of this Essay may be usefully consulted, as showing the discrepancies which exist between the Mosaical history and actual phenomena.

light"—light in the mind, for truth of a religious nature could now enter into it, and produce some faint degree of mental illumination.

THE FIRST DAY.

It is to be remarked that the phenomena of each day's creation are described as having been spoken into existence.* The view we are taking of this narration affords us a beautiful reason for this circumstance. All the evolutions of spiritual life are the results of the Lord's speaking. It is well known that all the good things of genuine religion have been communicated to us by what God has said. Wheresoever we behold any excellence, God has first spoken of it in his Word, and by that speech it has been brought into existence. The external or written Word is now the medium for these productions. It has spoken Christendom into being, with all its influences. God said, Let there be Christianity, and there was Christianity. But the full blaze of its intelligence was not suddenly displayed. We are not informed of the time it would require for realizing all its objects. The beginning is not to be mistaken for its maturity. The twilight is displayed before the sun rises to his meridian. God's Word has spoken of its magnificence, and His utterances cannot fail. This Word produces the light which we are commanded to let shine. That is the speech which brings into being the blade, the ear, the corn, and the fruit that we are directed to exhibit. That is the language which originates the sheep and the lambs which Peter was commanded to feed. This being the effect of God's Word now, we at once see why, in the case before us, the work of every day is prefaced by the sentence, "God said."† The things really treated of were the

---

* "In the beginning was the Word. All things were made by him; and without him was not any thing made that was made."—John i. 1-3.

† It may be useful to direct the reader's attention to the frequent occurrence of this manner of expression in all the Divine communications mentioned in the Scriptures, and especially in the prophetical portions of them: and it may not be impertinent to observe that it has been usual to infer, from the circumstance of God's speaking the world into being, that it was created out of nothing. But out of nothing nothing can be made; and the above mode of announcing the subject is rather a declaration that it was made from the Divine Love by the Divine Wisdom. Whatever might have been the *modus operandi*, these must have been the origin of creation.

actual results of that sacred speech. It was a divine dictate impressing itself upon the internal perceptions of men, and designed to bring into successive existence the higher sentiments of wisdom and faith, with all their charities and uses; which, however, are described in its own symbolical way.

The insemination of certain ideas of truth was among its first efforts. What God speaks is light to the subject which receives it, but more or less brilliant according to the state of man's reception. Without a right knowledge nothing truly useful can be done, and the attainment of that light is among the first efforts of unsullied love, because the communication of love without intelligence would be a blind impulse.

The Lord, then, imparted light,—this he "called Day, and the darkness he called Night." These definitions it is important to observe. As day and night are terms expressive of opposite conditions in nature, so they are significant of antagonistic states of mind. Whatsoever proceeds from the Lord admits of comparison with day, because it is accompanied by the light of truth; but everything arising out of man's ignorance is associated with moral mists and darkness, and therefore it is forcibly represented by the night. The night here treated of does not at all enter into the composition of that which is here called day, as is the case with the astronomical definition of that period. It is the light which God called day; this he is said to have divided (distinguished, is the more correct word) from the night to express that eternal separation which must ever exist between the truth which comes from Him, and the ideas which arise with us: hence he has pronounced it good, and declared "the evening and morning" of that light to be "the first day." By a day is spiritually signified a state, during the continuance of which certain mental and moral perceptions appear in the mind, and from which arise corresponding performances of duty. On this account Jesus said, "I must work the works of him that sent me, while it is day: the *night* cometh, when no man can work": * the day here alluded to is, plainly, a state favourable for carrying out the divine purposes. Such, also, is the day in the subject before us. It is generally admitted that it cannot there mean the ordinary idea derived from the diurnal

* John ix. 4.

motion of the earth, and some other interpretation of it is usually sought for. Many have thought that it denoted a period of indefinite extent. But that is by no means satisfactory. God does not employ words of definite meaning to express to men indefinite ideas. A notion like that could hardly be pronounced a revelation. Its true reference is to mental state and not to physical time: for the duration of a state is to the experience of the mind what the continuation of a day is to the experience of the body; and natural days of clouds and sunshine, of storms and serenity, have their correspondence in states of mental vicissitude. The six days' creation, then, are to be understood as so many successive states of religious advancement, in the last of which humanity became an image of the Divine. The insemination of the light of truth was among the first contributions to this high result, and it was the evening and the morning of this light which constituted the first day; for by the evening is denoted that dim aspect under which truth is at first perceived, but by the morning is signified the more clear and refreshing understanding of it.

It is remarkable that each of the six days spoken of in this chapter is described to have been constituted by the "evening and the morning"; night is entirely excluded from its composition. But from this more particular definition of the term day, we are not to infer that there is any disparity between it and that more general assertion which declared it to consist of light, for both the evening and the morning obviously include this idea. The reason why the evening and the morning are said to be a day, and why, also, the evening is put first in the order of the expressions, is, because the light of the divine truth which is proper to every state is, in its beginning, seen only as in the shade of evening, but afterwards it is perceived more clear and beautiful, and thus as the brightness of the morning, with all its dewy freshness and fertility. The order of our mental advancement is from obscurity to clearness. We do not pass from the evening to the night, and thence on to the morning. That is an order which belongs to the succession of natural time, but not to the progressions of spiritual state; and, therefore, the term night, proper to the vicissitudes of time, is carefully excluded from the description. Thus the very order and peculiarity of the expressions said to constitute a day afford a remarkable evidence that a description of spiritual things is the chief purpose of the narrative. We therefore pass on to

THE SECOND DAY.

"And God said, Let there be a firmament in the midst of the waters, and let it divide the waters from the waters—and it was so. And God called the firmament Heaven. And the evening and the morning were the Second Day."

By a firmament, in a merely literal sense, is meant the sky which is above us; but this, it is well known, does not constitute a partition for any of the waters of nature. Moreover, this firmament, brought into existence on the second day, is called "Heaven." Was this, then, another heaven, different from that which was originally created, for "in the beginning God created the Heaven"?? These facts suggest difficulties; but they exist only in the letter: viewed in a spiritual sense they entirely disappear.

By the firmament (more properly, expanse) which is now brought into being, is spiritually meant the development of some of those interior principles of thought which belong to the internal man. These constitute a mental expanse which exists somewhat above the terrestrial things of sense; and they discriminate between the knowledges which are of God and those which are of men: therefore it is said to divide (distinguish) the waters from the waters; the waters, as before observed, being significant of knowledges.

This firmament—these interior principles of thought—is now called heaven; not because the internal man, thereby signified, did not before exist, but because it was now first perceived. How many things are there belonging to our nature which actually exist a long time before we become properly aware of them! The internal man exists, and we may have this fact declared to us by infallible authority, still we have no right perception of its truth until we begin a course of interior thinking. By this man attains the evidence of its existence, and then believes; hence the evening and the morning of this state are the second day, for man is gradually led into this faith from things external to things internal, from the knowledges of earth to the intelligences of heaven, and thus, as it were, from the evening to the morning of every state.

THE THIRD DAY.

On the third day "the waters were gathered together unto one place; the dry land appeared; and the dry land was called Earth, and the gathering together of the waters, Seas; and the earth brought forth grass, the herb yielding seed, and the fruit tree yielding fruit."

That by waters are really denoted knowledges concerning religious things, is certain, from a variety of scriptural considerations. As, for instance, in his conversation with the woman of Samaria, the Lord said, "Whosoever drinketh of the water that I shall give him shall never thirst; but the water that I shall give him shall be in him a well of water springing up into everlasting life."* In this passage it is plain that, by water, is denoted those knowledges of religious truth which rise up in the mind from the acknowledgment of, and a faith in, the Lord. Again, the Holy Waters, seen by Ezekiel to issue from the sanctuary, and which rose first up to his ankles, next to his knees, then to his loins, and afterwards became a river large enough to swim in,† plainly denoted the successive increase and deepening of those divine knowledges which proceed from the sanctuary, or true Church of God. The Lord is said to "lay the beams of his chambers in the waters; ‡ because his chambers denote the interior principles of his Church, while the beams thereof signify their strength: these are said to be laid in the waters, because they rest and have their sure foundation only in the genuine knowledges of the Word, and therefore it is that the Word itself is described as "a pure river of water of life." §

From these considerations, it is evident that the gathering together of the waters unto one place denotes the collection of those moral and religious knowledges which had been diffusively impressed upon the mind, and storing of them up in the

* John iv. 14. † Ezek. xlvii.
‡ Psa. civ. 3. § Rev. xxii. 1.

memory as one place appropriated for their reception; but then, in consequence of their extent and depth, together with the intranquillity arising from apparent disagreements, they are compared to the sea.

Now it was that the dry land appeared, that denoting the unproductive nature of the merely external man. The external man, separate from internal and spiritual influences proceeding from the Lord, is as a dry and barren land: none of the good things of love and truth can spring up and grow therein. It is important that this characteristic of it should be known. The collection of religious knowledges, to which we have adverted, confers this information, and thereby the "dry land appears." This was called earth, that being the name conferred upon the external man at the beginning; but now it is spoken of as land, because in this process of spiritual development it first appeared somewhat conspicuous; nevertheless, in order to prevent any misapprehension concerning the quality of the external man, we are forcibly reminded that it is "earth." By original creation it is low and natural, nor will genuine knowledge ever cause it to appear in any other quality than that which the name "earth" suggests.

From the accumulation of these knowledges—for they had now become a sea—the duty was perceived of rendering this earth productive; to "bring forth grass, the herb yielding seed, and the fruit tree yielding fruit": which spiritually signifies the production of those orderly uses by which the moral life is to be sustained. The general idea here indicated is frequently reproduced in the Word. Thus the Lord described himself to be the sower, his Word the seed, and the diversity of moral results as fruits, according to the quality of the respective minds into which the seed had been cast.* He also described the progression of man's growth in spiritual things, as "the earth bringing forth fruit; first the blade, then the ear, after that the full corn in the ear."† There can be no difference of opinion as to the general facts here referred to; and how beautifully do those three expressions coincide with what are described as the productions of the state now treated of; namely, the "grass, the herb yielding seed, and the fruit tree yielding fruit"! The

* Matt. xiii. 19-23. † Mark iv. 28.

good which, when knowledge has been implanted, first springs out of "the earth," is somewhat low and delicate, and hence it is called "grass" (more properly rendered *tender herb*). After this succeed the performance of uses of a more vigorous kind, and these, because they are pregnant with a multiplication of delights, are compared to "the herb yielding seed." Then follows good of a superior kind, because acknowledging a higher origin, and this is pronounced to be the "fruit tree yielding fruit." * How striking are these correspondences! from what principle can it be denied that such a mode of explanation is the true one? They recognize and illustrate the canon of "Scripture interpreting itself." The moral and spiritual affections belonging to man at this stage of his upward progress are compared to the growing and fruit-bearing things of the vegetable world, because, as yet, he was somewhat insensitive to the great fact of their continued dependence upon the Lord: and thus that higher life and animation had not been attained, which the objects of the animal kingdom would more properly represent.

The collection of religious knowledges, planting them in the memory as the great storehouse of human information, causing the infertility of the merely external man to appear, together with the effort for rendering it, in some measure, more fruitful in the works of use, are what constitute the third day of the creation, and this, like all preceding states, advanced from a condition of shade to light, wherefore it is written, that "the evening and the morning were the third day."

THE FOURTH DAY.

The phenomena brought into existence on the fourth day are thus described: "And God made two great lights; the greater

---

* It is interesting to observe that there are only three phases of vegetable production here referred to, and that these, from the circumstance of their general utility to man, are such as to fit them for being employed in this symbolical manner. This must have been the main object of the statement, for, as the narrative does not contain the slightest intimation concerning that vast variety of genera with which the vegetable kingdom abounds, it cannot justly be regarded as having been designed to express their physical creation.

light to rule the day, and the lesser light to rule the night: he made the stars also. And God set them in the firmament of heaven to give light upon the earth, and to rule over the day and over the night, and to divide the light from the darkness." These words describe to us what are the great sources of all spiritual and religious illumination, the order which they establish, and the uses they promote. Light, indeed, had previously prevailed: it is stated to have been brought into existence upon the first day, when, also, it is said that God distinguished the light from the darkness: yet now we are told that upon the fourth day God made other, but superior lights,* whose office was also "to divide the light from the darkness." These, certainly, are embarrassing statements, viewed merely in their literal sense. Science has not seen how light and vegetation could exist before the sun. Ingenuity has ventured to suggest a plan, but philosophy has not been satisfied with the notion, nor can it ever be so, because the premises are wrong. The subject now treated of is concerning the development of the spiritual man; during this process, light is experienced under two distinctive aspects. The light which is seen by man in the early stages of his regenerating progress is very different in its quality from that which is experienced in his more advanced condition; in the former case it is external, partaking somewhat of the world; in the latter it is internal, deriving a quality from heaven. Thus the light which is treated of as existing during the first three days, represented that external and scientific truth which properly belonged to the early stages of spiritual development, and by which preparation is made for the reception of those more interior lights of love and faith: therefore it is said of those lights, that they were placed in the firmament, which God called Heaven; that is, in the internal man.

By the sun is represented the warming, enlightening, and fructifying principle of the Divine Love; and this is said to rule

---

* Though the sun and moon may be implied in this description, it is to be remarked that they are not so expressed. Astronomers inform us that some of the stars are at so great a distance from the earth, that their light which has reached us must, even at its amazing velocity, have taken hundreds of thousands of years. How plain is it, then, that they could not have commenced their existence on the fourth day, about six thousand years ago!

the day, to inform us that it should be a governing principle in all states of the truly religious character and conduct. By the moon is denoted the cooler and less luminous principle of truth, still truth derived from love (in like manner as the light of the moon, naturally, is derived from the sun); and this is said to rule the night, to teach us the proper dominion of truth in all states of mental obscurity and darkness. By the stars are signified those numerous and varied intelligences which distinguish a state so far advanced in religious life and excellence as that which is represented by the fourth day.

These significations could be extensively proved from the Scriptures; but as the most ordinary mind will perceive the analogies on which they are founded, the citation of a single passage must suffice. The Lord, when foretelling the consummation of the first age of Christianity, said, "The sun shall be darkened, and the moon shall not give her light, and the stars shall fall from heaven, and the powers of the heavens shall be shaken." * By the sun being darkened is meant that heavenly love would be eclipsed; the moon not giving her light denotes that spiritual truth would fail to illuminate; and by the stars falling from heaven is signified that religious intelligence would perish from the internal man: and thus, that the whole spiritual character of the Church would experience a convulsion, signified by the powers of the heavens being shaken.†

Now, those luminaries were placed in the firmament of heaven to give light upon the earth; or, in other words, spiritual love, truth, and intelligence were now fixed in the affection of the internal man, for the purpose of enlightening his perception, and giving life to the moral fructifications of the external man. One, it is said, was to "rule over the day," and the other "over the night," to inform us that love would reign when the states of illumination prevailed, and that truth would govern during the periods of obscurity. They were also "to divide the light from the darkness"; that is, they were to *distinguish* the one from the other. This, in the case of the first day, is said

---

* Matt. xxiv. 29.

† May not the remarkable condition of the Christian Church at this day be considered as the fulfilment of the above prediction, so understood?

to have been done by God, but now it was to be effected by those two luminaries. Here, again, the literal sense suggests a difficulty which nothing can remove but a perception of the spiritual fact. That fact is this. In the former case, as before observed, God is said to have distinguished the light from the darkness, "to express the eternal separation which must ever exist between the truth which comes from Him, and the ideas which arise with us." This distinction is not observed by man in his lower states; it is the result of a superior condition, when love, faith, and diversified intelligence confer their discriminating powers, and so distinguish that which is of man from that which is of God.

Moreover, they were to "be for signs and for seasons, and for days and years," to signify those delightful variations of state by which man in this superior condition was to be distinguished. Without such changes, life would be uniform, and the monotony would destroy its happiness: mutations of state are required to preserve it in activity. A continued sameness would blunt the faculties and produce a sort of death upon the intellectual powers. Man, by creation, is designed for the appreciation of beautiful variety, and hence the diversified existences of external nature are mercifully adapted to supply him with such enjoyment. Changes of state, then, are to result from the presence of those two luminaries in the mind. Such fluctuations are to be of a twofold character: love was to change the state of his delight; truth was to alter the condition of his knowledge,—and the former was to be for a sign and a season of his spiritual life; a sign to indicate its particular, and a season its general, condition: while the latter was to be for the days and the years of his intellectual vigour; the days denoting its particular, and the years its general, aspect.

Such, then, were the productions of the fourth day, together with their purposes. We recognize a spiritual idea, even in the minutest expression, when we consider the narrative as pointing out the process of human development; but find it exceedingly difficult to maintain one that is natural and consistent, when it is viewed as indicating physical phenomena.

THE FIFTH DAY.

The succeeding state, spoken of as the fifth day, is described to have consisted in causing the "waters to bring forth abundantly the moving creature that hath life, and fowl that may fly above the earth in the open firmament of heaven."

Here it is important to remark that it is the *waters* which were commanded to bring forth the creature that hath life: these waters, it was shown above, denoted the knowledges of religious truth; and now (the man of whom they were predicated having attained a superior elevation of character) they were endowed with the higher capability of bringing into active *moving* existence the living principles of religious virtue.

When the sun, the moon, and stars—love, faith, and intelligence—are set up in the affections of the internal man, and begin to impart their light and warmth to the external, then it is that all the vast variety of religious principles begin to live. Before those spiritual luminaries came into being, the man regarded the knowledges acquired and the good he had done as having resulted from the simple efforts of himself, instead of referring them wholly to the Lord. This was among the ignorances of his inferior condition; so long as that remained, his knowledge did not bring forth that which is alive; and, therefore, that state is compared to grass, the herb yielding seed, and the tree bearing fruit, which, after all, are but things inanimate. But when the man is enlightened by genuine love and faith, then his knowledges become the medium for a development of spiritual life, and he at once perceives that the truth he had known, and the good he had done, were operated in him by the Lord. This important knowledge is, therefore, the source through which his thoughts and affections acquire real life and animation; on which account they are now first compared to living things.

It is declared that "every good gift and every perfect gift is from above, and cometh down from the Father of lights"; * and also, that "without Him we can do nothing"; † He being "the light of life." ‡ It therefore follows, that whatsoever proceeds

---

* Jas. i. 17.   † John xv. 5.   ‡ John viii. 12.

merely from the selfhood of man can have but little of this living principle within it; and, consequently, it may be aptly signified by the insensible objects of the vegetable world; but when all man's thoughts and affections are derived from the Lord, and humbly acknowledged, then they must needs contain within them the principles of moving and imperishable life; in this case they may be most appropriately represented to us by the objects which really live: these are the reasons why the preceding inferior states are indicated by things of the vegetable kingdom, and the succeeding superior states by the objects of animated nature.

By the moving creature which the waters were to bring forth, is meant the living affections which pertain to the *scientific truths* of religion;* these were commanded to be brought forth abundantly, to denote the multiplicity of uses of which they are productive. But by the moving fowls are signified the living affections which belong to the *intellectual perceptions* of religion; and these were to fly in the open firmament of heaven, to denote the range and freedom which are proper to them in the now exalted condition of the internal man. The Scriptures furnish innumerable instances of animals being mentioned to signify affections; many examples will be adduced as we proceed: we shall here only refer to one, in which the Lord said, "I will make a covenant for them with the beasts of the field, and with the fowls of heaven, and *with* the creeping things of the ground." † It is plain that by beasts, fowls, and creeping things are meant certain classes of affections, because the Lord is said to make a covenant with them, which would be altogether unintelligible if applied to such irrational creatures.

---

* It is to be observed that fishes are the symbolical objects contemplated. The idea of their having been the production of the waters is here employed to represent the affections of scientific truth which belong to the external man. These affections are among the lower orders of religious things, and hence they are represented by fishes; these belonging to the inferior class of living nature. The reason why fishes signify the affections of scientific truth is, because they are creatures of the sea, the sea denoting the collected knowledges of the natural man. See p. 40. The extinction of this affection in the Church is, in the Revelation, described as the death of "the third part of the creatures which were in the sea, and had life."—Rev. viii. 9.

† Hos. ii. 18.

The Apostle also said, "All flesh *is* not the same flesh; but *there is* one *kind of* flesh of men, another flesh of beasts, another of fishes, *and* another of birds."* Surely it did not require an Apostle or a Revelation to tell us such common and ordinary facts as these are in their merely literal sense. We, therefore, infer that the principal object of those statements was to announce the existence of a variety of good affections and thoughts, which he considered to be symbolized by those respective branches of animated nature.

THE SIXTH DAY.

Such, then, were the phenomena of the fifth day, and we now arrive at the creations which transpired upon the sixth. This was begun by "God making the beast of the earth after his kind, and cattle after their kind, and everything that creepeth upon the earth after his kind; and seeing that *it was* good."

From this description it will be observed that the order of creation, or spiritual development, is now changed. In the preceding case the waters were commanded to bring forth the moving creatures that had life: but the mention of all mediate instrumentality is omitted in this instance, and God is said to make them. These distinctions are for the purpose of revealing to us the different orders, through which different classes of human affections come into being. Man first acts from the living *affections of scientific truth*, and so long as he so acts, it is the waters—the knowledges, which bring forth the moving creatures; but when he afterwards begins to act from the living *affections of spiritual goodness*, then it is said that God makes them, because all that is genuinely good comes to us directly from Him who alone is good. How bright and beautiful are these distinctions, and how true and consistent are they with religious experience! In the former case it was only the fish and the fowl—the affection of scientific and intellectual things —that began to live; but in the latter it is the beast, the cattle, and creeping things—the affections of spiritual good in different degrees—that began to live. The affections of the former state

---

* 1 Cor. xv. 39.

originated out of the commands of truth, and hence it is said that the waters brought them forth; but the affections of the latter state spring directly out of the influences of good, and, therefore, it is written that "God made them."

Hence we learn that the circumstances narrated in the chapter before us, preceding that which announces the making of man, are but particular parts of that general result, and descriptive of the successive states through which the human principles were communicated, enlightened, and made alive; and when so enlightened and made alive, he becomes intelligent and wise, and then a MAN is made. Thus the statement concerning the making of man does not, in our judgment, relate to the origination of his physical structure: we look upon it as the description of man in the possession of a high degree of spiritual perfection, to which a preceding series of mental and moral developments had contributed.

The ideas of what constitute a man will change with the aspect under which he is contemplated. If we take a low and corporeal view of him, we shall be led to think that he is a man by virtue of his form. If we look at him through military eyes, he will be pronounced to be a man in consequence of his prowess. The law says that he is a man when he has lived so many years; and there are many other points from which the conventionalities of society have so regarded him. But it is not to any such ideas as these that God attaches the term when it is used approvingly in his Word. That which is a man in the Divine estimation is intellectual and spiritual excellence. Hence the Lord, when speaking of the destitution of heavenly love in the Church, said, "I beheld the earth, and, lo, there was no man."* Again, it is written that Jerusalem would have been pardoned of her sins if "a man" could have been found therein;† where by a man is plainly meant internal superiority of character. This was induced by the Lord upon those human faculties which he has created for the reception of himself; and, in the proportion in which man received them he had life from the Lord, and so became an image and likeness of him: an "image" so far as he was in charity and faith, but a "likeness" so far as he was in love and wisdom. This is the

* Jer. iv. 25. † Jer. v. 1.

man about whom the Lord has made a revelation: and it is the things constituent of this manhood which required a revelation, in order that a knowledge of them may be perpetuated with our race. "God said, Let us * make man in our image, after our likeness": such was the divine proposition; but it is to be observed that the image only was now produced.† Those who have been accustomed to view the statements of the Word in some general external idea only, will not instantly recognize the particular distinction which those two terms are intended to convey, and which indeed they must express, unless we consider the Holy Spirit to have selected tautological and redundant words; which idea needs only to be named to be rejected. The nature of the distinction is the same as that which exists between things spiritual and things celestial. It is the spiritual man who is the image of God; the celestial man is His likeness: but that was a development that had yet to be educed, and of which we shall by and by have occasion to speak.

But after the general declaration that God made man in his own image, it is more particularly said, "Male and female created he them." That this cannot, consistently with the literal sense, be interpreted to mean the creation of the physical sexes seems evident; for, when we carefully consult that sense, it appears, according to the second of Genesis, that the woman was not created on the sixth day at all; that she did not come into being until after Adam was placed in the garden, and thus not until after the seventh day! The criticism which would have the description of woman's creation, as mentioned in the second chapter, to be regarded as only the detail of what is generally noticed in the first, does not remove these literal discrepancies. Moreover, such a view of the subject is founded upon the erroneous idea of these two records being fragmentary pieces relating to the same circumstance; whereas both ought to

---

* This plural pronoun may be interpreted consistently, as, indeed, it ought to be, with the idea of one single divine person in the Godhead, if we consider it to refer to what must have been the fact, namely, that a plurality of the divine attributes were specially exerted in the productions here treated of. See the Author's work on "*The Deity of Jesus Christ asserted*," pp. 23–27.

† See ver. 27.

be regarded, as we shall endeavour to show in the progress of our exposition, as the revelation of a series of distinct and progressive facts.

By male and female that were now created, are meant the complete evolution of the two characteristics of the human mind, namely, its intellect and its affection. These were designed to form one mind, and, therefore, it is afterwards said of them that they should *be one*, which, indeed, was realized when the celestial condition was developed. The characteristic of the intellect, from the force and vigour of its nature, is contemplated as male, and the affection, from the delicacy, grace, and beauty for which it is remarkable, is spoken of as female; hence they are distinguished as the sexes. These two faculties of the mind exist, indeed, in each of the sexes; but it is plain that they have been differently distributed, and it is the distinctive order in which they exist in each that constitutes their essential difference. The most conspicuous feature in the female character is that of will and its affections; her intellect is somewhat interior and perceptive. That which is most evident in the male is his understanding and intellectual energy; his will is more interior and subdued. It is those mental differences in the natural constitution of the sexes which fitted them to denote those two faculties in the human mind which their leading characters so much resemble. Hence that which has been popularly understood to describe the creation of the sexes is, when viewed in this light, found to be significant of the orderly development of the human will and understanding, and thus of the due preparation of those faculties for the reception of the divine love and wisdom, and by which reception they were afterwards to be merged into "one flesh,"—one flesh denoting their intimacy and union in the pursuit of all that is good and lovely.

These faculties being developed, it is now said that God blessed them; the blessing consisting, not in the utterance of a sentiment, but in the ability to enjoy those excellencies which had been communicated. They were also commanded to "be fruitful, and multiply, and replenish the earth, and subdue it." Fruitfulness is applied to the affections, and their prolifications in all manner of good works of love and use; but multiplication has reference to the increase of the knowledges of truth and wisdom: hence the Apostle, treating of the effects of the Divine Word upon the soul, says of the Lord, as the implanter of that "seed," that he will "*multiply* your seed sown, and increase the *fruits* of your righteousness." * By replenishing the earth is denoted the infilling of the external man with all the holy principles of intelligence and virtue; and to subdue the earth means to bring the external man into the order and submissiveness which an enlightened and spiritual love requires: hence was to result his "dominion over the fish of the sea, and over the fowl of the air, and over every living thing that moveth upon the earth": that is, in his spiritual character, as an image of God, he was to be capable of bringing into subjection all the inferior things of science and intellect, represented by the "fish" and the "fowl," together with all the lower affections and appetites belonging to his external man, and denoted by "every living thing that moveth upon the earth." These were to be the prerogatives of the man whose progressive development and elevation we have been tracing: they were to consist in the moral and mental government which the higher principles of his superior nature were to exercise over his inferior part.

Again, every herb and fruit is said to have been given to him, and to every beast, for meat; because the state secured would require to be sustained. By the man is now properly meant, that internal humanity which had been developed; and by the beasts, all the orderly affections belonging thereto. Both of these require to be sustained with appropriate food, and this is described to have consisted in herbs and fruits, because they signify the truths and good by which it is effected; the truths, or herbs, being for the beasts, or spiritual affections, and the good, or fruits, being for the man, as to his internal human delights.

Man being made, and these instructions given, it is then said that "God saw everything that he had made, and, behold, *it was very good*"; a statement beautifully expressing the Divine approbation of that high spiritual state which had been evolved, and which was emphatically the work of God, as is the case with all good things. Still this state was not one of equal brightness; it, like all the days which had preceded, had its

* 2 Cor. ix. 10.

shade as well as light, and therefore it is said, "And the evening and the morning were the sixth day." The work of human development, thus far advanced, was not ended till the seventh; but that is a subject which belongs to the succeeding chapter, and to which we shall next refer.

Thus the six successive days of creation, with all the circumstances mentioned to have transpired upon each, are representative of the six progressive states of human development, together with all the phenomena that were proper to the process; and, consequently, the narrative is descriptive of the degrees through which man passed out of the merest rudiments of humanity into the attainment of the Divine image.

Such are the subjects which we conceive to be treated of in the internal sense, which is the only sense, of this first portion of the Book of Genesis. Viewed as a narrative of physical occurrences, it is inconsistent with the facts and discoveries of science, and altogether unintelligible to the fair and free inquiries of reason. This is proved by the whole history of those interpretations which have taken that notion for their basis. But, regarded as a description of the mental and spiritual elevation of humanity, delivered in the form of figurative history, it is found to be in harmony with the best Christian experience, together with the soundest requirements of reason, and in beautiful consistency with all the disclosures of true philosophy concerning man's origin and nature.

CHAPTER IV.

THE SEVENTH DAY, A CELESTIAL STATE OF MAN.—*Gen.* ii. 1.

"There is one law of criticism, the most important to the thorough understanding of any work. It is that by which we should be led, by continued habits of mind and action, to approximate to that intellectual and moral condition in which the work originated.—The Bible has mind for its subject—that condition of mind which has heaven for its object,—and the Father of mind for its Author."— "*Growth of the Mind,*" by SAMSON REED.

A knowledge of things pertaining to the natural world is to be procured by the natural powers of men. Supernatural communications are not required to inform us of points in science, philosophy, or history. Narratives, literally expressing such things, may be employed as the vehicle for higher information, and thence derive a sanctity; the parties writing them may, also, have been sensibly directed in the selection of such external vehicles; nevertheless, they do not properly come within the idea of having required supernatural discovery.

A revelation is necessary to make us acquainted with spiritual things, because they are beyond the reach of the ordinary efforts of the human mind, nor can such things be expressed in natural language in any other way than as types and figures; hence what has been said concerning the "creation" is but a brief example of that representative and significant writing which prevails throughout every document that delivers an actual revelation. It is the spiritual truths contained within the letter of the Word which properly constitute a revelation from God, and the Scriptures are said to be inspired in consequence of the presence of such truths. Thus the Word itself is an inspired writing, apart from the abnormal or inspired condition of the individual by whose instrumentality it was produced. The letter is only the natural and symbolical continent employed for the delivery of spiritual truth to man.

We do not suppose that in the preceding exposition we have anticipated every objection that may be raised against the literal sense; or that we have so stated its spiritual meaning, as to remove every difficulty which may lay in the way of its immediate adoption: to effect these results, a more enlarged and particular treatment of the subject would be required than we proposed to undertake. What have been set forth are only a few of the general points contained in the chapter, leaving a very large amount of its particular arcana altogether unreferred to. The object has been to place the subject in such a light as to enable the ordinary thinker to see at least some general resemblance between the literal description and the spiritual process, through which a successive development of human principles finally resulted in man becoming an image of the Divine.

This process we have spoken of as a *development*. It might have been called *regeneration*, and we should have adopted that term if we had not contemplated some probable confusion by its use. Regeneration, indeed, considered in an enlarged and proper sense, is a development of all the human excellencies; but then it is commonly used to express man's attainment of those graces *after he had fallen;* and, therefore, in treating of that portion of the Scriptures which speaks of him before that calamity had taken place, it was felt that the expression, *development*, would exclude that idea, and so enable us to employ the word *regeneration* in its more general acceptation, when we come to consider the events by which that calamity was succeeded.

Hitherto we have considered the process by which man was successively raised, as it were, out of a state of non-existence as to spiritual life, into its full possession and enjoyment. The SPIRITUAL life of man is that in which all his affections and thoughts are regulated and determined into act, by a clear understanding of the laws and rules of religious duty. In other words, man becomes SPIRITUAL when he becomes *good by means of truth teaching him what good is.* In this case he becomes a practical reflector of the divine wisdom, and thence he is called the image of God. This was his condition upon the sixth day.

But a seventh day is next treated of, in which a higher state is contemplated. This was a condition of CELESTIAL life, in which are rest and peace, in consequence of the Lord having become the primary object of human love. He who loves the

Lord above all things, and *from that love perceives and does what are good and true in all the descending varieties of duty, is a* CELESTIAL MAN. It is a development of the highest condition of humanity on earth. To accomplish this was the great design of all God's providential works; and the realization of it is expressed as being the attainment of the seventh *day;* hence the Lord is stated to have ended his work, and rested thereon; also, to have blessed and sanctified it. That the seventh day is expressive of this exalted state of man, and thus a realization of the Divine purpose on earth respecting him, must be pretty evident to the reflecting. For God cannot be said to have "ended his work," and "rested," in any ordinary sense of those terms. The perpetuation of nature is as much a Divine work as that of its origination; and therefore, supposing the narration to refer to mundane things, the statement that he *ended* his work on the seventh day does not agree with the truth that he is continually working for its preservation. To this it may indeed be replied that the statement ought to be understood only as expressing the end of the work by which nature was originated. But if this were granted, the difficulty is not removed; for after this, God is described to have caused a deep sleep to fall upon Adam, to have taken a rib out of his side and built it into a woman. The expression, therefore, will not bear such a construction. Neither can it be supposed that *rest* could be required, unless we venture to predicate fatigue of the Omnipotent, which will scarcely be attempted.

It is easy, then, to see that by God ending his work, and resting on the seventh day, the idea is symbolically expressed, that the Divine purpose in human development was so far completed, and thus that the Divine love was satisfied; the rest not being a cessation of those active providences by which it had been brought about, but a holy satisfaction with their result.

It is admitted that the seventh day, in this narrative, cannot mean the seventh day in the ordinary sense of that expression, because what are described as the six preceding days are not days in the ordinary sense; and, therefore, the seventh day must be regarded as the emblem of some exalted state. Cruden observes that this word seven is used in the Scriptures as a number of perfection, and that in the sacred books and religion of the Jews a great number of events and mysterious circumstances are set forth by it.* It may be useful to cite an instance or two in which it is employed without any reference to its numerical import. Thus Isaiah, speaking of the future glory of the Church, says, "In that day *seven* women shall take hold of one man,"† where by *seven* women is denoted an exalted state of the affections, and by their taking hold of one man is signified their attachment to, and acknowledgment of, the Lord as that Divine Being, whom the prophet beheld as "one man."‡ Again, it is written, "She that hath borne *seven* languisheth,"§ to signify that the Church, in which sanctified affection had been conspicuous, was now declining. The Lamb which was beheld in the midst of the throne is said to have "had *seven* horns and *seven* eyes, which are the *seven* Spirits of God;"|| to denote the perfection of power and wisdom by which the Lord is distinguished: and thus it is evident that the number seven is used to denote completeness and perfection.

The seventh day was afterwards called the Sabbath, which word, in the original tongue, means rest: it also includes the idea of peace. The rest and peace which God is said to have had on the Sabbath day, signify that merciful repose and heavenly tranquillity which are experienced on the part of man, when he rests in the delights of superior wisdom, and enjoys the peace of exalted virtue; they are plainly the Divine rest and peace within him, and are predicated of God, to indicate that their existence in man is from him.

Almost every one has some idea, more or less distinct, of the number seven denoting something that is holy. This may have originated from the circumstance of the seventh day being the Sabbath; nevertheless, it cannot be the holiness of the day; for what distinction, in that respect, can exist among the seven? Therefore it must be some presumed states of holiness in man, specially exhibited on this day, which are the ground of the idea. Holiness, indeed, belongeth to the Lord alone, and, therefore, He is the essential Sabbath;¶ consequently, man, so

---

* "Concordance," Art. Seven.   † Isa. iv. 1.

‡ Dan. x. 5. Marginal reading.   § Jer. xv. 9. || Rev. v. 6.

¶ Mark ii. 28.

far as he is receptive of holiness from him, may also be considered as a Sabbath, by virtue of that excellence.

It is on account of this signification of the seventh or Sabbath day that, under the representative economy, it was commanded that no work should be done thereon. Those who attain the celestial state are not, like the spiritual man, to be engaged in the labour which attends the *learning* of spiritual truths and duty by an *external* way, because, possessing the love of God above all things, which is the highest sentiment of humanity, they will at once *perceive* what are wise and good from an *internal* dictate. Thus the law, which is prohibitory in the letter, declares a blessing in its spirit: and the prohibition was delivered in order to provide a means conducive to the blessing.

Under the same significant dispensation there was a law declaring that the transgressor of the Sabbath should be put to death.* This, indeed, appears a fierce and sanguinary enactment; but its letter was never designed for perpetual obligation. It was written for the sake of representing, and so revealing, a spiritual truth which every one may see to be rational in its nature, and continually in force. The Sabbath, in the highest sense, is the Lord himself, because He is himself that essential rest and peace which the word expresses: to violate the Sabbath in this sense is to reject the Lord, by sinning against him, and thereby to incur the penalty of spiritual death.

Hence, then, it is evident that the seventh day, in the subject before us, is mentioned to express the holiness of man on his attainment of the celestial state. Thus we learn that the second chapter of Genesis is designed to treat of man under an aspect superior to that in which he is spoken of in the first. It was seen that God's proposition was to create man in his own image and *likeness*, but it was the image only which was then effected: the production of the likeness was to be a subsequent work, and this is distinctly declared to have been accomplished.† It came into existence with man's sabbatical state. He was an "image" in his spiritual degree of life, because he was good from the teachings of wisdom; but he was a "likeness" in his celestial degree of life, because he was good from the impulses of love.

The first chapter of Genesis treats of the creation of the image,

---

* Exod. xxxv. 2. † Gen. v. 1.

or spiritual state; the second describes the creation of the likeness, or celestial state. This at once accounts for the circumstance of there being two descriptions of the creation, marked by somewhat different and distinctive features. Each treats of its own subject; and, therefore, we may observe even a difference of terms applied to both man and God. The Supreme Being, in respect to the spiritual man, is called by the single name *God*, but in reference to the celestial man he is called *Lord God*. Also, man's external nature in the former case is denominated *earth*, but in the latter it is spoken of as the *ground:* * and this is the man of whom it is said, "The Lord God breathed into his nostrils the breath of *lives;* and he became a living soul." † The living soul here spoken of does not specifically refer to that internal part of man to which his immortality belongs; ‡ that had been communicated before, and was obviously implied in his possession of the divine image; what is here more properly meant is, that external part of him which was now to be infilled with the living principles of heavenly life, which are the truths of faith in the understanding and the good of love in the will. These are the *lives* by which his character was now to be distinguished; they were to belong to him, and to be among the sources of his dignity and blessedness. They are proper to a high state of genuine religion; and Christianity contemplates their existence, for it is written "that man doth not live by bread only, but by every *word* that proceedeth out of the mouth of the Lord doth man live"; § here, by living, is not meant man's natural animus, but his religious life—the life of love in the will, denoted by the "bread," and the life of wisdom in the understanding, denoted by the "word that pro-

---

* The reader is desired to verify these remarkable facts by referring to the first chapter throughout up to the third verse of the second, and thence to the commencement of the fall.

† Gen. ii. 7. "Lives," plural, is the true rendering of the original.

‡ It is generally allowed that the import of the original words translated "living soul" is not the immaterial spirit of man, but the organic life of the animal frame; for the same words are rendered "creature that hath life," and "living creature" (see Gen. i. 20–24). This is the opinion of Grotius, Hewlett, Dr. Pye Smith, and other eminent scholars; and thus it very satisfactorily agrees with the spiritual idea advanced above.

§ Deut. viii. 3; Matt. iv. 4.

ceedeth out of the mouth of the Lord." When the soul lives from these principles, the seventh day is attained, and a celestial man exists. A wise and amiable love is the ground of his faith and action. He possesses a holy freedom, and the ends which influence him have all a regard to the Lord, his kingdom, and eternal life. What the Lord teaches him he perceives to be true and beautiful, because he has made a close approximation to that intellectual eminence which the Divine instructor proposed.

CHAPTER V.

ADAM A RELIGIOUS COMMUNITY.—EDEN, WITH ITS GARDEN AND EASTERN SITUATION.—HOW TO BE KEPT.

> "What if earth
> Be but the shadow of heaven; and things therein
> Each to other like, more than on earth is thought?"
> MILTON'S "*Paradise Lost*," *Book V., lines* 574-76.

The points in that most ancient history in the world, to the elucidation of which this and the two succeeding chapters are to be devoted, are thus described.

"And the Lord God planted a garden eastward in Eden; and there he put the man whom he had formed. And out of the ground made the Lord God to grow every tree that is pleasant to the sight and good for food; the tree of life also in the midst of the garden, and the tree of knowledge of good and evil. And a river went out of Eden to water the garden; and from thence it was parted, and became into four heads. The name of the first *is* Pison: that *is* it which encompasseth the whole land of Havilah, where *there is* gold; and the gold of that land *is* good: there *is* bdellium and the onyx stone. And the name of the second river *is* Gihon: the same *is* it which encompasseth the whole land of Ethiopia. And the name of the third river *is* Hiddekel; that *is* it which goeth toward the east of Assyria. And the fourth river *is* Euphrates."—*Genesis* ii. 8–14.

Here, to all appearances, we have described the first natural garden, and that the result of the divine planting, together with some intimation of its geographical locality and adjacent features. But if these statements be enquired into with the light and freedom belonging to a period when it has become allowable to examine intellectually the things of faith, we shall have the strongest evidence for believing them to treat of the religious states of living men, and not of the vegetable productions of insensible earth.

The primary object of the Scriptures is to make a revelation to man; to show him the things which pertain to his inner character; to disclose the philosophy and display the principles of spiritual life; to point out the nature of his future existence; and exhibit to him those causes which conduce to weal or woe in that other stage of being, for which this is but the preparatory world: and especially to keep before his mind's eye and inner life an intellectual faith in God, and practical charity towards mankind. These are the leading things of revelation; things which can be known to us by no other means than a revelation. The sciences and philosophies of nature cannot teach them. No acquaintance with physical phenomena, however extensive or profound, can unfold to us any information upon truly spiritual subjects. When they are divulged, natural philosophy may afford us materials for their illustration, but it cannot discover them. The utmost skill in the anatomy of the body has never enabled its professor either to detect or determine any fact about the soul. It is of a different substance, and belongs to another world—a world which God knows, and concerning which man could have known nothing if God had not consented to inform him. The means which he has employed to make these communications is the language of men so constructed as to embody and convey the mind of God. Nor is this all, but even the *genius of the language* which prevailed with men during that particular epoch when revelation was first vouchsafed to them, has been *bended into this merciful service*. Figure is the form in which the primitive genius of language has displayed itself. This to us, at first sight, may appear somewhat artificial; but a little reflection must show it to be genuinely natural,—so much so that it requires a considerable amount of art to construct a sentence without having recourse to it. The language of a primitive people must needs have been eminently figurative;* and, therefore, a revelation vouchsafed during its prevalence would, obviously,

---

* Dr. Hugh Blair was also of this opinion. His words are, "The style of all the most early languages, among nations who are in the first and rude periods of society, is found, without exception, to be full of figures; hyperbolical and picturesque in a high degree."—"*Rhetoric and Belles-Lettres,*" Sec. 6.

partake very largely of such a style. The mental genius and modes of expression that were extant, would be made to subserve the purposes of embodying divine ideas. If the antediluvian narratives be the most ancient in the world, and really refer to the aborigines of our race, and if it be true that the language of figure is the natural and spontaneous utterance of human thought; then it will follow that these documents ought to be so regarded. It is not consistent criticism to judge of the literary production of an ancient and highly poetic people, by that matter-of-fact standard of writing which is required in a prosaic and scientific age.

But supposing the occurrences to have been such as they are described; supposing that we saw no difficulties in the way of believing all the narrations to be literally true; supposing the circumstances mentioned harmonized with our knowledge of physics, and that they were in strict agreement with the perceptions and demands of reason; and supposing the history to express in the letter all the ideas that were intended: of what *spiritual* advantage would such knowledge be to man? Would it raise him one step upon the way which leads to heaven? We grant that it might satisfy our natural curiosity to know something certain about the beginning of things; we admit that our worldly information would be extended by it; we concede that, for the learning and scientific condition of the world, it would be useful; but of what real service would such earthly information be to our spiritual well-being?

If we knew that the world was created out of nothing; if it were certain that the first man was made from red earth;[*] if it were physically demonstrable that the first woman originated from his rib; if it were credible that life and knowledge once grew upon a tree; if it were evident that a serpent could talk: still, the utmost that could be said of such facts is, that they were extraordinary events peculiar to the natural world in its beginning: yet this would not raise man's thought above terrestrial things, or furnish him with any information con-

[*] Adam was so called, as critics and commentators suppose, from the *red earth* of which it is imagined he was formed.—*Robertson, On the Pentateuch*, p. 16.

cerning his spirituality, his futurity, or duty;* and when it is seen that all these things are the antagonists of good reason, it is evident that they can have no relation to man's inner consciousness, his spiritual condition, his religious development, or heavenly hopes. If we confine our ideas to the letter, it is plain that we limit them to the things of this world. We should endeavour to eliminate the spiritual things, which, as a revelation, they are intended to communicate. If we overlook this duty we shall lose sight of its practical character. The Apostle says, "The letter killeth, but the spirit giveth life";† which plainly means that the literal sense is of this world only, and that it is the spiritual sense which discloses spiritual life, and so points to its condition in the world to come. Moreover, the Lord has told us that "his words are spirit and life," ‡ a sentiment applicable to the whole Word, and not merely to the context in which it occurs; and consequently, to the antediluvian narrations.

The internal or spiritual sense of those ancient documents is their proper sense,—at least, we have not succeeded in discovering any other: that sense agrees with the designs of revelation, to disclose ideas upon spiritual subjects, and its truths are felt to be so, because they reach our human consciousness—they echo to the voice of intuition, and express the sensations of experience.

We have stated that the development—the spiritual creation of the human principles of religious life and actions, treated of under the figure of a natural creation, was a reality possessed and enjoyed by the man of the most ancient times. § The narrative teaches us not only the order by which, from being

---

* "Although the light of nature, and the works of creation and providence, do so far manifest the goodness, wisdom, and power of God, as to leave men inexcusable; yet they are not sufficient to give that knowledge of God and of his will, which is necessary unto salvation."—*Westminster Confession of Faith*, Art. 1.

† 2 Cor. iii. 6.   ‡ John vi. 63.

§ "When you talk of a man, I would not have you tack flesh and blood to the notion, no, nor those limbs neither which are made of them; these are but tools for the soul to work with, and no more a part of the man than an axe or a plane is a piece of a carpenter."—*Collier.*

"void" and dark, he was filled with spiritual principles and gifted with intellectual light, but it chronicles a fact which distinguished him as an early inhabitant of our world. It is historically true, understood in reference to his internal state. He was actually raised into that spiritual and celestial eminence so forcibly expressed by being in the image and likeness of God.

But in what sense are we to view this man? Is he to be considered merely as an individual, or to be regarded as a community? We think that the latter and not the former is the true idea connected with this subject; and we believe this idea to be clearly recognized in verbal expressions, as well as in more general statements.

Although the history is not to be taken in its literal sense, yet its language and intimations are constructed on the idea of extant society, and they may fairly be referred to as affording evidence upon this question, which must be received as important by those who insist upon the literal sense only. There are several circumstances so mentioned as to imply the existence of society apart from that of Adam, or his posterity. When, according to the common reading of these narratives, there were only three inhabitants upon the earth, we find that Cain, after the fratricide he had committed, said, "My punishment is greater than I can bear—and it shall come to pass, *that* every one that findeth me shall slay me.—A mark also was set upon him, lest any one finding him should kill him." * These statements evidently imply the existence of society: why should Cain fear every one that found him, if there had been none to find him but his parents? and of what use could have been the mark set upon him, if there had been none but Adam and his wife to see it and be warned by it? † They

---

* Gen. iv. 13-15.

† This difficulty has long been acknowledged ; but it is usually met by *supposing* that Adam might have had other sons and daughters, before this time, whose births are not mentioned, and from whom such a population might have descended.—See *Dodd, Bishop Patrick, Rev. J. Hewlett, &c.* Dr. A. Clarke *supposed* that Adam, at 130 years of age, had 130 children ; he next *supposed* each of these to have had a child at the age of 65, and that they continued to have one every succeeding year, which would, in the 130 years, amount to 1,219 persons, whom he *supposed* to have excited Cain's apprehen-

must have known him without such sign. These circumstances show not only that society then existed, but also that it was influenced by a moral sentiment which could reject and condemn a felon's crime.

But there is another fact equally strong, bearing upon this point. When Cain went into the Land of Nod, he is said to have had a wife and built a city, which he named after his first-born son, Enoch.* If there had not been society, where could he have obtained his wife, or procured the workmen necessary for such erections? Moreover, of what use could have been such a city, if there had been no society to inhabit it? From these facts, adverted to before,† it is fairly to be inferred that a people were then in existence, for whom no relationship can be traced to Adam, and of whose origin we have no history. The employment of Abel as a keeper of sheep is, also, favourable to the same conclusion; for what else but the existence of society could have originated such an occupation?

Now, if there were such a people,—and of this we think there can be no well-founded doubt,—why may not Adam indicate the existence of a community that had been gradually separated from the general mass, and had induced upon them those excellencies of character to which we have adverted? That which is apparently predicable of an individual may, with equal propriety, be said of a number of persons; and, therefore, the narratives relating to Adam, instead of being the personal history of one man, may be the spiritual history of a highly cultivated people, with whom a Church existed; and, because it is the oldest of which we have any record, may be called the most ancient Church. There is surely nothing irrational in this inference. But is there any more direct proof of such an idea? We think there is, and that it is afforded by the very name.

---

sion, and founded the city, which he has called the Village of Enoch.—*Commentary on* Gen. iv. 14. We should like to have been favoured with data for these suppositions of this pious and excellent man; they should be contained in the history, and we ask the reader carefully to examine it, and see if he can find them: we have made the effort, but have failed. Had we succeeded, it would not at all have affected the general view we are attempting to unfold.

* Gen. iv. 17. † Page 17.

When the Lord said, "Let us make man," the proposition could not refer to the individual, but to the race. Man is put for mankind, and so it is to be taken as expressing that wider sense: this, indeed, is evident, for it is immediately added, " And let *them* have dominion." * But the original word, translated man, is Adam, and this is distinctly asserted to have a collective signification, for it is written that the Lord "called *their* name Adam in the day when *they* were created "; † male and female are here, indeed, specifically meant; but there is an abundance of other instances in the Scriptures where the term is employed in the sense of mankind, or the human race in general. That this is its true import seems evident from the circumstance of its never being found in a plural form, though it is acknowledged that there is no grammatical difficulty in the way of its being declined by the dual and plural terminations and the pronominal suffixes.‡ Now, the term Adam occurs in the second and third chapters of Genesis no less than nineteen times, and in every case it is put with the definite article: as, then, it is not the actual appellation of an individual, but a nominal expressive of kind, it will follow that the terms, *the Adam*, or *the man*, must describe the people,—the community,—the society,—the Church, or whatever word else may be thought more fitting to signify the idea of a human association, possessing the solid acquirements of a genuinely spiritual religion.

It may be supposed that Adam's individuality is asserted by the Apostle where he says, "As in Adam all die, even so in Christ shall all be made alive." § This statement is both elliptical and symbolical. It is evident, however, that by the dying of Adam is meant the sin which was committed. But as this can be perpetrated by a community, and be spoken of under a collective name, it does not interpose any real difficulty in the way of the conclusion at which we have arrived. The fall of the Adamic Church caused sin; the establishment of the Christian Church is to promote deliverance. The Apostle says, "The first man Adam was made a living soul." ‖ In this

---

* Gen. i. 26. † Gen. v. 2.
‡ Kitto's "Cyclopædia," Art. Adam. § 1 Cor. xv. 22.
‖ 1 Cor. xv. 45.

there is nothing inconsistent with our view. "The first man Adam" is a phrase as applicable to the first community dignified by religious manhood, as to an individual: and "the living soul" of which he speaks was the holy genius by which they were distinguished. This is plain from what has already been said of the original passage to which the Apostle here refers.

The successive developments of character described of the Adam, were the progressive advancements of the community so denominated. They consisted of spiritual and celestial excellencies, which were actually enjoyed, not by an individual merely, but by a whole people, who lived in some exceedingly remote period of the past, and who, from the superiority of their character, constituted what we prefer to call a Church, and, consequently, it is the most ancient, because it is the earliest of which we have any revealed or authentic records.

Understanding, then, that by Adam is meant a highly cultivated and innocent community, we next come to inquire concerning the "garden eastward in Eden," where the Lord was pleased to put them.

It is evident, if Adam were a people, among whom a dispensation of divine blessings was received and enjoyed, that they must have occupied some position in the world's geography. But it does not follow that God has made the knowledge of that place a subject of revelation. Nor is any information concerning it derivable therefrom. There have been a great variety of positions claimed for it; these, however, are now reduced to *nine* theories,[*] not one of which answers to all the conditions which the problem demands. Travellers have sought for it with much industry and diligence, but no locality has been discovered which responds geographically to the antediluvian descriptions. It may be said to have had some of its original features so disturbed by the flood as to alter its identity. This is plausible, supposing the narrative to have been written with a view to geographical definition and the flood to have been really an inundation of water. These, however, are points which need not detain us now. We think that there is good reason for be-

---

[*] Rosenmüller's "Biblical Geography of Central Asia," translated by the Rev. N. Morren, pp. 91–98, Edinburgh, 1836.

lieving it to have been situated in some part of Southern Asia, but the precise locality is not so easily determined. It might have been in Palestine, as some of the best writers upon this subject have been led to believe.

If, however, we were sure of the precise spot, what would be its use, beyond the circumstance of adding another fact to our geographical knowledge? If we were influenced in our reflections concerning it by the mere letter of the Word, it might be turned to some account. We might say, In this spot Adam was placed before he was a week old, and, without the least experience, commanded to dress and keep the garden. It was here that the tree of life grew, and, hard by, flourished the tree of knowledge of good and evil. It was here that the first progenitor of our race lived but one day in the enjoyment of his felicity, in that he sinned, and was expelled the next. This was the place where the serpent, of whose existence and malicious capabilities man had not been informed, reasoned, and seduced the first pair. It was here that the Lord God walked, in the cool of the day, and called for Adam. It was here that the cherubim were placed, and the flaming sword which turned every way. Such, we say, might be the train of our reflections if we knew the geographical Eden, and were influenced in our meditations by nothing more than the mere letter of a figurative narrative.

But if we were under the persuasion of those popular theological speculations which have been educed from these remarkable narrations, we might still farther say,—Here it was where Adam, our federal head, transgressed the law, and induced the penalty of guilt upon unborn myriads of his race. This was the scene of that occurrence which aroused the indignation of the Almighty, and caused him to pronounce a curse upon the whole family of man. Here was the locality of that event which led God the Son to take upon himself the penalty of transgressors, and, in after times, to suffer as the victim substituted for their sin. It was here that the circumstance transpired by which God the Father was led to accept the sufferings of his innocent Son, in lieu of the punishment of guilty man, and which, by the persuasions of the Holy Ghost, they are to believe is justice. This, we say, might be the tenor of our remarks, if we actually knew the Eden of the world, and were influenced in our reflections concerning it by the mistaken theology of our day.

The place of the natural Eden is an undiscoverable spot, and, therefore, any advantages which might accrue from the above train of thoughts must come, if they come at all, independently of such information. To know it as a portion of the geography of the earth would not convey to us any knowledge of the principles of heaven. We could there see but little more of the finger of God, or the footsteps of the Almighty, than we may behold in the broad lands, the fertile fields, and cultivated gardens of our own country. We need not go to Asia in search of natural evidences of the wisdom and benevolence of our Creator: they are abundant in Europe, and we may discover them at our own door, if we be so disposed. It is the state of our souls which the Scriptures contemplate; it is that of which they treat; and the places of our bodies are sometimes employed to represent their condition. Such is the case with Eden and its garden on the East. Though we do not know their "local habitation," we are acquainted with the signification of their "names." We feel assured that the chief object of their being mentioned in the Scriptures, is to express that pleasurable condition of love and light which was enjoyed by the people of the most ancient Church, whose name was Adam.

It was when man had attained the seventh day—that state of holiness of which the Sabbath was significant—that "the Lord God planted a garden eastward in Eden." It is commonly supposed that the Lord did no work upon the seventh day; but this is not declared: it is said that he ended his work thereon, which plainly means that some was done. The work of the Lord consists of the influence of his grace to make man wise and good. The state of holiness represented by the seventh, or Sabbath day, was of a celestial quality, and thus somewhat different from that which was signified by the six preceding days. Those days denoted states of spiritual labour, in which it was first requisite to acknowledge the movings of the Divine care; then procure the light necessary to separate man from darkness; next educe the fruit-bearing principles of morality, afterwards admit the illumination of love and faith, then bring forth the living affections of religious intelligence, and the sixth day he became a spiritual man—an image of God. It was now that the "heavens and the earth were finished"; that is, the affections proper to the internal and external of the *spiritual* man were completed. Yet it was not until the seventh day that God ended his work. That was the day which God is said to have sanctified, because it was significant of the *celestial* man, who performs all the duties of religion from a principle of love; and love never feels duty to be a labour.

The distinction of these two states, and the circumstance of the former being treated of in the first chapter of Genesis, and the latter in the second, are spoken of above.

When Adam, the name which God employed to denote the most ancient people, reached to a celestial state,—when they became principled in love to God as the ruling delight of all their affections and thoughts,—they were obviously in the possession of a felicity arising from the tranquillity of purity and peace. This state is one of surpassing beauty. It is not merely that cessation from labour which occasionally attends the process of intellectual development, and which labour may afterwards have to be resumed; but it is a rest arising from having attained the summit of human excellence, and which nothing can produce but the interior life of loveliness and wisdom.

Now, it is the possession and enjoyment of this superior state of heavenly love which are denoted by Eden.* Hence the

* Dr. Adam Clarke observes that "it would astonish an ordinary reader, who should be obliged to consult different commentators and critics on *the situation of the terrestrial Paradise*, to see the vast variety of opinions by which they are divided. Some place it in the third heaven, others in the fourth ; some within the orbit of the moon, others in the moon itself; some in the middle region of the air, or beyond the earth's attraction ; some on the earth, others under the earth, and others within the earth ; some have found it at the north pole, others at the south, some in Tartary, some in China, some in the island of Ceylon ; some in America, others in Africa, under the equator ; some in Mesopotamia, others in Syria, Persia, Arabia, Babylon, Assyria, and in Palestine ; some have condescended to place it in *Europe*, and others have contended that it either exists not, or is merely of a spiritual nature, and that the whole account is to be spiritually understood."—*Com., Gen.* ii. 10.

The Doctor certainly believed that there was such a place, but he was not very certain about its locality. Does not all this show the necessity of seeking for it only in the state of a wise and happy people?

word, as a Hebrew expression, denotes what is pleasant and delightful: it also signifies tenderness, loveliness, and beauty. A pure and elevated love is always productive of high and sanctified delights, and it is God alone who can place man in the full enjoyment of them. When man loves God above all things, and lives in charity with all men, from the influence of His love, he resides in Eden, for it is then that he dwells amidst delights and pleasantness, loveliness and beauty. This we understand to have been the Eden of which the Scriptures speak, and into which the men of the most ancient Church were introduced. This is the Eden which we believe the Lord is desirous we should again know, and to the discovery of which he is wishful to direct our solicitude and attention.

But in this Eden there was a garden. These, however, are two different things. Love is not a solitary principle: it is always attended by its corresponding intelligence, and this is represented by the garden, which is said to have been planted eastward in Eden. We grant, indeed, that by God planting a garden may be meant his giving fertility, and causing growth, in some particular situation: and we admit that it is highly probable a superior people would be placed in some position favourable to vegetable luxuriance and beauty, because we think it is a law of mind, to express itself, not only in significant words, but to indicate itself by representative circumstances: nevertheless, we conceive that the true object of a garden being here mentioned, was to denote the existence of a cultivated intelligence; and this is said to have been in Eden, because its ground was in a purified love.

Surely every one may see that a beautiful garden is the appropriate symbol of an elegant mind:[*] what else but such a mind can in reality be the garden of God? Is not such a mind of his planting? Is not the fruit of such a mind of his culture? And is not the felicity arising from the possession of such a

---

[*] Origen asks, "Who is so weak as to think that God planted a garden, like a husbandman, and in it a real tree of life, to be tasted by corporeal teeth (tongue); or that the knowledge of good and evil was to be acquired by eating the fruit of another tree? And as to God's walking in the garden, and Adam's hiding himself from him among the trees, no man can doubt that these things are to be taken figuratively and not literally."

mind among his good and precious gifts? We instantly perceive the truth of this: it comes to us at once: the reason is, because, when the mind is enlightened by the suggestion, it passes, as it were suddenly and spontaneously, from the physical to the mental idea.

This general resemblance may be confirmed by more particular analogies. Thus, as the good and beautiful things of a garden grow to their perfection, only as they are set and taken care of by human industry and skill; so the true and useful things of the mind come forth in their completeness, only as they are planted and preserved by the wisdom and goodness of God. In a garden there is nothing cultivated but what is useful and delightful for the rational man; so in the minds of the intelligent, nothing is permitted to grow but what is requisite to promote some Christian grace.

The Lord Jesus Christ most certainly viewed the mind under this aspect, when he taught his beautiful parable of the sower. The "seed," said he, "is the Word of God"; and "he that receiveth the seed into good ground is he that heareth the Word, and understandeth *it;* which also beareth fruit, and bringeth forth, some a hundredfold, some sixty, some thirty."* Every one must see that this description of the mind, as arising from the reception and understanding of the Word, is founded in its resemblance to a garden. Moreover, the Scriptures on several occasions compare the Church to a garden. Thus, of the righteous it is written, that his *soul should be as a watered garden;* † and of the captive Israelites it was predicted that they should "plant gardens, and eat the fruit of them." ‡ which plainly means that the Church in bondage, which they then represented, would ultimately become intelligent and enjoy its advantages.

It is because the garden of Eden signifies the intelligence of love, as possessed by the Church of those ancient times, that it is written, "The Lord will comfort Zion, and he will make her wilderness like Eden, and her desert like the garden of the Lord." § Here, by Zion is meant the Church; the wilderness

---

* Matt. xiii. 23. † Isa. lviii. 11.

‡ Jer. xxix. 5. § Isa. li. 3.

and desert denote its deficiencies in truth and faith, but which, nevertheless, will become like Eden, when it is influenced by love; and like the garden of the Lord when distinguished by intelligence. They are said to be *like* the others, because they will, in some measure, be the reproduction of their excellence. But the prophet distinctly refers the wisdom and knowledge of the Church to the circumstance of having been in Eden, the garden of God. His words are, "With thy wisdom and thine understanding thou hast gotten thee riches;—thou hast been in Eden, the garden of God."* Upon this point, then, we need not farther dwell: we plainly see that the garden is employed as a beautiful symbol of that truth-bearing intelligence, which is the proper inheritance of the celestial man.

But this garden is said to have been eastward of Eden, to denote that the intelligence of the Adamic Church derived its illumination and warmth wholly from the Lord. For as the sun of nature is always ascending in the east as the earth is perpetually rotating upon its axis towards him; so the Lord, as the Sun of righteousness, is represented by the east eternally rising upon human minds, as men turn themselves to Him to receive the warmth of his love and the light of his wisdom. That the eastern sky at the time of sunrising is, from its splendour and magnificence, a beautiful representation of the Deity in his majesty and glory, may be easily perceived. The Scriptures frequently mention that region in this sense. A strong example is given by the prophet, where he says, "Behold, the glory of the God of Israel came from the way of the east."† The earliest traditions of all knowledge, whether human or divine, are associated with some ideas of the east: and wise men are said to have come therefrom,‡ to indicate

---

* Ezek. xxviii. 4, 13. † Ezek. xliii. 2.

‡ Matt. ii. 1. It deserves, also, to be remarked, that those wise men are said to have seen his star in the east (ver. 2). This is commonly understood to mean that they beheld the star in the eastern quarter of the sky. But this cannot be the true idea. (See *Campbell's* "*Four Gospels*," *translated from the Greek*.) The star which they saw must have been really in the west, for they were guided by it out of the east country westward, towards Jerusalem. The meaning, therefore, is that the wise men were in the east at the time they beheld the star. This agrees with the first verse; and it is necessary to express the spiritual sense, which is, that a state of illumination from the Lord is necessary to direct us where to find him.

that all genuine wisdom in man is communicated to him from the Lord. We also read, on several occasions, of the children of the east,* because they represented all those who are possessed of the knowledges of truth and good from the Lord. This idea is the source of that holy custom, which once prevailed, of turning to the east in times of prayer. It is also the origin of a similar observance in certain Christian churches at this day, on the repetition of their creeds; a circumstance which shows that a custom may exist long after the reason for its adoption has ceased to be attended to.

From these facts and considerations it is evident that the description of Adam's being placed in the garden eastward in Eden was intended to signify the state of his intelligence and love, together with his continued acknowledgment that those blessings came to him from the divine munificence and care.† This garden is said to have been planted by the Lord, to teach us that the insemination of every spiritual seed, and the growth of all celestial virtue, are derived from him: they are, as the prophet says, branches of his planting and the works of his hands, that he may be glorified. ‡ Such was the garden into which Adam—the most ancient Church—was happily introduced, and which he was mercifully required to "dress and to keep":—to enjoy, but to acknowledge that it was the Lord's, since it was only by such acknowledgment that the blessing could be kept.

We may also observe that commentators have felt great difficulty in discovering what is meant by the word *east*, as used in several parts of Scripture. Calmet confesses it on the ground that he was compelled to admit that it seemed to mean places *north* of India. (For a summary statement, see Cruden, Art. East.) Others have seen that it is sometimes used without any regard to the eastern quarter of the heavens. (See *Rev. J. F. Denham, M.A., F.R.S., Kitto's Bibl. Cyclopædia, Art. East.*) Of this there can be no well-founded doubt; the reason is, because it refers to the Lord, and the internal sense of the context required that it should be so employed.

* Judg. vi. 3; viii. 10; 1 Kings iv. 30.

† Dr. South thus nobly describes the understanding of man in Paradise: "It was then sublime, clear, and aspiring, and, as it were, the soul's upper region, lofty and serene, free from the vapours and disturbances of the inferior affections. In sum, it was quick and lively, open as the day, untainted as the morning, full of the innocence and sprightliness of youth; it gave the soul a full, bright view into all things, and was not only a window, but itself a prospect."—*Sears on Regeneration*, p. 31.

‡ Isa. lx. 21.

CHAPTER VI.

THE TREES OF THE GARDEN: SPECIFICALLY THE TREE OF LIFE, AND THE TREE OF KNOWLEDGE OF GOOD AND EVIL.

"Know that in the trees, fountains, and other things of the garden of Eden, were the figures of the most curious things by which the first Adam saw and understood spiritual things."—RABBI SIMON BAR ABRAHAM, *as cited from Hutchenson's Hebrew Writings, by the Rev. E. Madeley, in his "Science of Correspondences Elucidated,"* p. 125, *note*.

The peculiar language applied to the trees of the garden of Eden, and, specifically, the remarkable names given to two of them, contribute some additional evidence in favour of those views which we have attempted to establish in the preceding chapter. We shall now proceed to show that they are intended to represent some *particular* conditions of that intelligence and love, which we have seen to be the *general* inheritance of a superior people—the most ancient Church.

It is admitted that "much more seems intended" by those trees than appears upon the surface, and although, in some quarters, difficulties have been felt in determining what that is,* the cause of them is not so much in the things themselves as in the predisposition of certain minds to discover some physical meaning where it is not intended. The Jews interpreted the prophecies announcing the coming of the Messiah to mean the raising up of an earthly prince, in order to confer glory upon the worldly kingdom of Israel. They made up their minds with this mistaken idea, and thus produced a difficulty in understanding the true meaning of those predictions: so much so that they were actually fulfilled in the manifestation and mission of Jesus Christ, without their being acknowledged by that obstinate people. The confessed difficulty in comprehending what is meant by the trees of the garden, though different in kind, is the same in principle. Some physical notion has

* Dr. A. Clarke's Commentary on Gen. ii. 9.

been conceived concerning them, whereas some mental condition is really meant. "Life" and "knowledge" are not vegetable productions, they are spiritual and intellectual existences: and the attempt to find the former, in a narrative constructed only to express the latter, must be as fruitless as the endeavour to find

"Fire in ice,
Or darkness in the blaze of sunshine."

There existed in the garden four sorts of trees: *first*, those which were "pleasant to the sight"; *second*, those that were "good for food"; *third*, "the tree of life, which was in the midst of the garden"; and, *fourth*, "the tree of knowledge of good and evil." *

All who have viewed those statements in a merely literal sense, suppose the trees "pleasant to the sight" to have consisted in all such as are elegant in their structure, producing a beautiful variety of flowers, and exhibiting to the eye a rich magnificence of colour. It has also been thought that those which were "good for food" meant all such as were productive of luxuriant fruits, suitable for human sustenance and health.

There can be no well-founded objection to a belief that gardens did exist among the Adamic people, or that trees of a delightful and exuberant character grew within them. Still they must be higher facts than these which were intended by the description. These only contemplate the pleasure of the senses and the nutrition of the body. But revelation points to deeper and more interior things: it regards the delights of the mind and the sustenance of the soul; and, therefore, the elegancies of nature are borrowed and employed for their symbolical indication. That this must be the main object for which those trees are mentioned seems evident from "the tree of life," and "the tree of knowledge of good and evil," with which they are associated. The very names of these forcibly express the idea of spiritual and intellectual things.

We are aware that "the tree of life" has been thought to have been a tree possessing certain *medicinal* virtues, which were to be a means for the preservation of the body, and to act as an

* Gen. ii. 9.

antidote against death. We are likewise aware that "the tree of knowledge" has been considered as a tree distinguished by some peculiar property, which, when taken, was capable of increasing knowledge. But those notions appear to us as rather the efforts of a lively imagination than the result of a solid judgment. The idea of a *medicinal* shrub being called the "tree of life," or a stimulating esculent "the tree of knowledge," may be plausible to some, but we do not see how it can be truth to any. The former idea concerning the "tree of life" is founded upon the persuasion that man's natural body was intended for immortality. This is the notion which has suggested that invention; if such notion be taken away,—and surely science has most effectually done so,*—then it is instantly left without a resting-place, and so must perish. But the supposed perfection of man necessarily excludes the idea of this tree being a *medicinal* shrub. The latter notion, relating to the tree of knowledge, may have originated in the circumstance of opium, and other stimulants, having been employed for the purpose of exciting the imagination. It is, indeed, admitted that we know no other ground for such a suggestion; † but there is no analogy between the actual occurrence and the supposed fact. A vegetable stimulant, by which, it is said, man may be induced to *display* his knowledge, and the production of a tree, which is supposed to *communicate* knowledge, are two essentially different things. The one is to induce partial intoxication on the body, the other is to secure intellectual information to the soul. But

---

* "We find that all organized matter, that is, everything that has life, vegetable and animal, is formed upon a plan which renders death *necessary*, or something equivalent to death. The first step to life in the corculum of a vegetable seed, or the atomic rudiment of the animal body, in both cases so minute and recondite as to be inaccessible to human cognizance, commences a course of changes, which imply an inevitable termination. From dead organic matter the living structure derives its necessary supplies. The process of nutrition, assimilation, growth, exhaustion, and reparation hold on their irresistible course, to decay and dissolution ; in another word, to death. Some persons have dreamed of sustaining animal life by exclusively vegetable food, ignorant that in every leaf, or root, or fruit, which they feed upon, they put to death myriads of living creatures."—*Dr. Pye Smith. Scrip. and Geo.* Second edition, pp. 93, 94.

† Dr. A. Clarke's Commentary.

even if any resemblance could be established between the two ideas, and an argument founded thereon to favour the supposition, then it would remain to be shown how man could have been in a state of perfection, when he must have been destitute of the knowledge which this tree was adapted to communicate; and, also, how the eating of it should be a sin, which, as we learn from the sequel, it most distinctly was. These queries must remain unanswered. The obscurities, arising from a supposed natural sense, abide in all their force; they do not admit of being removed: examination on such grounds cannot eject them; and the attempt to do so will tend rather to increase their number than diminish their force. This, indeed, has long been felt by large and pious minds; and commentators who have been wishful to explain, have been compelled to apologize. It is, therefore, necessary to take some other ground—ground that may be more fertile in spiritual thought and rational satisfaction.

Trees are frequently mentioned in the Word in a purely figurative sense. They constantly refer to man, or to the things pertaining to him. It is said of the righteous man, that "he shall be like a *tree* planted by the rivers of water, that bringeth forth his fruit in his season";* but of the ungodly, that they are as "*trees* whose fruit withereth." † Now, a man is either good or bad by virtue of such principles, and it was of the operation of these, and their production in the characters of men, that the Lord said, "Every good *tree* bringeth forth good fruit; but a corrupt *tree* bringeth forth evil fruit. Wherefore by their fruits ye shall know them."‡ But the principles of good and evil are very various; and, therefore, we find some of them particularized by trees of a specific character. Thus, the Lord said, "All the *trees* of the field shall know that I, the Lord, have brought down the *high tree*, have exalted the *low tree*, have dried up the *green tree*, and have made the *dry tree* to flourish."§ Here by the "trees of the field" are denoted all the living perceptions of genuine truth; hence it is said of them, that they should know such things. To "bring down

---

* Psa. i. 3.   † Jude 12.
‡ Matt. vii. 17, 20.   § Ezek. xvii. 24.

the high tree," denotes the humiliation of intellectual pride; to "exalt the low tree," signifies the elevation of unpretending knowledge; to "dry up the green tree," is to bring desolation upon faith alone; and "to make the dry tree to flourish," is to render the solid knowledge of truth fruitful in all manner of good works of love and use. It was because the fig-tree was merely green with leaves and destitute of fruit, representing faith without charity, that the Lord said, "Let no fruit grow on thee henceforward for ever. And presently the fig-tree withered away." * Mere truth in the mind is as a dry tree, when it exists only as an intellectuality: without the moisture and flexibility of love it is severe and hard; nevertheless, it contains within itself the elemental properties of spiritual fruitfulness, and thus the capabilities of realizing the declaration of the Psalmist, that "the trees of the Lord are full *of sap*." † It is because trees in general signify such mental things as belong to the interiors of the mind, and because both the one and the other are so various, that so many species of trees are mentioned in the Word, every species signifying something different. Of this we have a striking and beautiful example in the parable of Jotham, in which the *trees* are described as going forth to anoint a king over them. ‡

The proximate historical sense of that parable relates to the circumstances in which the people of Israel had then placed themselves. The trees in search of a king, represented the people in their selection of a ruler. The refusal of the olive, the fig, and the vine-trees, denoted that superior men had declined to accept the government of such a stiff-necked and rebellious people; while its reception by the bramble was designed to express the consent of Abimelech, who was a baseborn and treacherous man.

This, however, could not be all that was intended to be stated by a parable which owed its origin to inspiration, and was designed to be a revelation. That sense only connects it with the outer and worldly history of a bygone people. As such it can only be the vehicle for bringing down some more interior truths, which may apply, and be instructive, to all future ages of the Church.

* Matt. xxi. 19. † Psa. civ. 16. ‡ Judg. ix. 8–1.

Viewed under this aspect, the trees which were in search of a king to anoint over them, represented the natural state of man, mentally acknowledging that some principle ought to reign in the mind and rule the conduct. The application made to the olive, the fig, and the vine-trees, denotes its confession of the fitness of celestial, spiritual, and doctrinal truth to perform this duty: but their refusal of that office signifies that the natural state of man is such that, however much he may make a mental acknowledgment of the fitness of such principles to rule him, he has as yet no spiritual state really capable of submitting to their mild and valuable laws. The only government which can be brought to bear effectually upon such a condition, consists in those appearances of truth which the letter of the Word exhibits, and in which God is spoken of as being fierce and angry, forbidding and unlovely: and these appearances of truth are the bramble. God appeared to Moses in a burning bush (bramble), to represent those appearances of truth in the letter of the Word, by which natural men were to be led and governed.

Thus we see that all the trees referred to in the parable signify different classes of mental perceptions; and so it is with innumerable other cases, which could be readily cited from the Word. But enough may have been said to prepare us for admitting that the trees of Eden must have been mentioned, to represent those varied and beautiful *perceptions* of truth, which filled with light and loveliness the minds of the people of the most ancient Church. By *perception* is here meant that interior capability by which the men of those times were enabled to acknowledge, that truth is truth and good is good, as soon as such things were presented to their thought, and so to dispense with those reasoning processes which, as it is well known, the men of after times have been compelled to use, in order to procure such knowledge. This *perceptive state* was that referred to by the Lord, when he said, "Let your communications be, Yea, yea; Nay, nay"; the *reasoning state* is intimated in that other declaration, "Whatsoever is more than these cometh of evil."* Reasoning is the result of an obscurity of thought, which is among the evils of the fall; perception per-

---

* Matt. v. 37.

ished in that calamity; true Christianity is adapted to restore the blessing, and re-plant the trees which were its ancient representatives.

The trees of the garden of Eden, then, were the perceptions and principles proper to the high intelligence of the most ancient people. The trees "pleasant to the sight," denoted the internal perceptions of heavenly *truth;* because all such truth is pleasant to the intellectual eye: and the trees which were "good for food," signified the internal perceptions of heavenly *good;* because all such good is the food and nutrition of spiritual and celestial life. These were among the distinguished inheritances of those superior men.

But their most remarkable perceptions are described to us as "the tree of life *in the midst of the garden,* * and the tree of knowledge of good and evil." It never would have been said that the Lord planted these two trees in the garden, one of which was to prove a stumbling-block to its inhabitants, unless the circumstance had been intended to sustain some spiritual representation, consistent with the true order of Divine Providence in respect to the interior things of men. It is easy to see that the "life," † which is here referred to, must mean the inmost influences of holy men; and the "knowledge" spoken of must be that very knowledge which had contributed to raise them into that elevated condition.

LIFE is an invisible, intangible possession, evidencing its existence by the production of consequences upon our organization; it is a growing and fruit-bearing principle in man, in which respect it may be called a tree; faint, indeed, and feeble

---

* At the 3d verse of the 3d chapter, the tree of *knowledge* is spoken of as being in the *midst of the garden.* The reason for these different statements is this:—So long as Adam continued in his integrity, the tree of life—the perception of love—was his inmost principle; but when he declined therefrom, as the third chapter describes him to have done, then the tree of knowledge —the perception of truth—became his inmost principle. The change which had taken place in his state altered the position of the trees, and so indicates the gradual manner in which he fell.

† *Chaiyim*—lives. The plural form is used in the original, because the religious life of the man, here treated of, was displayed under a twofold aspect—viz., the life of his *affections,* and the life of his *thoughts.*

in its beginnings, but successively sending out more vigorous developments and powers.

So the KNOWLEDGE of good and evil is a mental acquisition, gradually putting forth its tender shoots and stronger limbs, attaining greater height and showing more luxuriance, both in its utterances and its acts; in which respects it, also, is most aptly likened to a tree.

Now these inmost influences, which are here denominated the tree of lives, consist in love,—love to God, and love to man,—loves which derive their essential quality from the Lord, and so induce an intellectual faith concerning Him.

Every one who will seriously reflect upon this subject must conclude that such loves are not only the *life* of a religious man's will, but, also, the *life* of his understanding. Love is the primary life of such a man; without this there could be no living faith; man could not think if he were not first influenced by love to do so; he could not act if the love of action were removed. Whatsoever a man thinks, believes, and does, proceeds from love as its living cause. He is senseless, thoughtless, inanimate, and dead, to everything he does not love. As his love grows cold, his thoughts wax torpid; but if his love inflame, his imagination is illuminated, his utterances become forcible, and his actions energetic. Whatever a man loves pre-eminently, he thinks of continually, and it will more or less display itself in every act. The reason for all this is, because human love is the very life of the human character. To love God is the first great duty of all religion, and it is plainly intended by him to be in the midst of every other excellence in man; and thus it is a tree of life in the midst of the garden—a *tree*, because of its growing and fruit-bearing qualities; and a *tree of life*, because it imparts animation to every thought and every duty.*

It is reasonable to suppose that the love of God is the ruling

---

* Philo says, "By the tree of life is metaphorically meant love to God, the greatest of virtues, by which the soul is rendered immortal;" and by "the tree of knowledge of good and evil is signified that prudence which discriminates between things that are by nature opposite and contrary."—*De Mundi Opificio.*

Maimonides calls the law, "a tree of life."—*De Pœnitentia*, ix., sec. 2.

life of angels; and if so, how proper is it to be spoken of as the central life of celestial men—the life that was in the midst of their intelligence—their intellectual garden. That this is a correct view of the subject is evident, not only from its approving itself satisfactorily to our reason, but from the circumstance of the tree of life being yet extant, and the fruit thereof, conditionally, offered to the acceptance of universal man. In the Revelation it is written that the Lord said, "To him that overcometh will I give to eat of the tree of life, which is in the midst of the paradise of God."* To "overcome" means the successful resistance of what is evil; and then "to eat of the tree of life" plainly denotes, to be filled with the good of love, which is said to be in the midst of the paradise of God, to denote that it is the inmost principle of all heavenly intelligence and truth.

Seeing, then, that the tree of life was significant of the good of love to the Lord, as it existed in the most ancient Church, we are the more readily prepared to accept the idea that the tree of knowledge of good and evil was representative of all the truth of faith respecting Him. The proposition that the truth of faith is the tree of knowledge of good and evil, at once affects us as a lucid fact, which reasonings cannot brighten, but might obscure. The solid knowledge of the pre-eminently religious man is genuine truth, and this is the foundation of his faith; so that while his love of God is his "tree of life," his faith in God is his "tree of knowledge." These are the two essential things of true religion with the human race, and thus we learn, as it were in the compass of a nutshell, the bright and practical ideas intended to be represented by those two trees. The reason why the eating of one of them was prohibited we shall show in another place.

* Rev. ii. 7.

CHAPTER VII.

THE RIVER OF EDEN, AND ITS BEING PARTED INTO FOUR HEADS.

"The fairest test of a theory is its application to the solution of a phenomenon."—
JOHN BIRD SUMNER, M.A., *Records of Creation.* Second edition, p. 235.

If Eden and its garden were not intended to express geographical positions of the earth; if the trees of the garden did not mean productions of the vegetable kingdom; and if all these things be mentioned to signify internal states and principles, belonging to a highly cultivated condition of religious society; then it is easy to infer that by the river and its partings are not to be understood natural waters, but the source and order whence the several degrees of their intelligence were to be preserved in growth and fruitfulness.

Those who could compare a highly cultivated mind to a skilfully planted garden, and clearly perceive the general analogy existing between them, could also easily describe the more particular condition of such a mind, by some other more particular circumstances which such a garden would require for the maintenance of its fertility and beauty. When such a people talked of lands and rivers in connection with the spiritualities of religion, it was for the purpose of giving them a representative significance of internal things. They spoke of the geography of nature to express the conditions of intellect. They knew that the world of nature was in correspondence with the world of mind. Nor has this idea entirely vanished from the Church. How common it is for Christians to speak of Zion, Canaan, and Jordan, to signify some internal and religious things! In such cases they do not think of the mountain, land, or river, but some spiritual state, which they are conceived to signify. Those to whom the magnificence of nature was as a theatre, representing the gorgeous things of spiritual and heavenly life; those who could

> "Find tongues in trees, books in running brooks,
> Sermons in stones, and good in everything,"

would not only speak of the general condition of the mind by some general resemblance in the world, but they would represent its particular states by some particular features of physical nature. To such a people, a river, with its streams, would be eminently suggestive. In after times the beauty which they confer upon the landscape, the fertility which they induce upon their banks, their gentle flow, and sky-reflecting qualities, have originated poetic thought and writing: but the men of the most ancient times saw in such things something deeper than the modern poet; they beheld in such objects those interior and spiritual realities which are the soul and origin of poetry. With them the thought of a natural river was instantly changed into the idea of wisdom, and the varieties of wisdom they would indicate by giving names to its streams.* We need not descend into secular history for evidence of this fact; it is plentifully recognized in the Sacred Scriptures, there being numerous passages constructed on the circumstance of such a relationship being perceived. Those who are in the satisfactions arising from divine instruction are said "to drink of the river of God's pleasures." † The waters, also, which the prophet saw issuing from the house which he beheld in vision, are described to have successively deepened, until they became a river that could not be passed, ‡ to show how the divine truths which are proper to the Lord's Church are continually heightening, until they attain that elevation of wisdom which no man can pass. Again, the Psalmist says, "*There* is a river, the streams whereof make glad the city of God"; § where, by a river is meant the divine wisdom of the Holy Word, and by the "streams whereof," the numerous truths which descend therefrom; and these are said to "make glad the city of God," because they are productive of delight and

---

* The fables concerning the river Styx, Charon crossing the Stygian Lake, and the consecration of the fountains of Pindus, Helicon, and Parnassus to the Muses, with many other mythological intimations referring to rivers, their sources, and results, all took their rise from this perception.

† Psa. xxxvi. 8.   ‡ Ezek. xlvii. 1–5.   § Psa. xlvi. 4.

happiness to the Church. There is a remarkable similarity, in the general idea, between this passage and that which says, "A river went out of Eden to water the garden, and from thence it was parted and became into four heads." * "The garden" is as "the city of God"; the "river" and "streams" as the "wisdom and truths" which impart gladness and refreshing. It is likewise written, that "the earth is watered with the river of God," † which spiritually means that the external man is rendered fertile in his works of use through the inflowings of divine wisdom from the Word. John said that he was shown "a pure river of water of life, clear as crystal, proceeding out of the throne of God"; ‡ where the "pure river of water of life" plainly denotes the genuine truths of the Holy Word. These are they which impart spiritual life to man: hence the Lord said, "The water [*i. e.*, the truth] that I shall give him [the man who comes to him] shall be in him a well of water springing up into everlasting life." § Every one may perceive that it can be nothing else but divine wisdom which proceeds as a river from the throne of God, and also that its purposes must be to secure salvation and eternal life to all who will receive it. It is said to be clear as crystal, to denote that it is as pure as any spiritual illumination can perceive it.

Now it will be observed that the river of Eden is without a name: yet, as its uses were to water the garden and keep it in fertility, it may reasonably be considered as the river of life, which was the inflowing of wisdom from the Lord, in order to maintain, among the most ancient people, their state of religious eminence in its integrity and greatness. The reason why this river is spoken of without a name is probably because it represented the divine wisdom, as it is in itself, and which, as such, is inexpressible to finite thought. It is only when this river of wisdom becomes parted, by entering into the human mind, and there presenting itself to the distinct faculties by which it is distinguished, that it will admit of nominal description, because it is only then that we obtain distinct perceptions of it. Hence it was only when the river entered the garden that it was "parted"; it was then that it "became into four heads,"

* Gen. ii. 10. † Psa. lxv. 9.
‡ Rev. xxii. 1. § John iv. 14.

which were respectively called Pison, Gihon, Hiddekel, and Phrat.

It must be admitted that divine wisdom, as it is in itself, cannot fall into finite apprehension; and every one must see that, in order to its being understood at all by man, it must enter into some degree of his mind. These degrees are several; and divine wisdom is designed for all these, and to affect them all in the way of rendering them fertile in the things of use. These degrees, in general, are spoken of as *three*, and they consist of celestial, spiritual, and natural; but there is also the rational degree, which exists between the spiritual and natural; this is a medium principle, which communicates between the scientific things which act upon the mind from without, and the intellectual perceptions which operate upon it from within; and thus, in some measure, it belongs to both. The *celestial* pertains to the *will* and its affections; the *spiritual* to the *understanding* and its thoughts; the *natural* to *scientifics* and such common knowledges as are obtainable from the light of the world. The *rational* belongs to each of the latter two, and its office in religious things is, as it were, to open a door to let in spiritual influence upon the natural mind.

These, then, are the degrees or principles of mind which the river of divine wisdom is intended to affect with its fertilizing power. The *will*, so as to preserve in it the orderly affections of love; the *understanding*, with the view of keeping in it the illuminated intelligence of truth; the *reason*, for the purpose of keeping it pure and open for the descent of interior thought into exterior cognizance; and the *scientific*, in order to determine its purposes of use. This, also, is the order in which divine wisdom descends into celestial men, and so exercises its benign purpose upon their whole character; and these are the things signified by the river after it entered the garden, and then became parted into four heads, the streams from which are called Pison, Gihon, Hiddekel, and Phrat.* These names,

---

* Pison and Gihon are utterly unknown to geography, and the best scholars in oriental languages now consider them only as appellations signifying a stream in general : in this sense they may easily be seen as a beautiful figure of the inflowing of different graces into the human mind.

Hiddekel is commonly said to be the Tigris. About the truth of this there

as Hebrew expressions, are, in their literal sense, significant of ideas which bear very closely upon the spiritual meaning they were intended to sustain.

Thus, by PISON is literally meant a *changing* or *extending* stream; but spiritually, it denotes the influence of divine wisdom upon the will and its affections: through this the will is continually *changing* its quality by an upward ascent in holy things, and so directing its affections in the way of performing more *extended* uses. Every one sees that these must be the results of such an influence, and, also, that information concerning it comes within the scope and purpose of revelation to disclose. The will is the inmost of the human faculties, and it was created for the reception and throne of love or goodness. But love or goodness requires illumination from a stream of wisdom, in order to direct its impulse, regulate its attachment, and disclose its duties. Love without wisdom would be a blind feeling. It is by truth that good is taught and led into its activity. Good could not be developed if truth did not teach us what it was. We learn what is virtuous by the precepts which inform us; but truth completes its work only when it fixes the good which it inculcates as an enlightened affection in the will. This, then, is what is meant by the influence of divine wisdom upon the will and its affections, of which Pison

---

is no certainty. Scientific geography cannot reconcile the features of that river with the Scriptural account of Hiddekel. Etymological resemblances, rather than geographical features, have led to that opinion. It is thought to be the Tigris, because this river in Aramæan is called *Digla*, in Arabic *Diglat*, in Zend *Teger*, in Pelvi *Tegera*, whence it is said have arisen both the Aramæan and Arabic form, to which is to be traced the Hebrew *Dekel*, divested of its prefix *Hid*, which means rapid, so that Hid-dekel signifies the rapid Tigris. Phrat is said to be the Euphrates, for similar etymological reasons, into which we need not enter. The Scriptural account, however, of Hiddekel and Phrat is, that they were but branches of another river that flowed in Eden, and which was divided in the garden. The geographical facts concerning the Tigris and Euphrates are that they take their rise in the mountains of Armenia, fifteen miles apart, and so do not answer to the sacred description. The reason is, because the Scriptural account is not given for geographical purposes. It was written among a very ancient people, with whom, there is much evidence to prove, it was customary to compare wisdom to a river, and to represent its particular influences upon the mind by streams with descriptive appellations.

is significant. Hence it is said to have encompassed the whole land of Havilah,* where there is gold, to inform us that it includes all those characteristics of the *will* which are genuinely good. Every excellence of the human character arises out of the divine influences upon the human will when disposed to love; and love is spiritual gold, more or less pure, according to the exalted nature of the objects towards which it is directed; in this case, the gold is said to have been good, to express that its direction was towards the Lord: it, therefore, may be taken as a precise definition of its meaning. Besides gold, there were also "bdellium and the onyx-stone,"† to represent the truth and the faith that were in correspondence with that love.

Every one must have noticed that gold and precious stones are frequently mentioned in the Word to represent the spiritual riches of goodness and truth. There is a perceptible analogy between such natural and spiritual things. Pure gold is among the most valuable of worldly possessions, and so it is a fit representative of that genuine good which is the most precious of all heavenly gifts. It is on this account that the Lord said, "I counsel thee to buy of me gold tried in the fire, that thou mayest be rich."‡ The prophet, also, when describing the decline of good among the people, said, "How is the gold become dim! *how* is the most fine gold changed!"§ The genuine Church, the New Jerusalem, is described to be a City of Pure Gold, for no other reason than to represent the genuine good by which it will be influenced, and of which its establishment will be productive.

So, likewise, precious stones, because of the difference in their resplendence, are significant of truths in their diversified brilliancy. The twelve precious stones, which were the Urim and Thummim on Aaron's ephod, represented the divine truth

---

* There is nothing known of this land beyond conjecture. The word Havilah means to *bring forth;* this is what the divine wisdom is intended to accomplish,—to *bring forth* whatever is good and lovely.

† Dr. A. Clarke says that "it is impossible to say what is the precise meaning of the original words; and at this distance of time and place, it is of little consequence" (!!)—of little consequence to know the precise meaning of what God has caused to be written in his Word for our instruction!

‡ Rev. iii. 18.   § Lam. iv. 1.

in all its vast and magnificent variety; and they were set in gold, and worn upon the breast, to signify that they originated in love. * The foundations of the New Jerusalem were "garnished with all manner of precious stones," † to signify that the real Church of God is grounded upon every pure and genuine truth. So that, by the gold and precious stones which were in the land of Havilah, are denoted the affection of love, with its corresponding truths, implanted in the interiors of the mind. This is particularly confirmed by the statement of the Prophet, who, when treating of man in the possession of heavenly riches, says, "Full of wisdom, and perfect in beauty. Thou hast been in Eden, the garden of God; every precious stone was thy covering." ‡ Such, then, is the condition of the will of the celestial man, or Church, treated of under the generic name of Adam.

Again, by GIHON is literally meant a stream or *valley of grace;* but it spiritually signifies the influence of divine wisdom upon the understanding, and through which it promotes the intellectual perception of heavenly *graces*. But what is the purpose of this influential grace? Certainly, it is the purification and enlargement of human thought. It is when a stream of divine wisdom descends into our understanding that we are enabled to think with clearness and perspicuity upon things of a spiritual and heavenly nature. In this, we are at once enabled to perceive that truth is truth and good is good, when they are presented to our consideration and acceptance: and when this is effected, Gihon is said to compass the whole land of Cush, §

---

* Exod. xxviii.   † Rev. xxi. 19.   ‡ Ezek. xxviii. 12, 13.

§ *Cush*, the Hebrew. Our translation has it *Ethiopia*, because the Septuagint rendered it by Αἰθιοπία, and the Vulgate by *Ethiopia*, which has been followed by nearly all succeeding versions. But there is no satisfactory evidence to show, and, consequently, some reason to doubt, whether the ancient Cush is really the Ethiopia of modern times. Great disputes exist among Scripture geographers upon this subject. Bochart places it in Arabia, Gesenius in Africa, Michaelis and Rosenmüller have supposed it in both places. Others have sought for it in more northerly regions of Asia, as in the Persian provinces of Susiana, in Cuthah, and a district of Babylonia. Indeed, this inquiry is interminable, just because the name, in those ancient writings, is used in a figurative sense, and not to express a geographical locality. Ethiopia, so far as it expresses the idea of a country inhabited by the sable portion

to inform us that it includes all the characteristics of the *understanding*, and renders it fertile in thought and knowledge. The land of Cush is here mentioned, to signify the faculty of understanding, much in the same way that Zion and Canaan are sometimes referred to in the sense of holy and spiritual things. This faculty, before it comes under the influence of the divine wisdom, is dark; and Cush, by which it is here represented, literally signifies what is black; it is, therefore, an appropriate symbol of that faculty, requiring to be surrounded with a stream of spiritual light, which circumstance is described to have taken place.

But, thirdly, by HIDDEKEL is literally meant *a sharp voice*, and thus it becomes an apt representative of that stream of divine wisdom which illuminates the *reason*. Reason, considered in itself, is an obscure principle, which requires to be sharpened by the voice of revelation before it can know anything of spiritual things. The sages of Greece and Rome never discovered by it any of the genuine truths of religion, immortality, or heaven: reason attains such knowledges only so far as it is illustrated by revelation. The very process of reasoning implies, that the objects we would discover by its means are not self-evident and clear to the more inward perceptions of the understanding. Doubts and difficulties stand in the way of everything which is to be reached only by an effort of reasoning, and even when it has done its utmost, the result is, not unfrequently, far from being either satisfactory or convincing. What one man pronounces to be reasonable, and believes to be so, is by another denounced as a tissue of mistakes. This is the ground on which have arisen such varieties of religious sentiment and faith. Doubtless, every one believes his views on such matters to be reasonable; that they have been set forth and defended with what are considered to be reasonable arguments; and yet, after all, it is evident, from the opposite conclusions which have been arrived at, that reason has been

---

of our race, is the appropriate rendering of the Hebrew word Cush, as denoting blackness, and on this account, Ethiopia is afterwards employed in the Scriptures with the same spiritual signification. Cush is the same with Ethiopia only in the way of symbol; they cannot be shown to be the same geographical locality.

defective somewhere. This brief intimation of a common fact, which may be easily extended by the thoughtful, at once shows us how necessary it is that reason should be illustrated with revelation, which is one of the streams of divine wisdom: we cannot attain the knowledge of any spiritual things without it. Heaven, with the internal things of the Church, and spiritual futurity, are from that service, and all that the truly rational mind knows about them is derived from the divine wisdom affording it illustration. The stream Hiddekel is said "to go towards the east of Assyria," to denote the progression of divine wisdom, in the way of enlightening the rational mind. The enlightening is the *east*, whence all illumination comes; and the rational mind is here *Assyria*, as the understanding was *Cush*, and the will *Havilah*, as explained above. Assyria derived its name from Asshur, the son of Shem, and not from the son of Hezron; and the word properly means *beholding*, which circumstance well fitted the land so called, to be employed as the representative of such a *seeing principle* as that of the *rational mind*. It is on account of this signification that Assyria, like Israel and Egypt, is sometimes mentioned in the Scriptures without any natural application. One instance will be sufficient to produce. The prophet says, "In that day shall Israel be the third with Egypt and with *Assyria*, a blessing in the midst of the land: whom the Lord of hosts shall bless, saying, Blessed be Egypt my people, and Assyria the work of my hands, and Israel mine inheritance."* This is plainly a prediction concerning a state of the Church, in which its natural (Egypt), rational (Assyria), and spiritual (Israel), principles should exist in their proper order, and each be open to the divine blessing.

The fourth river was PHRAT, which literally means, to make fruitful; and this represents the influence of divine wisdom upon the scientific principle of the mind, so as to render it prolific in the works of benevolence and use.

The knowledges which exist in the natural mind are merely of an external and scientific kind. The natural mind is scientific, and adapted for scientific things merely. By these are not meant philosophical scientifics, but the external knowledge of religious things. Thus the doctrinals of the Church, its rituals,

---

* Isa. xix. 24, 25.

and their modes of administration—indeed, all things expressed in the letter of the Word, are mere scientific things, adapted to the natural mind; and as such they will remain, until, from some more interior light, man begins to see their spiritual origin and use. Most professing Christians know many things about the literal histories in the Word. They know something of the histories of Abraham, Isaac, and Jacob; also, about the house of Israel in Egyptian bondage, their deliverance thence, and their subsequent establishment in Canaan; likewise, of the government of the Judges, the rule of the kings, the denunciations of the prophets, and many other facts which the Word contains. But how few are those who can see, from any spiritual thought, that all these things are but external scientifics! Nevertheless they include within them celestial and spiritual principles, which prove the letter to be divine. This is a desideratum in the Church. We may believe these scientifics to be divine, because we have been taught that they are so, either by tradition or authority; but it is important we should see their truth from some interior conviction of our own; yet this is accomplished only so far as our natural mind is influenced and illuminated by that stream of divine wisdom denominated Phrat. This may serve to show the meaning of that river, as mentioned in connection with the most ancient Church.

From these considerations we learn that the river of Eden denoted the divine wisdom proceeding from the divine love, and that its division into four heads, upon entering the garden, signified their different influences upon the celestial, spiritual, rational, and scientific principles of holy and intelligent men.

That nothing natural could have been intended by those descriptions must be evident to every one who will venture to think above a common prejudice. Viewed in that light, they are full of difficulties, which neither ingenuity nor learning can remove. For instance, who does not know that it is physically impossible for a river to divide itself into four heads or sources of rivers? If two or more channels be presented to a running stream, it will not divide itself distributively, but pour its whole mass into the deepest furrow—it will naturally take the lowest level; and, moreover, there is no position known to scientific geography which at all answers to the Scripture narrative.

Those that are supposed to come nearest to the description, and which indeed are very distant, necessarily place the locality of Eden in Armenia, which is not at all mentioned in the Scripture. A garden into which one river ran, and which was then to be distributed into four other rivers, necessarily suggests the idea of a large tract of country, which we cannot rationally suppose the Lord would have required to have been "dressed and kept" by an individual Adam. We conclude, then, that these things were written, not to point out a geographical locality, but to represent the streams of divine wisdom entering into the minds of a wise and happy people, to irrigate their mental soil, and render it prolific in all that is good and estimable in the Divine sight.

By the divine wisdom of which we have been speaking, is meant that interior dictate which we believe can and does flow from the Lord into the will and perceptions of highly cultivated humanity. This, indeed, was the state of the most ancient people during the time of their integrity. They thought of nothing but what they loved, so that their intellectual and voluntary principles must have been in the closest connection, and, as it were, one in every thought and act. This is one of the reasons why that people were called *Man*, a dignity which does not appear to have been attained by any other community mentioned in the Scriptures! Some remains of this primeval excellence seem to have been recognized by the apostle, who, when speaking of the Gentiles, said, they "do by nature the things contained in the law—which show the work of the law written in their hearts, their conscience also bearing witness."* It is also declared that the "Lord would put his law in the inward parts of men, and write it upon their hearts; so that he will be their God, and they shall be his people."† It is, therefore, evident that there can be such an influx of intelligence from the Lord as is mentioned above. The means, however, to be employed for its communication, in the case just referred to, is the written Word. But such a medium does not appear to have existed among the Adamic people, nor could it have been necessary, so long as they remained in love to God above all things. The law and the prophets were given, after this love was lost,

* Rom. ii. 14, 15. † Jer. xxxi. 33.

with the view of assisting in its restoration: they "hang upon it." * In such a state they would receive instruction, in the way of internal dictate, immediately from the Lord. This would be inscribed upon their hearts, and thence there would be an influx of truth into their spiritual minds, next into their rational, and, finally, into their natural minds; consequently, into the natural scientifics which there existed: this would enable them to see the absolute distinction between spiritual and natural things; also, to perceive the correspondence which subsisted between them. Hence may be seen what is meant by the divine wisdom spoken of above, and its respective inflowings into the several orderly principles of human character which then existed.

With such a people, internal and heavenly things would be perceived in purer light than those which were external and worldly, because such things would occupy their chief attention. If such a people had read the Word which we possess, the internal sense of it would, doubtless, have been presented to their minds with greater clearness than the letter, because their states, as it were, lay entirely upon the heavenly side of this revelation. In after times this condition became reversed. Man, having descended from that elevation into external and terrestrial loves, can now see internal and spiritual things only in obscurity and shadow; hence the external sense of the Word appears to him in better light than its spiritual meaning: he having passed to the worldly side of revelation. This side of it has been mercifully provided for his state, and designed, by its peculiar construction, to raise him into the light and enjoyment of the other.

* Matt. xxii. 37-40.

CHAPTER VIII.

ADAM NAMING THE LIVING CREATURES.

> "Any theory, on whatever subject, that is really sound, can never be inimical to a religion founded on truth; and the part of a lover of truth is to follow her, at all seeming hazards, after the example of Him who came into the world that he might bear witness to the truth."—RICHARD WHATELY, D.D., *Archbishop of Dublin.*

The circumstance of naming the living creatures is one of religious importance, and it involves matters of peculiar interest. It is thus related:—"Out of the ground the Lord God formed every beast of the field, and every fowl of the air; and brought *them* unto Adam to see what he would call them: and whatsoever Adam called every living creature, that was the name thereof."* The careful reader will observe it is here stated that "out of *the ground* the Lord God formed every beast of the field, and every fowl of the air"; but if he will turn to the 20th verse of the first chapter, he will there find it written, "And God said, Let *the waters* bring forth abundantly the moving creature that hath life, and fowl that may fly above the earth in the open firmament of heaven." Thus, in the one case the *ground* is said to have been their source, and, in the other, the *waters*. Whence arises this discrepancy? It may be admitted that the command for the waters "to bring forth the moving creature that hath life," ought to be understood as referring only to the piscatory tribes, for we find that purely land animals are spoken of as having been created on the following day. The difficulty more particularly adverted to is this, that in the first statement the *waters* are distinctly said to have brought forth every *winged fowl*, whereas in the second it is as plainly written, that "out of the *ground* the Lord God formed every *fowl of the air.*" Now, what can be the reason of those apparently hostile statements, occurring, as they do, so

* Gen. ii. 19.

exceedingly close upon each other; and upon what principle are they to be reconciled? There is plainly a disagreement in the letter, which requires to be removed. The "Fragmental Hypothesis" would, perhaps, attempt it by supposing that they are merely the records of two different traditions of the same general circumstances, in which we are not to look for particular niceties of expression. But surely this cannot be satisfactory: under such a view of the case, what is to become of the fact of both being equally a revelation, and consequently a divine composition? Some higher ground than the literal sense must be taken, because some superior truth is meant to be expressed, and we have mentioned the circumstance, not because we think it a difficulty, but chiefly to draw attention to the truths intended to be stated.

It was observed above, that the first chapter of Genesis treated of the creation, or development, of the *spiritual man*, and all the living affections and thoughts which are proper to his condition; and also that the second chapter treated of the *celestial man*, and all the living affections and thoughts which are proper to him. Some reasons for those distinctions were likewise given; among others, that the man in the second chapter was no longer spoken of as "earth," but as "ground," and that the name of the Supreme Being was extended from "God" to "Lord God." Thus the two chapters treat of two different states which distinguished the most ancient people. To both of those states there belonged an affection for the intellectual things of an exalted religion, but they took their rise in different sources, and therefore their origination is differently described. In the first case, the affection for intellectual things (which are the winged fowls) arose out of the general knowledge of religion, and therefore it was commanded that "the waters" should bring them *forth;** but in the second case the affections for intellectual things (now called fowl of the air) sprang out of the prolifications of love, and hence they are described to have been made by the Lord God out of "the ground."

Every one must know that differences of religious character exist, and that they arise from different sources. It would not indicate the distinction to say that the inferior state sprang from

* See preceding page.

the same source as the superior; to describe them accurately we must employ distinctive terms, and this is precisely what revelation has done, in declaring the intellectual things of the spiritual man to have been created by God out of the *water*, and those of the celestial man out of the *ground*. There is, then, no actual discrepancy between the two statements, because they do not relate to the same, but to different circumstances.

In speaking of the fifth day's creation, it was observed that the objects of animated nature were chosen and frequently employed in the Word, to represent the living affections of men; farther evidences of that fact were likewise promised: an occasion is here presented for its fulfilment.

It is evident that some idea of the spiritual representation of animals must have been the reason why they were so extensively employed in the sacrificial worship, which, independently of that established among the Jews, was spread throughout the continent of Asia. This also must have been the source whence the Greeks and Romans adopted certain animals for sacrifices during some of their public festivities. We do not suppose those people to have attached any spiritual notion to such sacrifices; what we mean is that if they be traced up to the sources whence they were derived, that will be found to have been their origin. Sacrifices, considered in themselves, are most irrational modes of worship,* nor could they have been adopted until men had sunk so low in the scale of religious intelligence, as to suppose that the offering up of an animal to the Lord was the same thing as the dedication of that principle to his service, which it was originally understood to signify. The animal was mistaken for the principle which it represented, and the dedication of the principle to spiritual use was corrupted into a natural sacrifice. Their origin cannot be reasonably accounted for upon any other ground. This also explains why it was that several animals among some of the older nations became objects of such peculiar attention and respect. This circumstance was very remarkable among the ancient Egyptians. Herodotus says, †
"Both those which are wild and those which are domestic are regarded as sacred. If I were to explain the reason of this prejudice, I should be led to the discussion of those sacred sub-

---

* See Archbishop Magee on the Sacrifices and Atonement. † Euterpe, lxv.

jects which I particularly wish to avoid." · Here the historian distinctly connects their reverence of animals with some esoteric and religious views; and although he does not inform us what these were, there can be no reasonable doubt that, at some period of Egyptian history, the animals had been understood as the representatives of certain moral qualities, and that it was not until after a succession of corruptions, when their proper signification was lost, that veneration began to be attached to them. The worship of certain animals was a perversion of the respect once paid to the human principles of which they were significant.

It is impossible to read with care those portions of the Scriptures in which beasts and animals are mentioned, and not perceive that they have a symbolical meaning; they are spoken of, both generically and specifically, under circumstances in which it is evident that spiritual things, and not natural existences, are implied. For example, the prophet, treating of the peaceable character of the Lord's kingdom, says, "The wolf shall dwell with the lamb, and the leopard shall lie down with the kid; and the calf, and the young lion, and the fatling together; and a little child shall lead them. And the cow and the bear shall feed; their young ones shall lie down together: and the lion shall eat straw like an ox. And the sucking child shall play on the hole of the asp, and the weaned child shall put his hand on the cockatrice' den. They shall not hurt nor destroy in all my holy mountain."* Here we have no less than fourteen different animals, besides children, referred to, every one of which is certainly intended to represent some internal affection. There are, however, two classes of them, one tame and harmless, the other fierce and dangerous; the former plainly denote the affections which are good and innocent, and the latter those which are wicked and destructive; and by their all dwelling together must be meant a state in which the influences of the good will have subdued the pernicious tendencies of the evil, and kept them in subjection to its superior sentiments. It is also written that the Lord would "make a covenant with the beasts of the field, and with the fowls of heaven."† That "the beasts of the field would cry unto Him";‡ they are also exhorted

* Isa. xi. 6-9.   † Hos. ii. 18.   ‡ Joel ii. 20.

not to be afraid;* in which passages, by beasts cannot be meant beasts, but certain human affections, which they are meant to represent. These are the things with which the Lord effects his covenants; these are the principles which can cry unto Him, and may be benefited by his merciful persuasions. Ezekiel was commanded to "say unto every feathered fowl, and to every beast of the field, Assemble yourselves, and come: gather yourselves on every side to my sacrifice that I do sacrifice for you, even a great sacrifice upon the mountains of Israel."† Here, likewise, it is evident that natural beasts and fowl are not meant, but, instead thereof, the affections of religious life, and the sentiments of religious thought, since these alone can attend the invitations to a religious act. So, in the Psalms, it is written, "Praise the Lord from the earth, ye dragons, and all deeps: beasts, and all cattle; creeping things, and flying fowl." ‡ It is plain that we are not here to understand the irrational animals which are mentioned, but certain living affections and thoughts of men, to which they correspond; for every one must have observed that there is a conspicuous analogy between the natural qualities of some animals and some of the moral sentiments of the human character.§

Evidences of this kind could be extended to a considerable length, but these are sufficient; they suggest, somewhat impressively, that to maintain the statement that "Adam gave names to all cattle, and to the fowl of the air, and every beast of the field,"|| in a literal sense, is to mistake its meaning. There are certain facts and considerations in relation to such an idea, which are exceedingly embarrassing to those who will hazard an independent reflection upon the subject; and we conceive the real meaning of the apparent history is to be sought for in its spiritual sense. If we look upon the statement of Adam naming the creatures to signify the high character of that ancient people, impressing a peculiar quality upon those internal affections and sentiments, to which the objects of animated nature

---

* Joel ii. 22. † Ezek. xxxix. 17. ‡ Psa. cxlviii. 7–10.

§ Clement of Alexandria quotes verses from Xenophanes, the Colophonean, which state that every species of animal supplies metaphor to aid the imagination in its ideas of superior things.

|| Gen. ii. 20.

correspond, we have at once presented to us both an intelligible and a religious idea; and this can hardly be said of the notion which contemplates him as a zoologist.

It is said that *all* cattle and fowls, and *every* beast, were named by Adam. If the merely literal sense be insisted on to be the true and only design of this statement, then we are, at the very outset, compelled by science to curtail the signification of words which are employed with an unlimited meaning. For it is plain, from the discoveries which geology has made, that there were whole classes of animals which had existed at immense intervals of time, and had successively become extinct, long before there were any traces of humanity discernible. It is, therefore, demonstrable that Adam could not have named *all* and *every* creature. To this it may be replied that we ought not to interpret *all and every beast* to mean any more than those which were contemporary with him; but, if so, at what point are we to stop in putting a limited meaning on terms of unlimited signification? Such a view, if pressed with difficulties, may refuse to admit their application to all the animals then extant, and successively shrink them up to mean only those that were in Palestine, or Eden, or perhaps the garden only. It may be said that we should receive those documents as popular statements, and not expect to find them couched in language technically correct. To this we wish only to observe, that we do not believe them to have been loosely written, as the word popular would seem to imply; we regard the language of revelation to have been chosen with a care and deliberation, over the preservation of which the Divine Providence has been peculiarly watchful.

If we take a religious view of the intentions of God's Word, we must be led to see that this narrative, concerning the naming of the creatures, was intended for some spiritual instruction, altogether apart from the statement of the letter. For surely it is difficult to see what religious act could be involved in calling a lion, a lion; a bear, a bear; a sheep, a sheep; or a lamb, a lamb: nor is it easy to perceive how such an employment consisted with a religious state of mind, so extensively cultivated and highly developed as was that of Adam. If we suppose it to have been given him as an intellectual exercise, which is among the highest grounds that can be pretended for it, still we must inquire what possible relation it could have to spiritual and heavenly uses. To give a name to a thing that is without one, may be useful to distinguish it, and thereby to provide a verbal means for suggesting the idea of it to the mind; but it has very little connection with uses that are essentially religious. This is evident from experience, for it has happened that in these days of discovery men have not unfrequently been required to give names to extinct species of animals which it is certain Adam never saw, and yet in giving those names they have neither felt nor intended more than is included in the common sentiment attending the selection of an appropriate appellation.

It will hardly be pretended that the names, whether popular or scientific, of the animals which are now extant, are those which were pronounced by Adam. There is not the least evidence to show that society at any time, or among any people, adopted his supposed zoological vocabulary. To what purpose, then, was it given, if it did not come into use and obtain a currency? According to the common view, there was no coeval society, and therefore it could not have been for their use and information; nor is there the slightest intimation of his having instructed posterity in the names, which a mistaken view of this narration has led men to suppose, he gave to the creatures.

But supposing it could be satisfactorily proved that the Hebrew names of the various beasts mentioned in the Scripture were really those which had been given to them by Adam; and supposing that we conceded, which indeed we do, that those names were founded on a knowledge of some prominent feature or remarkable characteristic of the creatures to which they are applied, then we should possess some evidence of the man having been distinguished by a superior genius in respect to this particular department of nature. But why in this department only? If the circumstance of giving names to all cattle, fowl, and beasts were a display of intellectual eminence, why was it not also exhibited in respect to the fish? If all the creatures of the earth could have been collected in the garden, with the view of receiving their names, why might not all the fishes of the sea have been gathered in the river of that garden for the same purpose? What was possible in the one case could not have been impossible in the other. Why, also, were the objects of vegetable nature omitted to be named? Surely a knowledge of the distinction between different plants and trees must have been a subject of much concern to Adam, particularly as his attention had been distinctly drawn to the subject through the naming of two trees by the Lord himself: also, by his having been commanded to dress and keep the garden, and told that he might freely eat of every tree but one. Certainly, if names for any objects were of importance to distinguish them, they must have been so in the vegetable department of nature. But to these we do not read of any names being given by Adam. If the giving of names to animals were an intellectual exercise, the giving of names to vegetables could not have been otherwise. There must have been some reason for this omission, and what other reason can be offered besides this,—*That they were not suited to the representative purpose of the narrative, which treats of a higher state of interior and intellectual life than the fishes or the objects of the vegetable kingdom were adapted to represent?*

We see that the whole subject, viewed from a literal aspect, is full of difficulties,—difficulties of a religious, moral, and scientific nature,—difficulties not of that class which industry and research may be capable of removing, but of a character which neither learning nor ingenuity can surmount. The source of them is that erroneous ground of interpretation, which consists in mistaking the descriptions of a figurative narrative for their literal sense.

The creatures, agreeably to a style of expression which prevailed among the ancients, and which originated in a perception of the correspondences which exist between natural and spiritual things, are significant of certain classes of affection and thought which distinguished celestial men. Of this, some examples and expositions have been given from the prophetical writings, the style of which took its rise from that which existed with a more remote and superior people.

The order in which the creatures are mentioned is,—cattle, fowl, and beasts. The word rendered "cattle" should have been *beasts*,—implying, indeed, those of a peaceful nature; and that which is translated "beast" should have been *wild beasts*, to indicate such as were of a less pacific character. These creatures are frequently spoken of in the prophetical Word, and they are, in all cases, most carefully distinguished. Now, by beasts—the tame, the peaceful, the pacific—are represented the good affections of the will of the celestial man; by the fowls of the air are denoted the true perceptions of the understanding of the spiritual man; and by the wild beasts are signified the general affections of the natural man, which, from their greater remoteness from the Lord and closer adjacency to the world, always require the influence of superior principles to preserve them innocent and harmless. These particulars could be proved by numerous citations from the Word; we, however, will only adduce, for each, one confirmatory instance.

That *beasts* represented the good affections of the celestial man, is evident from its being said that "beasts were in heaven," and that "four *beasts* fell down and worshipped God, saying, Amen; Alleluia."* These circumstances cannot be predicated of natural beasts, but only of the good affections of celestial men which they represent.

That *fowls* denote the true perception of the spiritual man is plain, for similar reasons:—An "angel cried with a loud voice, saying to all *the fowls* that fly in the midst of heaven, Come and gather yourselves together unto the supper of the great God."† This invitation was not delivered to irrational, irresponsible birds, but to the intellectual perceptions of the spiritual man of which they are significant. That by the *wild beasts* are signified the general affections of the natural man, which are preserved in order by the influence of superior principles, appears from this declaration;—"The wild beasts of the field shall honour me: because I give waters in the wilderness, and rivers in the desert, to give drink to my people."‡ Wild beasts give no honour to God on account of the blessings which he bestows upon mankind; but they are said to do so, on account of the representation they were selected to sustain.

Now the living creatures which were brought to Adam were

---

* Rev. xix. 4. See, also, Rev. vii. 11. † Rev. xix. 17.

‡ Isa. xliii. 20. This passage, in the Authorized Version, has simply *beasts ;* but the original word here, and in several other places where it is translated beasts only, properly means *wild beasts,* as, indeed, the context commonly shows.

of three descriptions:—they consisted of celestial affections, spiritual perceptions, and natural delights; and the Lord is said to have formed, and brought them unto him, to reveal that he is the author of their existence, and the giver of them to men.

They were, however, brought to Adam for a particular purpose,—to see what he would call them; that is, to observe the quality which he, in the exercise of his freedom and responsibility, would impress upon them. To call by a name, and to give a name, are forms of expression which frequently occur in the Scriptures, but they do not always mean to pronounce a word; their design is to indicate a quality. Thus the angel who wrestled with Jacob said unto him, "Thy name shall be called no more Jacob, but Israel."* This change of name was intended to express a change which had taken place in the quality of his character, hence it is immediately added, "For as a prince thou hast power with God and with men, and hast prevailed." So, again, when the Lord said of the Church, "I have called thee by thy name; I have surnamed thee, though thou hast not known me,"† the meaning is that a new quality had been imparted, and yet its advantages had not been appreciated. The Lord said he would write his new name upon him who overcometh,‡ to show that a new quality will be given to the spiritual character of those who conquer in temptations. Those "whose names are not written in the book of life"§ are plainly those whose internal qualities are such as to exclude them from the heavenly kingdom. Hence it is evident that to give a name denotes to impress a quality upon the object of which it is predicated; and this, also, is its meaning in the case of Adam naming the creatures.

The circumstance will admit of illustration from experience. It frequently happens that some good affections and true ideas are suddenly introduced into the human mind. They come under circumstances in which we did not expect them, and we are enabled to perceive their excellence. Doubtless, these spiritual beasts and fowl are of divine origination, and surely they are brought to us by infinite wisdom to see what we shall call them; that is, to give us the opportunity of receiving, and impressing upon them, such a quality as we, in the exercise of

---

* Gen. xxxii. 28. † Isa. xlv. 4. ‡ Rev. iii. 12. § Rev. xiii. 8.

our freedom, may choose to adopt, and which quality, when so impressed, remains upon them so far as our own individuality is concerned; a circumstance which the representative history thus expresses,—"Whatsoever Adam called every living creature, that was the name thereof."

Such we conceive to be the meaning of the narrative of Adam naming the living creatures. Under this view it is brought home to the business and bosoms of religious men. It is beautifully consistent with the Word of God, and eminently practical. The experience of men presents a counterpart of it, and so a rational interpretation.

CHAPTER IX.

ITS NOT BEING GOOD THAT ADAM SHOULD BE ALONE.—HIS DEEP SLEEP.—THE TAKING OF A RIB FROM HIM, AND BUILDING IT INTO A WOMAN.

"It requires but little attention in any one to discern that woman was not formed out of the rib of a man; and that deeper arcana are here implied."—SWEDENBORG. *Arcana Cœlestia*, n. 152.

It is written, that "the Lord God said, It is not good that man should be alone; I will make him an help meet for him.—And the Lord God caused a deep sleep to fall upon Adam, and he slept: and he took one of his ribs, and closed up the flesh instead thereof; and the rib, which the Lord God had taken from the man, builded he a woman, and brought her unto the man. And Adam said, This is now bone of my bones, and flesh of my flesh: she shall be called Woman, because she was taken out of man."*

These statements are remarkable, not only on account of their apparent singularity, but for other reasons, when considered as a literal history. In that point of view there are several difficulties, which could hardly have existed if the narrative had not been constructed with some more recondite design than appears upon the surface.

As already remarked, the first chapter of Genesis informs us that the female was created upon the *sixth* day, and at the conclusion of that day's work it is said, that "God saw everything that he had made, and, behold, it was very good." But in the second chapter we find, that after the *seventh* day, when Adam had been placed in the garden, it was discovered "not to be good that he should be alone," and that this circumstance originated the woman.

For the solution of these discrepancies, it is requisite to admit that the two chapters treat of two different conditions of the man

* Gen. ii. 18, 21-23.

of the Church in these early times. Of this we have already spoken. These different descriptions have led to curious results. Some have considered what is said of the creation of man—namely, "male and female created he them"—to mean that Adam was originally distinguished by both sexes; and this was thought to derive confirmation from the peculiar circumstance of Eve's creation, afterwards related. Others have conjectured that man and woman were, indeed, created upon the sixth day, but by some means fastened, something like the Siamese twins, sideways to each other, so that she was as a rib to him; and that her separation from him during a deep sleep, with her subsequent presentation to him as a separate individual, are what are meant by taking from him a rib, and making it into a woman.* All this is curious enough, and, doubtless, the literal sense will admit of these and other equally unreasonable conjectures, and this, surely, is sufficient to suggest the duty of taking other grounds from which to view these narratives.

It is, indeed, popular to consider the history as "wise, benign, and simple"; and with a view to the maintenance of its literal character, it is asked whether the " imagination can frame a mode of origin so well adapted to endear her to her conjugate, as that the creative power should form her out of his actual bodily substance."† We could have understood this argument, whatever we might have thought of its force, had it been employed in reference to the first child, but what it has to do with the first conjugate it is difficult to conjecture. Such a method of defending the history suggests the idea of Adam being the mother of Eve rather than her husband! If this mode of origination were really intended to supply the motive for endearment, which is assumed, what has become of it? When was it lost? Why has it not been perpetuated? How has it happened that such myriads of attachments are formed and continued, irrespective of such a motive to their existence? It is gone, and whenever the statement is adverted to, there is felt more of the buoyancy of a smile than the solemnity of belief. The supposed argument has no foundation in truth. The question, however, is not whether the imagination can form a more suit-

* Cruden, Art. Woman.
† Dr. Pye Smith, Scrip. Geo., Second Edit., p. 285.

able idea of the origination of woman, but whether that which is commonly understood to be the description of it is really so. We may fail in a conjecture of this sort, but that would not prove the literal sense of such a description true, and therefore the narrative remains just where it was. It must be judged of from other grounds.

We have traced the rise and progress of the Adamic Church into the full enjoyment of Eden with all its blessings. We have seen that that garden and those blessings consisted in the religious intelligence, high principles, sound virtue, and distinguished character of that people. We have ascertained that they received instructions in duty from their Maker, and there can be no reasonable doubt that these were for a time carefully and happily obeyed. How long the people continued in their integrity there is no record. We are only informed of the fact, and not of its duration. It is highly probable that it might have been maintained for several generations; but this is a matter with which we have not to deal: we find that in process of time, while they were yet in the garden, the discovery was made that it was not good for the man to be alone.

Now, we hold that this cannot be reasonably construed to mean that he was the only existing human individual. If the literal sense must be received as evidence, the male and female are of the same age, and Adam is their generic name.* The woman is distinctly declared to have been created in the same day as the man,† nor is there anything in the statement to preclude the idea that it was at the same moment. Moreover, a command was given to them to "be fruitful and multiply, and replenish the earth,"‡ *before they were placed in the garden;* it is therefore plain that Adam could not have been there alone, in the sense commonly understood by that term. Besides, the woman knew the command of God concerning the forbidden tree;§ there is no intimation of Adam having communicated it to her, and therefore it is to be inferred that she was present at its delivery, which was before the time he is stated to have been *alone:* and which therefore requires that this expression should not be understood to mean that there was no woman then in existence. That statement is intended to furnish us with infor-

* Gen. v. 2.   † Gen. i. 27.   ‡ Gen. i. 28.   § Gen. iii. 2, 3.

mation relating to some new internal condition of the most ancient Church. It is an intimation concerning their decline from innocence and purity; in the record, that a period had arrived in that remote dispensation, when it was *not good* for man to be alone, we have presented to us the germ of that catastrophe called the Fall. That circumstance was not a sudden calamity, it was the result of successive downward steps. Those who had been gradually raised into the possession of every blessing, and so gifted with experimental evidences of their value, would not be instantaneously precipitated into flagrant guilt: that catastrophe was small in its beginning, and therefore it is delicately spoken of as not being good to be alone. It is expressive of an incipient disinclination to remain under the exclusive guidance of God. That is what the Scriptures treat of when they speak of man being *alone*. Those who submit themselves wholly to the divine guidance are said to be alone, because they are governed solely by the Lord. Hence Balaam's prediction concerning some future happy state of Israel was, "Lo, the people shall dwell alone." * Moses, also, in speaking of a similar circumstance, said, "Israel shall dwell in safety alone."† The prophet likewise said, "Arise, get you up unto the wealthy nation, that dwelleth without care, saith the Lord, which have neither gates nor bars, which dwell alone."‡ Now, the Adamic people, during the period of their integrity, had dwelt in "safety alone." They had been led and influenced solely by the Lord: but with some of their posterity there arose an inclination to selfhood,—a desire to possess an individuality apart from the Lord. This was necessarily attended by the experience of influences from two different sources,—those which come from the Lord and those which spring from the selfhood of man: and so they clearly prove that a cessation had been put to the *single* leading of the Lord. This was the state which he beheld, and said of it, "It is not good that man should be alone." It is not a sentence expressing deficiency in God's creation, but a revelation to us that men had then begun to pervert its excellence. They desired to be not alone, and it was permitted; because, to have prevented it would have required an interference with that liberty of

* Numb. xxiii. 9.   † Deut. xxxiii. 28.   ‡ Jer. xlix. 31.

man which God holds inviolable, in order to preserve him responsible.

But although for this reason God allowed them to descend into such a state, he did not abandon them. He is ever merciful, and always grants what the state requires. Hence, when Adam ceased to be content under His exclusive influence, he said, "I will make an help meet for him," which is afterwards described to have been "a woman"; because she represented the selfhood to which he had inclined, and which had now become dear to him.

This selfhood may be described as that individuality, or proper-self,* which man as a finite creature necessarily possesses. It belongs to his highest nature, and is inseparable from every other condition of his existence; it will be good or evil, according to the quality of his character. By the most ancient people, during the period of their integrity, it was inherited as a genuine good: but it was not intended that they should love it; this, however, they began to do, when they were not content to be alone. This new circumstance of man brought into activity new mercies on the part of the Lord. As the selfhood of the man at this time was of such a quality, it was not only permitted him to love it, but it was afterwards provided that it should be orderly for him to do so. The statement, "I will make an help meet for him," † was a promise to render the selfhood a resemblance of all his other excellencies, so that it might be proper for his attachment. Hence this suitable help was subsequently represented by a woman.

It is to be observed, that between the time of this promise and the period of its fulfilment there are related three remarkable circumstances,—the naming of the creatures, the sleep of Adam, and the taking from him the rib and building it into a woman. The creatures were brought to Adam to be named, when he began to incline towards himself, that he might review

---

*The Latin word *proprium*, or the French *le propre*, but especially the former, best expresses the idea here intended to be conveyed. The above definition is adopted, that the general reader may not be embarrassed by the use of a word not yet Anglicized.

† The original, *ezer kenegdo*, strictly means a help as with him; and this, with the context, implies a new assistance from within him.

the quality of all his interior affections and thoughts, and so remember their origin and value. They were all pure graces communicated from the Lord, and, therefore, the man could not find among them that which is spoken of as the help meet for him. Nothing of the selfhood was discoverable; his inclination led him to look for it among them, but it was not found. This circumstance beautifully reveals to us, that all the virtues and graces of a genuine religion acknowledge God to be their exclusive author, and eschew everything of man.

But the disposition not to be *alone*, and the inclination to consider that self had something to do with the production of the above excellencies, had made some inroad upon men's character; hence the result, in process of time, was that they were led into great obscurity and darkness of thought concerning them. This state was represented by the deep sleep that fell upon Adam. Now the time had come for the Lord to realize his promise. The manner of it is thus described:—"The Lord God took one of his ribs, and closed up the flesh instead thereof; and the rib, which the Lord God had taken from the man, builded he into a woman, and brought her unto the man."* Now, if we remember that it is the religious, and not the physical, condition of the man which is here treated of, the difficulty in perceiving the true meaning of these statements will be considerably lessened. The leading ideas so expressed are, that something was taken from the man, raised into a new condition, gifted with new life, and then presented to him as an object that might help him, and to which he might be affectionately attached.

That which was taken from him is called a *rib*, because it represented selfhood without spiritual life; this is said to have been built into a woman, to denote that it was afterwards raised into the condition of such a life; it is then declared that she was brought unto the man, to signify that the selfhood thus vivified

---

* Gen. ii. 21, 22. The common version is, "made he a woman," but "*built* into a woman" is the more correct rendering of the original, and, indeed, recognized in the marginal reading. It is used in contradistinction to the terms *creating* and *making*, previously employed in reference to the development of man, in order to indicate the idea of raising up something that had fallen.

and introduced to his affections would help to sustain his character and maintain his happiness. In other words, this significant history means, that when this posterity of the most ancient Church began to think holy things might have arisen with themselves, and thus fell into states of obscurity (deep sleep) about their genuine origin, the Lord, during its continuance, mercifully effected the removal of that unspiritual selfhood (rib), and endowed it with a new capacity, by which it was enabled to know truth, and do good, as from self, still always preserving the acknowledgment and belief that they are from the Lord: under this aspect, selfhood became an object that might be loved and cherished; and, therefore, it is represented by the woman brought unto the man; whereas, under its condition as a *rib*, it was separated and taken from him.*

These facts will admit of some degree of illustration from the state of human selfhood now. This, with merely natural men, is such, that they regard it to be the chief thing of their existence.† They think that all they know of truth or feel of goodness has come from self, and thus they are in a deep sleep as to the real truth, that all such blessings descend from the Lord. This selfhood, like the hard and bony structure of man, is scarcely possessed of any spiritual life; it, as it were, surrounds his heart, and so it is represented by the *rib* which is adjacent. Before his elevation can be effected, this rib must be taken away. It must be raised into a new condition, and be animated by another life; it must come to see that truth and goodness are to be believed and done by man as of himself, yet always under the acknowledgment that they are from the Lord. When this takes place, it is soft and yielding, fair and lovable, and hence compared to a woman beautiful and innocent.

That *bone*, which the *rib* is afterwards called, denotes the selfhood of man, may be made evident from many passages of the

---

* "This part of the history, where Eve is said to have been made from the rib of Adam, might have been a hieroglyphical design of the Egyptian philosophers."—*Dr. Darwin's "Temple of Nature," Additional Notes*, 10.

† Rochefoucault, Esprit, and their disciple, Mandeville, have contended that self-love was the origin of all those virtues mankind most admire: and teach that the highest pretensions to disinterestedness are only the more artful disguises of self-love!

Scriptures. The Psalmist says, "Make me to hear joy and gladness, that the *bones* which thou hast broken may rejoice";* where the bones which are broken denote the selfhood humiliated, when spiritual happiness may be obtained. It is to be observed, that the breaking of the bones is here somewhat analogous to the removal of the rib—that separation implying the idea of a breaking—a breaking, however, only in the sense of humiliation and dejection, with a view to subsequent exaltation. Again, it is written, "Heal me, O Lord, for my bones are vexed";† "all my bones are out of joint";‡ "my bones are consumed";§ "neither is there any rest in my bones";|| all of which sentences imply states of anxiety and trial which the selfhood was undergoing. But when this selfhood is made somewhat alive by an infusion of the Divine Spirit, it is said, "All my bones shall say, Lord, who is like unto thee?"¶ and, for a similar reason, it is promised that "your bones shall flourish like an herb."** Passages of this nature could be extensively increased; they not only show that the term bones was employed by the ancients in a figurative sense, but they also show that figure to be the selfhood of man, from the intelligibility which the sentences acquire on the application of that idea to the word.

The vivified *bones*, spoken of in the two passages last adduced, are not called *woman*, as in the case of the animation given to Adam's *rib*, because the quality of both the selfhood and vivification treated of is of a different nature: they relate to what is spiritual; that of Adam's to what is celestial. Nevertheless, the prophetical Word does furnish some approximation even to that idea. Ezekiel, relating his vision of the valley of bones, teaches that the bones heard the word of the Lord, received his breath, and became alive, and thereupon they are declared to be the whole house of Israel.†† Thus, *bones* are distinctly said to have been raised into *a whole people, consequently some of them into women*. Of course, this inference from the vision, like the vision itself, will not be understood in a natural sense; the vision was designed to represent the impartation of a new prin-

---

* Psa. li. 8. † Psa. vi. 2. ‡ Psa. xxii. 14. § Psa. xxxi. 10.
|| Psa. xxxviii. 3. ¶ Psa. xxxv. 10. ** Isa. lxvi. 14.
†† Ezek. xxxvii. 4, 5, 11.

ciple and character to the selfhood of a degenerated people. Viewed under that aspect, it is somewhat parallel to the narrative of Moses: he is treating of a people who were not content to be alone, and upon whom a deep sleep had fallen; and, therefore, it was mercifully provided to remove the selfhood which had attended this condition, to infuse into man a new life, and give it a new form, which is described as taking a rib from the man and building it into a woman. This is perfectly consistent with the circumstance of Adam's stating that it was bone of his bone; it was a new selfhood in the external man, raised out of that which the internal man had furnished as the basis. Hence it is said to have been taken out of man, and then called woman. In consequence of the change of state that was now induced upon this posterity of the Adamic Church, it was permitted them to recede from internal things, and attach themselves to what were pure and good in things external. This is what is meant by man "leaving father and mother and cleaving to his wife." The father and mother who might be left, were those internal things from which they had receded; and the wife that might be cleaved to, was the selfhood to which celestial and spiritual influences were now adjoined. It is then said that they were both naked and not ashamed, to teach that the *wisdom*, which constituted the *man*, and the *selfhood*, represented by the *woman*, were still in innocence and free from guilt. Thus it is a figurative and not a literal history: it proceeded from a peculiarity of intellectual genius, some remains of which are traceable in the mythology of after times, and in which there are some apparent histories of a similar kind. For instance, Venus is said to have risen from the froth of the sea; Gigantes to have sprung out of the blood which issued from the wound of Cœlus their father; and Minerva from the brain of Jupiter, whose head was opened by the axe of Satan. Surely every one may see that it is no less difficult to receive these relations as literally true, than that which states a woman to have been built up from the rib of a man. Those Greek fables were framed by men who possessed merely the wreck of that exalted genius which had been employed in the construction of the divine narrative; nevertheless, a sufficient amount of the original remained, to assure us that its written utterances were singularly figurative. It is plain that the ideas and circumstances of primeval men were very different from those which subsequently existed; and also that their method of expressing them must have been less literal than that which was afterwards adopted. It is, therefore, evident that we cannot arrive at correct notions concerning the written sentiments of the former, by the same kind of judgment as that which we bring to decipher the productions of the latter. What they wrote was from internal perception; what has subsequently been written has been from external information. The one relates to internal things figuratively expressed; the other to external things literally described. By overlooking this distinction, and judging of the documents of the former by a standard proper to be applied only to the writings of the latter, a meaning has been claimed for them which they never could have been intended to express. We are aware that the long acceptance of such a meaning may raise a difficulty in the way of its being relinquished. The mind, when once familiarized with an inconsistent notion, does not readily discover its perplexities. It is like a vicious habit, the disorder of which is hidden from the perpetrator by long continuance. However, the question is not whether the literal interpretation of the narratives has been long accepted, but whether it be true: if it be not true, its antiquity can have no claims upon our respect, and the sooner it is abandoned the better will it be for the interest of an enlightened and spiritual religion. The narrative is commonly spoken of as an artless statement; this we believe to be a mistaken idea. As a divine composition, it must be looked upon as a work of God; and cannot, therefore, be an artless production: it must be the result of the most consummate skill, and so correspond with every other work that is divine.

CHAPTER X.

THE SERPENT AND ITS DECEPTION.

"Inquire no longer, man! who is the author of evil; behold him in yourself.—Take away everything that is the work of man; and all the rest is good."—ROUSSEAU.

The subjects treated of under the representation of a serpent and its deception are of deep and melancholy interest to humanity. Great difficulties have always been experienced in the way of a satisfactory understanding of them. The letter has been contemplated, and the spirit overlooked. We shall endeavour to avoid that course, and present the truth which lies beyond it. The meaning is not that which at first appears. We cannot believe in the existence of a talking serpent; we do not think that God ever endowed a reptile with the capability of reasoning; nor can we conceive that mankind were seduced from their propriety by the utterances of a snake. At these views, prejudices may be shocked: we cannot help it; reason will rejoice: error may be alarmed, but truth will be strengthened and advanced. Truth will find her responses in the inner sensations of humanity, if they be fairly permitted to unfold themselves. We appeal, with our interpretation of the Word, to the consciousness and intuition of rational nature, as to the very counterpart of revealed and spiritual wisdom. There is such a phenomenon as feeling a thing to be true, even though there may be difficulties in the way of its clear utterance and demonstration. This we call perception,—a faculty superior to reason, for it is the response of nature, and not the cogitations of art; and there is a harmony existing between those responses in man, and a right exposition of God's Word. It requires care and erudition to comprehend and grasp an argument intended to elaborate a truth for those who are not disposed for its acceptance; but the honest and good heart, which loves truth for its own sake, will perceive it more clearly in the proposition than in the argument. If men would only give their hearts and consciences fair play, they would soon be delivered from many of the fetters which have so long bound them to a misunderstanding both of revelation and of themselves. Let us, then, attend to those approving impulses which arise, and strive to retain the impressions they make upon our minds, as we proceed in the examination of the subjects before us.

In preceding chapters we have traced the progressive development of human excellence, and ultimately found mankind raised to the very pinnacle of religious greatness. From this they fell. The manner of that calamity, together with its immediate consequences, are thus detailed:—"Now the serpent was more subtle than any beast of the field which the Lord God had made. And he said unto the woman, Yea, hath God said, Ye shall not eat of every tree of the garden? And the woman said unto the serpent, We may eat of the fruit of the trees of the garden; but of the fruit of the tree which is in the midst of the garden, God hath said, Ye shall not eat of it, neither shall ye touch it, lest ye die. And the serpent said unto the woman, Ye shall not surely die: for God doth know that in the day ye eat thereof, then your eyes shall be opened, and ye shall be as gods, knowing good and evil. And when the woman saw that the tree was good for food, and that it was pleasant to the eyes, and a tree to be desired to make one wise, she took of the fruit thereof, and did eat, and gave also to her husband, and he did eat. And the eyes of them both were opened, and they knew that they were naked.—Therefore the Lord God sent him forth from the garden of Eden to till the ground from whence he was taken." *

---

* Gen. iii. 1-7, 23. Dr. Adam Clarke remarks on this narrative, "That man is in a fallen state, the history of the world, with that of the life and miseries of every human being, establishes beyond successful contradiction. But *how*, and by what *agency*, was this brought about? Here is a great mystery; and I may appeal to all persons who have read the various comments that have been written on the Mosaic account, whether they have ever yet been satisfied on this part of the subject, though convinced of the fact itself. *Who* was the *serpent?* of what *kind?* In what *way* did he seduce the first happy pair? These are questions which *remain yet to be answered.* The whole account is either a simple narrative of facts, or it is an allegory." An allegory certainly! The Doctor, however, considered it as a " narrative

To understand this account of man's fall, we must remember that the eminent condition from which he descended had been successively procured. His primeval state is declared to have been as the earth, without form, and void; and also, as darkness being upon the face of the deep: thus his original condition was the lowest degree of human life; from this he was gradually elevated into the highest degree of human excellence. That low degree of life, in which he originally stood, was doubtless of a sensual nature, but not of an evil quality; for evil had not then come into existence. It was an orderly degree of life proper to man; it had the capacity of elevation latent within it, and it was upon this that his higher degrees of life had a foundation. This is the life into which man now first comes, though its quality, in consequence of the fall, is more or less tainted with hereditary evil. Nevertheless man, as an infant, is the mere creature of sensation, and the life of the senses is first developed, and must be so, before the higher degrees of intellectual and moral life can be unfolded. Thus Adam was not constituted by one principle merely, but by several.* His highest or inmost was celestial, the next was spiritual, and after these came the natural and sensual. The existence of these several principles in him is proved by the fact that they are all, in some measure, capable of being redeveloped in us; and also in the circumstance, that they are more or less in activity in every mind which cherishes respect for truth and virtue. The internal principles of human life, called celestial and spiritual, are superior to those more external principles

---

of facts," and, after the use of much Hebrew and Arabic learning, arrived at the conclusion that the serpent was an orang-outang, and that the chattering and babbling, of which it is now capable, are the remains of the speech with which it was once endowed, and of course the evidences of the curse. From this we dissent. He, however, was not quite certain that this opinion was correct, nor do we wonder at his doubt. Speech is the exclusive endowment of humanity, and it is attributed to the serpent only in the way of figure. But the Doctor farther says, "If it is an allegory, no attempt should be made to explain it." Indeed! no attempt to be made to explain what God has allegorically revealed! what a commentary on commentators and himself!

* "It cannot be doubted that the first man was created with a great variety of instinctive or inspired knowledge."—*Sir H. Davy.*

denominated natural and sensual; the former belong more to the things of heaven, the latter relate more to the things of the world: and this is as true of man in his primeval state as it is of his condition now: though then the exercise of his lower principles was only instrumental to the purpose of his higher ones; but in after times this instrumental purpose became perverted; the delights of the sensual principle began to be cultivated, irrespective of superior ends, and his perceptions of spiritual and heavenly things were successively closed.

This distinction of principle in man is of the utmost importance to be known, if we would attain to any clear comprehension of the subject before us. The men of the most ancient dispensation had not only the higher principles of celestial and spiritual life, but they had also the lower principles of natural and sensual life. So long as the people continued in their integrity, and maintained their innocence, so long all those principles existed in their proper order, the lower contributing to the purposes of the higher; but when man fell into disobedience and guilt, a disruption took place among them, and the lower principles began to usurp the places of the higher, and thereby to paralyze their functions. Hence it is easy to see that the quality of man's sensual nature before his fall was very different from that which it became after. Before the fall, it was such that it yielded willing obedience to the dictate and impulse of the higher principles of his inner life. It was as a servant ministering to the attainment of superior ends, always acknowledging its subordinate position; but after that catastrophe men began to prefer the sensual things of the body to the intellectual and spiritual things of the mind, and thus the instrumental became the principal, so that the whole order and series of life, which had been successively developed, were changed. This is the state of man now; sensual things are uppermost with him; and the design of religion, its influences and leadings, is to regain the order which has been lost.

The senses are but inlets for certain knowledges,—doors through which information concerning the outer things of the world pass into the mind. The elevation and enlargement of the mind are ends, for the accomplishment of which the senses are among the appointed means. Some persons hear, see, and taste, merely for the sake of hearing, seeing, and tasting; they live a long life, with a very limited extent of intellectual acquirements, because they have scarcely proposed to themselves any higher object than the gratification of their senses. Whereas those who have employed their sensual powers as the ministers to higher uses, with a view to produce superior ends, are found to possess enlarged and comprehensive knowledges of men and things. These circumstances may, in some faint degree, enable us to form an idea of the difference between the quality of the sensual principle of man before and after his fall. But the distinction is admissive of illustration and explanation by other facts known to general experience.

For instance, when we are earnestly endeavouring to understand the meaning of a speaker, the words give us little concern: we hear them, indeed, yet they affect the sense of hearing very slightly, because of the interest we are taking to collect the meaning: nor is this all, for if we think a little more interiorly, and pay attention to what is really transpiring in our mind, it will occasionally be found that we do not always gather the meaning as intellectual sentiments, in consequence of our chief aim being to catch and comprehend the feeling which urges the discourse. Some persons hear the words, but do not grasp the sentiment; they say the language was good and the discourse powerful, but can scarcely give an idea as to what it was about: with such the sensuality of hearing is the chief thing. Others hear the words, but listen to them only as the instruments for communicating the ideas of the speaker; with them the activity of the sensual principle is directed to a higher use: with others, however, the sense is but imperfectly collected, in consequence of the attention being so deeply engaged to comprehend the feeling of the utterer: with such the sensual principle is directed to a nobler end. This latter was a use which the men of the purest times made of their sensual principle, while the former are characteristics that have been engendered in later periods. We call attention to these distinctions, because the Scriptures have presented both conditions of the sensual principle to us under the emblem of a serpent. When the sensual principle is circumspect, and employed as a means for the acquisition of useful knowledge, then is fulfilled the divine injunction, " Be ye wise as serpents";* but when it is used merely for the purpose of securing sensual gratification, then it is declared to be the "serpent more subtle than any beast of the field." †

There are few facts better attested by historical evidence than that the serpent has, by all the nations of antiquity, been regarded as a type, and employed symbolically. It is conspicuous in their history, stands out in their fables, and is visible in their religion. Herodotus informs us that it was sacred at Thebes; ‡ and the hieroglyphics which have been brought to light in our own times abundantly show that it must have been used in an emblematical way among the ancient Egyptians. Bryant, also, asserts that in the first ages the serpent was extensively introduced into all the mysteries that were celebrated; and that wherever the Ammonians founded any places of worship, there was generally some story of a serpent. There was a legend about it at Thebes, at Colchis, and Delphi. Even the Athenians had a tradition that the chief guardian of their Acropolis was a serpent.§ It is sometimes presented under a variety of ideal forms, nor is it uncommon to find it represented with a human head.‖ It is impossible rationally to contemplate these circumstances, and doubt that the serpent sustained some symbolical character. The facts at once suggest that such must have been the design of the serpent said to have been more subtle than any beast of the field: and here we raise the question, Of what was it significant?

The various nations by whom it was symbolically used do not appear to have viewed it under the same aspect. Uniformity of idea, in this respect, would not long continue after that knowledge had perished which originally directed its selection for a symbolical purpose; and when men were left, with no other guide than a fallen fancy, and no sounder principle than a dim caprice, to conduct them in the profound matters of religion and its objects. The serpent is said to have been worshipped, from the circumstance of its having been mentioned

* Matt. x. 16. † Gen. iii. 1. ‡ Euterpe, lxxiv.
§ Bryant on Serpent Worship, vol. i., p. 476, &c.
‖ See Montfaucon's Antiq., by Humphreys. Chimæra is said to have been a black-eyed nymph in her upper part, but downwards a frightful serpent. *Hesiod's Theogony.*

and set apart as one of the objects associated with the religion of Egypt. This was the opinion of Eusebius and others: and it might have been the case in the most corrupted periods of Egyptian learning. That is, it might then have become the symbol of something to be worshipped; but, although it was always a symbol, that was not always the object of it. The serpent came to be spoken of as sacred, only from the circumstance of its having been associated with religious sentiments; it was not at first set apart to be worshipped, or for any good it could bestow, but rather to be dreaded for the mischiefs it might originate. It was the symbol of something that might, if not guarded against, be disastrous to mankind. Hence we find it so frequently referred to in the legends of remote antiquity, as having exercised an unfavourable influence upon the destinies of the people. Every one knows that the figure of a serpent biting its tail is very ancient; it is commonly regarded as the emblem of eternity: but is it not rather a representative of evil punishing itself? In Phœnician mythology we read of a serpent surrounding an egg, plainly implying the danger with which life is beset by sensuality from its very beginning. Among that of the Greeks, we are informed of the hair of Medusa being transformed into serpents, because she had violated the sanctity of the temple of Minerva. The serpents are evidently employed to represent the sensuality she had indulged. The serpent Python, which is fabled to have sprung out of the mud left by the deluge of Deucalion, was an emblem of the evil occasioned to Greece by the inundation of Thessaly. The serpents which the infant Hercules strangled in his cradle were, unquestionably, a representation of innocence conquering the blandishments of sensuality; and the hydra, which he afterwards overthrew, was a representation of those evils which the labours of energy and fortitude may overcome. So, also, the Caduceus, which was a rod entwined by serpents, and with which Mercury is said to have conducted souls to the infernal regions, plainly symbolized the evils which cling to a misdirected power, and so conduce to misery. Esculapius, the medical attendant on the Argonauts, is always represented with a serpent entwined about his staff, to denote the power of the physician over the diseases of humanity. Many other instances of the emblematical use of the serpent might be collected from the writings of the ancients, but these are sufficient for our purpose: they plainly show that the emblem of that whereby man fell was preserved among mankind for a long time after the reminiscence of its definite signification had passed away. They retained the emblem, with some general idea of its meaning, but had lost sight of its precise signification. For this we must go to analogy and the Scriptures. Those are the only sources whence satisfactory information can be drawn, and they will show us that the serpent was the sensual principle of man.*

"Of all the objects of the animal kingdom, the reptile tribe is the lowest, of which serpents of various kinds and species are the most conspicuous. Of all the degrees of man's life, the *sensual* and *corporeal* are the lowest; because they are nearest to the earth, and are actuated by merely earthly appetites, influences, and causes. These lowest degrees in man's nature partake the least of what is truly human in man, and the serpent, their corresponding emblem, is of all animals the most remote from the human form. As the serpent crawls upon the earth, so the sensual principle in man is nearest akin to the earth, which, if not elevated by the rational and spiritual principles of his nature, may be said to crawl upon the earth in like manner. As sensual things have a tendency to fascinate and charm the mind, because sensual delights are more vividly experienced than any others, so certain kinds of serpents, especially the more malignant, are said by naturalists to fascinate and charm their prey before they devour it."† The general analogies, so satisfactorily presented in this extract, assists us in perceiving

---

* The Rev. J. Hewlett, B.D., in his "Annotations," observes, "St. Paul, in addressing himself to the Corinthians, says, 'I fear, lest, as the serpent beguiled Eve, through his subtlety, so your minds should be corrupted from the simplicity which is in Christ.' Now the city of Corinth was notorious, even to a proverb, for its devotion to pleasure, for the grossest sensuality and voluptuousness; and as the holy apostle draws a parallel between them and the temptation which seduced Eve, it may be supposed that he favours the allegorical interpretation of those who consider the serpent as the well-known emblem or symbol of sensual pleasure."

† A writer under the signature of "Minus," in the "Intellectual Repository" for 1843, p. 53.

certain general resemblances between the serpent and the sensual principle of man.

Now the serpent* which was in Eden, we believe to have been the sensual principle that was connected with Adam's character. For a time there was with him a realization of the Lord's injunction to be "wise as serpents." The sensual principle, at first, was right and orderly, because it stood in its proper relation to the dictates of his higher nature. It was among the objects upon which the Divine approbation had been pronounced: for the Lord declared the *creeping* things to be " good," yea, " very good." This, then, was a characteristic of the serpent, or, more literally, of the sensual principle of Adam, as declared of it by the Lord himself.

So long as it was employed *instrumentally* to promote the ends of spiritual use and order, so long it was wise; but when it was directed *principally* to secure the gratifications of corporeal nature, it became most subtle. The *wisdom* of the serpent is the circumspection and prudence of the sensual principle of man; the *subtlety* of the serpent is its artifice and deception. In neither case was a literal serpent meant. The very circumstances of the narrative having given to it speaking and reasoning powers, ought to have preserved mankind from the belief of such a crudity. If it once could speak, when and how did it lose the power? The Scriptures furnish no answer. Theology has suggested that it was the devil, and not the serpent, who spoke. But the Scriptures do not say so. They express no idea about the then existence of the devil: † how could he have come into

---

* The Hebrew word here translated serpent is *Nachash*. Much learning has been bestowed upon this term, for the purpose of determining who or what the serpent was, but without any very satisfactory results. The principal reason is, because a sense has been sought for it which it was never intended to express. Forbes, in his "Oriental Memoirs," says, "A great nuisance at Benares is the number of Yogees, Senassees, and *Nanghas*, or religious mendicants, who go about entirely naked: we occasionally meet with a few of these people at other places, but here they abound." (Vol. iv., p. 86.)

† "This question may be asked,—If such be the case, how came the opinion so general respecting fallen angels, and whence was it derived? There can be no doubt respecting the source whence it was obtained. The first notion of the existence of a fallen angel is found in the Zendavesta. The

being before evil had been perpetrated? The Scriptures most distinctly assert that it was the serpent which spoke: nor is there, throughout the whole narrative, the slightest intimation that it was any other being. The faculty of speech is attributed to it because it is significant of the sensual principle of man; which is, indeed, a speaking principle, uttering wisdom when it is used as the instrument of spiritual order, but discoursing artifice when separated therefrom and directed to worldly indulgence.

Man is formed, not by one principle only, but by many; he has not lost any of them by the fall: that calamity destroyed their quality, and perverted the order of their existence, but it obliterated none. Hence humanity, in its primitive perfection, must have had principles distinguished by higher and lower degrees of excellence; the interior being allied to the things of spirituality and heaven, and the exterior to the objects of corporeity and earth.

Now, one of the distinguished characteristics of the Adamic people was their freedom. When placed in the garden, they had a choice given to them to obey or transgress the divine commands. It was said to them, "Of every tree of the garden thou mayest freely eat: but of the tree of knowledge of good and evil, thou shalt not eat of it." This freedom must have been very perfect, because their condition is pronounced to have been very good. From this state they must have known the truth, for it is a law that those who know the truth, "the truth shall make them free."* Moreover, the Spirit of God was present with them, and the apostle has declared that "where the Spirit of the Lord is, there is liberty." † They had been raised to the summit of their excellence by the use of freedom in that direc-

---

later Jews became conversant with the Persian mythology, and introduced this, with various other notions, into their writings, and it seems to have been adopted by the early Christians, without any inquiry into the Scriptural authority upon which it rested. Our immortal countryman, Milton, by clothing this fiction of the Persian mythology, in all the beauty and attractions of poetry, has so recommended it to our imagination, that we almost receive it as of divine authority; and we feel a reluctance to be convinced that all his splendid fabric is based on falsehood."—*John Lamb, D.D. Hebrew Characters derived from Hieroglyphics.* Pp. 118, 119. *See. ed.*

* John viii. 32. † 2 Cor. iii. 17.

tion. But this did not *compel* them to remain there. They did not forfeit their freedom by the attainment of their superiority: it was enlarged and perfected as they ascended.

While the men of the most ancient times employed this freedom in co-operating with the Lord to develop the interior resources of their orderly humanity, it was exercised in a wise and right direction; but by that very freedom they could again descend the mountain they had climbed: yet to do so would necessarily be attended by a curtailment of their freedom. "He who doeth sin is the servant of sin." * Freedom is rightly used when it causes all the principles of men to look inwards and onwards to the attainment of superior states: but it is abused when it permits them to look outwards and backwards to the delights supplied by inferior things.

Now, the tendency of man's lower sentiments and disposition is towards the world, while the impulses of his spiritual nature and inclination are towards heaven: and, so long as the former remain under the influences of the latter, so long order is preserved, and all their respective relationships are good: but who does not know that the inferior principles strive to relax the vigilance of the superior? Who has not occasionally experienced the lower principles of his nature proposing doubts as to the reality of those objects which the higher principles believed and sought after? Who has not sometimes permitted his judgment to be formed only by the testimony of the eye, or the evidence of some other sense, and yielded belief only to those things which he could see and touch, and has cherished doubts about those interior subjects which are to be known only to the inner convictions, by means of the mental sight and higher feelings of our nature? These are no uncommon circumstances. They come home to the general experiences of men: and, surely, it is easy to see, when our sensual nature is endeavouring to separate itself from the light and guidance of our spiritual nature, that the serpent is attempting to deceive us. The sensual principle endeavours to persuade us that the objects of the outer senses are more real than the things of intellectual perception; and thus it would induce us to prefer the pleasures of the world to the felicities of heaven. Do we not, in this fact, even now,

* John viii. 34.

experience the temptation of the serpent? Does it not make an effort to weaken our regard for God's commandments, and is it not frequently insinuating, that the gratification of the passions of our lower nature is preferable to the delights anticipated by our higher principles? Is not this fact the common experience of men, and does it not suggest a reasonable exposition of the serpent saying, "Ye shall not surely die"? The serpent of natural history cannot say this, but the sensual principle of man practically does so whenever it begins to act independently of higher powers; and this we conceive to have been the very serpent by which Adam was seduced from his propriety, and led into transgression!

The serpent is said to have been "more subtle than any beast of the field," not to teach that it has any remarkable sagacity beyond what is common to the instinct of animated nature, for no such fact is known to naturalists; but this is said of it to inform us that the sensual principle is the lowest and the least to be depended on of all the other affections belonging to our external man: it is requisite to watch over it by the higher powers of our minds, and to direct it by superior principles, or it will be sure to lead us into a forgetfulness of our highest duty, and finally plunge us into disobedience. The reason is, because it dwells as it were upon the outer extremes of human life. It thus readily receives impressions from the external world, by which the memory is furnished with information, which it can wield with a persuasive art in favour of the delights and pursuits of worldly things. It reasons with shrewdness and dexterity, because its thoughts are so near the tongue: it thinks that intelligence consists in speaking from the memory concerning things collected from without, and views the understanding of things implanted by the Lord with doubt and disrespect.

There is nothing so deceptive as the senses. If we trust to them only for information, our judgment and conclusions must be full of error. There is a proverb that "seeing is believing"; but it is not always true. We have to correct the impression which we receive from without, by the higher faculties of our minds, in order to reach the truth. How various are the fallacies of vision! The sun appears but a small body, formed to rise and set upon the earth, which seems immovable. The stars, also, appear to be fixed in the same extended plane, and moving from east to west in the vast expanse; but these things are not really so; they are mere fallacies of the sight, which we correct by another and superior power! If the sensual principle be not so corrected, it remains in fallacies, and it will be found to appeal to the testimony of the senses for evidences that the appearance is the reality. The subtlety of the serpent consists in the fallacies which sensuality induces. All its reasonings are grounded in worldly things; and by these it would lead us to believe that there is nothing worthy of our attention or attachment, but what we can see, feel, or taste: and there is a force and plausibility about such reasonings, which fits them for the purposes of seduction.

Any one capable of seeing how the higher powers of the mind correct the fallacious impressions which outward and worldly things make upon the lower senses, will readily perceive how it was that all the faculties and powers of Adam, during his integrity, existed in harmony and order. For a time, his sensual principle was as wise as a serpent, because it admitted into it the correcting light of spirituality and intelligence. Still it was not removed from the influences of the world; and he possessed both the power and freedom, if he chose to incur the responsibility, of listening to its suggestions. This, according to the history of the temptation, was actually done; thereby the light, by which his sensual nature had been previously illuminated, began to be diminished in its force, and the consequence was that fallacies were received and believed as truths, and thus the way was opened for evil to begin its deadly work.

The fall of man, as thus effected, was a gradual event. It began by his commencing to love the good of his inferior principles, in preference to the good of his superior ones; successively descending, until he finally sunk into the persuasions and delusions of his sensual nature. This was the circumstance in which evil had its origin, and men will obtain a tolerably correct idea of that disastrous event, if they will but carefully attend to the beginning of their own actual guilt. Every one knows that this had its commencement in freely yielding to the suggestion of his sensual nature, to gratify some selfish love. It was near to him, and promised immediate satisfaction, whereas those which were of a superior nature seemed to be at a greater distance, and to exert a feebler influence. The serpent which seduced the inhabitants of Eden from their innocence and wisdom is the same as that by which transgression and guilt have been perpetuated. Man is its exclusive author, and not anything extrinsic to him. The attempt to charge it upon some other being is only another act of self-delusion. It is the endeavour of man to excuse his own misconduct, by heightening the criminality of another; but this he cannot do until after the perpetration of his own guilt.

But Adam did not at once sink into every evil: the depth of his criminality, like that of the guilt of men in subsequent ages, was a progressive result. The first intimation of it is given in the preceding chapter, where it is said that "it was not good for man to be alone," of which we have already spoken. At first he only inclined towards the impulses of his sensual nature; he afterwards began to inquire whether it was not lawful to prefer its desires and suggestions, and at length he yielded to its solicitations. Nevertheless, the evils into which he fell were mild and few, compared with those which were perpetrated in after times. His transgression was only the beginning of that catastrophe by which the fall of man was made complete. Successive ages added to the enormities which he began, but the atrocity of the fall could not have reached its depth, until the Lord Jesus Christ came into the world,* in order to bruise the

* It may be a matter of surprise to some to hear that the fall of man was not completed before the time of the Lord's manifestation. This, however, we think is very plain, from a careful consideration of the Scriptural History of man. The extreme of the divine mercy was adopted when the extreme of human necessity had arrived. Still, the state of Rome, in respect to its refinements in literature, the arts, and general civilization; its successful and extensive conquests, together with the circumstance of its having been the Augustan age, when peace was so settled with all the world that the temple of Janus (Patulcius) was shut up, may be urged as facts difficult to reconcile with the above statement. But no condition of merely natural civilization, however eminent, if it be destitute of true religious grounds, can be of any weight in an argument of this kind. That the civilization of Rome, or of any other of the nations, had no ground in genuine religion, is the uniform testimony of all history. The fall of man was complete when he was separated by pride, ambition, selfishness, and all their attendant evils, from divine and heavenly influences: and there is evidence to prove that

head of the serpent which had occasioned that calamity. In the acts attendant upon that coming, he fulfilled the prediction which was delivered immediately after the temptation became successful. But how did he fulfil it? Was it by bruising any natural serpent's head? Certainly not. As the prediction was

these features distinguished the nations at the period of our Lord's manifestation more than at any other time in the history of our race. The awful character which Jesus draws of the Jewish nation is a representation of the Church as it then existed with mankind at large. Sismondi, in his history of the "Fall of the Roman Empire," speaking of the Julian family, says, "it is that of the 'dictator Cæsar'; his name was transmitted, by adoption, out of the direct line, but always within the circle of his kindred, to the five first heads of the Roman Empire. Augustus reigned from the year 30 B.C. to the year 14 of our era; Tiberius from 14 to 37 A.D.; Caligula from 37 to 41; Claudius from 41 to 54; Nero from 54 to 68. Their names alone, with the exception of the first, concerning whom there still exists some diversity of opinion, recall everything that is shameful and perfidious in man,—everything that is atrocious in the abuse of absolute power. Never had the world been astounded with such a variety and enormity of crime; never had so fatal an attack been made on every virtue which men had been accustomed to hold in reverence."—*Cabinet Cyclopædia*, Vol. I., p. 28. We may be reminded that the world had become exceedingly wicked at the time of the flood; and also, that after that catastrophe, the atrocities of men, indicated in the overthrow of Sodom and Gomorrah, were exceedingly revolting; and from these facts it may be argued that men had fallen at those periods, quite as low as any degradation observable in their history at the time of the Lord's advent into the world. But those who hold to that conclusion are not yet in possession of all the facts and circumstances of the case.

The fact of the Antediluvians having perished through the evils which oppressed them, is no more evidence that the fall had reached its greatest depth, than the crucifixion of the thief is a proof that he was the worst of men. The remarkable way in which the Antediluvians perished, shows that there were some circumstances peculiar to their case, but it does not show the completeness of the fall. Their minds were originally constituted from the reception of heavenly influences by an *internal way*, and it was the effectual closing up of that way which brought about the deluge: when men so circumstanced ceased, as it were, to respire with heaven, they perished; but there was another and more *external way*, by which holy things might obtain access to the mind; this, not being opened out with the Antediluvians, they did not pervert. This way for the entrance of holy things into the mind was opened out with the Noachic people; it belonged to that new covenant that was established with them, and it was not until after this was closed that the fall became complete.

The fall of man is not to be considered simply as a fall into criminal acts, but chiefly as the corruption and wreck of all his human principles, and thus not so fulfilled, is it not evident that it could not have been any natural serpent which caused the temptation? The serpents of that time were the sensualities of fallen humanity, for the Lord distinctly asserted the Jews to be "serpents, and a generation as the perversion of all his inclinations to receive and retain all the spiritual sentiments of purity and heaven.

The human principles are celestial, spiritual, and natural: it is these which distinguish man from the beast; and the two former fell into depravity before the latter was entirely corrupted. They are distinct degrees of human life, to which respectively belong the sentiments of love, faith, and duty; and that which was pre-eminent in each principle stood out as the characteristic of mankind in the best times of the Adamic, Noachic, and Israelitish people. In each of those periods, a Divine Dispensation was established, suited to the prevailing genius and requirements of the people to whom it was vouchsafed: the first, however, was associated with a more interior life, even in its visible character, than the intermediate and the last. How plain is it that the condition of religion which was begun with Adam was much more eminent than that which had its commencement with Noah; and how certain is it that this was superior to that which was established with Abraham and his descendants! The reason is, because the first was adapted more to the loving or celestial principle; the second, to the believing or spiritual principle; and the third, to the obeying or natural principle of the people. It is well known that each of these churches declined and fell, but the peculiar nature of these falls was that the people of each successively corrupted that principle in themselves, to which its teachings were specifically addressed. Thus the celestial principle in man was closed when the divine things proper to the Adamic dispensation ceased to be perceived, and its ruin is revealed to us by the calamity of the flood. The spiritual principle was corrupted when the divine things proper to the Noachic dispensation ceased to be acknowledged, and its wreck and desolation are represented by the confusion of tongues and the dispersion of mankind; and the natural principle was defiled when the obedience proper to the Israelitish economy ceased to be observed, and its fall is shown by the termination thereof at the coming of the Lord Jesus Christ.

Hence we learn that the cessation of each Church was accompanied by, or rather that it resulted from, the corruption of that distinctive principle in man for the development and maintenance of which it had been mercifully provided. Consequently, the fall consisted in the successive defilement of each distinct principle of human life. Thus, although the criminal acts which were perpetrated in the early ages of our race were quite as atrocious as any that were committed in subsequent periods; yet, as in each of these periods such acts proceeded from the corruption of the different principles that were peculiar to each, it is certain that there must have been a difference in the quality of the atrocities which prevailed; and consequently, the first dispensation, in this respect, must have been more enormous than those that

of vipers."* The Lord's bruising the serpent's head, then, consisted in his subduing the power and ascendancy which the sensual principle had obtained. He did this by opening out fresh influences from Himself, which are called "a new and living way,"† from which time men have been capable, as all history attests, of thinking and acting from higher grounds than they had done previously, and thereby of discovering and exposing the fraud and deceptions which the merely sensual nature would impose upon us. This is what is implied in the promise made unto believers, namely, "I will give you power to tread on serpents";‡ "they shall take up serpents."§ Power over these things naturally, was originally vouchsafed; nor is there any intimation of its having been lost by man's transgression: on the contrary, we find savage nations display it with considerable energy. The Lord did not come into the world for such a purpose. The power to *tread on serpents*, which he then conferred, was a power to subdue our sensual nature; and the power to *take up serpents*, was the ability to elevate our sensual nature, by placing it under the purifying influences and directing energies of the loftier principles of spirituality and religion.

There are several historical narratives in which serpents are mentioned in a truly literal sense. In those cases, however, their representation is the same as that which they sustain in factitious history; consequently, they may be cited as affording confirmatory evidence of it. For instance, the rod of Aaron, on the occasion of his interview with Pharaoh, is stated to have been cast down, and it became a serpent. ‖ Because the rod of Aaron denoted the power of spiritual good, by casting it down

---

followed : the people sinned with more open eyes, and so brought ruin upon a more interior principle than any of the rest ; hence that dispensation perished in a catastrophe more terrible than any of the rest. So, when it is said that the fall of man was not completed until "the Lord God of Israel visited to redeem his people," the meaning is that at that time the lowest of the remaining human principles had been forced into its final corruption ; that "darkness covered the earth, and gross darkness the people." The enormities of the ancient world, therefore, oppose no real difficulties to the doctrine which maintains that the fall did not reach its deepest depths until "God became manifest in the flesh."

* Matt. xxiii. 33. † Heb. x. 20. ‡ Luke x. 19.
§ Mark xvi. 18. ‖ Exod. vii. 10-12.

was signified its degradation; and by its becoming a serpent was represented, that such a power, with the Egyptians, had become altogether sensual. The circumstance of the rods of the magicians also becoming serpents, was a confirmation of that truth which the transaction of Aaron had representatively revealed; and the rod of Aaron swallowing up those of the magicians, was a farther representative revelation that such disorderly power would be taken from them.

When the people of Israel "spake against God and against Moses, fiery serpents were sent among them, so that much people of Israel died." This was done to represent the sensual loves with which they were beset, and through the influences of which so many of mankind spiritually perish. Moses, complying with a divine command, "made a serpent of brass, and put it upon a pole: and it came to pass, that if a serpent had bitten any man, when he beheld the serpent of brass, he lived." * Every one must perceive that this was done for a representative purpose. It is evident from the circumstance of the Lord having said, concerning it, "As Moses lifted up the serpent in the wilderness, even so must the Son of man be lifted up: that whosoever believeth in him should not perish, but have everlasting life." † The Lord Jesus Christ, as to the good of his sensual nature, was signified by the brazen serpent. He was so represented before the Israelites, because they were merely in a sensual state, and did not elevate their thoughts concerning God above that low condition. Its being lifted upon a pole, signified

---

* Numb. xxi. 5–9.

† John iii. 14, 15. This passage is commonly regarded as a prefiguration of the crucifixion of Jesus Christ, which men are to believe was a suffering substituted for that which is due to their own guilt! But the student whose mind has not been pre-occupied with that idea, will find it difficult to establish any analogy between such a supposed type and antetype. Surely there is no correspondence between Moses, who lifted up the serpent, and the wicked authorities who crucified Jesus! nor can anything but fancy find any resemblance between the pole and the cross. There is nothing answering to the crown of thorns, the nails, the spear, &c., &c. The reason is, that it was not such a type. The raising of the brazen serpent related to the glorification of the Lord, but the crucifixion to the humiliation of the Lord: these were two distinct acts connected with his manifestation in the world for the redemption of mankind.

the glorification of the Lord's sensual nature. For those who were bitten by the serpent to look upon that which was of brass, and receive a cure, denoted that those who feel the stings and wounds inflicted by sensual loves, and look up to the Lord for deliverance, will be sure to receive the communication of spiritual life for effecting it.

Other cases could be easily adduced, and, like the above, summarily explained; but what has been observed must make it evident that the serpent of Eden was the sensual principle of the Adamic people, and that its temptations consisted in presenting before their higher faculties the fascinations of worldly objects and delights; so that, in process of time, their higher principles and powers were seduced to favour them, and being lulled into a forgetfulness of superior duties, they gradually sunk into the indulgence of their lower principles, irrespective of a higher guidance, and, therefore, lost possession of their intelligence; and this is what is meant by their expulsion from the garden.

This view of the subject presents the narrative to us in an intelligible form. It comes home, in a good measure, to our experience; we see its reasonableness, and at once recognize the subtlety* of the serpent in the occasional experience of its suggestions; also the fallacious aspect under which it presents worldly and selfish ends. We perceive that its influence must be attended with a fatal withdrawing from all spiritual good, unless it be vigilantly watched and carefully resisted. It reasons fallaciously, because the materials of its argument are drawn from the things of time and sense. It does not consult the inner dictate and superior suggestions of the mind. The sensual man says, "This is my nature; why should I resist its propensities, and not enjoy the pleasures which they promise? God, if there be such a being, must have given them to me, and certainly I cannot sin against him when I use them." These deceptive reasonings illustrate the serpent saying, "Ye shall not surely die." But how transparent is the subtlety of such suggestions! Although God has given to man a sensual nature, because he was to be a resident in a physical world, yet it was given

---

* The original word translated "subtle," though it may denote insidiousness and craft, yet here it rather means the power to insinuate and ingratiate.

in connection with superior powers, and was intended to be employed under the direction of higher principles than itself. Again, the serpent is reported to have said, "In the day that ye eat of the forbidden fruit your eyes shall be opened, and ye shall be as gods, knowing good and evil." To eat of the forbidden fruit is plainly to transgress a given law. The tree of knowledge is a divine gift, by which men are enabled to perceive the truths of faith: the fruit of this tree is the good of life. When men, from sensual persuasions, are led to think that any virtues they may possess are self-derived, they eat of the fruit of the tree of knowledge: they believe their eyes are open, because they can see with approbation the delights of the world; and they conceive that they are as gods, knowing good and evil, because they think they guide themselves in the prudence they observe: but these are fallacies utterly destructive of all genuine faith in spiritual and celestial things!

Look at the effects of such reasonings as they are exhibited in worldly and sensually guided men. Who are so strongly persuaded as these, that their eyes have been opened by having abandoned the teachings of religion, and plunged into the fascinations of the world? "They think that as gods they are wise, knowing good and evil, because they may be capable of distinguishing between the pains and pleasures of sense; and yet who, in reality, are as blind as they to all the knowledges which relate to spirituality, futurity, and heaven? They do not acknowledge an eternal life, for they believe that when they die they end: neither do they acknowledge the Lord, but worship only themselves and nature. Those amongst them who wish to be guarded in their expressions, say that there is a Supreme Being, of whose nature they are ignorant, and who rules over all. These are the principles in which they confirm themselves by numerous sensual and scientific arguments, and if they dared, they would openly proclaim these views before all mankind. Such persons, although they desire to be regarded as gods, or as the wisest of beings, would, if they were asked what it was not to love themselves, reply that it was the same thing as to have no existence. The idea of living from the Lord they conceive to be a mere phantasy; and if interrogated as to their knowledge of conscience, they would say it is a mere creation of the imagination, which may be serviceable in keeping the vulgar under restraint: if interrogated as to their knowledges of perception, they would laugh at your question, and call it enthusiastic. Such is their wisdom; *such open eyes they have, and such gods they are:* on these principles, which they imagine clearer than the day, they ground all their reasonings and conclusions concerning the mysteries of faith; and what can be the result but an abyss of darkness? These are the serpents, above all others, who seduced the world." * This principle, having gained a successive influence over the Adamic people, caused their fall. It may be questioned whether the generation with whom its seductions began, descended into all the enormities contemplated in the above extract, though there can be no doubt that they were fearfully realized by their posterity before the flood.

*Arcana Cœlestia, 206.

CHAPTER XI.

THE EATING OF THE FORBIDDEN FRUIT, AND EXPULSION FROM EDEN.

> " 'Twas man himself
> Brought Death into the world: and man himself
> Gave keenness to his darts, quickened his pace,
> And multiplied destruction on mankind."
> DR. PORTEUS, *Bishop of London.*

From the considerations which have been adduced, we learn that the people, treated of under the collective name of Adam, were distinguished by a variety of principles, the whole of which, during their integrity, existed in order and operated for happiness. The sensual principle was among the lowest of this variety; the circumstance of its existing upon the outermost range of the mind, and, as it were, dwelling so close upon the world, is the reason why it is described as being more subtle than any beast of the field. Hence it was seen that the tendency of this principle was outwards and downwards, in like manner as the desires of the higher principles were inwards and upwards; consequently man, by the freedom of his nature, was capable of giving ascendancy to either, by cultivating the one in preference to the other; therefore the success of the serpent's temptation consisted in man's sensual nature favouring the excitement induced upon it from without. It has also been intimated that this catastrophe was not a sudden but a successive work; that it began by inducing inclination to prefer the outer pleasures of the world to the inward delights of heavenly things; *then* by insinuating doubts as to the existence of things spiritual, because they could not be seen or handled by the physical senses; *next,* by suggesting that natural things might be the only realities, because they only came under the cognizance of the eye and the touch; and, *at length*, by producing the consent of the inner powers to the indulgences of sensual love. Such we conceive to have been the general process of the temptation, and the transgression finally induced. The period which was occupied in this decline and fall is not announced. Still there can be no reasonable doubt that it was the work of several generations. It is the existence of the fact, rather than the period occupied in its production, which it is of importance to know.

Having these general views of the superior state of man, and the way of his decline and fall, before us, we can now proceed to investigate the nature of the law he is stated to have broken by that transaction. It is thus written: "Of every tree of the garden thou mayest freely eat: but of the tree of the knowledge of good and evil, thou shalt not eat of it: for in the day that thou eatest thereof thou shalt surely die."* The manner in which it was transgressed, though cited in the preceding chapter for the sake of having the whole transaction then before us, was not there explained: for this purpose it is now again produced. "When the woman saw that the tree was good for food, and that it was pleasant to the eyes, and a tree to be desired to make one wise, she took of the fruit thereof, and did eat, and gave also unto her husband; and he did eat. And the eyes of them both were opened, and they knew that they were naked.—Therefore the Lord sent him forth from the garden of Eden, to till the ground from whence he was taken." † Eating is the act forbidden, and we think it much more natural to regard it as the interdiction of some irregular process of the mind than as the prohibition of a particular act of the body. If a physical act were intended by the proscription, surely we may fairly ask why the tree was placed in the garden? Why it should have appeared so good for food, pleasant to the eyes, and a tree to be desired to make one wise, if, after all, it were not to be tasted? The common answer to these inquiries is, that it was planted in the garden with a prohibitory law, to test the fidelity of the parties who beheld it. But who does not perceive that this idea makes the tree a stumbling-block, and God the tempter for

* Gen. ii. 16, 17.   † Gen. iii. 6, 7, 23.

having put it there.* It plainly represents the tree as a temptation, and supposes God not to have foreseen its consequences. Surely the Lord does not try the constancy of his people by giving them, upon the one hand, a law to observe, and, on the other hand, by placing in their way a temptation to transgress it. The supposition is shocking, and should be avoided. . The whole notion about God trying the fidelity of his people, by placing them in difficult circumstances, requires revision. It is an apparent and not a genuine truth.

God is essential goodness, and he has always watched over the welfare and happiness of men with the utmost care: he would have removed the fruit out of Adam's reach, and hindered the serpent from persuading him to eat it, if they had been things extraneous to his nature. But they were not; they were things which belonged to him as a man, and to have removed them would have been to have taken away his manhood. This sensual principle was necessary to complete his nature, and fit him for residing in the world: the knowledge of good and evil was necessary to encourage him in the way of obedience, and to act as a hindrance to his transgression. Freedom was indispensable to employ those knowledges agreeably to his own choice. How could a man be a man without a sensual principle! How little would man have been distinguished from the brute if he had been deprived of the knowledge of good and evil! and without freedom he would have been a mere creature of impulsive instinct.

Adam was endowed with all these excellencies. He possessed information of the highest kind. He was in the life of obedience, and so in the knowledge of good; thence he would have a perception of its opposite, and so acquire the knowledge of evil. This was a tree distinguished among the other intelligences of his intellectual garden. It was an enlarged possession of genuine

* Byron, in his terrible poem, "Cain," makes him say, in reference to the temptation of Adam,—

"The tree was planted, and not for him?
If not, why place him near it, where it grew,
The fairest in the centre? They have but
One answer to all questions, ' 'Twas *his* will,
And *he* is good.' "

knowledge, proper to his high condition. But he was not to eat thereof. Eating was the prohibited act. Why was this, when he was so freely permitted to eat of every other tree? We shall find the answer to this interrogatory if we consider the signification of the term.

That it does not mean natural eating is evident, because taste is the chief species of knowledge which it is capable of inducing, and that is among the lowest class. The notion of the fruit having possessed some property that was capable of exciting the mind to greater action, and so to procure additional information, we think to be unworthy of a serious thought. Stimulants will inflame the imagination, but they do not increase our wisdom! They may excite and disorder the mind, but they cannot increase and strengthen it. Surely knowledges, superior to those which Adam in his integrity possessed, were not to be procured by the eating of some peculiar fruit! If so, Adam could not have been so wise as is supposed, because there were certain knowledges withheld from him, and which the fruit of some remarkable tree was capable of furnishing. But what dreams are these!*

Eating is a term of frequent occurrence in the Scriptures, and, in the really historical portion of them, it literally denotes what it expresses; but there are many occasions on which the word is used without such meaning; yet in every instance it has an internal sense. We select the following examples. The Lord said, "I am the living bread which came down from heaven: if any man *eat* of this bread he shall live for ever." "Except ye *eat* the flesh of the Son of man, and drink his blood, ye have no life in you." "He that eateth me, even he shall live by me."† In these sentences, it is plain, that by eating is not meant eating, but that internal act of the mind by which it appropriates, in an orderly way, the good things of religion, and thereby acquires spiritual nutrition for the sustenance of the soul. It was for the same reason that the Lord said by the prophet, "Hearken diligently unto me, and *eat* ye that which is good, and let your soul delight itself in fatness."‡ The Lord also said, "To him that overcometh will I give to eat of the tree of life, which is in the midst of the paradise of

* See pp. 77, 78.   † John vi. 51, 53, 57.   ‡ Isa. lv. 2.

God ":* where, by the tree of life, is meant the perception of love; for love is a fruit-bearing principle with men; and this is said to be in the midst of the paradise of God, when it is made the centre of all the religious duties of the Church; while to eat of the tree, clearly means to appropriate the perception of love to our spiritual use and benefit. The act of eating, as of natural food for the nutrition of the body, is named, because it corresponds to the act of appropriating spiritual good for the sustenance of the soul. There is a food for the mind as well as for the body. The soul must be fed with the good of love, in order that it may live in spiritual health, in like manner as the body must be supported with the bread of nature, in order to maintain its physical vigour. The love of what is good, and the perceptions thence arising, were the food by which Adam was instructed to sustain his eminent condition: this is what is meant by that portion of the law which says, "Of every tree of the garden thou mayest freely eat": the reasons for the exception will presently appear.

Every one is, as to his internal quality, precisely what his love is: it is this, with its consequent perception, which constitutes his individuality. A man's character springs from his love, and he is judged and estimated according to the nature of its quality and developments. This love and perception are, as to the individuality which they form, the man's own: they distinguish one man from another. In this respect each one is himself alone. He has a distinctiveness of nature which belongs to no one else, and this is acquired by his having appropriated, incorporated, cherished, or spiritually eaten of some peculiar love. If it were not so appropriated, it would pass away and vanish. It is only by such appropriation that his individuality remains. As he appropriates good in any of its varieties, the distinctiveness of character thereby imparted cannot perish. So that he may "eat of every tree of the garden, but of the tree of knowledge of good and evil he must not eat of it"; this is forbidden for reasons which regard his truest welfare.

The knowledge of the spiritual things of faith, duty, and heaven, is not of man; it is the Lord's. It is communicated to the world by revelation, either through an internal dictate to its

* Rev. ii. 7.

immediate subjects, or by means of a written Word. Without such revelation, man must have been utterly ignorant of such knowledge. Every one may be sure, if he be so disposed, that all his knowledge of such things has come to him from a source superior to himself. He feels that he is incompetent for such discoveries, and, therefore, that he ought to live under the continual acknowledgment, that all he knows of holy and religious things is not from himself, but from the Lord.

Now, as eating is significant of mental appropriation, to eat of the tree of knowledge denotes that mental appropriation of it, by which men are led to believe that it is the result of their own self-derived intelligence. Adam was forbidden to eat of it, in order to guard against this consequence; therefore, we cease to wonder at the prohibition. We see that it was done for a wise and merciful purpose, and designed as a medium for preserving man in the humble acknowledgment of the Lord, as the source and giver of all intelligence and truth; also, to teach him, that if he ceased from such acknowledgment, he would necessarily fall into transgression. Is it not so? Do not those who are wise in their own conceits, who pride themselves upon their presumed intelligence, and consider it as a meritorious acquisition of their own, reject the Lord, and so transgress his law?

But there is another important reason why the eating of the tree of knowledge was prohibited. Knowledge is a means to an end. It is given for the improvement and formation of character. The more eminent the knowledge is, if applied to life, the more exalted is the man. All knowledge has respect to life, and it is intended for the promotion and establishment of good. Therefore, to eat of the tree of knowledge is to appropriate information for the enlargement of the understanding merely, without due regard to its holier uses. How frequently is that which is denominated genius, found to be disorderly! How often are clever men discovered to be crafty! Does it not sometimes occur, that men with enlarged understandings have narrow souls and selfish hearts? Is it not true that learned men are sometimes wicked? that they perpetrate their ills with sagacity—"plate their sins with gold"? Doubtless these are facts; but whence do they arise? Simply because such men have eaten of the tree of knowledge, devoured information with a greedy appetite, regarding knowledge as the end, and desiring to be clever rather than good. The mischievous tendency of such a course is evident. It places the perpetrator in the position of "that servant which knew his Lord's will, and prepared not himself, neither did according to his will, (and who therefore) shall be beaten with many stripes."* How wise, then, is the command, "Ye shall not eat of it"! and if men do so, how certain is their fall—a fall into a criminal neglect of the laws of order, propriety, integrity, and virtue!

Does not experience prove that this is the course which the sensual appetite invariably suggests? It desires to separate itself from superior guidance, and to be left to its own control. It strives to prevent knowledge from exercising its salutary influences upon the lower affections: it would persuade us that its only province is the head,—that men are wise in many things, because they know something of a few,—and so leave the heart untouched, to mistake its way. Thus we conclude that the prohibition was founded in such good reasons as men may see the value of. The prohibition is as binding upon us as it was upon Adam; and a violation of the command will also be attended with fatal consequences. It is lawful to SEE the tree of knowledge—to comprehend what is wise. God planted it for this purpose; but to EAT of it was forbidden, because to do so would be to regard intellectual sustenance as the end of it, and so induce a state which would permit the heart to grow corrupt.

But the tree was eaten of, and this consequence resulted: still, as it has been said, it was not accomplished by the first sallies of the tempter. Men who have attained to any eminence in virtue do not fall into evil on the first excitement. They think upon the subject, revolve it in their minds, and for a period, they, to some extent, resist it: but by and by they incline towards, and afterwards look at it with desire, whereupon the suggestions of the higher sense are weakened. Then they experience a struggle between desire and duty, and give way only when the exciting object appears to the affection as the tree of knowledge did to the woman, namely, "as good for food, pleasant to the sight, and to be desired to make one wise." Men do not partake of that which is forbidden until they have been

* Luke xii. 47.

persuaded it is *good:* they do not plunge into transgression until the delights thereby proposed to be obtained appear somewhat *pleasant to the eye*—that is, agreeable to the illusion under which they labour; neither do they enter upon a career of guilt until they have begun to cherish it as a means to something *that is wise!*

These are the circumstances under which men in general pass into the perpetration of crime in these our days, and they serve forcibly to illustrate the narrative which describes the process of Adam's guilt. His fall was, in its general nature, somewhat similar to that of ours when we are tempted into transgression. The principal differences lie in the degrees of its enormity. He fell into evils with a larger amount of knowledge than it is our lot to possess: he began to decline with a purity of character which does not belong to us. He transgressed with more open eyes, and sunk into an abyss from a loftier summit than we have ever gained. Hence his posterity, in a few generations, perished in that terrible calamity described as a flood.

Having descended into evil by the process we have indicated, he must needs have begun to view all moral things under a perverted aspect: and, finally, he would have misgivings as to the existence of spiritual and heavenly things, because they could not be conceived of sensually and scientifically: the result of this incredulity was the inversion and overthrow of all his excellence. Evil was thought to be good, and falsehood truth; to describe which the forbidden fruit is, under the influence of the temptation, said to have appeared "as good for food, pleasant to the eye, and to be desired to make one wise."

The consideration of these facts will aid us in seeing the *rationale,* and tracing the process of Adam's fall. We at once see that it was not accomplished by a talking reptile that was out of man, but that it resulted from the fallacious reasonings of the sensual principle within him, the existence of which was proper and necessary to his being. These fallacious reasonings consisted in confirming appearances to be realities. They were small in their beginnings, but fatal in their growth and consequences. It was like a particle of dust falling upon the pupil of the eye, and preventing it from seeing the things of nature with certainty and clearness: self-guidance was preferred to a dependence on the Lord, concerning which the prophet says, "Woe unto them that call evil good, and good evil; that put darkness for light, and light for darkness; that put bitter for sweet, and sweet for bitter! Woe unto them that are wise in their own eyes, and prudent in their own sight!"*

Such was the state brought about by a series of perverse sensual reasonings. We do not consider it to have been the work of one man, or of the first generation, but as a result consummated by some of their posterity during the age of the Adamic Church.

But this state led to other consequences, the painful nature of which may also be illustrated by the common experience of mankind. All know that there was a period in their personal history when they had not fallen into the actual perpetration of those sins which now so easily beset them, and that the first effect of having done so was to awaken them to a sense of the danger they had incurred. The act which first succeeds a deed of guilt is timidly to look about to ascertain whether it has been watched by others. Conscience, also, by its pangs in after times, effectually proves to them that their innocence is gone. These experiences, like that of Adam, *open their eyes, and let them know that they are naked.* To open their eyes meant that they now saw their guilt; and to know that they were naked denoted a consciousness that their innocence was lost. It is well known that the Scriptures speak of "nakedness" in the sense of degradation.†

It was said of them before they fell, that "they were naked and not ashamed," to teach that they were innocent and felt no guilt: but after their transgression, they saw the disaster they had incurred, and became ashamed. Where there is no innocence, nakedness is a scandal and disgrace; but it is not so where innocence exists, as in the case of infants; here, therefore, nakedness is the symbol of innocence. But to know it with shame, as in the case of Adam, implies the presence of a sense of guilt; consequently, he was sent "forth from the garden of Eden, to till the ground from whence he was taken."

To be sent forth from Eden was not an arbitrary act of the Almighty: he does not deprive man of any felicity which he is

* Isa. v. 20, 21. † Rev. iii. 17.

qualified to enjoy; and, therefore, his expulsion from paradise was a natural consequence, arising from the unfavourable change which had now taken place in his character. His position in Eden, as shown in the preceding chapter, denoted the pleasure and delight which arose from an orderly love; but of these his transgression necessarily deprived him. It was his own act. By listening to the suggestions of his sensual nature, and misusing his freedom, he withdrew himself from the sacred influences of genuine goodness, just as the vicious are still known to keep aloof from virtuous society.

But although Eden is necessarily lost to every man who transgresses the rules and discipline of virtue, yet he is watched over with unabating diligence by the divine mercy of the Lord. "Though a good man fall," says the Psalmist, "he shall not be utterly cast down."* Adam was preserved in a condition to "till the ground from whence he was taken." Providence does not abandon the sinner; it is always benignant and merciful: it reminds him that all the virtues which he might have possessed were communicated graces, and that they were sown into his nature, specially created for their reception, by teaching and training. Man is lifted into spiritual eminence by cultivating the moral ground in which he may be placed. This was the ground whence Adam had risen into the distinction he attained: he fell, and so passed back to it again: but he was not then forgotten; he was taught a duty—he was "to till the ground from whence he was taken." In other words, he was to cultivate the ground from which he had risen, and to which he had descended, by the inseminating of truths into it; to watch over their growth with solicitude and care; to be attentive to the fruits they were intended to produce, and thus strive to regain the eminence he had lost. The capacity to do so was still preserved in him, and perpetuated to all his posterity.

* Psa. xxxvii. 23, 24.

CHAPTER XII.

THE CURSE UPON THE SERPENT—THE SORROWS OF THE WOMAN—AND THE CURSE UPON THE GROUND FOR MAN'S SAKE.

> "God made not death: neither hath he pleasure in the destruction of the living. For he created all things, that they might have their being: and the generations of the world were healthful; and there is no poison of destruction in them, nor the kingdom of death upon them: but ungodly men with their works and words called it to them."—Wisd. i. 13-16.

The circumstances of the fall of Adam and his expulsion from Eden were attended by other calamities, to which it is requisite to refer. A curse was pronounced upon the serpent; the sorrows of the woman, in conception and parturition, were to be multiplied, and the ground was cursed, that man might eat of it in toil and sorrow all the days of his life. These subjects are thus set forth in the sacred narrative:—

"And the Lord God said unto the serpent, Because thou hast done this, thou art cursed above all cattle, and above every beast of the field; upon thy belly shalt thou go, and dust shalt thou eat all the days of thy life: and I will put enmity between thee and the woman, and between thy seed and her seed: it shall bruise thy head, and thou shalt bruise his heel. Unto the woman he said, I will greatly multiply thy sorrow and thy conception; in sorrow shalt thou bring forth children; and thy desire shall be to thy husband, and he shall rule over thee. And unto Adam he said, Because thou hast hearkened unto the voice of thy wife, and hast eaten of the tree, of which I commanded thee, saying, Thou shalt not eat of it: cursed is the ground for thy sake; in sorrow shalt thou eat of it all the days of thy life. Thorns and thistles shall it bring forth to thee; and thou shalt eat the herb of the field. In the sweat of thy face shalt thou eat bread, till thou return unto the ground."*

* Gen. iii. 14-19.

The leading idea presented in this narrative is the curse. In what sense is this to be understood? That disastrous consequences followed the transgression cannot be doubted: but were they the natural results of disobedience, or the specific inflictions of the Almighty? The latter is the common idea, though the history does not say so. To the serpent, God said, "Thou art cursed above all cattle"; and to the man he said, "Cursed is the ground for thy sake": thus it simply represents God as declaring its existence, and not as producing it. He mercifully revealed the state, but did not inflict the misery. Calamity follows sin as death does poison; but as God does not originate the sin, or administer the poison, he cannot be chargeable with the calamity or the death. Although he is described as saying to the woman, "I will greatly multiply thy sorrows," under certain events; yet it was not the sorrow, considered in itself, but the *multiplication* of it, which was the evil announced. Sorrow, it would appear, attended these events under the best condition of humanity, yet it was to be increased; and God is represented as its author: but, under the circumstances, may not this have been a blessing? We can easily conceive a wise Providence placing difficulties in the way of attaining what a degenerate mind thinks to be desirable, in order to promote some genuine good. Pains and trials are no proofs of God's displeasure; we know that they tend to soften, humiliate, and bless; and, therefore, the multiplying of the woman's sorrows may come within the scope of mercy rather than malediction.

An idea that God became angry with the human race when the first man transgressed, very extensively prevails. The above passages are considered to declare it. But this cannot be correct. Anger is no attribute of God; it must be as foreign to the Divine Nature as sin itself; and, therefore, those passages of Scripture in which it is predicated of him are designed rather to express the aspect under which he appears to perverted minds, than to declare a genuine truth. To the jaundiced eye all things are yellow; but they are not really so; it is only an appearance arising from the action of physical disease. The moral disorders of men cause them to view the character and providences of God under an aspect contrary to their reality. We never read of God being angry, or declaring a curse, but in connection with something disobedient on the part of man. Under such circumstances, it is true that he appears angry, yet it cannot be true that he is so. If we desire sensible information concerning the felicities of heaven, the reasonable course is to consult those who have experienced some antepast of its happiness, through obedience to its laws. How unwise, then, is it to seek, in those passages of the Word which are addressed to the wicked only in accommodation to their perverted views, real truths concerning the Divine character! The fire by which Sodom was destroyed is said to have come down from heaven;* but heaven is not really the reservoir of that fire which punishes and destroys the wicked; nevertheless it is so said, because it so appeared to that abandoned people. In God there is no fury:† and the Psalmist says of him, "With the upright man thou wilt show thyself upright; with the pure thou wilt show thyself pure; and with the froward thou wilt show thyself froward."‡

If God were angry at any time, he would be imperfect, for anger is an infirmity in man. If he were once angry, he must be always angry, because he is unchangeable. If he be at all angry, he must be infinitely so, because all in him is infinite. How are the ideas that he is infinitely angry and infinitely loving to be reconciled? It cannot be done so long as both are considered to be realities.

To imagine that God can become angry, is to suppose him liable to disappointment, and, consequently, that man can do something which He had not foreseen. But how impossible is this! The whole Scripture is constructed on the principle that "God is love": this attribute is infinite in him, and so necessarily excludes every opposite sentiment. He has declared that he loveth man with an "everlasting love." § How, then, can he be angry, and curse both him and the circumstances in which he is placed? He has told us to "love our enemies, to bless them that curse us, and do good to them that hate us."|| Can we doubt that he will do to us that which he has commanded us to do to one another? If he loved only those who loved him, he would resemble "sinners, for they also love those that love them." ¶

---

* Gen. xix. 24. † Isa. xxvii. 4. ‡ Psa. xviii. 25, 26.
§ Jer. xxxi. 3. || Matt. v. 44. ¶ Luke vi. 32.

The excellence and beauty of the human character consist in its resemblance to the divine perfections. "Be ye perfect, as your Father in heaven is perfect";* "Be ye merciful, as your Father in heaven is merciful." † Still, man's highest attainments in these imperishable virtues are but faint shadows and images of the divine purity. In him every excellence is infinite: nor are their sweetness and placidity to be disturbed; their immutability is not to be changed by human disobedience. God "knoweth our frame, and remembereth that we are dust," ‡ and, with this knowledge and remembrance, "his mercy endureth for ever." The good man realizes the evidences of this fact in his own experience; the bad man does not, because of his perverted nature. All the displays of divine love are to induce men to become wise and happy. The wicked are made to feel the influence of this love, in the restraints which it mercifully imposes upon their vicious pursuits, and so the very goodness which God would promote is felt by them in those restraints, as if it were the unfoldings of anger.

An enlightened survey of nature presents no intimation of the anger of God: the reason is, because there is no such principle in his character.§ The universe furnishes no analogy suggestive of such thought. The sun is acknowledged to be a beautiful emblem of the Deity: hence God is called "a sun."‖ But there is nothing observable in that glorious luminary which can be said to answer to the notion of divine anger. Lowering and darkness are not in him: such phenomena are occasioned by the interposition of clouds, and the diurnal motion of the earth. The sun forever shines in brightness and in beauty. He never frowns, even upon the wicked: he shines upon the evil and the good. It is so with the divine character: anger is opposed to all that is divine, but it is predicated of God, because man, in an inverted state, sees him so. The wicked man thinks that God must be angry with the transgressors of his law, be-

---

* Matt. v. 48. † Luke vi. 36. ‡ Psa. ciii. 14.

§ It is sometimes said,—
  "A God all mercy is a God unjust;"
but this is an unreasonable and perverse assertion: the truth is, that if he were not all mercy, he would be unjust.

‖ Psa. lxxxiv. 11.

cause he believes that if he were in God's place he should be so; and as an evil being he certainly would: but this is not the character of God. In a perverted state, spiritual and holy things appear contrary to their reality, as the sun seems red and fiery when beheld through a murky atmosphere.

This is a principle which should not be overlooked in considering those passages of revelation in which God is spoken of as being angry, sending forth his wrath, and executing vengeance. God is the author of the laws of order: if a man transgresses them, disastrous consequences follow; but of these the man, and not God, is the author. The serpent was told that it was cursed because it had transgressed. The ground was pronounced to be cursed for man's sake, because the man, now fallen, may be presumed to have withheld from it those orderly labours which are necessary to maintain its fertility. The sorrows of the woman were, under certain circumstances, to be multiplied, because, by a withdrawing of the mind from the divine guidance, some natural law of the body might have been infringed. There is, then, no necessity for fixing the authorship of such calamities on God, in any other way than as an appearance, even if the statements of them were to be regarded in a literal sense: so far as they are evils, they are fairly and rationally chargeable on transgressors only. But let us examine some of the particulars in which these curses are said to have consisted.

Of the serpent it is written, "Upon thy belly shalt thou go, and dust shalt thou eat all the days of thy life: and I will put enmity between thee and the woman, and between thy seed and her seed." It is true that some serpents of natural history may be said to go upon their belly; also that all civilized society usually associate with the idea of them a sentiment of disgust. But it is not true that any eat dust all the days of their life; or, indeed, eat dust at all.* Nor is there any evidence to show that the form, habits, and instinct by which they are now distinguished are not those with which they were originally endowed.† No condition into which an animal is created really

---

* The food of serpents consists of young birds, mice, frogs, and fruit.

† Many things have been related to set forth the subtlety of the serpent (see Cruden, Art. Ser.), but some are mere puerilities, and others are evidently false; nor is there any fact established to show that they possess any

comes within the idea of an almighty curse. All are as happy as their organization will admit of, nor are any of them sensible of any deficiency arising from an inelegance of form or filthiness of habit. Serpents that crawl without legs have no sense of inferiority to the saurians which have them; and commentators are not agreed as to which kind it was that received the curse: nor can they ever be so: there are no data for determining the problem. The difficulty is considerably increased when it is asked why the serpent should have been cursed at all, when, as commonly supposed, it did not really effect the seduction, but the devil, who had either entered into it, or assumed its shape? The only way of avoiding the embarrassments which attend such considerations is at once to concede the allegorical signification of the narrative.

The circumstance of the Lord having spoken to the serpent most certainly shows such to be the case. Man cannot conceive the idea which the literal statement expresses. But taking the serpent to be a representation of the sensual principle of man, we can understand the fact intended to be revealed. Under such a view of it, we see that by the Lord speaking to the serpent was denoted divine teaching concerning the evil which the sensual principle had produced: and therefore the serpent is said to have been cursed above all beasts; thus that all the affections by which man had been happily distinguished, were now become partakers of a common corruption, but that the serpent was sunk into deeper degradation than the rest. It is now first described as going upon its belly, because it had now first ceased to look upwards to heavenly things; it no longer walked uprightly, but crawled close to worldly and terrestrial objects, when dust became its meat, because it now began to live on earthly and corporeal loves. The enmity between it* and the woman with her seed, denoted the separation then effected

---

remarkable sagacity. Their character for cunning and deceit has been derived from its description in the temptation, and not from natural history. It was *the* serpent that was subtle, not the whole species so denominated.

* Dr. A. Clarke says, "It is yet to be discovered that the serpentine race have any peculiar enmity against mankind, nor is there any proof that men hate serpents more than they do other noxious animals.—But we are not to look for merely literal meanings here."

between the sensual principle and the heavenly selfhood, represented by the woman and her seed. Every one knows that such a separation exists. The apostle referred to it when he said, "The flesh lusteth against the Spirit, and the Spirit against the flesh: and these are contrary one to the other":* and also in the declaration, "When I would do good, evil is present with me." † These are the common experiences of religious men, which practically show the enmity between the serpent and the woman with her seed.

But to the woman it was said, "I will greatly multiply thy conception; in sorrow shalt thou bring forth children; and thy desire shall be to thy husband, and he shall rule over thee." This, like the malediction on the serpent, can be satisfactorily understood only in a spiritual sense. Inquiry has resulted in showing that the former part of this announcement does not universally apply: and it would be somewhat difficult to prove how the latter part comes within the meaning of a curse. Although it may be admitted that the fall infringed certain laws, which so affected the female constitution as to increase the natural sufferings attending parturition, yet it is well known that they are very unequal in their severity, which they should not be on the supposition of their being a divine infliction, and if God be impartial in its distribution. Montaigne says, "This curse, as it is called, applies only to a certain species of females; whole nations of females being entirely free from it." ‡ Another writer observes, "Whatever may be the cause or causes, the fact seems to be, that women of colour have easier parturition in general than white Europeans." § Travellers assert that it is comparatively easy among the Indians, under the equator, and particularly in Tartary.‖ Goldsmith states, "The women of Africa always deliver themselves, and are well in a few hours after." ¶ Thus it is evident that climate and physical constitution have very much to do with this matter; and the discoveries

---

* Gal. v. 17. † Rom. vii. 21. ‡ Essays, i., c. 14.

§ White's "Regular Gradations in Man," p. 73.

‖ Terry's "Voyage to India," sect. xvii., p. 430 ; and Thevenot, part iii., ch. 24, p. 47.

¶ "History of the Earth," &c., vol. ii., p. 47.

of science* have made great progress towards affording entire relief under what is usually found to be so painful in the northern regions of the world. Supposing the application of such discoveries to become general, which is by no means unreasonable, since a great number of particular cases have already occurred, then what is to become of the idea that the sufferings were the result of execration? Must we believe that the curse was inflicted for a time only, and that God has at last mercifully enabled men to discover a physical means which, by putting a stop to its existence, enabled them to determine the period of its duration? This would hardly be satisfactory; nor, indeed, can any other view of the subject, except that which brings us back to the acknowledgment of its symbolical character.

The declaration that the woman's desire should be towards her husband† will hardly be construed by the chaste into a melancholy consequence. Such will consider a steady and undivided affection to be among their best enjoyments: and are there not multitudes of instances in which it would have been a solid blessing? If the circumstance of the woman's desire being towards her husband were a portion of a curse, then the existence of an opposite affection may be inferred to have been a blessing, and, in that case, how came the enactment, "Thou shalt not commit adultery"? To interpret it as a curse, takes reason far beyond its depth, and quite submerges it. But what is to be said of the assertion, "He shall rule over thee"? As Christianity is true, that statement, even supposing it to treat of the relative position of the sexes, cannot mean to declare the

---

* The use of chloroform is here referred to. When first introduced into the practice of the accoucheur, it was vehemently objected to on the part of some of the clergy of Scotland and others, on the ground that it was unlawful to prevent the due course of that which God had pronounced to be a curse. Many pamphlets were written in defence of this absurd opinion.

† This is sometimes construed to mean, "thy desires shall be thy husband's," a dative for a genitive case. But, admitting this, which nevertheless is not the true idea of the original, an affectionate wife would rarely consider her reception of the orderly desires of her husband any very deplorable circumstance. She would most likely regard it as a means of binding herself more closely to his love. Are not the thousands of instances existing, in which his desires are not so received, proofs that such is not the meaning of the sentence?

dominion of a master, but the guidance of a protector. Where, then, is the malediction? If these things were calamities to the woman, how were they to affect the man? He can hardly regard the information by which he learns the intense attachment of his wife, and the dignity of his own position in respect to her, as an indication of anathema. It never once occurs to him that woman's undivided love, or that the protection which he extends to her, is the result of an almighty curse! It cannot be so. It is plain that to view the history in such a light is to mistake its purpose; and even if this were less obvious than it is, intelligent piety would be compelled to acknowledge, that human degradation and its painful consequence were not of God, but from man, by his perversion of God's good things.

The narrative is intelligible and satisfactory only when viewed in a spiritual sense. The circumstances related in it represent those spiritual consequences which the fall induced upon the people of the Church of those most ancient times.

It has been shown that the woman, who was given to the man when it was discovered not to be good that he should be alone, was the symbol of that selfhood which the Lord mercifully granted, when discontent under the divine guidance began to appear.* This selfhood, like a pure and lovely woman, was then good and innocent, being vivified by the Lord. But it consented to the persuasion of the serpent, and consequently fell. Hereby that selfhood, which had primarily been directed to the Lord, and had been filled with the delight of heavenly things, was turned towards the world, and became enamoured of its pleasures. Its character was changed; and sensual influences were so brought to bear upon it as to endanger the ease and freedom with which spiritual things had previously been conceived in the mind, and brought forth in the conduct. Her sorrows were to be multiplied† in conception and bringing forth: the sorrows in conception‡ were the difficulties that were

---

* See page 113.

† It deserves to be remarked, that the sorrows were now to be multiplied; thus implying that they had, to some extent, previously existed. The reason is, because the fall was not a sudden but a gradual decline, and the severity of the consequences was now in the process of being increased.

‡ "Conception." The Septuagint version omits this clause altogether;

now to be experienced in the apprehending of interior truth; and the sorrows in bringing forth were the pains and temptations that were to be endured in introducing them to life. The Lord is said to be the author of them, because they become perceptible, through his pressing, as it were, to be received and loved. Every one knows these sorrows to exist, and that they are the peculiar inheritances of the fallen selfhood of humanity. In this sense the statements are of universal application, and experience furnishes the interpretation. The same is true of the assertion, "Thy desire shall be to thy husband, and he shall rule over thee."

Before the fall man had wisdom and intelligence, and these were denominated *man;* but by that event those blessings were corrupted, and reason, another principle, took their place. Hence it was called *husband*, and not man. The change of terms denotes an alteration in condition. Every expression in God's Word is peculiarly significant. That which had been man was now husband; that which had been wisdom now was reason. Hence, by the woman's desire being towards her husband is denoted the continual inclinations of the selfhood toward the reason with which it is conjoined; and by his having "rule over her" is signified the dominion which that reason ought to exercise.

In reference to the man it is said, "Cursed is the ground for thy sake; in sorrow shalt thou eat of it all the days of thy life. Thorns and thistles shall it bring forth; and thou shalt eat the herb of the field. In the sweat of thy face shalt thou eat bread." This is usually interpreted to mean that the fertility of the soil was impaired, so that henceforth man should not derive his natural subsistence from it without laborious cultivation: and, also, that during the raising of the crops he should be afflicted with anxieties, arising from the fear of mildew, insects, unfavourable seasons, and other causes by which their safety would be endangered. Now, it is true that such labour is required, and that such anxieties exist, yet we cannot conceive them to have sprung out of divine anathema! They are not universally

perhaps because the translators inaccurately supposed it was sufficiently comprehended in what follows. This, however, neither the original nor the spiritual sense allows.

felt. They pertain directly to that portion of mankind only whose employment is agriculture. There are whole classes of society entirely exempt from them. Moreover, the inflictions are very unequal on those by whom they are experienced; they are found to vary very much with latitude, locality, and other physical causes. With how little labour, and with what an absence of solicitude, is abundance of corn produced upon the banks of the Nile! That river does for Egypt much of that which manual labour is obliged to supply in other countries. It has always been celebrated for its fertility. "Joseph gathered corn as the sand of the sea, very much, until he left numbering; for it was without number."* Pocock informs us that it is sometimes necessary to temper the richness of the soil by bringing sand to it. Herodotus, speaking of Babylonia, says, "Of all the countries which have come within my observation, this is far the most fruitful in corn. The soil is so particularly well adapted for it, that it never produces less than two hundred fold; in seasons which are remarkably favourable, it will sometimes rise to three hundred."† Norway is the reverse of this fertility; its inhabitants, therefore, raise scarcely any grain or vegetables: they import most of what they use, and in seasons of scarcity are obliged to mix the ground bark of trees with their bread.‡ These facts show that the differing conditions of the land render manual labour, for the production of food, very unequal in its amount; which is difficult to understand if the universal ground were cursed, in order to exact a laborious toil from man to render it productive. Why should it not have been uniform in its action? There is no hint given that it was to be partial in its operation; which we think would have been the case if the literal sense had been intended for our faith. Moreover, these differences are traceable to natural causes,§ and the labour which an inferior soil requires may be considerably reduced by the appliances of art. ‖ But the ground was to bring forth "thorns and thistles;" and it does so. When was

---

* Gen. xli. 49. † Clio, cxciii. ‡ Goldsmith's Geography.

§ It may be said that God is the author of those natural causes: so far as this is the case, he operates in the way of general blessing, and never in the way of partial curse

‖ Consult Professor Johnson's work on Agricultural Chemistry; also Liebig.

it otherwise? It cannot mean that it was then for the first time to do so. The species are not named, but geology shows us the existence of some that must have flourished long anterior to the creation of man. We feel it difficult to reconcile these facts with the common notion of God having, six thousand years ago, pronounced a curse upon the ground for the punishment of his people. It is a shallow inference, and not a divine truth. The idea of God having, upon the one hand, taken from the ground that which had rendered it luxuriant in the production of human food; and, upon the other, to have imparted that which was to make it fertile in *whins* and *briars*, cannot be rationally sustained: nor is it requisite to uphold the character of God's justice, or to maintain the divine purpose of the narrative. It was written with an entirely different design,* which we shall endeavour briefly to explain.

By the ground is denoted that orderly external of man, by which he was distinguished when the development of his religious character became complete.† By the fall its excellence was necessarily impaired, and so it became less prolific in the good things of use. "To eat of it in sorrow," denotes to live from it unhappily: "to eat" is to appropriate, and so to live; and every one may see that to appropriate the false sentiments and evil affections, which had now taken hold of the external man, must needs have been attended with anxiety and sorrow. Experience shows that it is so, and satisfactorily explains the passage.

The ground was now to bring forth "thorns and thistles," to denote that the external man would now engender evil and false principles. Evils are the thorns, and false principles are the thistles. Hence the Lord, when treating of the distinction between the good and the evil, and the faithful and disbelievers, said, "Do men gather grapes of thorns, or figs of thistles?" ‡ To "eat the herb of the field," signified that he would live a worldly life; and "to eat bread in the sweat of the face," was to partake of heavenly things only through toil and exertion.

---

* St. Austin says, "No Christian will venture to affirm that these things are not to be taken in a figurative sense."—*Preface to his Twelve Books on the First Three Chapters of Genesis.*

† See page 58.   ‡ Matt. vii. 16.

These ideas could be easily proved by citations from the Word, but we cannot dwell on the detail. The reasonableness of these views, briefly as they are stated, will commend themselves to the thinker: those who will not think need not expect to know.

From what has now been stated it will be seen that by the condemnation of the serpent is denoted the evils which the sensual principle had brought upon itself; by the sentence upon the woman was signified the evils to which the voluntary selfhood had become attached; and by the anathema upon the man was represented the evils to which his intellectual part had consented. These respective evils were the curses; and, as man brought the evils, so he must have been the author of the maledictions, and of his sufferings therefrom.

CHAPTER XIII.

CAIN AND ABEL, WITH THEIR OCCUPATIONS.

> "It is consonant to the history of Moses to suppose that God wished him to give mystical representations of the more sublime subjects of theology; because that style of writing was suited to the hieroglyphical learning in which he had been instructed."—Dr. Spencer, *De Legibus Hebræorum.*

The history by which we are informed of the births of Cain and Abel, with their occupations, is exceedingly simple and compendious. "Adam knew Eve his wife; and she conceived, and bare Cain, and said, I have gotten a man from the Lord. And she again bare his brother Abel. And Abel was a keeper of sheep, but Cain was a tiller of the ground."* If we were to regard this as literal history, it would, nevertheless, be reasonable to think that, as a revelation, something more was designed by it than first meets the eye; and this it would be our duty to investigate and endeavour to learn. Although there might have been in early society such individuals as Cain and Abel, engaged in agricultural and pastoral pursuits, yet it is difficult to suppose they would be referred to in any other way than as affording ground for the construction of a symbolical history, relating to matters of a much more extensive and serious nature than the mere letter can possibly express. As the history which precedes that of Cain and Abel is only representative, we think that their history is of a similar character. The manner in which those histories are connected seems to us to establish this opinion. As Adam is a generic name, expressing the idea of a community, the names of Cain and Abel, who are described to have descended from them, must be similarly construed; for a community of persons cannot be said to give birth to individuals in their general capacity. The people of one generation originate the people who succeed them; but each individual springs from his own particular parents. It would be absurd to say that all

---
* Gen. iv. 1, 2.

the inhabitants of Rome were the father and mother of Julius Cæsar; and yet this is much like supposing the societies called Adam and Eve to have been the personal parents of Cain and Abel, considered as individuals. One generation, called Adam, gave birth to other generations, called Cain and Abel; but as the former was a collection of men, so were the latter: as the former constituted a church, which afterwards fell, so the latter constituted separate communities, which distinguished themselves by different religious sentiments and life.

It is no uncommon thing for a single name to be employed to express the idea of a whole people. It was customary among the ancients, it is found in the Scriptures, and occasionally it is had recourse to in modern times. Thus, in countries, whether monarchical or republican, the king or president is named to express the acts and opinions of a whole cabinet. France, England, and other countries are sometimes mentioned, not to signify their geographical existence, but to denote their living populations. In the Scriptures, Egypt, Judea, Philistia, Sidon, Jerusalem, and many other places are mentioned, not to indicate localities, but their inhabitants. Every one knows that the single names of Jacob, Esau, Joseph, Benjamin, and other descendants of Abraham, are frequently employed, not to express individuals, but a whole people, who were influenced and directed by certain views of a religious or economical character. The following instances will suffice to show this:—"I will visit Jacob according to his ways"; "Jacob shall rejoice, and Israel be glad"; "He leadeth Joseph like a flock." Multitudes of cases of this kind may be found in the Scriptures, and those of Cain and Abel are to be classed among them. They do not signify individuals, but communities, in whom were developed certain features of religious sentiment and feeling. They descended from the people called Adam, and the principles by which they were morally influenced were derived from the same source.

These statements will appear remarkable to all who have been accustomed to regard those names as significant of individuals only. Nevertheless, it is evident that at this time more than four persons were in existence. Indeed, it is usual to concede this fact by supposing that there might have been other descendants of Adam, whose births are not recorded. But, apart from this idea, society must have been considerable. Some reasons for this opinion have been already adduced; others may now be added. The occupations assigned to Cain and Abel, if understood in a literal sense, require the admission of this idea. Tilling the ground and keeping sheep were distinctive employments, that must have sprung out of the requirements of society. Although the cultivation of a little land might have been required for the maintenance of four individuals, yet it is difficult to see why the keeping of sheep should have been requisite for so limited a number. Such distinction of employments would scarcely have been recorded if there had not been society sufficiently extensive to require their uses. However, Cain's attention was not wholly directed to agriculture. We find that he had acquired some knowledge of the art of building; for he is afterwards described to have erected a city in the land of Nod: both this knowledge and the city must have been called into existence by the requirements of society. It must have been such society that provided him with his wife, for there is no account of her origination.

But for what purpose were the sheep to be kept? It does not appear that they were used as food. To suppose that they were kept for the sake of their wool, implies the existence of a much larger society than that with which the letter of the history makes us acquainted, and to which its uses, in the way of being converted into articles of clothing, must have been well known. If we conjecture that it was for sacrificial purposes only, this obviously implies the prevalence of a religious community for whose offerings they were preserved. The offering of Cain was of the *fruit of the ground.* What was this? was it brought in a natural or prepared state? The original word *minchah* is thought to be explained in Leviticus, and to mean an offering of *fine flour, with oil and frankincense.** If Cain's offering were really of this description, how can we reasonably account for the existence of those arts by which fine flour and oil were prepared, but on the supposition of society being more numerous than is usually thought of?

The very circumstance of offerings being spoken of, unaccom-

---

* Lev. ii. 1. See Dr. A. Clarke.

panied by any command enjoining them, is presumptive evidence that the idea of such a practice had been obtained by these brothers from a church or people previously extant. Sacrificial worship was not *commanded* by God, nor is it any spontaneous offspring of the human mind. It must have originated out of the perversion of some divine law or institution, for it is most unreasonable considered in itself;* and therefore, granting the offering of Abel to have been a natural sacrifice, that fact implies the perversion of some holier things that had been known to his predecessors.

Both Cain and Abel brought offerings unto the Lord; this indicates a publicity in their worship, which idea the notion of the presence only of the two parents and two sons is not sufficient to supply. "The Hebrew word rendered *brought* is never used with respect to domestic or private oblations, but always for public sacrifices."† The circumstance, then, of their having *brought* offerings obviously denotes the existence of society, and consequently that there were two classes of men, each of which was most attentive to its own views concerning them. But the unquestionable fact that Adam was a people, and not a single person, renders it unnecessary to dwell upon merely collateral circumstance to prove that it is the religious state of society, and not the worldly vocation of individuals, which is represented by the occupations of Cain and Abel.

The Adamic Church having fallen by the transgression of its members, different views of faith and duty would, in the process of time, obviously arise among them. Having eaten of the tree of knowledge, they would begin to think and act from self. Self is not a uniting, but a dividing, principle. Under such circumstances, sectarianism would break out among them; and the sects, with their different branches, would for a considerable period be capable of being traced to the original stock. The fallen Adamic Church was the parent whence they all descended. It was customary in ancient times to speak of one

---

* See Dr. Magee on the Atonement. Bishop Patrick says, "It is not probable that Adam would have presumed to invent a way of worship by killing beasts and burning their fat; especially as we cannot perceive any inclination to it in nature."

† Bishop Patrick.

condition of the Church as being conceived and born of another, and so to form a sort of genealogy concerning its successive states, and to give them names accordingly. This is the principle involved in the description of Adam's descendants. There are a conception and birth of religious opinion as well as of persons. Every one who is at all acquainted with the history of the Christian Church knows when the principles of Protestantism were born, and who were their parents; for we have only to look abroad upon society, and we shall behold their progeny in a hundred sects. In the Church, one thing is, as it were, conceived and born of another in the way of spiritual generation. The apostle says, "Now abideth faith, hope, and charity; but the greatest of these is charity." * Charity, then, according to this authority, is the firstborn principle of the Christian life, faith is next, and hope succeeds. If charity became extinct among a people, the light of faith is necessarily endangered; and then how feeble and precarious must be their hopes! It is easy to see how one imperfect state of the Church may, as a parent, beget another: the idea is distinctly expressed in the Revelation, which describes a woman as the mother of harlots: † it plainly means a false religion originating abandoned principles.

Now if the narrative of Cain and Abel be viewed under this aspect, we shall perceive that they are names expressive of two different classes of religious principles, which descended from the Adamic people, after they had partaken of the forbidden tree. The same view is to be taken of their other descendants. ‡ This is somewhat evident from what is stated of the age of Adam. He is said to have lived eight hundred years after he begat Seth; a circumstance that may be fairly doubted when interpreted of an individual man, but which is very rational when it is supposed to treat of the continuance of a religious dispensation. Considered in this light, parallel cases can be adduced from religious history. The Jewish economy has lasted for nearly three thousand years; and Abraham may, in a certain sense, be said to have lived all this time, in the religious principles and

---

* 1 Cor. xiii. 13.   † Rev. xvii. 5.

‡ "All the personages whose histories are so earnestly related in Eastern countries never existed, and are nothing more than the ancient symbols personified."—ABBE PLUCHE's *History of the Heavens*, vol. i., p. 142.

physiognomy which have been perpetuated to his descendants. But we must not here anticipate what we have to say on the longevity of the antediluvian patriarchs. It is sufficient now to observe that the nine hundred and thirty years recorded as the duration of Adam's life were significant of the states and periods of the dispensation so denominated; but that it, like the Protestant religion during the three hundred years of its existence,* was broken into a variety of sects, among whom Cain and Abel were the first and most distinguished.

So long as the Adamic dispensation continued in its integrity, all the faculties of its people acted as one. The will loved what the understanding perceived to be true, and they worked harmoniously in promoting the virtues of a holy life. But when the people fell, those two faculties ceased to be united. This condition of them is one of the legacies which that event has bequeathed to posterity; and experience proves it to have been faithfully transmitted. We have a distinct consciousness that the will and the understanding act separately from each other. We think one thing, which may be true;—that is of the understanding: we love another, which may be opposite thereto;—that is of the will. These two faculties, in our unregenerated state, do not act in unison: they, so to speak, turn their backs upon each other, and look in opposite directions. This fact is a proof that man has broken in upon the harmony of his moral creation, and destroyed the unanimity which it originally possessed. Every one is aware that in religious things there are some persons who know truth much better than they do it; and, also, that there are others who feel truth much more correctly than they know it. The understandings of the former are always on the alert to seize on any information which is likely to increase their power: the will of the latter will be found docile, and responsive to certain qualities of good. These distinctive classes are among the results of that separation which has taken place in these two faculties of humanity, and were first displayed

---

* Protestantism is referred to for illustration, because the facts concerning it are better known in this country. History shows the Roman Catholic religion not to have been exempt from similar divisions. What is called the Eastern Church is separated into three great parts, the Greek, the Roman, and those who differ from both.—MOSHEIM, Cent. xvi., chap. 11.

under the representative characters of Cain and Abel. By Cain were represented those who intellectually knew their Master's will but did it not: by Abel were denoted those who felt goodness to be superior to knowledge, and so cultivated it with the greatest ardour. Such classes have always prevailed within the pale of a declining church. The Lord informed us of their existence among the Jews, by the cases of the Pharisee and the Publican.* They both went up to pray, but the Pharisee, in the pride of his intellect, thanked God that he was not as other men are; while the Publican, in the humility of his heart, said, "Lord be merciful to me a sinner"; and this man was justified rather than the other.

Traces of similar characters are to be found in Christendom. It is well known to observers that there are those who are self-satisfied with their intellectual possessions; who can converse with fluency about the things of religion; who can argue its positions with acuteness, and defend them with sagacity and power; but who, nevertheless, show, by their conduct and behaviour, that they have hard hearts and questionable morals.

Who is not aware that there are others, but slightly acquainted with the doctrinal sentiments of religion, that can only converse imperfectly about the spiritual truth of revelation, but who, notwithstanding, have about them that simplicity of character which assures the observer that they love and cherish what is good? The former strive to conceal the deformity of their character by the brilliancy of their intellect; the latter, possessing no such talents, at once let you behold their hearts, and you see that they have respect for order and for virtue.

Now, it was two classes of sentiments of this description, and, consequently, of persons by whom they were respectively held, that came into existence in the Adamic Church under the two names of Cain and Abel. They both professed to serve the Lord, but each from a different principle, and therefore, with different results.

But we will endeavour to investigate the character of each, under the light of true Christian teaching. First of Cain.

As the Adamic people, by eating of the forbidden tree, chose knowledge in preference to obedience, and so placed the cultiva-

* Luke xviii. 10-14.

tion of intellect above the purification of the heart, it is easy to see that the first results of such a course must have been the conception and birth of faith,—yea, faith only, as a means of acceptance with God. Cain was the representative of this principle; and, consequently, of all those persons who acquired and possessed it. The name, as a Hebrew word, denotes acquisition or possession. They believed that the possession of religious knowledge was more necessary to secure the divine favour than the excellency of a virtuous life. They knew much, for they were tillers of the ground,—the planters of knowledge in the intellect; but they went to the Lord with their understanding chiefly, and so attempted to serve him with only one half of their minds. They neglected the duty required by the invitation, "My son, give me thy heart."* They overlooked the important circumstance that knowledge is only a means to virtue as an end, and thus they rested their salvation upon the faith of thought, rather than upon the purity of life. They did not sufficiently attend to the fact, that, as light without heat produces no fruit, so faith without charity can secure no acceptance.

A doctrine somewhat of this character, was propounded in the Christian Church at the time of what has been called the Reformation. It is thus expressed : "We are accounted righteous before God, only for the merits of our Saviour Jesus Christ, by faith, and not by works and deservings ; wherefore, that we are justified by *faith only*, is a most wholesome doctrine, and very full of comfort": † but there is no such doctrine as this taught in the Sacred Scriptures. They, indeed, inculcate the necessity of faith, as one of the ingredients of the Christian character; but they never, like the above Article, represent it as the exclusive virtue: and herein lies the error; which the

* Prov. xxiii. 26.

† Book of Common Prayer, Eleventh "Article of Religion." The plain meaning of this article is felt by the learned to be opposed to the plain teachings of the Scriptures ; and therefore Dr. Burnet says of it, " By *faith only* is not to be meant faith as separated from the other evangelical virtues ; but faith as opposite to the rites of the Mosaical law."—*Exposition of the XXXIX Articles.* This, though not very clear as an explanation of the article, is satisfactory as a renunciation of the false doctrine which it expresses.

apostle sufficiently exposes, when he says, "What doth it profit, my brethren, though a man say he hath faith, and have not works? can faith save him? Faith, if it hath not works, is dead, *being alone.* Ye see how that by works a man is justified, and *not by faith only.** The doctrine of *faith only* has been very disastrous to the Church, and contributed very extensively to the dangers by which she has been assailed. Although it is now, happily, becoming a mere theory, which most sensible persons are abandoning, yet it was not always so. Luther said, "The ten commandments do not belong to us Christians, but only to the Jews: we will not admit that any the least precept of Moses be imposed on us. Therefore, look that Moses, with all his law, be sent a packing *in malem rem*—with a mischief":† and the Church sometimes acts as though it still believed this abomination. This is conspicuous in the case of great criminals, who, having forfeited their lives by a transgression of God's commandments, are told to have faith, and expect salvation.

A regard to faith, as the chief thing of the Church, was the first heresy of the Adamic people. It was conceived when the woman ate of the tree of knowledge, and born when Eve said, "I have gotten a man, Jehovah."

There are two things which belong to a church, its wisdom and its love. With the good, wisdom is as a husband, and love as a wife. The Church, at the time here treated of, was, as to its wisdom, represented by Adam, and as to its love, by his wife. But we are informed that "Adam called his wife's name Eve," ‡ that is, "life." The word Eve is a contraction of the Hebrew *charah*,§ and answers very closely to the word *Zoe*, by which it is rendered in the Septuagint, both of which signify "life." Now, why was she so called? It will be replied, "Because she was the mother of all living": but surely something more is meant by this than what is so expressed. There

---

* Jas. ii. 14-24.

† Luther's Works, vol. 1, published at Würtemburg, p. 147, cited in the "Intellectual Repository" of 1828, p. 80. And in continuing the paragraph, he says that Moses "should be held suspected for a heretic, cursed and damned, and worse than the Pope or the devil."

‡ Gen. iii. 20. § See Marginal Reading.

is only one fountain of life, that is, the Lord: it is because He lives that we live: * it is in Him we live, and move, and have our being.† In a merely literal sense, there is no more reason why she should be called *life*, from the circumstance of being the first mother, than that Adam should have been so called, on the ground of his having been the first father; and for other reasons, if the literal sense had been meant, it might have been equally appropriate.‡ The fact of this name having been given to her, shows that something more recondite is intended. Adam called his wife's name *life*, because the Church, as to wisdom, knows that the Church, as to love or affection, is *life;* it is a living thing with men, and so the spiritual mother of all its living excellence. It is well known that the Scriptures speak of the Church as a mother: the apostle distinctly asserts, that it is "the mother of us all":§ so that the idea which Moses, in respect to Eve, has symbolically indicated, the apostle has literally expressed.

Now, a church can give birth to nothing but such things as pertain to faith and charity; but the quality of those descendants will depend upon the character of the parent. A corrupted fountain must send forth a turbid stream. Grapes do not grow on thorns, nor figs on thistles. Eve had fallen, and her first offspring was Cain, or faith, concerning which she said, "I have gotten a man, Jehovah," to express the idea that faith, without charity, was now considered to be sufficient for the purposes of the Church. Before this time, faith had not become a separate object of thought; it was united with love, and formed one with it. But now it began to exist as a distinct principle in the mind, and also to be espoused by a people as the essential thing for their salvation. The Church, having acquired the doctrine of faith, is described as "getting a man."

---

* John xiv. 19. † Acts xvii. 28.

‡ Swedenborg states "that the soul is from the father, and the body from the mother; for the soul is in the seed of the father, and is clothed with a body in the womb of the mother; or what amounts to the same, all the spiritual part of a man is from the father, and all the material part from the mother."—*True Christian Religion*, No. 92.

§ Gal. iv. 26.

and to indicate its relation to the Lord, the term "Jehovah" is appended thereto.*

By Cain, then, is to be understood, the doctrine of salvation by faith separate from charity, and, consequently, a people by whom this tenet was held. In this we discover what was the first heresy, and who were the first heretics. This doctrine was an enormity, and, therefore, God is recorded to have had no respect to its offerings. That which constituted their faith was actual knowledge. They saw the objects in which it was necessary to believe, with certainty and clearness, but they rested in their knowledge as an intellectual possession, considering it the all of religion, and so allowed the affections to go astray and to revel in their lusts.

But the doctrine of *faith only*, which has sprung up in the Christian Church, is not precisely of this character. Its members do not see that the objects in which they are taught to believe are really true. Indeed it is openly stated, that they are mysteries for faith, and not matters for comprehension: thus it is the dictate of authority, and not the result of knowledge. If a thing be not understood, how is it known to be true? What assurance is there that it is not false? To say that God has said so, and that, therefore, it is to be believed, is assuming

---

* The Authorized Version represents Eve as saying, upon the birth of Cain, "I have gotten a man *from the* Lord." The original does not express the idea "from the Lord": there is nothing answering to the word *from*. It is *eth Jehovah, i. e.*, the Jehovah; and not *meeth Jehovah, i. e.*, from the Jehovah. The passage is considered to be one of great difficulty. The former sentence is thought to have been an elliptical mode of expressing the latter idea, so that the whole is interpreted to mean, that Eve had gotten a man *through* the blessing of the Lord. The Septuagint and Vulgate so render the original. This construction might be satisfactory, if the premises on which it rested were not suppositions; but that being the case, we are at liberty to doubt. Besides this conjecture, it has been said, because the name Jehovah is sometimes applied to places (see Gen. xxii. 14; Exod. xvii. 15; Judg. vi. 24. &c.), and is also admissive of being represented by the term Lord, which is frequently applied to men, that Eve's statement, "I have gotten a man from the Lord," is a mere acknowledgment to her husband of Cain's paternity: but this notion has no foundation in true criticism. The correct translation is, "I have gotten a man, Jehovah"; in this sense it might indicate an acknowledgment in the form of "Jehovah, I have gotten a man." Under this view it agrees with the spiritual sense given above.

the very point in question. Has God really said what is generally, required to be believed? Has He declared unintelligibilities for the faith of man? That which is not rationally seen to be true does not contribute anything to the development of affection or to the enlargement of thought: and hence we find religious society at a standstill in every situation where it has been touched with the paralyzing wand of *faith only*. But though this doctrine in the Christian Church (because arising from an obscurity under which the things of faith are contemplated) is less malignant in its nature than that which was represented by Cain, still it is the same in kind, and must be fatal in its results.

Much ingenuity has been exercised in the defence of this extraordinary tenet. But the inventions of talent cannot successfully maintain what is essentially false. It is possible, by avoiding some main point of an inquiry, to make a show of argument in favour of any falsehood, and so, for the moment, to embarrass even truth itself. Men who are disposed to believe the worse to be the better cause, will find assertions to defend their notions. It is possible to make black appear white, by looking at the feathers of a raven in a certain angle with the sun. But all such courses are delusive, and they will terminate, like the offering of faith alone, in disappointment and rejection. That doctrine is similar to the light of the sun without its heat; like summer without its fruits; like winter, cold, fierce, and chilling.

Here, however, by faith alone we do not merely mean the tenet as it is propounded by certain branches of the professing Christian world; because we can see that it may practically exist within the pale of a genuine church. Persons may join her community and learn her truths so as to know them with a rational persuasion, and yet they may not love them so as to realize the virtues to which they point. It is this practical view of the case, rather than the mental persuasion, which is the real antitype of Cain.

Faith cannot bring an acceptable offering to God, unless it be conjoined with charity; and charity is not a theory, but an act. Faith is the knowledge and consciousness that certain things of religion are true; for if they be not true, they are not worth believing. If men believe without a persuasion from such sources, their faith is blind: and if, in such a state, they should rely upon something that is false, it must necessarily exercise an injurious influence upon their intellectual life. Faith then, considered in its solitary character, is the mere knowledge of truth; and this faith is more or less expansive and enlightened, as the truths which form it are more and more abundantly increased.

Here it may be inquired, If the knowledge of truth be one of the constituents of faith, why are its offerings not acceptable to God, seeing that, as truth, it must have originated in Him?

The answer is, that although truth does originate in God, yet it does not descend from him as a solitary principle. In him it is eternally associated with good, and with this it comes from Him to man: man has separated them. He has put asunder what God has joined together, and, in rejecting the principle of good, on which the quality of truth depended for its excellence, there can be only a dead, and not a living faith. Moreover, the truth which is necessary to the formation of faith is only a means to an end, and the end cannot be secured by a mere belief in the means. All believe that a good day's work may be done by industry and diligence: this is believed because experience has proved it true; yet it is certain that mere belief will not do the work. The case is similar in religious things. We must employ the truths we know to obtain the goods they teach, before they can become an acceptable offering to God. A further reason why mere faith cannot present an acceptable offering to Him is, because it is not morally beneficial to us. Nevertheless, faith is the first principle to which the Church gives birth—like Cain, it is first-born;—a man must first learn to speak and think, then to investigate and know the things of religion; but to stop at this point is to consider that religious principles are formed, when, in fact, they are only known; and this is to resuscitate the character of Cain. Faith, without charity, is nothing: for the apostle has most eloquently said, "Though I have the gift of prophecy, and understand all mysteries, and all knowledge; and though I have all faith, so that I could remove mountains, and have not charity, I am nothing."*

Much difficulty has been experienced by the Church in deter-

---

* 1 Cor. xiii. 2.

mining whether faith or charity was the primary principle. This is a consequence of not distinguishing between faith as being the first in respect to time, and charity as being chief in respect to end. It may now be easily removed, and the facts familiarly illustrated. For example: in building a temple, the first thing, in respect to time, is to lay the foundation, erect the walls, cover them with a roof, and afterwards provide the altar and raise the pulpit; but the chief thing in respect to end is, that God may be worshipped therein. So, again, with regard to the building of a house: the first thing in regard to time is to build the external parts of it, and then to provide the requisite conveniences within; but the first thing in regard to end, is a commodious dwelling for the master and his family. Illustrations of this kind are abundant. They show, most conclusively, that faith is first with respect to time, because it is a means to charity as an end: and hence Cain, by whom this faith is represented, is described to have been first born.

This representation of Cain is farther sustained by the occupation in which he is said to have been engaged. He was a tiller of the ground; and by this is spiritually signified a planter of knowledges in the understanding merely. That this was the character of Cain—that is, of all those people of that most ancient time who adopted the heresy of faith separate from charity—appears from all the circumstances which are related of him, and especially from these, that his offering was rejected, and that he slew his brother.

This brings us to inquire concerning Abel. Ancient writers abound in observations on his mystical character,* and he has very commonly been regarded as the representative of the pastoral tribes, in like manner as Cain has been considered the author of the nomadic life. Thus, his representative character seems to be admitted, though some obscurity may be felt as to what he

---

* Chrysostom, *Hom. in Gen.* xviii. 5; Augustin, *De Civitate Dei*, xv. 1; Irenæus, *Contra Hæres.*, iii. 23, so speak of him. Dr. Darwin, in his *Botanical Garden*, Art. *Portland Vase*, speaking of the opinions which have been held concerning the early personages of the Bible, says, "Abel was the name of an hieroglyphical figure representing the age of Pasturage, and Cain the name of another hieroglyphical symbol representing the age of Agriculture."

signified. From what is written concerning him in the Word, we think it is evident that he was the representative of charity. Abel, as a Hebrew term, denotes humility, also weakness: *humility*, to denote a characteristic of charity, and *weakness*, to express its modesty and sweetness; as well, perhaps, as to indicate the limited number of society by whom it was loved and practised. Abel is said to have been the brother of Cain, to inform us that charity is a near relative to faith. The Scriptures continually speak of the intimate connection between these two principles of the Church, and man has been mercifully gifted with two faculties for their reception: the will for charity, the understanding for faith. But although there is a spiritual brotherhood subsisting between these two principles, the universal experience of mankind is, that the things of faith are more forward and urgent than the affections of charity. Charity, though the sweeter and more gentle excellence of the Church, is too frequently lorded over by the more daring and presumptuous influence of faith. The affections of good are well known to be more feeble than the perceptions of truth. Abel is modest and retiring, Cain is bold and confident. Faith struggles for command and mastery, and it is too frequently inattentive to the weaker but inner sensations of charity. Most persons have felt a desire to do good when a suitable opportunity has been presented, but how many have had it set aside by the influence of some selfish persuasion! How frequently does talent endeavour to place itself as a substitute for virtue! Cleverness has sometimes been mistaken for goodness. These facts are too common to have escaped the attention of those who observe what is taking place around them. But it may have occurred to them that, in these phenomena, they were beholding the struggles of two spiritual brothers: the efforts of faith to secure an ascendancy over charity: the sternness of Cain displaying its prowess to subdue the modesty of Abel; and which circumstance, in after times, was also represented by Jacob taking away the birthright and blessing of his brother Esau,* by Pharez gaining the primogeniture from his brother Zarah,† and by Ephraim obtaining the position which belonged to his brother Manasseh.‡

* Gen. xxvii. 36.   † Gen. xxxviii. 27 to the end.   ‡ Gen. xlviii. 18 to the end.

It is because Abel represented charity, and, consequently, those who were principled in it, that the Lord called him "the righteous Abel,"* and that the apostle spoke of his offering as being the "more excellent sacrifice."† His occupation, as a "keeper of sheep," will farther exemplify this fact.

The Scriptures very frequently employ the idea of a shepherd, as well as the expression, to denote one who exercises the good of charity. It is on this account that the Psalmist said, "The Lord is my shepherd; I shall not want." ‡ He is essential charity; and from this principle he is perpetually engaged in watching over the welfare and providing for the wants of mankind: hence, also, it is written of Him, "He shall feed his flock like a shepherd: he shall gather the lambs into his arms, and carry them in his bosom, and gently lead them that are with young"; § a passage beautifully expressive of the Lord's affectionate tenderness for the people of his pasture, and his charitable solicitude for the sheep of his hands. Peter was contemplated as a shepherd, when the Lord directed him to feed his sheep: || he was expected to exercise an enlightened charity in the apostolic office to which he was appointed. Ministers of the Gospel are sometimes called pastors, that is, shepherds, for the same reason. He who leads and teaches what is good is called a shepherd, and those who are led and taught, are called the flock. The Scriptures represent the good shepherd to love his sheep, and to care for the safety and unity of the flock; but the hireling shepherd is described as one who leaveth them, and in times of danger fleeth, so as to allow them to be scattered. The Lord Jesus Christ said, "I am the good shepherd, and know my sheep, and am known of mine": ¶ and the Church he called a sheepfold.** The reason for these descriptions is that a shepherd is the emblem of that charity which carefully watches over the things of innocence, gentleness, and purity, in the human mind: and this is said to have been the occupation of Abel, because he was a representative of this excellence.

Thus we learn that by Cain, as a tiller of the ground, was

---

* Matt. xxiii. 35.   † Heb. xi. 4.   ‡ Psa. xxiii. 1.
§ Isa. xl. 11. || John xxi. 16.   ¶ John x. 14.
** John x. 1.

denoted faith, engaged in planting knowledge in the intellect merely; and that by Abel, as a keeper of sheep, was signified charity, chiefly employed in promoting the good things of use: consequently, that they represented two classes of persons in the most ancient Church, to whom those principles respectively belonged. These conclusions will be corroborated by other evidences to be adduced in the succeeding chapter.

CHAPTER XIV.

THE OFFERINGS OF CAIN AND ABEL: WHY THE OFFERING OF ABEL WAS RESPECTED, AND THAT OF CAIN REJECTED.

"Truth is like the dew of heaven; in order to preserve it pure, it must be collected in a pure vessel."—St. Pierre.

The offerings of Cain and Abel are the first intimations of divine worship that are recorded. The subject is thus related: "In process of time it came to pass, that Cain brought of the fruit of the ground an offering unto the Lord. And Abel, he also brought of the firstlings of his flock and of the fat thereof. And the Lord had respect unto Abel and his offering: but unto Cain and to his offering he had not respect."* Now whence could the idea of divine worship have originated? It can be satisfactorily accounted for only by admitting that a Church existed, to which a knowledge of that duty had been communicated. It is true, we do not read of any command having been given upon this subject; this was not requisite, because we think it was implied in the offering, and necessarily included in the process by which the Church was developed; of which we have previously treated. The worship of the Lord must have been one of its conspicuous features; it naturally belonged to the Paradisiacal state of the Adamic people. Their fall would induce a neglect of the essential things of this duty, but not a complete forgetfulness of it: that calamity would also lead to a difference in the quality of the worship, but not to its entire abandonment. Cain and Abel, therefore, must have learnt the duty of divine worship from the Church that was extant, and the difference in their offerings must have originated in the different perceptions of that duty, then in the process of being manifested.

But how are we to understand their offerings? Are they to be interpreted as meaning the physical things described, as was

* Gen iv. 3–5.

afterwards the case in the Jewish Church, or are they mentioned only because they are the symbols of certain things of the mind, by which all worship must be performed? We think the latter, and not the former, is the view which ought to be taken of the case. Although men had fallen, they had not forgotten that natural things were the emblems of spiritual sentiments and love, nor had they yet ceased to speak of them as such; these were subsequent occurrences. A really ceremonious worship did not come into existence until men had lost all spiritual ideas of worship: when this took place, they began to worship the Lord with those objects which their ancestors had only spoken of as the symbols of those mental affections and thoughts with which they had worshipped. Having lost sight of the spiritual reality, they began to worship with the natural representation; and this was the origin of that ceremonial worship subsequently arranged among the descendants of Abram. It was then instituted, not only as the shadow of better things to come, but, also, as the types of those precious things which had perished.

At the time of Cain and Abel, the people had not sunk into so low a condition as that which afterwards required the establishment of a ceremonial religion: worship of the Lord from some interior principle still prevailed among them; and as all such principles were known to them to have their correspondence in natural objects, such objects would be mentioned in connection with their worship, to signify spiritual things only. If they spoke of the firstfruits, or of a lamb, as offerings to the Lord, it would not be to indicate those natural things, but symbolically to express some internal sentiment of truth and love: this we conceive must have been the case with the offerings of Cain and Abel.

It is well known that offerings, under the ceremonial law, were acts of worship; that is, not worship in themselves, but types of those spiritual and heavenly principles from which it must arise. This must be obvious to every one who will reflect. The offering, apart from the sentiment which it represented, could be of no religious value. In such a case it would be an external without a corresponding internal, like a body without a soul, or a dumb idol. External acts of worship are mere ceremonies, unless they are sanctified by the adoration of the heart. What are the prayers of the lips but mere babbling, unless the affection of the mind be in them? All such acts are valuable only so far as there is a corresponding intention in them: they must be attended with an internal love to give them sanctity, and render them acceptable. The offerings, then, as forms of worship, were significant of mental and spiritual affections, in which the real virtue and efficacy of the worship consist.

Offerings are presents: this is the idea which the word literally expresses; and the original may with propriety be so translated. But presents in general are intended to testify the esteem which we entertain for those to whom we give them; and the will or intention is regarded by him who receives them as of greater value than the thing presented. If this be true, then the things which are presented to God must be tokens expressive of such sentiments of gratitude and love as are cherished by the offerer; and God must be considered to receive them, not for the value of the things themselves, "for the world is his, and the fulness thereof,"* but wholly for the sake of the affections by which they are accompanied. It is upon this principle that the Lord said, "If thou bring thy gift to the altar, and there rememberest that thy brother hath aught against thee; leave there thy gift before the altar, and go thy way; first be reconciled to thy brother, and then come and offer thy gift."† Here it is plain that the offering was considered as the symbol of an inward sentiment of love and charity, because reconciliation with a brother was necessary to render it acceptable.

Seeing, then, what an offering to the Lord involves, we may readily perceive that the things which were arranged for this purpose under the representative law were intended to signify particular states of the affection and thought of those who worshipped. We find that lambs and rams, sheep and oxen, goats and calves, doves and pigeons, and flour and oil, were directed to be presented to the Lord. Moreover, some of them were to be offered under special circumstances. There were sin-offerings, meat-offerings, drink-offerings, heave-offerings, wave-

* Psa. l. 12.   † Matt. v. 23, 24.

offerings, peace-offerings, and trespass-offerings, to each of which specific ceremonies were attached. These various offerings were evidently intended (or why else were they so many, and one thing selected for their celebration in preference to another?) to show forth, in a representative manner, the several states of affection and thought which, under various circumstances, become characteristics of the worshipper.

The offerings under the Levitical law seem generally to include the ideas of death and consumption by fire. These, however, were the results which attended the introduction of sacrificial worship, rather than the natural concomitants of the primitive offerings; *they* did not involve those circumstances, and therefore they are not mentioned in connection with those of Cain and Abel; this may be taken as evidence that they are stated only for the sake of the symbols which they afforded. We are merely informed of what they consisted, but not of the manner in which they were presented: it is then simply the meaning of those offerings into which we have to inquire. First of Cain's:—

Cain, or the religion of faith without charity, has its offerings, that is to say, its modes and principles of worship. It was in the process of time " that Cain brought of the fruit of the ground an offering unto the Lord." From this it would appear, that the characteristics of the worship which now distinguished Cain were not developed all at once: they were results brought about *in the process of time*. Thus it was not so far separated from charity in the beginning as it afterwards became. The last state was worse than the first: it was about this period when "Cain brought of the fruit of the ground an offering unto the Lord." What, then, is meant by the fruit of the ground? It will be remembered that Adam, when sent forth from the garden of Eden, was to till the ground whence he was taken; and, in treating of that circumstance in a preceding chapter, it was shown that the ground was significant of the external man. *That* is the ground on which the spiritual and celestial things of the internal man rest, as a house upon its foundation. It is compared to the ground, because it is to the things of the mind what the earth is to the body. The apostle says, "That which is first is not spiritual, but natural;" and then of this first he says, it is "of the earth, earthy."* The Lord said, "The kingdom of God is as if a man should cast seed into the *ground;*† and also, in explanation of the parable of the sower, he said, "He that received seed into good ground is he that heareth the word, and understandeth it; which also beareth fruit, and bringeth forth, some an hundredfold."‡ In these instances it is plain that by the ground is meant the external man, and to sow seed therein denotes to implant truths, that they may grow up and produce the leaves of faith and the fruits of love.

Now it is to be remarked that Cain did not bring for an offering the *fruit of those seeds.* Although he was a tiller of the ground, yet he only brought of the *fruit of the ground,* and not of the fruit of the seeds, which, as a tiller of it, he had sown therein. This is a distinction of the highest consequence, to be carefully observed, in order rightly to understand the subject. The sentiments of revelation are couched in choice expressions; and the fruit of the ground is spoken of as the offering of Cain, because it denoted the works of the merely external man.

What is the external man? It is not the physical structure, but all those knowledges and affections which are gathered thereby from the outer world, and which then form, as it were, the external of his spirit. The natural body is only the outermost covering, within which, the external of which we are speaking, and the spiritual man, reside during its location in this world.

The internal man is so constituted that it can perceive and love the things of heaven, and the external is such that it can learn and delight in the things of the world. With the good these two act as one, the internal illuminating and guiding the external, as the efficient cause of all its works of use and order. With those who are not good it is not so. In that case, the internal is more or less closed, according to the quality and extent of the evil that is loved, and the *external* man only remains in activity; this it derives from the love of self and the love of the world. A man in such a state is not necessarily deprived of religious information: he may store his memory with its doctrines, become acquainted with its duties, and acquire the ability of speaking of them with fluency and force, but his motives in doing these

* 1 Cor. xv. 46-49. † Mark iv. 26. ‡ Matt. xiii. 23.

things will wholly arise from the loves of self and of the world. The quality of the external man, when separated from the internal, is worldly; and all that it produces is with a view to selfish ends.

This, then, is the ground, and such is the fruit thereof. The religion of a man like this is obviously nothing more than knowledge and its forms: it has no soul from above, its life is from below. How can the fruits of this ground be acceptable to God? We see at once that it cannot be respected. It rejects the great principle involved in the invitations, " My son, give me thy heart;" " Let thy heart keep my commandments."* These circumstances, then, fully explain the case of Cain's offering not being respected.

But it may be asked what evidence there is to prove that Cain was merely an external man? The apostle says, he was of the wicked one: † it is also presented in all the circumstances related of his character, and from which it has been seen that he represented faith only. The tendency of that doctrine is, to produce such a result upon the human character. When a man believes faith to be the principal thing of the Church, he will gradually recede from charity, for that in process of time will perish; in this case he will, as it were, have lost the kernel, and merely retain the husk, which will also be endangered. Faith is an external principle, of which charity is the internal, and, therefore, it is plain that those who are in faith only must be merely external men, whose faith is not faith, but mere science and persuasion. Confidence, which may be called faith in an eminent degree, cannot be given to those who are not in charity. How can those have genuine confidence who have lost the good by which it is inspired and made alive? Charity is as a flame, and faith the light which it emits: when the flame expires the light perishes, or, if any remain, it is dim and doubtful. These, then, are the reasons why the Lord had not respect to Cain, or to his offering. Faith only is no object of the divine regard, neither are its offerings, these being nothing else than the self-derived intelligence of the external man.

By these representative descriptions we are informed of the moral state and spiritual danger of all those persons among

---

* Prov. xxiii. 26; iii. 1. † 1 John iii. 12.

whom the heresy of Cain prevailed; which is confirmed by the divine declaration made to him, namely, "If thou doest well shalt thou not be accepted? and if thou doest not well, sin lieth at the door." It is plain that he did not *do* well, and that, therefore, both he and his offering were rejected.

But why had the Lord respect to Abel and to his offering? To Abel, because he was the representative of charity, which prevailed with another community, and which is an internal and sanctified principle, inducing all that is good and lovely in the human character. This view is recognized by the apostle, who, speaking of Abel's works, says they were righteous.* But of what were his offerings significant? Under the ceremonial law the sacrifices were supplied from two sources, the *flocks* and the *herds*. Those of the flock consisted of lambs, sheep, rams, and goats; and those of the herd, of oxen, heifers, and calves. By those of the flock were represented the good affections of the internal man, and by those of the herd were denoted the good affections of the external man; or, in other words, by the former were denoted the good things of love and charity, and by the latter, the good things of truth and faith. Hence arose the proverb, "Know the state of thy flocks, and look well to thy herds;" † and also the declaration concerning backsliding Israel, namely, "Shame hath devoured their flocks and herds." ‡ The Lord likewise called those who affectionately followed him a "little flock," and said unto them, "It is your Father's good pleasure to give you the kingdom." § Now Abel's offerings were of the firstlings of his flock, and the fat thereof; which may be taken, in the representative sense, to mean a lamb, and the fat thereof.

The significant character of a lamb is abundantly shown to us in the Scriptures. The Lord's command to feed His lambs; || His sending forth the disciples as lambs among wolves;¶ and the circumstance of His Humanity being called the "Lamb of God;"** sufficiently prove that this term is used in a symbolical sense; and the same facts clearly dictate that it is employed as the representative of innocence. The truth of this idea is per-

---

* 1 John iii. 12.   † Prov. xxvii. 23.   ‡ Jer. iii. 24.
§ Luke xii. 32. || John xxi. 15.   ¶ Luke x. 3.
** John i. 29.

ceived almost by intuition; and from this circumstance has grown up the affectionate custom of speaking of children in their innocence as lambs.

Innocence is of two kinds: the innocence of infancy, and the innocence of manhood. By manhood, we mean that sound condition of humanity which is induced by religious influences and teachings. The innocence of the infant is the innocence of ignorance; it is of a mere negative quality, arising from the unconscious presence of any guilt, and thus it is merely the ground on which all the future states of religious life are raised. It is not a possession which the infant can appreciate: it is a necessary result of his condition, and towards which, neither his intellectual nor his voluntary powers have at all contributed. But the innocence of the man is the innocence of wisdom: it is, as it were, the innocence of the infant grown into a man, developed, and made alive by the instructions of truth and goodness. In this case it becomes an appreciable possession; so that the distinction between the quality of the innocence with the infant and the man is, that with the former it is an inheritance of which he is unconscious, but with the latter it is an enlightened and sensible possession. Thus, the state of infancy is not a state of religious innocence; because, with the infant, it does not exist as a spiritual quality, perceptible to the subject: but the innocence of the man is a religious principle, implanted as he receives good and becomes wise.

Goodness and wisdom are essential innocence. It was on this account that the Lord Jesus Christ, as to His Humanity, was called the "*Lamb* of God," and described to have "grown in wisdom and favour with God." The disciples are called lambs for a similar reason. Such, then, being the signification of a lamb, it is easy to see that the offering of it to the Lord meant the worship of him from the good of innocence, and a consequent acknowledgment that it had come from him, and was properly his.

Every one must perceive, that in all good there must be innocence; it is that which makes it good; for if innocence be removed, then in comes guilt. Charity without innocence cannot be charity: as, then, Abel was the representative of charity, and, consequently, of all those in whom it exists, it is plain that innocence must have been a quality essential to its existence. If, then, a lamb really denoted the quality of religious innocence; and if by the firstling of the flock be meant a lamb, then it follows, as an irresistible consequence, that the offering of Abel was designed to signify the worship of the Lord by and from that innocence.

It is called the firstling of the flock because innocence is among the first things of man, which is afterwards made alive by the insemination of religious good; and the fat thereof is intended to express the superiority of its quality, and the beauty of its developments. The fat of the lamb represented the essential things of innocence, which is the principle of celestial good itself. Hence the Lord said, "Hearken diligently unto me, and eat ye that which is good, that your soul may delight itself in fatness;"* and again, "I will fill the soul of the priest with fatness, and my people shall be satisfied with my goodness."† It is plain that, in these passages, fat does not mean material fat, but that which is essentially good from the Lord.

With these views before us, we can be at no loss to discover why it was that the Lord had respect to Abel and to his offering. Charity, and the good of innocence, with which those who are principled in it worship the Lord, are acceptable things to him. They involve a faithful obedience to the laws and duties of revelation, and whosoever cherishes and observes them will be sure to obtain admission into the heavenly kingdom, and so realize those blessings which are associated with the divine respect for them.

But by what evidences were Cain and Abel made acquainted with the results of their respective offerings? There is no statement given by which they were to be guided into such knowledge. It has been conjectured that fire came down from heaven and consumed Abel's offering, but passed by that of Cain's, in like manner as fire is said to have descended on two or three other occasions, after the establishment of the Levitical law.‡ This supposes the offerings of Cain and Abel to have

---

* Isa. lv. 2. † Jer. xxxi. 14.

‡ See Lev. ix. 21; 1 Kings xviii. 38; also Judg. vi. 21. To support this idea, Theodotian has translated the Hebrew *shaah* (have respect) into Greek by the word *enepurisen*, he set on fire.—*Bayle's Dict. Hist., Art. Egnatia.*

been identically similar with the Jewish sacrifices; Whereas in their offerings there is no intimation of sacrifice in the way of killing an animal and presenting it upon an altar. But if any weight were attached to this notion, we should still have to inquire, how they knew that burning of the victim was a sign of the divine approbation? Had they learnt it by experience, or were they taught it by revelation? There is no written information by which these questions can satisfactorily be answered; nor need they be urged when it is known that their offerings are not mentioned in order to be understood in a physical sense: the whole difficulty arises from that view of the case, and it can be removed only by other considerations.

It is plain that both Cain and Abel must have known, by some means, the divine estimate of their respective offerings: as there is no information of any external token being given of the circumstance, it seems certain that it must have been afforded them by means of some internal evidence. Is not that the only real evidence which a man can have of his position in the Church of God? The divine acceptance or rejection of human worship is made known to the internal sensations of the worshipper, rather than by any external signs. Those people must have known, from the satisfactions and delights which attended their worship, whether it was acceptable or otherwise. So far as it was genuine, it must have been admissive of a holy influence from the Lord, and so of an indication of his respect; but when it was not genuine that influence could not enter into it, and surely that would evince its rejection. The worshipper is still gifted with some tokens of this description, which testify the sincerity or imperfection of his love; and his experiences in these respects will serve to show how Cain and Abel must have known the estimation in which their offerings were held. If a man's heart be not set right towards God, he is made to know, by his consciousness of that fact, that his offerings cannot be regarded. He feels his affections tending downwards rather than upwards; he knows that his thoughts wander in the world, while his words may be expressing the sentiments of holiness; he is fully aware that he dwells in nature only, and offers nothing but the fruit of the ground.

The experience of this consciousness on the part of Cain is thus described: "He was very wroth, and his countenance fell." This circumstance unfolds his character: it shows that charity was gone; anger could not otherwise have possessed him. It proves that a gloomy state was induced upon his mind, or his countenance could not have fallen. The feeling of wrath is opposed to the sentiment of charity, and a falling of the countenance only takes place when some unfavourable change affects the interiors of its subject. Anger is aroused when self-love is opposed, and that love is contrary to the love of God. The existence of the former proves the absence of the latter: so, also, the countenance, which is bright and pleasing when enlightened and influenced by a benignity within, becomes sad and falls when the consciousness of impurity is felt. Such was the character of Cain; and by his history we are informed of the internal state and spiritual danger of all those people among whom the heresy of his religion prevails. That his state was of such a quality is farther confirmed by its being said to him, "If thou doest well, shalt thou not be accepted? and if thou doest not well, sin lieth at the door:" he did not do well, therefore he was not accepted; his offering was the form of worship without the essence: and similar disappointment and rejection await all those who, like him, know their Master's will, but do it not; who know the way, but walk not in it; who think they shall be heard well, because they speak much; who have enlarged minds, but guilty hearts; who have the faith of knowledge, but not the charity of love.

CHAPTER XV.

THE DEATH OF ABEL.—THE CURSE ON CAIN; HIS FUGITIVE AND VAGABOND CONDITION.

"During the first eight centuries the Greek and Roman churches were in communion with each other; but in the ninth century their disputes became so violent, that a final separation took place between them. A Patriarch was elected for Constantinople, as the head of the Greek Church; he was soon excommunicated by the Pope, as the head of the Romish Church; the Pope, in return, was excommunicated by the Patriarch."—*Jones's "Dictionary of Religious Opinions,"* p. 76.

The circumstances recorded to have constituted the successive decline of the Adamic or most ancient Church are, as to kind, very similar to those which have produced the corruptions of other religious dispensations mentioned in the Scriptures. They are also illustrated by facts, which history assures us have brought about the extinction of various institutions of a religious character, and which, at the time of their origination, were intended to promote some general good. For a period they have satisfactorily flourished in the accomplishment of the purposes for which they were established, but by-and-by their quietude has been disturbed: some persons, influenced by the love of pre-eminence, have sought to rule, and they have rudely broken in upon the order and the happiness which previously existed under such institutions. Having partaken more largely of knowledge than humility, men sought to be as gods; and in the prosecution of their designs they have originated dissensions and divisions: one party has obtained ascendency over another: temporary success has stimulated the arrogance of selfishness, until it has wickedly attempted to crush the modesty of right and justice,—in which it has too frequently been successful.

In such historical facts we have the general counterpart of those events which brought about the catastrophe of Abel's death; and, viewed under this aspect, we perceive, in the antediluvian narrative, a history of the development of human passions, when once evil had introduced its unhallowed presence among them. The narrative, in having responses in after-history, not only treats of the lawless activity of man's fallen nature among an ancient people, but it may also be regarded as describing circumstances which have been enacted over and over again in the wide domain of religious society; it is not only the written picture of events which have frequently distinguished such society, but it is also a caligraphic portrait of the states of individual men. Do we not find them abusing the privileges they are permitted to enjoy, and so preferring personal gratification to religious obedience? Do not our experiences assure us that we have produced a separation between our knowledge and our duty? and have we not acted as though we considered them to be distinct things, instead of regarding them as one? Religious knowledge exists for the purpose of conducting men to spiritual obedience: but every one knows that he has permitted the love of information to acquire an ascendency over the love of duty; and it is no uncommon case to find that the desire of duty has been extinguished in the pursuit of knowledge, and thus that Cain has slain his brother Abel.

It is only when we can see the Word of God to have a universal, continual, and particular application to the moral experiences of men, both in their collective and individual conditions, that we possess the genuine evidence necessary to convince us that it is what it professes to be—a revelation from God. It must have been the Divine Mind which caused the construction of the narrative we are considering, because it describes, in a consecutive series, facts which, when viewed in their internal sense, have their counterparts in the experiences of religious men. None but God knoweth what is in man; none but He could have looked into futurity, so as to have beheld the workings and displays of disordered humanity, and thereupon to have caused the production of a work which should describe them with the minutiæ and accuracy which His book can be proved to do. His Word is for all time and for all men. To suppose that it was merely the history of a particular period and of a peculiar people, is to take away from it the majesty and eternity of its purpose, as well as to overlook the infinity and spirituality of its origin. It is written of God, that without a parable spake he not.* The most marvellous and accomplished parable of revelation is that which is called the Antediluvian History; and we now come to that part of it which informs us of the death of Abel by the hand of Cain. The catastrophe is thus related: "And Cain talked with Abel his brother: and it came to pass, when they were in the field, that Cain rose up against Abel his brother, and slew him."† This result sufficiently indicates that their talking together is to be understood as expressing the idea of angry disputation. This was the natural consequence of two different sects, which had branched off from the most ancient Church, one of which was seeking an ascendency over the other.

It is no uncommon circumstance for rival parties in religion to be found in the bitterness of controversy. Although they may be in the same field together,—or, what is thereby signified, although they may profess to belong to the same general religious dispensation,—yet the particular views which each has taken of some of its doctrines and discipline have brought them into collision, and they have not unfrequently conducted their controversies more in the spirit of conquest and the world, than under the influence of truth and heaven. The history of the Lutheran, Calvinistic, and Arminian parties in the Christian Church, displays these facts with sufficient clearness. They have talked together, but they have talked vehemently. Luther denounced Erasmus as a vain, inglorious animal, because he exposed some of the religious crudities which "the Reformer" had published: ‡ Calvin caused Servetus to be put to death, because he dared to differ from him in religious opinion.§ The

---

* Matt. xiii. 34. † Gen. iv. 8.

‡ His words are, "That exasperated viper, Erasmus, has again attacked me; what eloquence will the vain, inglorious animal display in the overthrow of Luther!"

§ "When Servetus had escaped from his prison at Vienna, and was passing through Switzerland in order to seek refuge in Italy, Calvin caused him to be apprehended at Geneva, in the year 1553, and had an accusation of blasphemy brought against him before the council. The issue of this accusation was fatal to Servetus, who, adhering resolutely to the opinions he had embraced, was, by a public sentence of the court, declared an obstinate

controversies founded on the doctrines of Arminius involved Switzerland in years of discord; and other branches of the professing Christian Church, which have had greater power and more audacity, have not scrupled at any means by which they could subdue their antagonists in religious things. Sometimes they have had recourse to violence and blood, rather than not attain the supremacy to which they aspired. This has been the case not merely with individuals, of which the martyrdoms are a sufficient evidence, but it is true of whole parties. History most distinctly informs us of several instances in which one sect has wickedly attempted to exterminate another, not by the persuasions of truth and reason, but by the weapons of cruelty and murder. The Albigenses were a people who, in the eleventh century, attempted to effect some reform in the Church as it then existed; their views, however, were condemned in council by the ecclesiastics of the time, and an effort was thereupon made to exterminate them by the most violent persecutions.* Another instance of a similar kind is presented to us in the history of the Waldenses;† and that of the Huguenots, in the seven-

heretic, and, in consequence thereof, condemned to the flames."—*Mosheim, Eccl. Hist.*, cent. xvi., par. iv. Dr. A. Maclaine, the translator, observes, that "it is impossible to justify the conduct of Calvin in the case of Servetus, whose death will be an indelible reproach upon the character of that great and eminent reformer. The only thing that can be alleged, not to efface, but to diminish his crime, is, that it was no easy matter for him to divest himself at once of that persecuting spirit which had been so long nourished and strengthened by the popish religion, in which he had been educated. It was a remaining portion of the spirit of Popery in the breast of Calvin that kindled his unchristian zeal against the wretched Servetus."

* Limborch's History of the Inquisition, translated by Chandler, vol. i., pp. 42–70.

† "The injuries and insults they suffered at the hands of many orders of men, and more especially of the Jesuits, are not to be numbered. In Poland, all those who ventured to differ from the Pope found, by bitter experience, during the whole of this (17th) century, that no treaty or convention that tended to set bounds to the authority or rapacity of the Church was held sacred, or even regarded, at Rome. For many of these were ejected out of their schools, deprived of their churches, robbed of their goods and possessions, under a variety of perfidious pretexts; nay, frequently condemned to the most severe and cruel punishments, without having been even chargeable with the appearance of crime. The remains of the Waldenses that

teenth century, discloses unparalleled atrocities. They were a sect of Protestants which rose up in France, and, for having separated from the dominant party of the Romish Church at that time, were denounced as objects of hatred. Mosheim informs us that, "after having groaned for a long space of time under various forms of cruelty and oppression, and seen multitudes of their brethren put to death by secret conspiracies or open tyranny and violence, they were at length obliged either to save themselves by clandestine flight, or to profess, against their consciences, the Romish religion."*

With such facts of history before us, it is no difficult thing to conceive that the dispute of Cain with Abel, when viewed as religious parties in the most ancient Church, should have terminated in the more bold and daring effecting the destruction of the more modest and unresisting. This is one of the unhappy consequences which attend a Church during the process of its decline from wisdom and purity; it is then that evil and false principles effect an entrance and perpetrate their mischiefs. The sweetness of charity is sacrificed to the austerity of faith. Creeds have triumphed over virtue; innocence has suffered in the struggle to establish an opinion; guilt has flourished for a time, and, under the injured name of truth, has perpetrated murder. This we conceive to be the general idea which the history of Abel's death by the hands of Cain was intended to convey to posterity. How many disasters would have been prevented in society, if the moral of it had been practically learnt! But, alas! it has not been so. The narrative describes a calamity which must attend the presence of false principles in the Church during the process of its decline and fall; it is also a revelation of their consequences, which have been verified in after ages by a hundred facts.

lived in the valleys of Piedmont were persecuted often with the most inhuman cruelty (and more especially in the years 1632, 1655, and 1685), on account of their magnanimous and steadfast attachment to the religion of their ancestors; and this persecution was carried on with all the horrors of fire and sword by the Dukes of Savoy."—*Mosheim*, cent. xvii., part 1, par. viii.

* Eccl. Hist., cent. xvii., part 1, par. ix. See also the second chapter of the second part throughout.

While we can see the general principle involved in the declaration of Cain talking with his brother Abel, and subsequently slaying him, let us endeavour to examine the subject a little farther, in order to comprehend the statements in their more particular form. Their talking, as it was said, plainly indicates an angry disputation: the result proves the truth of this induction. Divisions having broken in upon the unity of the most ancient Church, doctrinal disagreements would, in the process of time, manifest themselves in various forms, more or less malignant. Cain—or, what is the same thing, those who maintained that faith grounded in the knowledge of truth constituted the excellency of religion—would talk authoritatively, and wield an intellectual power over Abel—or, what is the same thing, those who were influenced by the docility and gentleness of charity. Those who love charity love peace. They prefer to let their lives, rather than their words, speak of the uprightness of their heart and the integrity of their character. The intelligence of their faith shows itself in the purity of their works: what they know of truth fixes itself in amiability and loveliness of conduct. They are actuated by an affirmative principle, and, in their communications on points of difference, will say little more than "Yea, yea; Nay, nay;" because they are well assured that whatsoever is more than these has come of evil. Their religion is exhibited in the meekness and moderation of their deportment. They will give to every one that asketh them, a reason for the hope that is in them; but they cannot enforce their views by contention and the strife of words. They cannot talk rudely, and so irreverently, about heavenly things. They remember the sanctity of goodness, and endeavour to preserve it with every care. If opposed by those who are in the pride of intellect, they will state their views of truth with lucidity and candour, but they will carefully eschew the risings of an angry disputation. They fear lest they should imbibe an ungenerous spirit, and prefer that their opponent should acquire the reputation of a conqueror, rather than to endanger the good they may possess by entering into the heat and virulence of controversy. "Charity suffereth long, and is kind; charity envieth not; charity vaunteth not itself, is not puffed up, doth not behave itself unseemly, seeketh not her own, is not easily provoked, thinketh no evil; rejoiceth not in iniquity, but rejoiceth in the truth; beareth all things, hopeth all things, endureth all things. Charity never faileth."* Those who are led by this holy principle care not so much about the talking part of religion: they regard the doing of their duty in all the relationships of life to be of the first importance. They are ever attentive to acts of benevolence and use, and experience happiness in the diligent performance of them; and they will be found to submit to sufferings and persecution for righteousness' sake, rather than be driven into resistance by violence and oppression. Such were the characteristics of the people called Abel.

But Cain, or those who believe that the knowledges of faith are the principal things of religion, are not satisfied with so mild and amiable a course. They cannot endure that any should hold sentiments different from their own; and every one whose views do not harmonize with their ideas of faith is considered as an adversary, and regarded with disdain. They dispute with vehemence, and break into anger in the midst of argumentation, because they are destitute of the charity that would keep them placid. They pretend that charity is only the ornament of religion, and not necessary to the salvation of the believer. With them, faith, and not virtue, is the essential thing. This has been the ground of those supposed conversions which certain wicked persons are said to have experienced, when under the influence of affliction or the fear of death. Such persons, because they could serve themselves no longer, are then persuaded to have faith in God, and to believe that this alone will save them. But of such the Lord has said, "Depart from me; I never knew you." From the same pestilential source some criminals, who have forfeited their lives by the atrocity of their conduct, have been said to have become religious, and to have died in penitence and hope; so that the scaffold has not unfrequently been exhibited as no obstacle in the way to heaven. Merciful God! to what detestable results have men been led through the adoption of false principles in religion, and which, in their audacity, they have said were thine!

* 1 Cor. xiii. 4–8.

Those who suppose that faith only—that is, faith separate from charity—is the essential thing of the Church, and so the principal thing in man's salvation, overlook this circumstance,— that no one can procure genuine faith who is not first in the love of something that is good; also, that good cannot be obtained but in a state of liberty, or fixed in the life until it be practised. Faith, then, is the offspring of charity, for charity is good, and thus the living and essential thing of religion and salvation. But the belief of these truths is no part of the Solifidian's faith. His great effort is to set the speculations of faith above the excellences of virtue. He struggles incessantly to obtain pre-eminence for faith. He entertains no kindly sentiments for those who differ from him. He cherishes no affectionate regard for spiritual good: he asserts that it is impossible to obtain it; and so he does not look upon charity as his spiritual brother, but disputes with those who think it is so, rejects their arguments, and neglects their virtues. The non-resisting character of those who are in charity is construed by him into a want of confidence in its superiority. He treats the humility of charity as the docility of ignorance; its submissiveness is pronounced to be cowardice, and then it is destroyed. It is thus that Cain rises against his brother, and Abel perishes!

When Abel is slain,—when men destroy the life of charity in themselves, by rejecting it as no essential thing of religion or salvation,—when they think works of virtue will not aid their upward progress, they are not far from believing that acts of vice will not prevent it; and so the doctrine of "*faith only*" is no safeguard against the perpetration of any enormity which their lusts may prompt. Hence it was that Cain, by whom this doctrine was represented and sustained, is recorded to have committed the highest crime. Men do not fall into guilty practices toward their fellow-men until they have wounded charity in themselves. The inquisition, the rack, and the fagot, were the inventions of those in whom the sentiment of genuine charity had perished. In having recourse to these enormities, they professed, indeed, to be actuated by a principle of religion, but then it was only in the shape of a creed, and not in the form of love. It was something which they regarded as faith, without its amiable and forbearing brother; hence they persecuted and destroyed their neighbour, under the horrid persuasion that, by so acting, they were doing God service.

These considerations help us to see, that by Cain's slaying his brother Abel is denoted, that those who were in the mere doctrinals of faith rejected the life of charity, and thus admitted all those evil influences implied in the curse which was pronounced upon him.

We now come to notice some other circumstances which the narrative reveals concerning Cain. First, the Lord said unto him, "Where is Abel thy brother?"*

The Lord is frequently treated of in the Scriptures as speaking to various persons; but by this we are not to understand oral communication, like that which takes place between man and man in the expression of his thoughts. The Lord does not so effect his intercourse with men. By his speaking, especially to the guilty, is meant, in general, an internal dictate, produced either through the human perceptions or conscience. Conscience is the peculiar inheritance of man: it is one of the evidences of his spirituality, and by which he is distinguished from the brutes, who have it not. It is formed in man during the early years of his existence, by means of the affections, attentions, and moral instructions of his parents and friends; but more particularly by the teachings of what are good and true: and all goodness and truth are the Lord's, communicated to man through such mediums as his state requires: that medium is now the Word. When man at any time transgresses those principles in which he has been trained, he is made to feel internal pain and reproof. The pain arises from a mental sense of the violence which has been done to something that is good; and the reproof, from a perception of the injury which has been inflicted on something that is true: this mental sense is the Divine voice, uttering its complaints within. It speaks a sensible and a nervous language, and leaves impressions not readily forgotten. We know that such experiences do not come to us from without: we feel that they originate in a dictate from within, and thus that they come from a higher and a holier source than ourselves. It is easy, then, to see that the

* Gen. iv. 9.

Lord speaks with men in the dictate of some internal principle, formed and disciplined by means of the Divine teachings.

This dictate to Cain, in the instance before us, was made upon his perception, and it concerned the violence which he had done to charity. It is thus expressed: "Where is Abel thy brother?" It was an internal impression, inquiring what was become of the innocence, the peace, and tranquillity, that were enjoyed before charity was slain; it was a spiritual investigation, giving the assurance of guilt by the sensations of pain. The case, with Cain, was similar to that which the guilty have experienced in after ages. They know that this description of their state is true: but what is their practical answer to such an inquiry? It partakes of the false position in which their guilt has placed them; and it is forcibly expressed in the reply which Cain is declared to have made, namely, "I know not: Am I my brother's keeper?" Those who are not willing to be connected with or influenced by charity, strive to make light of the guilt that has extinguished it. Those who produce the death of Abel are therefore brought into a state which, in some measure, prevents them from seeing the enormity of their crime. The criminal does not see his wickedness in so hideous a form as society, who have suffered from its malignity. Those who cherish ill-will and hatred towards their neighbour think very lightly of the enormity they are committing: such persons see in their neighbour nothing but inferiority and fault; they know him not, nor do they conceive why they should be regarded as his keeper. They practically reason with themselves, and say, Why should they serve him? Why should they be inquired of concerning him? Why should he stand in the way of their success? Such base reasonings as these express the depraved conditions of their hearts, from which they strive to remove every obstacle to the foul dominion which they seek, so far as they can command the power, and use it with safety to themselves.

Thus it is, that those who are principled in the doctrine which Cain represented, like him, make light of charity, even when it is inquired after: and that they entirely reject it is signified by his contemptuous inquiry, "Am I my brother's keeper?"—in other words, What have I to do with charity?

Nevertheless, this daring on the part of Cain did not suppress the urgency of the inner dictate: it forcibly accused him of having offered violence to charity, and strongly convicted him of the crime, by making him conscious of his guilt; which circumstances are described by the Lord saying to Cain, "The voice of thy brother's blood crieth unto me from the ground." "The voice of thy brother" denotes the complaint of charity; his "blood" is intended to express the idea of its rejection and death; and this is said to have "cried from the ground," to inform us that the destruction of charity arose from the heresy into which the people called Cain had fallen; and, therefore, they are pronounced to have been cursed.

Now all cursing comes from evil: God is not, cannot be, the source of it. Man produces it, by turning himself away from God; and he does this whenever he prefers his own will to God's teachings. The sun is not the author of darkness; he is ever shining : but darkness comes by the earth's rotating from him. Those who, like Cain, know truth, and do it not, turn themselves away from God, and so become averse to what is good. All blessing comes to men as they love the good of charity: all cursing overtakes them as they banish and extinguish it; for, in this case, cruelty, unmercifulness, and hatred enter in; and thereupon the bond is broken between man and God: consequently, the means of blessing is dissolved, and the opposite state is that of being cursed; for, as it was said, all cursing comes to men through the entering in of evil, which faith *alone* cannot prevent. That man may be in such a faith, and yet in a state of condemnation, is plain from its being written, "The devils believe, and tremble."* It is a fearful state, to know what is right and do it not. The Lord has thus described it: "Every one that heareth these sayings of mine, and doeth them not, shall be likened unto a foolish man, which built his house upon the sand: and the rain descended, and the floods came, and the winds blew, and beat upon that house; and it fell: and great was the fall of it."†

But the nature of the curse which befell Cain is more particularly described by its being said to him, "When thou tillest the ground, it shall not henceforth yield unto thee her strength:

---

* Jas. ii. 19.   † Matt. vii. 26, 27.

a fugitive and a vagabond shalt thou be in the earth."* Adam was told that the ground was cursed, and would bring forth thorns and thistles; and now Cain is informed that it should not yield her strength. Every one who will reflect must see that the statement is not intended to express any hindrance to the natural prolification of the land, but that something of a spiritual character must be meant. Natural laws and spiritual laws operate distinctly from each other. The spiritual laws by which a man becomes good, and the natural laws by which his land becomes productive, are of two different kinds. There may be an analogy between them, but they are not dependent on each other for their effects. It is a natural law, that if the earth be tilled it will produce its increase, whether the man who tilled it be good or bad. The good man's garden will not afford him fruits, if he be inattentive to the natural laws of production. The bad man's ground is not barren, if he duly attend to the requirements of the soil. It is plain, then, that the statement made to Cain, namely, "When thou tillest the ground, it shall not henceforth yield unto thee her strength," is designed to announce, not a physical result, but a consequence of the action of some spiritual law. What this is will presently appear.

It will be remembered that, in a former chapter, it was shown that the ground was an emblem of the natural state, or mind, of the celestial man; also that his fall consisted in his descent from his celestial condition into that natural state, or mind, again; and thereby carrying into it the seeds of transgression. It then became his work to till this ground, which denoted the rooting up, by means of repentance, of the weeds and briers, the thorns and thistles, of transgressive life, and the cultivation of the natural mind for the reception of the seeds of truth and goodness. But this important duty, by which it was intended to raise him out of his corruptions, had not been properly attended to. The people, it was seen, became divided into sects, and that of Cain cultivated the ground of the natural mind, so as to produce the erroneous persuasion, that faith was all that was necessary to form the religious character and to realize religious hopes. By this they fell into the deeper

* Gen. iv. 12.

wickedness of extinguishing all spiritual good,—they rose against Abel, and slew him. Hence their faith became a heresy; for the faith that rejects charity as a means of acceptance with the Lord, is not from heaven, but from fallen man. The ground of Cain was still the natural mind of the people so called; but by the destruction of charity it became infested with false notions, both of religion and themselves.

The will having become corrupt, the understanding partook of the depravity. When men commence to love what is evil, they soon begin to think what is false. The head is soon seduced when the heart is foul; so that heresies arise among mankind from the prevalence of evil. Men are expert in reasoning in favour of the things they love,—they strive to believe what they desire. Cain's love had now become the love of self, for he had hated and destroyed his brother; hence all his notions and opinions acquired a tincture from this iniquity, and thus his faith became a heresy. It was the heresy of believing that mere knowledge and persuasion would save, which now constituted the ground of his natural mind. To till this ground was to cultivate this heresy; but he was told that it would not yield its strength. Providence mercifully interrupts the course of the wicked; and God designs that interruption to be a blessing, but they receive it otherwise. It disturbs their loves, it hinders their pursuits, and so retards the progress of malignity. Is not this an actual blessing? Most certainly it is! Still, it is regarded as a misfortune and a curse by those who are its subjects. The people called Cain tilled their ground,—they cultivated the heresy into which they had fallen: they were informed that it should not yield her strength, —that it could not bring forth acceptable fruits. In other words, they were told that the good and excellent things of heaven could not grow out of a perverted mind. We cannot gather grapes of thorns, nor figs of thistles.

Religious heresies have never been productive of any real good to society: it is impossible, in the nature of things, that they should; because, in such case, the ground of the natural mind is not tilled to bring forth virtue, but to grow arguments and opinions for the maintenance of the schism. How many have quarrelled, fought, and died in the defence of an opinion, which time, and the advancement of knowledge, have proved to be false! How many heresies have arisen in the Church, which have successively perished, with the sole exception of a name in history! Their professors tilled this heretical ground with assiduity and zeal, but it did not improve the condition or enlarge the virtues of society: it served rather to increase their subtlety, and to impart severity to their characters, and hence the heresies have passed away. This result is in agreement with the apostolic statement, "If this council or this work be of men, it will come to nought: but if it be of God, ye cannot overthrow it; lest haply ye be found to fight against God."*

The natural mind, infested with schismatical notions about religious things, however it may be cultivated, does not yield its strength: falsehood and fallacy weaken its powers, and prevent it from going to those sources which furnish information. The cultivation of error, instead of yielding the intellectual strength of the mind, develops its weakness; and this, together with its non-production of benefits and use, bring it into merited disgrace and ruin: in these facts we learn in what the curse of Cain consisted. When the heresy which destroyed charity in the Church began to be cultivated by itself, it was found to produce no fruits of moral and spiritual use, and to yield no strength of intellectual knowledge. Cain's water was nought, and his ground was barren, so that he became "a fugitive and vagabond in the earth." †

These things are predicated of the religious state of Cain, rather than of their physical and outer condition. A fugitive is one who runs away from the demands of duty, and a vagabond is a wanderer who has no settled habitation. The people called Cain had these two epithets applied to them, with the view of expressing the idea that they had, as to their will, run away from the love of goodness; and that, as to their understanding, they had no settled conception of truth. The same words are applied in the historical portion of the Scriptures to other parties, with a like signification. The terms *fled* and *wander* also denote the same ideas; which an instance will sufficiently illustrate. The

---

* Acts v. 38, 39.

† Septuagint renders this passage, "groaning and trembling on the earth." The above, however, is the more correct expression of the original Hebrew.

prophet Isaiah, speaking "of the valley of vision," says, "All thy rulers WANDER together, they are bound by the archers: all that are found in thee are bound together, which have FLED from far."* Where, by the valley of vision, is represented the phantasy of a religion of faith without charity: the *wandering* of its rulers denotes the unsteady condition of its knowledges: all that were found in it under such circumstances are mere perversions of good, and hence they are said to have "fled from far." The Lord, and all genuine goodness, are far away from such a state. Thus Cain was called a fugitive, to denote that his affections had run away from goodness; and he is pronounced to be a vagabond, to signify the wandering character of his understanding in respect to truth; whence we learn that all those who, like him, profess and cherish a religion of faith which is not grounded in charity, are pronounced to be fugitives and vagabonds in the Church.

* Isa. xxii. 3.

CHAPTER XVI.

CAIN'S COMPLAINT AND APPREHENSIONS.—THE MARK SET UPON HIM FOR HIS PRESERVATION.

"The goodness and love of God have no limits or bounds but such as his omnipotence hath; and everything that hath a possibility of partaking of the kingdom of heaven will infallibly find a place in it."—LAW's *Appeal*, p. 88.

When men turn their affections away from what is good, and their thoughts from what is true, they are necessarily brought into a state in which pain must be experienced and danger apprehended. We say this is the necessary consequence of such a procedure, because it is a Divine law that a sense of happiness and security springs out of the love and practice of what is wise and virtuous; and, consequently, that a departure from that law must be attended with opposite results. This was a condition of which Cain had now become sensible, and, to record it, he is said to have exclaimed, "My punishment is greater than I can bear."*

Perception, which then stood in the place of that which was conscience in after ages, was not entirely destroyed; there yet remained some of its correcting impulses and suggestions, and these gave rise to those utterances of deep despair. Nor were the painful sensations of their present state the sole cause of their hopelessness: they had a foresight of calamity in the future, and hence Cain is described to have said unto the Lord, "I shall be driven from thy face; and it shall come to pass, that every one that findeth me shall slay me."† Such were the natural anticipations of a religious community, who were in the process of being convinced that they had extinguished the good and falsified the truth, which God had mercifully entrusted to their care and observance. It is plain that the dread which is declared does not relate to the fear of natural life being destroyed, but to the alarm occasioned by a perception of the

---

* Gen. iv. 13. † Gen. iv. 14.

danger to which spiritual life was exposed. According to the literal sense, there was only Cain himself, with Adam, and his mother, then in existence. Whom, then, was he to fear? By whom could such a deed of death be done?*

But on the admission that there were other persons, of whose origination and existence the history does not distinctly speak, we can hardly suppose that every one of them would have been so exasperated by his iniquity as to be ready to take upon himself the power of inflicting judicial vengeance. In our own time the great mass of mankind shrink in dismay from such an idea. An executioner is instinctively felt to be a horrid character. This, however, is not the subject treated of, as will be very apparent after a moment's attention to the peculiar structure of the sentence which expresses the fear, namely,—"Every one that findeth me shall slay me." Now "every one" that found him could not do it; † he had but one life to lose, and this could not have been taken by every one with whom he came in contact. It is therefore evident that the statement does not relate to the infliction of natural death, and that we must refer, for its true meaning, to the phenomena which take place with the inner life of fallen man. It is there alone that we can find the realization of those sensations of which Cain's language is expressive. Those who are principled in evils of any kind thereby expose their spiritual life to spiritual assailants. Infernal influences and thoughts rush into every avenue which is opened in the mind by human wickedness, so that they will soon become a legion. It is the evils which pass into the hearts of guilty men that make them fear. There is a well-known proverb in the Church, which says, "Be sure your sins will find you out." These infest the guilty with trepidation and alarm, because they

---

* In the note at page 65 is cited the supposition on which a large number of persons may be considered as existing in the time of Cain. Those who have adopted that view, to avoid the difficulty which the literal sense of this portion of the history suggests, seem not to have observed that by such an opinion they are in collision with the Apostle, who asserts that Enoch was the *seventh* from Adam (Jude 14).

† Cain's words may be thought to be only a general and loose expression of his fears that some *one* would avenge himself upon him; but no one who considers that revelation is verbally accurate, and that every expression is significant of an appropriate idea, can reasonably adhere to such a notion.

threaten the entire extinction of all spiritual life. The language of Cain's fear of every one, then, expresses the internal consternation which was experienced by that people upon the entrance of every evil influence to which they had exposed themselves. Having perverted the truth of faith, and destroyed the good of charity, as its spiritual brother, they were brought within the sphere of terrible temptations. These met them on every side, and, entering into them, effected their distresses. Their fears for the dangerous condition of their spiritual life sprung out of the severity of their temptation. Their power over the means for the preservation of spiritual good had become exceedingly weak. They felt that every source of happiness was fast departing; for having destroyed charity, they possessed no power for its retention. Thus they were reduced to a state of the most painful anxiety and deep disquiet.

These ancient experiences have had their counterpart among transgressors in after times. Do we not know that every violation of the laws of goodness has been attended with fears, both external and internal: external fear lest we should be discovered and exposed; and internal fear lest our spiritual disquiet should result in the destruction of that happiness which man regards to be his inner life? Thus, if we fall into the guilt of rejecting charity from our affections, we open out the way for a multitude of evil desires and false persuasions to enter in, every one of which brings its poison, and threatens us with death. The experiences of the men of the Church in our times satisfactorily explain the statement of Cain's fears. Evil is alike in its consequences at all periods, and it only differs in the degree of its enormity. It produces similar results among all men; more or less severe, as the conscience may have been more or less accurately formed. The punishment of which Cain complained was a condition of moral agony produced by the presence of evil, admitted through the destruction of charity; and his fear lest every one finding him should slay him denoted the distress that was occasioned by every temptation that found in him a plane upon which it could operate its malignity. Evil and falsehood slay the spiritual life of religion in the souls of its professors, and cause them to have nothing of genuine happiness or heaven within them. The fear of this had now produced a miserable influence upon that branch of the most ancient Church called Cain.

The Scriptures speak of similar states having come into existence under the Jewish dispensation; and those who were their subjects are described as fearing and flying from the sword. Thus Moses, speaking of those who persisted in their transgression, says, "Upon them that are left alive of you I will send a faintness into their hearts in the lands of their enemies; and the sound of a shaken leaf shall chase them; and they shall flee, as fleeing from a sword; and they shall fall when none pursueth."* Here it is evident that the pain of evil desires, and the fear of spiritual death thereby occasioned, are the subjects treated of. So, again, Jeremiah, speaking of the judgments of the Ammonites, says, "Behold, I will bring a fear upon thee, saith the Lord God of hosts, from all those that be about thee; and ye shall be driven out every man right forth; and none shall gather up him that wandereth."† This denouncement is nearly parallel, both in sentiment and expression, to that recorded of Cain: he feared all those that were about him, and was driven out from the face of the Lord. The wicked cannot do otherwise than fear: the loss of innocence, with the consciousness of guilt, afflict them with it. They can have but little hope of spiritual life hereafter, when they reflect that the doors of heaven are shut against iniquity. It is written, that "without are dogs, and sorcerers, and whoremongers, and murderers, and idolaters, and whosoever loveth and maketh a lie."‡ This is a law which must remain perpetual in the Church. Men may try to reason away its force, by supposing that the Divine justice will be satisfied through the sufferings of a victim substituted for the sinner, and so abstract from it its practical importance. Still they will have the evidences of intuition, that heaven is only for the good, and that none are faithful but those who are obedient. The faith that does not remove the mountains of evil which afflict humanity is of little worth.§ Faith, to be of real value, must

---

* Lev. xxvi. 36.   † Jer. xlix. 5.   ‡ Rev. xxii. 15.

§ Jenyn sensibly observes, "The true Scriptural meaning of the word faith seems nothing more than a docility or promptitude to receive truth; and the Christian faith, to believe the divine authority of that religion, and to obey its precepts; in this sense surely too much merit can never be imputed to it:

have its ground in truth, and thus possess the power of making men good. If it have not those properties, it has no pedigree in heaven, because all that proceeds thence is intended to make men wise and happy.

It is easy to understand, as a general principle, that the state of a people who had destroyed within themselves the life of charity must have been fearful and distressing; nor is it difficult to perceive that their anguish was much greater than it would have been had they been an ignorant people. This they were not. There are certain sensibilities which attend the possession of knowledge that are exceedingly acute: they are blunted and deprived of much of their poignancy by ignorance. Cain represented an enlightened but an uncharitable people. The wicked can be clever, but the circumstance of knowing what is right, and doing what is wrong, augments the severity of the punishment which ensues: the sin of ignorance is less enormous in its consequences than the sin of knowledge. The Lord said, "He that knew not, and did commit things worthy of stripes, shall be beaten with few *stripes*. For unto whomsoever much is given, of him shall be much required."* This latter state was that of Cain; they transgressed the laws of goodness, and knew it; they pursued their own uncharitable course with open eyes. They were not ignorant of their duty to man, but thought that a certain faith in God would be accepted in its stead. They substituted knowledge for virtue; extinguished charity, and trusted to solitary faith to gain for them admission into heaven. Hence came that particular condition which the trepidation and

but since this denomination has been so undermined, that no two ages, nations, or sects have affixed to it the same ideas; and so absurd, that under it every absurdity that knavery could cram down, or ignorance swallow, has been comprehended; since it is still capable of being so explained as to mean anything that an artful preacher pleases to impose on an illiterate audience; the laying too great stress upon it must be highly dangerous to the religion and liberties of mankind: but the proposing it as a composition for moral duties is, of all others, the most mischievous doctrine; as it unhinges all our notions of divine justice, and establishes wickedness upon a principle; and it is the more mischievous, as it cannot fail of being popular, because, as is usually intended, it is, in fact, nothing more than offering to the people a license to be profligate at the easy price of being absurd—a bargain which they will ever readily agree to."—*Jenyn's Works*, vol. i., p. 219.

* Luke xii. 48.

alarm of Cain were intended to teach us. He had the faith of knowledge, but not the practice. This is the trait of character which, in all our consideration of Cain, we have endeavoured to keep in sight, as being that which was both possessed and represented by him.

But who does not see that the existence of religious knowledge is endangered by the life of evil? The faith of knowledge in religious things is placed in jeopardy by the rejection of charity. By the faith of knowledge we mean a belief in what is understood to be true; but if men destroy in themselves the practice of religious good, their belief in religious truth is placed in peril. The truths of religion live and acquire their perpetuity by being embodied in acts of usefulness to society. Truth becomes good by use. The truths of religion are to teach men how to live; if this purpose of them be extinguished, they become mere intellectual things; and as such are like the faith of Cain, exposed to death. The machine rusts when it is thrown out of employ; to preserve the mechanism bright and clean it must be kept in use. The religious knowledge which exists merely in the head will soon expire; and so the death of truth is to be feared when the life of charity has been destroyed. This is the particular idea of which the recorded dread of Cain is intended to inform us. Charity having perished, faith was placed in great danger. Cain, having slain his brother Abel, now began to fear a similar calamity. How can those preserve their faith who have abandoned virtue? Men do not long remember what they cease to practise. Cain's fear of death was intended to shadow forth to us the danger in which truth is placed when good is lost. The orderly and affectionate course of a good man preserves his faith in health and vigour; the vices and immoralities of the wicked endanger its existence. Every evil to which they are tempted inflicts a new blow, and threatens to destroy it: the reason is, because they do not resist these evils, but fall therein, whenever they are assailed. These are truths of experience, and how closely do they resemble the state indicated by Cain's expressions! They present the history to us under a practical aspect. It comes home to what is very generally known and felt to be the case. It is not merely a fact which distinguished an ancient sect, but it is a revelation of certain religious experiences in after times. Every man knows that the retention of his belief is endangered when he does not practise its instructions: we cannot long believe after we have ceased to do; and the Apostle has most emphatically informed us, "that faith without works is dead." *

From these considerations we see, with remarkable accuracy, that the agony of Cain, and his fear of death, represented the danger to which truth among that people was now exposed, in consequence of its not being reduced to life. This brings us to another point in this investigation, which is thus expressed: "Whosoever slayeth Cain, vengeance shall be taken on him sevenfold. And the Lord set a mark upon Cain, lest any finding him should kill him." †

The first general remark which these statements educe in connection with what has been previously explained is, that faith, even though it be in a state of separation from charity, is to be held as a sacred and inviolable principle of the Church. For if Cain really represented a state of faith, which at this time had dissolved its brotherhood with charity, then it follows, as an irresistible consequence, that the strong prohibition of his death was intended to express the necessity for its preservation. The faith founded on truth was not to be destroyed. We have all along insisted that the faith of those people was of this character: it was preserved to them by instruction from their immediate predecessors who had enjoyed the intelligence of Eden. Their faith was founded on truth, and therefore it was to be preserved. The existence of Cain was to be maintained. The knowledge of spiritual truth and faith therein is of the utmost importance to the Church. It is a sacred and holy principle, and as such it must be preserved to men. Woe to those by whom it is destroyed! The reason is because faith in truth is a means to good; and, indeed, the proper source through which it is to be obtained. Before men can do good they must learn the laws of truth which teach it; before they can live in charity with all men, from a religious principle, they must have learned the law which says, "Thou shalt love thy neighbour as thyself." Faith precedes charity, as the means to an end. To erect the temple, we must first lay the foundation: we must know the way to

* Jas. ii. 20. † Gen. iv. 15.

virtue before we can walk in it; and this it is the office of faith to teach. Faith does not save, but it points out the way to that which does: it is this which constitutes its value and importance, and this is the end for which it was to be protected and preserved. "He that cometh to God must believe that he is, and that he is a rewarder of them that diligently seek him."* Thus faith in the Divine existence, protection, and truth, is an essential ingredient in the formation of the religious character. It is a valuable principle in God's Church, and required to be held in high esteem by men, because it is the appointed means to every good; and these are the reasons why it is said that Cain should not be slain.

Of course it was possible to effect this. God does not take away the liberty of men. Those who had destroyed charity were not deprived of the power to extinguish faith; but if they did so, vengeance sevenfold was to be taken on them: which plainly denotes that a full and complete punishment would result. Can we not see the *rationale* of this announcement? The punishment was not the arbitrary infliction of God, but he has revealed it as the necessary consequence of a certain extremity of wickedness on the part of man. Do we not perceive, that if men destroy the knowledges of faith, they thereby entirely separate themselves from truth, and consequently abandon both its illumination and guidance? What must be the condition of such persons? Do they not thereby fill up the measure of their iniquity? The man who destroys within himself the faith of truth, deprives himself of the means of learning what is good; and thus intelligence, as well as virtue, perishes. Truth and good are human principles, and men are more and more human as they receive and cherish them; but if they reject them, they slay the essential things of manhood, and thereby rush into the characteristics of a devil: and this is what is meant by the sevenfold vengeance that was to be taken of those who extinguished the truth of faith, and which would have been represented by the slaying of Cain. The Lord revealed the consequence, that men might eschew the cause. Here, again, we recognize the instructive character and moral bearing of this narrative. We see that it is founded on the very nature of

* Heb. xi. 6.

moral delinquency, and perceive the equity of the declaration, "If thou doest well, shalt thou not be accepted? and if thou doest not well, sin lieth at the door."*

To prevent this disastrous consequence, so far as it could be done without hindering the activity of human freedom, we are informed that "the Lord set a mark on Cain, lest any finding him should slay him." Of course this mark was intended to make him known, to testify who he was, and to operate as a preventive against any attempt at his destruction. What, then, was the nature of it? Those who contemplate the narrative in a literal sense merely, consider it to have been some physical distinction; but that idea we conceive there is every reasonable ground for rejecting. Such a mark could not have been necessary for pointing him out to those of whom the history informs us; they must have known him without it; and if there had been no other persons in the world, the safest way to avoid their revenge would have been to absent himself from the family. That opinion of the narrative plainly includes the idea of there being other persons who might have heard of his crime, but to whom he was not known; also, that his wandering or vagabond condition would bring him into contact with them, and that they were to be warned against offering violence to him. The fact of a larger community existing than the letter of the history expresses must be conceded. The setting of the mark might have deterred men from slaying him, if they had been informed that it was set with the view of preventing such a crime; still it may be asked whether it was not the most likely way to have called attention to his character, and thus to have rendered him a subject of general abhorrence. While, therefore, it may be said to have been the means for the preservation of his life, it must likewise be said to have been the cause of giving publicity to his crime, and so to have realized some of those distresses which he is considered to have apprehended. This point of view takes away that idea of mercy and forbearance which the affixing of the mark at first sight supposes; and other difficulties may be raised against the physical sense of it; on which, however, we need not dwell.

The many curious conjectures which have been seriously ex-

---

* Gen. iv. 7.

pressed as to what this mark was, will show the necessity for having recourse to a different view of the subject. Some have imagined that he was rendered *paralytic;* * and others have supposed that God impressed some *letter* upon Cain's forehead, taken either from the name of Abel or Jehovah.† Others say that it consisted of *three letters*, which composed the name of the sabbath; and a few assert that it was the sign of the *cross*. Some have thought that it consisted in a *wild aspect, with bloodshot eyes rolling in a horrid manner;* ‡ and others assert that it was the Hebrew letter *tau* marked on his forehead, and that it was to signify his contrition, because it is the first letter in the Hebrew word *teshubah*, which denotes repentance. There are those who have thought that it was *Abel's sheepdog*, given to him for a travelling companion; § and others have maintained that it was a *horn*, which grew out of his forehead.‖ It has been said that the mark was a circle of the sun rising upon him; ¶ also, that it meant that "a sword could not pierce him; fire could not burn him; water could not drown him; the air could not blast him; nor could thunder or lightning strike him."**

It is useless to increase these "curiosities of literature" on the subject, or to offer any comment. It is enough to say that

---

* This idea seems founded on the Septuagint Version, which has rendered what the English translation called a fugitive and vagabond, by words which signify groaning and trembling. We have remarked on this version of the original in a preceding note. See page 203.

† The Targum of Jonathan ben Uzziel.   ‡ See Bayle's Dict. Art. Cain.

§ Abravenel.   ‖ Rabbi Joseph.

¶ The author of Bereshith Rabba, a comment on Genesis.

** The author of an Arabic Catena, in the Bodleian library, cited by Dr. A. Clarke. See also Dr. Shuckford, on the general subject of Cain's mark. Dr. Thos. Brown's "Vulgar Errors" may also be consulted. Matthew Poole remarks, "What this visible token of the Divine displeasure was God hath not revealed to us, nor doth it concern us to know." Here the mark is called a mark of "Divine displeasure"; whereas the whole history of the circumstance shows it to have been the means of protection, and so of blessing! The writer says it does not concern us to know what it was! we do not believe there is anything mentioned in God's Word of which it does not deeply concern us to know the meaning, and which it is not our duty to endeavour to learn.

not one of these speculations has fastened itself upon the credibility of the Church; nor will any other that is founded on the idea of physical distinction be more successful. For a more prosperous issue in this inquiry, other ground must be taken.

The Hebrew word *oth*, which in our version is translated *a mark*, also signifies a *sign*, or *token*. The bow* was to be *leoth, for a sign*, or *token*, between the Lord and the earth; therefore the original, rendered, "And the Lord set a *mark* upon Cain," might have been translated, And the Lord appointed to Cain a *token* or a *sign*, by which he was to know that a special providence protected his life. Although this version may not be free from every objection, yet it sets the inquirer upon the right path: it contemplates the mark to have been of a mental or moral kind; and if we view the subject from this aspect, we shall be able to see both its utility and its nature.†

The setting a mark upon Cain is not the only instance of such a circumstance being mentioned in the Scriptures. The prophet was commanded to "go through the midst of the city, through the midst of Jerusalem, and set a mark upon the foreheads of the men that sigh and that cry for all the abominations that be done in the midst thereof."‡ Here the marking is not mentioned to express the idea of fixing any physical impression, but rather to notice the sorrowful condition of those who saw and lamented the wickedness of the people: the mark, therefore, by which they were distinguished, consisted in some spiritual love for propriety and goodness. This mark is said to have been in the forehead, because that, as the supreme part of the face, in which the affections are reflected, corresponds to love. This was the mark to which the Apostle pressed forward for the prize of the high calling of God in Christ Jesus.§ In the Revelation, we read that the locusts should hurt "only those men who have not the seal (mark) of God in their foreheads."‖

---

* Gen. ix. 13.

† Dr. Raphall translates the passage, "The Lord appointed a sign unto Cayin"; and remarks concerning it, that "commentators have exercised their skill and inventive faculties to discover the nature of this sign, but have offered nothing satisfactory on the subject."—"*The Sacred Scriptures in Hebrew and English.*"

‡ Ezek. ix. 4.   § Phil. iii. 14.   ‖ Rev. ix. 4.

Every one who is so disposed may see that the mark of God is the impress of some spiritual excellence, distinguishing the characters of those of whom it is predicated. The mark of the good is the meekness of their virtues; the mark of the intelligent is the strength of their knowledge: and these marks are the gifts of God. Here it is of importance to observe that the mark set upon Cain was the mark of the Lord. It is distinctly written that the Lord set a mark upon him. It was a mark, not to indicate a curse, but to distinguish for preservation. It is not said to have been affixed to any particular part of his person, because it was intended to characterize all the faith of which he was the representative. Those who destroy charity, mark themselves; those who cherish the knowledges of truth, retain thereby the mark of God. The mark of those who destroy charity is, in the Revelation, described as the mark of the beast.* When false principles of religion are imbibed, they impress upon man's character the moral scars and evidences of his defection. The mark which Cain set upon himself was indicated in the falling of his countenance, and in the kindling of his anger: it consisted in the impure state of his affections, arising from his having rejected the influences of good. The external mark of wicked men is a disorderly life; the internal mark is impurity of love. Outward vice is a sign of the decay of inward virtue. The conduct of men is a mark by which we distinguish one class from another. It is by this that we discriminate between the good and the bad. The Lord has told us, "By their fruits ye shall know them." Thus it is easy to understand the nature of the mark which Cain may have set upon himself, in consequence of the death which he had inflicted upon charity. But the mark which was set upon him by God was of another kind. This had reference to that characteristic of faith, of which we have seen he was the type. He, or, what is the same thing, the people under that name, knew the truths of religion, although they had discarded its virtues. This knowledge was of great value and importance, therefore it was to be regarded and preserved. It was the ground and pillar of faith; on this account it was to be esteemed as a sacred thing —the monitor of virtue, the directing staff to heaven. It is

---

* Rev. xvi. 2.

essential to the right development of every other principle of the Church. It is the lever which, when put in motion, is to lift men up to the land of blessedness. The knowledges of truth constituted the faith which was represented and maintained by the people called Cain; and although its existence was endangered by the destruction of charity, yet it was to be respected and preserved, because it was to be a means whereby the gifts of God might be communicated. That people knew that what they believed was a reality. They saw the evidence, and understood that it was true. Their faith did not consist in believing certain propositions because some persons in authority had taught them, or because they had become mere dogmata in the Church; but they believed the propositions of religious truth, because they fell within the grasp of their understandings. They comprehended what they believed, either on the testimony of facts or by the light of perception. Their faith was founded on truth, clearly and definitely seen to be such; and this is the mark by which God has mercifully distinguished it. The internal consciousness and intellectual certainty that the subjects of faith are true, constitute the mark by which faith was to be known in after ages. It is given by God, that men may know it, and that, by knowing it, they may be led to respect it, and so be preserved from the danger which must follow its destruction. Men were to know that their faith was truth, through an understanding of its subjects. This was to be the mark for distinguishing between truth and error; and if we do not recognize it in our belief about spiritual things, then we are without the evidence by which it has been marked by God himself. He wishes men to understand what they believe: he desires that their knowledge should be correct; and hence he has caused it to be written, that "they who worship him must worship him in spirit and in truth."*

The religious things which were known to Cain were the results of an internal perception peculiar to the most ancient Church, answering the same use with them as the revelation, which has been subsequently vouchsafed, does with us; and those knowledges were retained, though their virtues had been neglected.

* John iv. 24.

In order that man may now know what Divine truth is upon religious subjects, the Lord has mercifully provided him his holy Word, and endowed him with the ability for comprehending it. The Word and the human understanding are both God's good gifts, and therefore they cannot be designed to repel each other: if in any case they are found to do so, we may rest assured either that the understanding has been corrupted, or that the meaning of the Word has been perverted. The Word is given for man rationally and intellectually to understand its teachings: the faith which is thus perceived is the faith of truth, and this is the characteristic which God has set upon it, and which he is wishful to preserve: every one, therefore, may see that to destroy it with such a mark of its origin, utility, and importance, must needs be followed by that calamity which is described as sevenfold vengeance.

These considerations lead us into a more intimate acquaintance with the nature of faith as a means to goodness; they show us that the constitution of faith is truth, marked and characterized as such by God himself. If we see this mark upon any religious doctrine which is propounded for the acceptance of mankind, we should be careful that we do not slay it. To do so is to peril the safety and satisfaction of our intellect. Whenever God permits us to see a religious truth, he designs that we should preserve and cherish it. Such a sight is an act of his particular providence, intended for our especial good. Let us, then, endeavour to bring this subject home to our business and our bosoms. Does the reader see that these interpretations of the Word bear upon them the impress of truth? Do these views of the narrative affect him as being reasonable in themselves, in agreement with the teachings of the Word, the purposes of God, and the means to virtue? If so, it is the mark intended to distinguish them for his respect and preservation. This is the only mark of faith which can be given, and what other would a rational man desire? To extinguish it after the recognition of the evidence of its existence, is to destroy the dictate of man's rational nature, and evince the most criminal indifference concerning the particular providences of God!

CHAPTER XVII.

THE LAND OF NOD.—CAIN'S SON.—THE BUILDING OF A CITY, AND CALLING IT AFTER THE NAME OF HIS SON ENOCH.

"The Hebrew narrative is more than human in its origin, and consequently true in every substantial part of it, though possibly expressed in figurative language; as many learned and pious men have believed, and as the most pious may believe without injury; and perhaps with advantage to the cause of revealed religion."— SIR W. JONES' *Works*, p. 137.

Moses concludes his account of Cain in these words: "And Cain went out from the presence of the Lord, and dwelt in the land of Nod, on the east of Eden. And Cain knew his wife; and she conceived, and bare Enoch: and he builded a city, and called the name of the city, after the name of his son, Enoch."* The circumstances mentioned in these statements have not engaged so much critical attention as some other parts of the Antediluvian history which have been considered. They are, however, not the less interesting on that account. We shall find that they describe important events in the moral history of a declining Church. The histories in the Bible are the special histories of the human mind, written under the superintendence of a particular providence, and designed to reveal some of its most remarkable activities and developments. Though they appear to have respect to particular times, and to relate for the most part to a privileged people, yet in reality they belong to all periods, and are adapted for the instruction of all men. There is nothing obsolete in the Bible. Its truths are always fresh and powerful. Its histories, the rites and ceremonies which it commands, together with the idolatries and transgressions which it denounces, are such as may be realized over and over again in the states of the affections and thoughts of men. This is the reason why the Lord has said that his "words are spirit and life"; they relate to the inner sensations and living principles

* Gen. iv. 16, 17.

of men: these have contributed to the outer histories of the Word. The visible aspect of a society or of a nation is derived from the principles, opinions, and feelings of the people: and *men*, who write these histories, describe chiefly their visible events and consequences; but God, who has superintended the production of the written histories of his Word, has caused them to be so constructed that they might also represent the spiritual motives in which such effects originate. The histories of men regard outer things; the histories of God refer to inner things, and to the things which are without, only as the means for representing those within: the former relate mostly to the natural, the latter principally to the mental world.

The good which may be implanted in human nature will ever present the same general phase to the world, allowing only for that peculiar distinctiveness which it must acquire by coming in contact with our idiosyncrasies. The evil which men may cherish will always exhibit the like distorted features to society, more or less modified in their enormity by the personal fears or darings of the individual. Men of love are amiable and benevolent; men of hate are severe and wicked. The Bible is designed to encourage the former, to warn the latter, and thus to treat of both conditions under their respective varieties. Observe it treats of them not so much in respect to their outward position as to their inward condition. The Word always has been, and always will be, a powerful exhibition of the state of the Church with men under all possible circumstances. It is thus a revelation informing us of the extent of the Divine presence and its blessings, together with the nature of the apparent Divine absence and its consequences. The exposition of the subjects which belong to this chapter will, in some measure, serve as additional confirmations of these views of the holy Word. We do not, however, regard this Mosaic description in the light of merely external history; we receive it only as a portion of that grand allegory under which the Antediluvian period is represented.

Every one must see that the description of Cain's going out from the presence of the Lord is purely figurative; no one can be separated from the Omnipresent in any real sense; for the Psalmist has said, "Whither shall I go from thy spirit? or whither shall I flee from thy presence? If I ascend into heaven, thou *art* there: if I make my bed in hell, behold, thou *art there*. If I take the wings of the morning, *and* dwell in the uttermost parts of the sea; even there shall thy hand lead me, and thy right hand shall hold me.—Yea, darkness hideth not from thee; but the night shineth as the day: the darkness and the light *are* both alike *to thee*."*

It has been considered, from the above statement concerning Cain, that the Lord had a special presence with Adam and his immediate posterity, somewhat resembling what the Rabbins have expressed by the term Shekinah.† The circumstance of Adam and his wife having directly after their fall "hid themselves from the presence of the Lord amongst the trees of the garden,"‡ is thought to be the expression of that idea. This, however, cannot be well supported. The Church, indeed, is the special dwelling-place of the Almighty; that is to say, it is there where his presence is more distinctly recognized: hence He may be said to have had such a presence with Adam as has not been experienced by any other people. In this sense he has also had a presence with the Jews unlike that which existed with the Gentiles, and likewise with Christians different from that which has prevailed with those who are not so. Under this aspect we at once see, that to go out from the Divine presence must denote the cessation in man of those sentiments by which alone the Lord can be perceived; and this furnishes us with a rational interpretation of Cain's going out from the presence of the Lord.

It is, however, to be observed that the original does not really speak of the *presence*, but of the *face* of the Lord: it was from the *face* of the Lord that he went out; and consequently it was the fulfilment of his own declaration unto the Lord, "From thy face shall I be hid."§ The Scriptures do frequently speak of the Lord's presence, and also of his face; but each term is in-

---

* Psa cxxxix. 7-12.

† By the Shekinah is understood the visible symbol of the Divine presence, which rested over the propitiatory in the shape of a cloud, and from which God gave forth his oracles when consulted by the high priest.

‡ Gen. iii. 8. § Gen. iv. 14.

tended to set forth its own idea. The Lord's *presence* is perceived by means of *truth*, but His *face* is known only by means of *love*. Now Cain yet retained many knowledges of the divine truth, and consequently he could not yet have actually departed from the Lord's *presence;* but he had relinquished the sentiments of Divine love, and therefore he really did go out from the Divine face.

The face of man indicates every emotion of the human heart: he may prevent his thoughts from appearing in his conversation; but the most consummate dissimulation cannot prevent his face from disclosing any real and earnest affection he may possess. Offend modesty, and it will blush; accuse the guilty, and they become pale. Thus love and anger, fear and hatred, joy and sadness,—in short, every passion which may seize the heart, will be seen to impress itself, with more or less distinctness, upon the face. Hence the face of the Lord is mentioned to represent His love; that is, His essential and never-varying character. "God is love." Those who are in faith observe His presence; but those who are in love perceive His face. Those who give up that love, as we have seen was the case with Cain, necessarily depart from that face, and in consequence of this they dwelt in the land of Nod, on the east of Eden.

What, then, is the land of Nod? Was it a geographical locality? Of course the people were inhabiting a specific country; but it is a change of their state rather than a change of their dwelling which is the subject treated of. Nod literally means, the land of exile, a vagabond: spiritually it means the destitution of goodness and truth—as we shall presently see. The Septuagint and Josephus call it *Naid*, and they seem to have regarded it as a place. But where was Naid? An altered reading of the Hebrew term offers no explanation; and no one knows anything more about the one than the other. Regarded as a place, it could not have received the name *Nod* until after Cain had entered it; because by that term, as just observed, is meant a vagabond; it is the untranslated Hebrew word for that idea; and we can hardly conceive that society had as yet set apart any particular land for the special residence of its vagabonds. There are no grounds for supposing that jurisprudence had then so far advanced as to have provided a land for the transportation of criminals. Surely there was no penal settlement in those early times at all answering to the "Hulks" or the "Botany Bay" of modern history. Why, then, is it said that there was a land whose name was significant of this idea? St. Jerome and the Chaldee interpreters are said * to have taken a view of this subject by which this inquiry is in some measure met. They thought that Nod ought to be understood only as the appellation of Cain; and that his being said to dwell in the land of Nod merely meant that he dwelt in the land a vagabond. This indeed removes part of the difficulty contemplated; nor do we see that it is any essential departure from the Hebrew text: still it explains no more of the circumstances in which Cain stood after he went out from the face of the Lord, than is included in the fact of his having been declared a vagabond before that departure took place; and surely something more was intended to be conveyed by the statement.

But it is useless criticism to endeavour to attach a geographical idea to a name that is plainly the appellation of a state which had overtaken the faith of a degenerate people. Those denoted by Cain having become vagabond in respect to the sentiments of faith, are said to have dwelt in the land of Nod, in order to describe that they had lost all *settled convictions* about what is good and true, and that they were living in a state of exile from them, and uncertainty concerning them. Those who fall into doubts about the truths of faith are obviously in a wandering condition respecting them; and so long as they are in such a state, they dwell in that which the land of Nod was intended to express. When good goes out from the mind, doubt enters into it; and therefore the things of faith come to be regarded as objects of speculation merely; and however true those things may have been in their beginnings, they are soon unsettled by the evils of life which follow the rejection of charity, and a turning away from the Divine face. Men cannot long retain a belief in truth, after they have extinguished the love of goodness. Their notions about religion and spiritual things are continually wandering. The faith of the disobedient is necessarily changing. Transgression is sure to produce doubt. Evil doers are driven about by every wind of doctrine; and

* Rev. J. Wood's "Dictionary of the Bible," Art. Nod.

whenever they fall into disgrace and danger, will embrace any ideas which may promise them relief from suffering, or protection from calamity. They will be found more attentive to the promises of security than to the means of attaining it. Their minds are occupied about relief and deliverance as an end, rather than about the necessary means by which they are to come. This fact has thousands of proofs, both in the lives and deaths of the wicked. The sinking man grasps at straws; but they do not save him. So the faith which has extinguished charity is a weak, unsteady thing: it leaves the heart open to the sallies of every lust; and hence the bonds of truth are broken: whereupon men pass from the face of the Lord, and dwell in the land of Nod,—that is, they live in a state of mind which is vagabond and fugitive in respect to all good things.

In this light the statements come home to our experience. In disclosing the moral condition of Cain, they are also a revelation and a warning to all men. They show us consequences which must result to our faith, whenever we disregard the life of charity and avert ourselves from the face of God. Nod has not a place in this world's geography, and hence men have never found it there, but it is a state in the mind's degeneracy which multitudes have discovered: and it is said to have been *towards the east of Eden*, to signify that the state now treated of had respect to the understanding. The east is the Lord, and Eden is love;* consequently, the east of Eden is the Lord regarded as the supreme object of love. But this love was departed from Cain, and another sentiment had usurped its place. Still it was provided that the understanding, wherein the principles of faith resided, should, notwithstanding their fugitive condition, be preserved in the capacity for knowing truth and goodness, and so be *toward* the east of Eden. The understanding, amidst all its embarrassments, has had preserved to it this capacity; and, although it may be driven about by every wind of doctrine, this capacity will keep it in that direction. How many persons have lived for a considerable period in states of fluctuation and uncertainty about the things of spiritual truth, and so, in the land of Nod! and how many have had their

---

* See p. 74.

faith rescued from that condition, and been made regenerate! thus proving its position to have been *towards the east of Eden*. How satisfactorily, then, does experience illustrate the statement!

Now it is that we are first informed of the wife of Cain. Before this there is no mention of any other woman being in the world but Eve; although it is plain, from the series of things contemplated, that others must have existed. The reason, however, why they are not noticed, is because they were not required for the representative purpose of the narration. Nor is Cain's wife now mentioned with the view of recording the existence of a woman, but to signify that the people called Cain were distinguished by an affection in correspondence with the state of their faith, and he is said to have known her, to express the conjunction and confirmations which now took place between the fallacies of the understanding and the affections of the will. The faith of the understanding is as a man, and the corresponding affection of the will is as his wife. Cain now rendered conspicuous his affection for the heresy into which he had fallen, and this is called his wife. That term is well known to express one of the tenderest attachments of humanity, and, as such, it is sometimes employed in the Scriptures to denote, in a spiritual sense, the affections of those of whom it is predicated. Affection is the very nature of woman, and, therefore, it is easy to see the propriety of selecting her to be its living symbol. It is on this account that the Scriptures invariably represent the Church by a woman,—the true Church under those terms which express her most amiable condition, such as a virgin, a bride, a wife, and mother; but the false Church under those names which denote the abandoned portion of the sex, such as an adulteress and a harlot. The people of the true Church have an affection for God and their neighbour; the people of the perverted Church have an affection for themselves and the world, so that their affections are conjoined to their opinions: they are united, as it were, in the bonds of a spiritual marriage; and hence has originated the popular remark that certain persons who are strongly attached to their opinions are wedded to them. Such had now become the case with the people called Cain. The false persuasions into which they had fallen had united themselves to a corresponding affection, and the result was, the conception and birth of a new heresy, called Enoch.*

Cain, as it has been seen, were a people with whom arose the first heresy in the Adamic Church; and they, in process of time, having added to their number, separated from their original parents, and constituted a sect. They also, in their turn, became the parents of other schisms, of which Enoch was the first. Heresies are communicated from mind to mind; and at last they are found to acquire some definite form, through the open espousal of them by the people. Wherever one exists, it is sure, in the process of time, to beget another; and these are spoken of in the antediluvian history under the form of a genealogy of sons and daughters; of sons, in reference to the birth of persuasions and opinions; and of daughters, in respect to the manifestation of affections and delights.

Heresies are productive things. Like weeds, they grow apace. No ordinary vigilance can hinder their propagation. The reason is, because falsehood is congenial to a corrupted heart. He who tells a falsehood will give utterance to many more, to maintain consistency for the first, and each assertion will require a similar process: how prolific is a lie! It is upon these general grounds that we find the birth of Enoch is described to have been succeeded by other births descending from him. Thus, "Unto Enoch was born Irad: and Irad begat Mehujael: and Mehujael begat Methusael: and Methusael begat Lamech," &c.† There is no consistency in error. It has none of the elements of unity; it has no steadiness of purpose; it is a vagabond principle, aiming at division; and whenever it once obtains admission into the Church, it will be found to spread itself in various forms, and separate the people into different communities. The several names which immediately follow those of Enoch, and who are all stated to have descended from Cain, were intended to express the several heresies by which the Church at that time was torn and broken up, until at last *faith*

---

* The Rev. J. Hewlett says "that there were an ancient people, called by Pliny, Heniochii; by Mela, Eniochi; and by Lucan, Enochii; some of whom lived so far eastward, that Sir Walter Raleigh fancies they might have been the posterity of this people!!" How were they saved from the flood?

† Gen. iv. 18.

perished at the hands of *Lamech*, as *charity* had previously done by the hands of *Cain*. By the name Lamech is denoted what is poor and stricken: and, considered as the designation of an heretical sect, it signifies what is low and base; consequently, a condition of the Church in which *vastation** was experienced: hence he is represented to have said, "I have slain a man to my wounding, and a young man to my hurt. If Cain shall be avenged sevenfold, truly Lamech seventy and sevenfold."†

* A church *vastated* is such that it knows what is true, but is not disposed either to understand or to love it.

† Gen. iv. 23, 24. The literal sense of this speech of Lamech, introduced as it is with so much abruptness, has always been considered a very difficult point in this history. Most commentators think that it is vain to conjecture what was the particular occasion which gave rise to it. Considerable ingenuity, and some straining of the original text, have been resorted to, in order to make it indicate some intelligible story. Thus, Hobigant, whose view is countenanced by Dr. Lowth, translates the first part of the verse, "I being wounded have slain a man;" and so considers the speech to be an apology for committing homicide in his own defence. The words *Le-petzangi* and *Le-chaburathi*, to my wound, and to my hurt, are paraphrased to mean, because of the wound, and because of the hurt which I received. Our version, in the second part of the verse, speaks of his having slain a young man, but the original of that denotes a child. It is difficult to see how such a one could inflict or threaten an injury, which demanded such a vengeance. Others, supposing the circumstance spoken of to have been very close upon the invention of *edged tools* by Tubal cain, have concluded that Lamech had become blind, and using one of these tools, in ignorance of its power, committed homicide on one of his sons, and that his address was to claim the forbearance of his wives! These, with other criticisms which could be produced, have hindered the generality of scholars from adopting the above view of the subject. Dr. Shuckford resists it with an opposite opinion. He thought that the family of Cain were fearful lest other branches of the descendants of Adam should avenge on them the murder committed by their ancestor. He conceived Adah and Zillah to have been specially haunted by this fear in respect to Lamech, their husband, and that he made the speech to them to show that their fears were groundless:—that, as God has pronounced a sevenfold vengeance on any who should slay Cain, who had been really guilty, He would certainly inflict a much greater punishment on any who should injure them, who were entirely innocent of Cain's enormity; and that, therefore, there were no grounds for any such alarm as is supposed to have existed, and to have originated the speech. Hence the Doctor read it interrogatively, "Have I slain a man to my wounding, or a young man to my hurt?" and this he paraphrases to mean, "I have not killed a man that I should be wounded, nor a young man that I should be hurt." Thus, two

Every one, who is so disposed, may perceive the similarity between the two cases of Cain and Lamech. Both are contemplated to have done violence to human life. Cain's act, as we have frequently observed, denotes his destruction of charity; but Lamech's signifies his destruction of *faith*, and also of the good that had been associated with it; for he not only slew a man to his wounding, but likewise a young man to his hurt. He perpetrated a double homicide; the former brought desolation on the things of faith, and so inflicted *a wound* upon his understanding; the latter induced desolation on the things of good, and so produced *a hurt* upon his will, which circumstances resulted in the complete devastation of the Church. Thus, they not only suffered the sevenfold vengeance, which it was predicted should come upon those who slew Cain, but also the utter rejection and condemnation implied in the seventy and sevenfold.

We need not go farther into those details: it is a clear fact, that faith must perish when there is no charity to cherish and uphold its use. How can the evil long believe? They have no proper motive, either to extend or to preserve the knowledge of truth about spiritual things: such truths will exhibit to them their own moral deformity, and, therefore, they shun them to avoid a discovery of the hideousness of their own characters. With such, one truth of religion perishes after another; at last they all drop out of the mind, and faith becomes extinct. Experience proves this to be true of individuals; and reason

dignitaries in the same Church furnish two essentially different interpretations of the same text; both, however, are compelled to add to, and paraphrase, the sense expressed in the original, in order to make it harmonize with their respective opinions. Others have thought that Lamech was apprehensive of danger for having two wives, which being the first recorded instance of polygamy, may also have been the first case that had occurred, and that, by his having thus violated the institution of marriage, he had incurred the resentment of his kindred, and, consequently, that his speech is the announcement of his having retaliated their insults! However these things might have been, we do not think there is any good reason for supposing them to have been contemplated in the narrative before us. The sense of the original is very fairly given in the authorized version of it, and it is constructed with the view of setting forth the spiritual ideas indicated above, rather than to record any such natural occurrences as these views seem to express.

shows that it is equally correct in respect to communities, whenever heresies obtain admission among them: they lead to divisions, and to the destruction of fraternity. When men extinguish charity, the uniting principle is gone, and, however true might have been the propositions of faith in the beginning of the disruption, they are sure to be attenuated and corrupted by the self-derived intelligence of men, and so will perish. The genuine truths of faith cannot be maintained among any people who have renounced the life of charity. They have no congenial state into which such principles can flow and live. In such cases men cease to view truth through the soft and subduing influences of love: they originate notions and opinions of their own, and so prefer their own thinking to God's teaching. This state of things becomes more and more enormous, until faith itself perishes amidst the general corruption. This was the condition of the Church among that branch of the antediluvian heresies called Lamech. It was the condition of all the Churches of which the Scriptures speak as having come to an end. The Jewish Church perished, because the people had no true faith in the Word of God, but instead thereof substituted the traditions of the elders. It was, in consequence of its impurities and selfishness, broken up into sects, of which the Pharisees and Sadducees were the most conspicuous. The Essenes * and Herodians were others of inferior importance; all, however, partaking of the same common depravity: they had no faith in the teachings and predictions of the Divine Scriptures; they had perverted the meaning of the prophecies, which declared the nature, manner, and objects of the Messiah's coming, and hence they slew him when he came. The like destitution of faith is to be a characteristic with the people of the Church at the period of the Lord's second coming; wherefore he inquired, "When the Son of man cometh, shall he find faith on the earth?" † It is easy, then, to see how it was that faith perished in the posterity of Cain, by whom charity had been first extinguished.

* The name of this sect does not occur in the Scriptures, but their manners, rites, and doctrines are described by Josephus. *Antiq.* xiii. v. 9, and xviii. i. 5.

† Luke xviii. 8.

The people originated notions of religion which had no higher authority than their own speculations, and which were set up for the gratification of themselves and the adoption of others. Those others did not long see them in the same light, and therefore they produced new ones themselves; so that "Cain begat Enoch, and Enoch begat Irad, and Irad begat Mehujael, and Mehujael begat Methusael, and Methusael begat Lamech." Similar genealogical successions of heresies could easily be pointed out as having taken place during the history of the Christian Church; but on these we cannot enter now. The people of those ancient times divided to rule; and acting upon this maxim of the father of lies led to the begetting of Lamech, with whom the principle of faith and all the little remaining love of goodness perished; wherefore he is declared to have slain a man to his wounding, and a young man [*i. e.*, in Hebrew, a child] to his hurt.

How terrible are the consequences of heresies in the Church! How injurious are they to the common weal of man! What hindrances do they oppose to human progress! How successfully do they weaken and break up all the ties of spiritual affection! What fallacies have they forged to restrain the freedom of human thought! The vain imaginations of perverted minds, having let loose the activities of a corrupted heart upon society, brought in disaster and dismay upon the Church. From these considerations we learn that Enoch was the first heresy which Cain begat. Of the nature of it we are not informed: the narrative merely states that he was born and begat Irad, and then we read no more about him. He was not the Enoch who is described to have walked with God, and who the Apostle tells us was translated that he should not see death.*
This Enoch was not a descendant of Cain at all: he was the offspring of Jared from the line of Seth, who is spoken of as Adam's third son. This race was altogether of another quality to that of Cain. There was also a Lamech from the same race.†
It is requisite to notice these circumstances, in order to prevent a confusion which might otherwise take place from the identity of the names. Schismatic churches possess the true names of things that have to be believed; but then they attach false

---

* Gen. v. 22; Heb. xi. 5. † Gen. v. 25.

notions to them. The thing is not to be judged of merely by the name: the name must be examined and explained to be understood. There are certain sections in the Christian Church, which retain common names for the doctrines they profess, yet they believe very differently concerning them. Thus the Godhead, atonement, mediation, faith, and some others, are general names received by all; but men differ very widely in the ideas which are attached to them: so that false ideas in the Church are expressed by the same names as those that are true: therefore we need not be surprised at finding that there was an Enoch who was a heretic, as well as an Enoch who walked with God. Concerning this latter Enoch we shall have occasion to speak again.

These remarks bring us to consider what is meant by the circumstance of Cain building a city, and calling it after the name of his son.* That a community influenced by certain prejudices and opinions should separate themselves from their brethren, and emigrate to some other locality, with the view of building a town for their future residence, may be easily conceived. Modern history furnishes examples of a similar character. Nevertheless we do not conceive this to have been meant by the narrative before us: a fact of this nature may have suggested the employment of such a history as the suitable basis for denoting some spiritual circumstance, without intending thereby to express what appears upon the letter. But without dwelling upon this point, it is plain, from the series of things treated of, that by the city which Cain is said to have built, is to be understood the preparation of something for the mind to dwell in, rather than erections for the residence of the body.

By a city, in a spiritual sense, is meant the doctrinal views of religion which are entertained by the persons of whom it is pre-

* It is curious to observe the oversights into which commentators are sometimes led. Ptolemy is said to mention a city *Anuchtha*, in Susiana, or Khuzestan, a country lying eastward from Chaldea; this the learned Huet believed to be the same city, under a Chaldean name, as Hanakh or Enoch, built by Cain. See "*Univ. Hist.*," vol i., p. 151. But surely it must occur to the most superficial thinker to inquire, how a city built before the flood should have remained after it, if all things perished in that catastrophe, with the exception of Noah and his family, as was believed by Huet, and the writers of the "Universal History"?

dicated. Men live in their opinions: they are, as it were, the houses in which their affections dwell, and a number of opinions constitutes a spiritual city: "a city of holiness," if the opinions be doctrinally true, but "a city of destruction," if they be heretical and false. Men who believe what is true, and live therein, are contemplated as dwelling in the "city of God." Solomon wrote, that "the rich man's wealth is his strong city,"* because a rich man is one who knows truth; and this spiritual wealth is a strong city. The cities of refuge† appointed under the Mosaic dispensation, for the protection of those who unintentionally did injury to another, represented the doctrinal truths of religion to which those are to flee, who, through ignorance, may have done some harm to society. Such truths both teach and protect those who adopt them with a view to life and safety. The cities of Judah so frequently mentioned in the Word, and others, considered to have been the cities of Israel, likewise represented the doctrinal truths of the Church: the former, those truths which relate to our duty to God; and the latter, those which treat of our duty to man. The "city of habitation"‡ signifies the doctrines of the Church, which teach men the way to live for heaven; "the cities without inhabitants"§ denote doctrinal truths without their corresponding goodness.

Cities naturally are such by virtue of the people who inhabit them, and thence they are found to possess certain characteristics of their own. Every one may be acquainted with this fact who knows how to observe men and things. How frequently do we hear those residences of men spoken of under some cognomen intended to express their general feature! Some are said to be *commercial*, some *manufacturing*, some *low*, some *proud*, some *ignorant*, some *learned*, some *industrious*, some *idle*. In short, the idiosyncrasies of cities differ as much as the individualities of men: they acquire a distinctiveness from the principles which influence them: for a city is, as it were, a man, a larger man than the individual, nevertheless a man as to all his moral activities and intellectual operations; so that a city, as a collection of men, actually exhibits the doctrinal

---

* Prov. x. 15 † Numb. xxxv. 6–12.
‡ Psa. cvii. 7. § Isa. vi. 11.

views and sentiments which may have contributed to the production of the cognomen by which it is known. This may serve to illustrate the circumstance of cities being mentioned in the Scriptures to represent the doctrinal opinions of the people of whom they are predicated; and why, also, certain appellations are sometimes applied to them. Jerusalem is said to be "builded as a city that is compact together," * to express the unity and solidity of those doctrinal truths of the Church of which it is the type: hence also it is called the "heavenly Jerusalem," † and described as the holy city coming down from God out of heaven. ‡ It is not a natural city of men and houses which is to come down, but a disclosure of the doctrinal truths of the Word: these come down from heaven to guide men thither: and the Lord said, "A city that is set on a hill cannot be hid," § to teach us that the doctrines of truth, when grounded on the elevated principles of love, will always be conspicuous for their brightness and their beauty.

Thus it is plain that by a city is denoted doctrinal things. Let us then apply this signification to that which Cain is said to have built. It will at once occur to the reflecting, when they remember the series of spiritual things treated of, that this circumstance was intended to represent the people collecting together the various materials on which they had grounded their heretical opinions, and thereupon arranging and constructing them into a doctrinal form for their future use. This idea may be illustrated by many circumstances which have taken place in the Christian Church. This has been broken up into numerous sects, some of which have stood in the relation of parents to others. It was predicted that one would be "the mother of harlots." || The state of the people during the decline of all Churches is pretty much the same: they corrupt the truth and build other sentiments, which they attempt to fortify by inventions of their own. For example, let us take the doctrines of Predestination and Grace.¶ Whatever truths might

---

* Psa. cxxii. 3.   † Heb. xii. 22.   ‡ Rev. xxi. 2.
§ Matt. v. 14. || Rev. xvii. 5.

¶ The correct idea of *Predestination* is, that God "created every one for His glory," Isa. xliii. 7; that is, for the enjoyment of His blessings, so far as they comply with the means placed within their power. *Grace* is the Divine mercy which saves mankind according to appointed means.

have been originally expressed by those terms, it is quite evident that, in the process of time, they became entirely perverted, and that errors were substituted for them. A controversy concerning them was begun in the ninth century (they had then existed about four hundred years) by the Saxon, Godoschalchus, and it was continued with more or less severity for a period of seven hundred years. During all this time the people were wandering in their faith concerning these things. They had no settled convictions upon the subjects which those terms were intended to express; but in the sixteenth century a new champion arose, who, with the materials of this controversy, constructed as it were a new city, which has not been called after the name of those who founded it, but after *Calvin*, their son in the faith.* The case of Cain building a city, and calling its name Enoch, was something similar to this.

It will be recollected that those people had become fugitive and vagabond in reference to the things of faith. Their notions about spiritual and holy things had no coherence with each other, because they had departed from the face of the Lord, from whom alone all excellence and consistency descend; and therefore they are described to have dwelt in the land of Nod, which is a state of wandering and uncertainty about the principles of faith. Now, to secure the credibility and adherence of the people, it became requisite to re-examine the sentiments which had led to the production of such unsteadiness of life and opinions; to cast away all those notions which had fastened themselves as excrescences upon their general principles; and so to re-arrange and construct the whole of their doctrinal views of religion, that they might appear as a new and more compact city. Thus the description of Cain building a city and calling it Enoch, *i. e.*, *instruction*, was intended to represent those who held the heresy of Cain, striving to render it attractive. In our own day we speak of attractive speculations as "castle building." Surely, then, we need not wonder at its being said, by those among whom figurative language was so prevalent, that the construction or arrangement of certain doctrinal views of religion was the *building of a city*. We speak also of *building* up an opinion, and of *fortifying* our sentiments; and to describe

---

* See Mosheim, cent. v., sec. 23; cent. ix., sec. 22; cent. xvi., sec. 13.

the confidence of some men in the notions they entertain, it is sometimes said of them, that it is the city in which they dwell.

When, therefore, we see that by Enoch, as the descendant of Cain, was denoted the origination of a new heresy, it is easy to perceive, from these reasonings, facts, and illustrations, that the building of a city, and calling it Enoch,—instruction,—were intended to represent the erection and building, in an attractive form, of certain doctrinal notions of religious things for the reception and faith of that people. The teachers of truth are the builders of the city of God; they, by the divine assistance, erect the walls of Jerusalem, and cause her to be a praise in the earth; whereas the teachers of error are the builders of the city of destruction—the architects of the synagogue of Satan.

These circumstances, together with the errors which afterwards arose from that of Enoch, and especially the extinction of all faith in spiritual things produced by the heresy of Lamech, terminate this branch of Antediluvian History. We read no more of Cain: nothing further of his life; no record of his death is preserved. The whole narrative concerning him concludes towards the end of the fourth chapter, because, as we have seen, the things of the Church were ended with his fifth descendant, Lamech.

CHAPTER XVIII.

THE BIRTH OF SETH—THE LONGEVITY OF HIS DESCENDANTS— AND THE "TRANSLATION" OF ENOCH.

> "The notion of a man's living to the age of 600 or 1,000 years was Egyptian.— How is this reconcilable with their precise knowledge of a solar year, and with their fixing the age of men, one with another, to the term of 28 years?—This has suggested a supposition, that by 600 or 1,000 years in question, they meant the duration of a *tribe* or *dynasty*, distinguished by the name of its founder."— WEBB'S "*Panto.*," p. 275.

On the cessation of that division of the most ancient Church called Cain, we are informed that "Adam knew his wife again; and she bare a son, and called his name Seth: For God, *said she*, hath appointed me another seed instead of Abel, whom Cain slew."* Now as Abel represented the principle of charity, which had been regarded by an earlier people of the most ancient Church to be the chief thing of religion, and as Seth was appointed as *seed* in his place, we reach the fact at once, that Seth represented a principle of faith out of which charity was to be developed; and consequently that it was given by God for the adoption of another branch of the Adamic descendants. This seems evident from the circumstance of its being said of his posterity, that they began to call upon the name of the Lord;† that is, to worship Him from a principle of love and charity. The state of charity which now began to be cultivated does not appear to have been precisely of the same exalted quality as that which prevailed with Abel, because, in its communication, it passed through another medium. With Abel charity entered into the affections by a more internal way than with the posterity of Seth. With the former it arose out of an impulsive love which is an internal principle; but with the latter it sprung up from an intellectual dictate, which respectively was an external principle. But this merciful provision

* Gen. iv. 25. † Gen. iv. 26.

for the development and security of charity did not continue in its integrity, for we are immediately informed of successive descendants, each of whom is intended to express some change which the perceptions of truth in respect to charity were undergoing among them, until they finally perished among a people called Lamech. The people with whom that faith perished, which had its commencement with Seth, bore the same name as those with whom ended the faith which had begun with Cain. They were distinct races, but are called by the same names, because they represented principles of a similar character, with like results. From these considerations it is plain that, in the times now treated of, there were a great variety of doctrines and sects that separated from the Adamic Church, each of which was distinguished by its appropriate appellation; and that, owing to the peculiar genius of the people, their sentiments and heresies must have been exceedingly subtle, fascinating, and dangerous, much more so than any which have existed in after times; and hence it is that the people professing them are described to have perished in so calamitous a manner.

Now as Seth was significant of a new faith, and consequently represented the people to whom it was given, and by whom it was embraced, it will follow that all who are described to have descended from him in the genealogical series, are the appropriate names of so many distinct branches and separations from the faith so called. This circumstance at once suggests an idea which will assist in explaining in some measure what is meant by the extraordinary ages of those who are usually called the Antediluvian Patriarchs. That the ages of mankind in those times were not so great,—some of them amounting to many hundreds of years; Jared and Methuselah to nearly a thousand,—may appear obvious to those who will venture out of that track of thinking on this subject which so commonly prevails.

Antediluvian longevity is one of those subjects which has been felt to be full of difficulties in most ages of the Church, whether Jewish or Christian. Josephus abides by the letter, and cites several authors of Egyptian, Chaldean, and Phœnician

history, to show "that the ancients lived a thousand years."*
They, however, prove no such thing. It is not certain that those writers allude to the ages of individual men. He does not produce their evidence, and it is highly probable that they refer either to some poetical idea or to dynastic existence.

Christian commentators, notwithstanding considerable ingenuity has been displayed upon this inquiry, have not been able to offer any explanation of the subject. Some, indeed, with the view of reducing the duration of human life down to the standard which general history assures us was its common extent, have thought that lunar years are meant.† But this suggestion, though it might be supposed to remove some of the embarrassments, is found to create others equally difficult. It would make the whole period from Adam to Noah only about one hundred and forty solar years, and many of these Antediluvians must have been parents in their infancy. According to this method of calculation, Enoch would have been exactly five years old when he became the father of Methuselah. It is plain, therefore, that this view of the case does not offer the right solution. Men feel, that to believe in such extraordinary ages is a large draft upon their credibility; still they try to persuade themselves into the idea. Some say that vegetable food,‡ and the purity of the atmosphere in those early times of the world, contributed to this happy result. We can easily

---

* Josephus, "Antiquities of the Jews," book 1, chap. iii. 9.

† Plutarch observes, that "the Egyptians introduce an infinite number of years into their genealogies, because they reckon months for years." Another author (when making this extract, we omitted to transcribe his name) says that "they reckoned the years by the inundations of the Nile, which overflowed *twice* in every *solar* year." This latter view would reduce the antediluvian ages one-half; but we have not met with any writer who has ventured to adopt this speculation. St. Austin (De Civitat. Dei, lib. xv., cap. 12) mentions that some ancient writers supposed the year to be divided into ten parts, and that each of these decimals was taken for one year. This of course would reduce these extraordinary ages to one-tenth of their present amount; so that the nine hundred and sixty-nine years of Methuselah would be ninety-six years and nine months.

‡ Beverovicus, a German physician, attributes the longevity of the patriarchs' lives to their feeding upon raw flesh!—*Rev. J. Hewlett, B.D.*

conceive that such circumstances would have a tendency to maintain the health and prolong the life, yet it is not always so. Science does not teach us that a superior quality of food prolongs the life of man more than that which results from an inferior quality, provided it be wholesome. The poor, whose diet is coarse, supposing they have enough, live as long as the rich, who fare sumptuously every day. This objection is answered by the suggestion, that the original constitution of men, in those early times, was more robust and sound. Of course, all this is mere conjecture. The Scriptures do not furnish us with such reasons for the supposed results. Some have imagined that because God had newly formed mankind, he willed that they should be long livers; and that this circumstance is sufficient to account for such extraordinary duration of human life.* We must close the argument with those who would refer the fact in dispute to God's peculiar will, until they have produced the evidence on which their acquaintance with that will, in this respect, is founded.

Such long life is said to have been required for the peopling of the earth. This, however, is a mere invention; there is no Scriptural statement to that effect. If that had been the intention of such longevity, how did it happen that some were so late in beginning to be fathers? Seth was one hundred and five years old when he begat his first son, Enos;† and Methuselah was a hundred and eighty-seven before he begat his son Lamech,‡ who is mentioned as his first descendant. Surely, if the population of the earth had been one of the purposes of this longevity, we should not read of circumstances which indicate delay.

Some have supposed that those ancient people were peculiarly dear to God, and that this was one of the principal causes of their remarkable ages. It is true that God loves his creatures; and it is equally true that men may be more sensible of this love in one age than another, because they may, by greater obedience to his laws, be distinguished by superior virtues. But it is not true that God ever intended that the number of men's years should measure the extent of his love. If so, the

---

* Josephus, "Ant.," book 1, chap. iii. 4, adopted by Dr. Dodd.

† Gen. v. 6.   ‡ Gen. v. 25.

death of infants would imply that he did not love them; or, if so, it is so little, that when compared with that bestowed upon the aged, it is scarcely to be mentioned. We see, however, that the young and virtuous are frequently cut off in the bloom of their hopes and the prime of their usefulness; while the wicked are not unfrequently permitted to continue to an advanced age in a profligate career. It is plain, then, that those passages of Scripture which promise length of days as the result of righteousness,* and that portion of the Decalogue which commands us to honour our father and mother, that our days may be long in the land,† are not to be taken as promises that natural life will be extended by the observance of such duties. We see persons removed every day, notwithstanding the excellence of their piety, and the devotedness of their attachment to their parents. The length of days that is to be the result of those virtues will consist in the perpetuation of those spiritual states which they induce. States have the same relation to the soul of man that days have to his body: hence days are significant of states. Every new state in the life of religion is a fresh spiritual day, which is mercifully prolonged to the possessor by the beneficence of God. The land which He giveth us is the possession of some enjoyment in His own kingdom; and the duties of filial affection are among the means by which it is to be obtained.

But the condition of goodness among the antediluvians continually decreased, and that which was preserved, remained only among a few; the great mass of the people having fallen into those general corruptions which are stated to have occasioned the deluge. Their longevity, then, supposing it to have related to individual men, cannot, with any consistency, be interpreted as evidence that God loved them better than the subsequent generations of our race. And, therefore, another reason sometimes put forth to account for the supposed great ages of those people—namely, to afford them opportunities for obtaining high degrees of spiritual and intellectual excellence— must fall to the ground. It did not answer the supposed purpose. They did not attain those virtues. They appear to have been worse in their age than in their youth, or the catastrophe

---

* Psa. xxi. 4 ; lxi. 5, 6. † Exod. xx. 12.

in which they were finally overwhelmed would not have occurred.

That those ages were not intended to be expressed of individual men is farther evident from the third verse of the sixth chapter of Genesis, where it is written, "The Lord said, My spirit shall not always strive with man, for that he also is flesh: yet his days shall be a hundred and twenty years." Here some arcana apart from what is mentioned in the literal sense are plainly meant, for the statement of man living a hundred and twenty years has no literal connection with what precedes, nor had it any general realization in the history which follows. Noah lived three hundred and fifty years after the flood.* Shem, his son, lived five hundred years after he begat Arphaxad; Arphaxad lived four hundred and three years after he begat Salah; and Salah lived, after he begat Eber, four hundred and three years; and Eber, after he begat Peleg, four hundred and thirty years.† From these facts it is plain that the declaration, "yet his days shall be a hundred and twenty years," could not have been intended to predict what should be the period of human life in the world.

It is indeed thought that this remarkable passage was designed to express the time which should elapse between the date of its utterance and that of the flood; and thus, that it was the period of respite which God granted to the people for repentance, before the execution of that calamity.‡ But this view of the case, to be reasonable, should agree with the Scripture chronology, which it does not! Noah was five hundred years old when he

---

* Gen. ix. 28.

† Gen. xi. 11-17. Hesiod, speaking of the golden age, says, "The growing child was nursed an hundred years by his careful mother, very infantine in his home."—"*Weeks and Days*," v. 126. The longevity here implied, like the period to which it is assigned, is doubtless a poetic statement, and not a literal circumstance; and therefore it is no collateral evidence of the personal longevity which Sharon Turner, in his "Sacred History of the World," has supposed it to be.

‡ Dr. Geddes reads the whole passage thus:—" I will never unawares pronounce or execute judgment on mankind. They shall not be punished without a warning; they are but frail flesh, and shall have one hundred and twenty years given them to repent and amend their lives."

begat Shem, Ham, and Japheth.* It was a considerable period after this before the supposed respite was uttered; yet it was "in the six hundredth year of Noah's life that the fountains of the great deep were broken up;"† so that no such period did elapse as the passage is supposed to promise; and, therefore, it cannot be the correct view of the subject.

The fact is, that those days which were to be a hundred and twenty years, were not intended to refer to the duration of natural life at all; but those numbers are made use of because, according to the ecclesiastical computation of those early times, they signify the lowest condition of spiritual life that could remain with man, and which is afterwards so frequently called a remnant, out of which a new dispensation of religious truth and goodness was always to be raised, when the corruption of a former one should bring it to its end. When a church has so far declined that its principles of faith and action have been rejected by the general mass of the people, then a new dispensation has always been raised up by the special interposition of the Divine Providence. This we find was the case with the antediluvians. They continually decreased in their attachment to the good and excellent things of religion, until they were found to remain only among a few, when a new church was raised up under the name of Noah. A similar falling away distinguished the Noachic dispensation; and when it was dispersed, at the building of Babel, another new church was begun with Abraham and his descendants, who it is reasonable to suppose were among the best of those that remained of the preceding dispensation. The Jewish Church continued, with various vicissitudes, until the fulness of time arrived, which was the completion of its corruptions; and then it was made to pass away, as to all the vitality that had ever belonged to it, by the manifestation of the Lord Jesus Christ, by whom another new church, called the Christian, was begun. In all these cases the commencement of the new was effected through the instrumentality of those persons in whom any good of the old yet remained. It is this peculiar circumstance, which has been verified in the history of the decline and establishment of churches, that is designed to be represented by the words, "His days shall be a

* Gen. v. 32. † Gen. vii. 11.

hundred and twenty years." It denotes the lowest estimate to which the good of the church could be reduced, and that, when so reduced, another dispensation should be commenced through its instrumentality. In this sense it symbolically expresses the state of every church and people, previously to the commencement of another, and in no other sense has it any historical significance.

Those who consider numbers in the Scriptures only in the light of arithmetic or chronology, must needs have a very worldly view of the subjects treated of, whereas the true idea which ought to be attached to them is spiritual. This, indeed, must be evident from the circumstance of the disaster which was inevitable on David's *numbering* the people.* It is difficult to see what crime was involved in ascertaining the numerical strength of his kingdom. Most nations have thought it useful, and adopted it, for the purposes of the state, without intending thereby to perpetrate any offence against the Divine laws. But it was a representative history; and when it is known that such *numbering* was significant of man attempting from himself to ascertain the quality of faith and virtue in the Church, which can be known only to the Lord, we at once see the heinousness of the offence represented, and, consequently, why it was that such calamities resulted. In the Revelation it is said, "Let him that hath understanding count the number of the beast," † which signifies, that he whose mind is enlightened from the Word may know what are the nature and quality of those doctrines by which the Word has been falsified. The falsification of the Word here more particularly alluded to, is that whereby charity and good works have been separated from faith, and the latter set up as the only essential for salvation. This is the beast: and his number is said to be six hundred threescore and six, to denote how fully such a doctrine perverts all the truths of revelation.‡

---

* 2 Sam. xxiv. 2-13. † Rev. xiii. 18.

‡ The Greeks expressed numbers by the letters of their alphabet, and therefore it has been supposed that the number of the beast, as the number of a man, referred to some individual, the letters of whose name, considered as numerals, would make 666. On this ground great pains have been taken, and some ingenuity displayed, to find the number in some persons or cir-

The Psalmist says, "The days of our years *are* threescore years and ten; and if by reason of strength *they be* fourscore years, yet *is* their strength labour and sorrow; for it is soon cut off, and we fly away."* It is true that seventy or eighty years are the average of what is now called a good old age; but it must be plain to the reflecting, that this passage does not treat

cumstances connected with the Popish religion. See *Lowman* and *Archbishop Newcome*. The views most generally received for this purpose are two,—*first*, the sentence, VICARIVS FILII DEI, on the frontlet of the triple crown of the Pope, is thought by some to be very conclusive in pointing him out to be the beast, because the letters employed as numerals in that sentence, when selected and added, make up the sum 666. *Second*, the name LATEINOS, mentioned by Irenæus, and made use of by the Greeks to express the circumstance of the Romish Church having *latinized* everything pertaining to it, has by others been considered the name of the beast, because it contains the number spoken of ; and this view is thought to be corroborated by the fact of the Hebrew name for the Roman kingdom being ROMIITH, the Hebrew letters for which, considered as numerals, make the same number, thus :

LATEINOS.		ROMIITH.	
Λ	 30	ר	 200
A	 1	ו	 6
T	 300	מ	 40
E	 5	י	 10
I	 10	י	 10
N	 50	ת	 400
O	 70		666
Σ	 200		
	666		

These coincidences are certainly remarkable, but then it requires something more to assure us that such are the facts referred to : and especially it would require that such coincidences were peculiar and isolated ; but such is not the case. The Rev. Robert Hindmarsh, in his *Letters to Dr. Priestley*, p. 181, says that he had made out about a "hundred and fifty names, that could no more be supposed to have any connection with the contents of the Apocalypse than the man in the moon," and, among others, he has mentioned "*Joseph Smith, Tomkins*, and *Benjamin Bennet.*" This certainly shows that the number of the beast cannot mean the person whose name may happen to contain the numerals which make up the sum 666. The intention of this number is to express the complete falsification above alluded to, wherever and with whoever it may exist, but especially that section of the Church with which it has become a doctrine.

* Psa. xc. 10.

of such a subject. More than two-thirds of the human race die in childhood; more than two-thirds of the adult population die before they reach the age of sixty; not one-half of the remaining third continue on to eighty; and very few have their lives prolonged to ninety. What, then, becomes of the literal sense of the passage, on the supposition that it treats of the duration of human life? Is it a revelation only to a few, not one of whom can ever know that it will apply to him? It may be replied, that the passage is not designed to teach us that all will arrive at such an age, but that its purpose is to express a limit beyond which we cannot reasonably expect to live. This, however, had been taught by many ages of experience, during which some had lived beyond the asserted limits, and, therefore, its purpose, as a *revelation*, must be to inculcate something else. The subject which is really treated of is the spiritual age or state of man—the age of the soul, not the age of the body; and this age is measured, not by the times attendant upon natural life, but by the states and conditions which distinguish a religious life. The soul may be young in heavenly things when the body is old in worldly age. Our bodies may be comparatively young in natural life, and yet we may have attained to considerable age in spiritual life. Youth, in spiritual life, is feebleness of thought, and the want of experience in heavenly goodness: age, in spiritual life, is clear perception of truth, and an ardent love for all that is pure, wise, and lovely. This cannot be reached suddenly or at once; there are progressions in the states which conduce to wisdom, as there are successions in the years which effect longevity. We cannot pass from a state of ignorance to a condition of wisdom, without going through the discipline of instruction, experience, reasonings, temptations, conquests, and confirmations in good; all of which are so many spiritual years by which man's interiors are advanced into the gravity of that wisdom which constitutes the age of heavenly manhood. From the succession of these states, he who is so disposed may see, among many other wonderful things of the Divine Providence, that a prior state is the plane of that which immediately follows,—the old state must be gone through before the new one can begin; also that the opening and arrangement of the thoughts and sensations of the outer man, proceed from the unfolding and development of the perceptions and delights of the inner man. It is by passing through those states that the age and stature of the soul are measured. The old age which the Scriptures represent to us as venerable, refers not to the infirmities and decrepitude of the body, but to that state of gravity, wisdom, experience, and resignation to the Divine will, which ought to be possessed when the body begins to bend beneath the weight of advancing years. Age is venerable on these accounts, and these are the things to be respected and admired. An old man living in a state of wickedness is an odious spectacle: vice in age puts on its grimmest and most horrid aspect. Age should be the companion of that wisdom which can look backward, with satisfaction and gratitude, upon the conquests which have been effected over vice and error, and look forward with a well-grounded confidence in the Divine mercies, and cherish an enlightened resignation to the Divine will. The aged man, in whom Christianity has been enabled to fix her illustrious and lovely principles, charms and delights us. A wise and good old man is one of the most holy and happy objects in created nature. But, then, both his happiness and holiness belong to his inner life, and they have been attained through a succession of states, trials, temptations, and conquests, which are so many spiritual years that have contributed to produce so venerable a development of religious placidity and excellence. It is to express the pleasing aspect of this state that the life of man is said by the Psalmist to be threescore years and ten, for the number seventy denotes what is holy, and, consequently, a state of holiness in those of whom it is predicated. It was in consequence of this signification of that number that there were seventy elders chosen for Israel,* and that the Lord also appointed seventy disciples.† The propagation and establishment of the principles of holiness were the objects and ends of the seventy in both cases. When Peter inquired, "How oft shall my brother sin against me, and I forgive him?" and suggested "seven times;" the Lord replied, "I say not unto thee, Until seven times; but, Until seventy times seven," ‡ which number plainly denotes that the principles of charity

* Exod. xxiv. 1. † Luke x 1. ‡ Matt. xviii. 21, 22.

are to be continually active under every circumstance. Thus the life of man is pronounced to be threescore years and ten, not to express the duration of his natural life in the world, but to denote that condition of spiritual life of which holiness may be predicated. But it is farther said, "If by strength they be fourscore years, yet is their strength labour and sorrow; for it is soon cut off, and we fly away." The number eighty, in this connection, and because it is associated with the ideas of labour and sorrow, signifies those deep temptations by which man is introduced into a more intimate conjunction with the Lord: *labour* is the temptation which the understanding sustains as to its reception of the truth, that all wisdom is the Lord's; and *sorrow* is the temptation which the will experiences in its admission of good, under the pure acknowledgment that it is the Lord's: but these temptations soon pass away from those who have obtained the strength derivable from holiness, and they enter into the enjoyment of more perfect liberty, hence it is written that they are "soon cut off, and we fly away." Immediately following this passage the Psalmist says, "Teach us to number our days, that we may apply our hearts unto wisdom;" * which is not to be understood as the expression of a desire to ascertain how long we shall live, that we may prepare ourselves for death just before the event. No! The Lord teaches us to number our days, because, by the instructions of his Word, we are influenced to arrange our knowledges of truth and goodness for the purposes of spiritual life: and this is the application of our hearts to wisdom.

These considerations relating to what the Scriptures say of the number of years, which we see are but apparently applied to the age of man, must tend to show that the numbers and ages which are recorded of the so-called Antediluvian Patriarchs do not express the duration of the natural life of individuals, but denote the state and quality of the respective branches of the Adamic Church, of which we have seen their names to be significant. We have only to change our ideas from that of the duration of the life of a person to that of the condition of a religious dispensation, and the whole difficulty which those incredible ages suggest vanishes at once. This is a solution of

* Psa. xc. 12.

the matter in perfect consistency with the spiritual purpose of the narrative as a revelation from God, which is to inform us of the qualities of the spiritual states that distinguished the heretical branches of the most ancient Church. The years that they lived denoted the states under which they existed; by their begetting sons and daughters is signified the sentiments and affections which they engendered; and by their dying is represented the extinction of such states.

It is true that as those various heresies and doctrines were embraced by societies, they must have been maintained for some considerable time in the world—probably much longer than it was the lot of any individual to live; and therefore the ages which are assigned to them might have some foundation in historical truth. Although we do not think this to have been the principal aim of the narrative, we see no good reason for rejecting the idea. It aids in the reduction of the embarrassments which the notion of individual longevity induces. Opinions live in a community, after the parties who invented them have passed away, and their followers and proselytes are for a long time called by the names of their founders. *Israel* and *Edom* were the appellations by which all their descendants were distinguished throughout their generations. In this sense, Israel, up to the time of the coming of the Lord, may be said to have lived upwards of eighteen centuries. This view produces no surprise: historical parallels abound, both in the Jewish and Christian Churches, showing the great ages to which heretical branches of them have lived. The Essenes among the Jews sprang up at the decline of the Babylonish captivity, that is, about five hundred years before the Christian era; and the Pharisees and Sadducees had then existed upwards of two centuries, and were conspicuous and powerful as sects in the time of the Messiah. So also in Christendom; the two parties, Arians and Athanasians, arose in the fourth century, and now the age of each is nearly fifteen hundred years, for they are living still.

This view suggests another consideration. It is to be observed that it is only Seth and his descendants of whom longevity is predicated. We do not read of the age of Cain, or any of his progeny. Although the true reasons for these circumstances are purely spiritual, still other probable grounds, taking their rise in those reasons, may be assigned. Seth being the seed that was given instead of Abel, and so representing a church in which charity was to be developed, would needs acquire, and impart to its descendants, a longer life than faith alone, or any of its offspring, by possibility could reach. Faith soon dies in that mind which is not imbued with charity. That which depends upon memory only for its being has but a fleeting existence, but that which enters into the affections lives and long continues. What a multitude of religious notions have lived just long enough to die! But, on the other hand, principles which have regarded the good of mankind continue from generation to generation, and become venerable for their antiquity. The good of Christianity has lived, through various vicissitudes, for eighteen hundred years: a thousand faiths have been framed and pretended to be Christian during that period, and all have perished. The circumstance, then, of Seth being a church in which charity, as in the dispensation of Abel, was to be continued, suggests a reason why longevity is predicated of his generation. Those branches may have reached the advanced ages which are recorded of them, though, as it has been said, we consider that the chief design of such numbers is to indicate their quality as to faith and charity: and as every one of them was in a different state as to these things, arising from the distinction of genius and temper, hereditarily acquired, therefore their ages were so various; numbers, agreeably to the perceptions of the ancient times, being employed to express them. A more particular idea as to what is meant by the qualities of churches will appear in the consideration we have to offer concerning Enoch, and his so-called translation.

The quality of the several churches which descended from Adam, through the line of Seth, was derived from the perceptive capability of the people. The perception of a church consists in the ability of its members to perceive from the Lord what is good and true; not so much what is good and true as to civil society, but what is good and true with respect to love and faith towards the Lord. Those who have a faith in truth confirmed by the good of life, may form some idea of what this ancient perception was.

So long as the people called Seth remained in their integrity, they were enabled to know, by an internal impulse, whatever was good and true in reference to the things of God, heaven, and religious duty. They arrived at this result, it is to be observed, not by an external way of thinking, but by an internal dictate and impression. The Lord talked with Adam, which means an internal dictate as to what is good and excellent. The other churches which proceeded from him experienced a similar perception, though, in consequence of the fall, its force and clearness were diminished. Divisions in the process of time took place, and the internals of the minds of those who embraced impure sentiments became successively closed, by the misdirection of their affections to unworthy objects, and thus one degree of perception perished after another; which circumstances are expressed by the recorded decease of Seth, Enos, Cainan, and others.

These facts assure us, that the knowledge of what was genuinely true and good was in the process of passing away, and that the faculty through which it had come was being perverted. It was during this decay that Enoch was born; that is, a branch of the declining Church, under that name, came into existence. The object of that people was to prevent the dissipation of those religious knowledges which they saw was threatened. They therefore collected the information which the several preceding churches had derived from perception, and which tradition had preserved, and thereupon they arranged them into a doctrinal and perceptive form; so that the truths of religion, which were ceasing to be perceived by an internal way, might be taught by an external way. The people called Enoch saw the changes which were taking place in the moral constitution and religious character of society, and thereupon undertook the duty of correcting it, by becoming themselves instructors. This work was according to their genius, and therefore it was identified with them. Hence it is that they constituted a remarkable point amidst the decline of those ancient churches. Although the internal perceptions of men were decaying, the truths which had been perceived were, by Enoch, in process of being preserved. It was the collection of these truths into rules of life, and teaching them, which constituted the delight of that branch of the declining Church called Enoch. Hence the name means to instruct and discipline; and therefore, also, it is that we find the Apostle speaking of this Enoch, the seventh from Adam, as prophesying,* that is, teaching. Every one acquainted with biblical literature is aware of the great interest which has, upon several occasions, been attached by scholars to an apocryphal Book of Enoch, found in the Abyssinian version of the Scriptures, several copies of which have been brought to Europe by oriental travellers. How far this book possesses the antiquity or authority which its name implies, cannot be now determined, though there can be no doubt of its being a production long anterior to Christianity: but the very circumstance of the existence of such a document proves that a tradition must have prevailed, down to the time of its production, that Enoch was distinguished by those characteristics which we have stated. This is why he is said to have "walked with God"; for it is well known that to walk with God means to live according to his precepts. Truth is the way which God has laid down for men to walk in; it is the high road that leads to his kingdom: he is himself this way: indeed, he says so; † consequently, the men who walk in it also walk with God. This, then, was a distinguished feature of religion among the people called Enoch. The fact is twice stated; ‡ and in the latter case there is added this remarkable clause, "He was not, for God took him." This is popularly understood to mean that he was taken to heaven without the experience of natural death; not that the sentence contains such an idea, for the very same phrases occur respecting the supposed death of Joseph, and also in reference to the death of Rachel's children: § but it is founded on the statement of the

---

* Jude 14. "In several of the Fathers, mention is made of Enoch as an author, not only of a prophetic writing, but of various productions. The Book of Enoch is alluded to by Justyn Martyr, Irenæus, Clement of Alexandria, Tertullian, Origen, Augustine, Jerome, Hilary, and Eusebius." It seems to have been known to them through a Greek translation, the original language in which it was composed being either Hebrew or Chaldee; the Ethiopic version, discovered in Abyssinia, appears to have been made from the Greek, and not from the original.—*See an interesting article on this subject by the Rev. S. Davidson, LL.D., Professor of Biblical Literature and Oriental Languages in the Lancashire Independent College, in Kitto's* "*Bib. Cyclopædia.*"

† John xiv. 6. ‡ Gen. v. 22 & 24. § Gen. xlii. 36; Jer. xxxi. 15.

Apostle, who says, "By faith Enoch was translated that he should not see death."* But by *translation* he must have meant a change of state, disposition, or bent of mind (for he is treating of the effects of faith), and not the removal of an individual, with his body, into a place unfitted for its existence, for that body, as flesh and blood, he has said, cannot inherit the kingdom of God.† The view, therefore, which ought to be taken of the term translation, is somewhat similar to that which the Apostle elsewhere expresses by the word *transform*, as when he says, "Be ye transformed by the renewing of your mind, that ye may prove what *is* that good, and acceptable, and perfect will of God."‡ By Enoch's not seeing death is denoted that he did not experience condemnation. How should he, if he walked with God? The character of his faith prevented it! The original description is, "He was not, for God took him:" where, by the sentence, "he was not," is simply meant that the doctrines of truth which were collected by the people called Enoch, for the instruction of posterity, were not theirs; nothing of their mind was in them; they were Divine things, which spoke of the glory of God, and adapted to promote the intelligence of the people. By the phrase, "God took him," is plainly meant that the truths so collected were preserved by Divine Providence for the use and edification of all future conditions of the Church. The correctness of this view of the case is proved by the fact that all subsequent ages, conditions, and diversities of the actual Church of God have been instructed by means of documents embodying the rules, teachings, commands, and promises of Divine truth.

* Heb. xi. 5. † 1 Cor. xv. 50. ‡ Rom. xii. 2.

CHAPTER XIX.

THE CORRUPTIONS OF THE ANTEDILUVIAN WORLD. — THE SONS OF GOD TAKING TO THEMSELVES WIVES OF THE DAUGHTERS OF MEN.

> "On different senses different objects strike,
> Hence different passions more or less inflame,
> As strong or weak the organs of the frame:
> And hence one master-passion in the breast,
> Like Aaron's serpent, swallows up the rest."
> —Pope's *Essay on Man*.

The moral and intellectual corruptions of the most ancient people are historical circumstances, easily to be perceived, as a general idea, even though the narrative expressing them is written in language of a purely figurative character: general truths, in the Scriptures, frequently stand out very conspicuously amid the symbolical details in which they are embodied. Still, as such, they are surrounded with haze and mist, and they will remain so as long as the mind rests merely in generality. General ideas are comparatively obscure, like distant objects in the twilight of the morning; they become clear only as particular truths shine in upon them, and afford lucidity for the development of their forms. These are as beams from the rising sun, successively breaking in upon the uncertain outline of objects in the western vista, revealing to us their nature, their forms, their colours, and all their loveliness.

Although the first few verses of the sixth chapter of Genesis suggest a general idea concerning the corruptions of the ancient world, still it is evident that this general idea, if we do not carefully examine the sentences through which that impression may have been derived, will be more or less uncertain. The idea of corruption may, indeed, not pass away; but the nature of it, how it was instigated, and why it should have produced results that were never to occur again, remain unravelled; and so, one of the great objects of revelation, which is to impart clear and decisive thoughts on the subjects on which it treats, is not obtained.

General ideas, not grounded upon particular information, are not only imperfect, but liable to be lost. They are like a candle introduced into a murky atmosphere, the light of which grows dim, and so is in danger of being extinguished. We cannot be certain that our general ideas are true, unless we have been careful to form them on the consideration of particular and specific knowledges: just in the same way that the general notion of being a sinner is a very undefined notion, so long as it remains unfounded on the fact and consciousness of having perpetrated particular sins. Most persons will freely acknowledge themselves to be sinners in a general sense, but how few will confess to the guilt of particular transgression! The general assertion of being a sinner has a meaning in the faith of the utterer, no farther than he has searched out his particular sins. Again, how common is it for men to acquire a general prejudice, for or against certain things, without having furnished themselves with any particular reasons for the adoption of such prejudice. This is found to operate, not only with respect to persons and circumstances in the world, but likewise in reference to the statements and purposes of revelation. Some men are well known to entertain certain general ideas about a variety of subjects mentioned in the Word of God, although they may have never candidly examined the particular evidences on which they rest, or the conclusions to which they conduce. For instance: every one has a general idea that the antediluvian people became exceedingly corrupt; but how few are they who have any particular idea of the wickedness into which they fell, although it is evident that it must have been of a very peculiar nature, or it could not have brought about so terrible a result as it is related to have done. Again, most persons have some general idea that the catastrophe called the flood was an overflow of water and a drowning of the people; but whenever the particulars of science and theology are brought to bear upon this general notion, the whole matter becomes a dim and doubtful thing; so that, in order to retain any faith in the occurrence, as popularly understood, it is found requisite to refer the matter to Omnipotence. Of course, when false conceptions of this

Divine attribute are brought into a subject, the right activities of reason will go out of it. Omnipotence cannot be without its laws of order, nor can God transgress them.

The grounding of our general ideas of theological truth upon particular conceptions of it, is of the utmost importance to the intellectual well-being of the Church. It is in consequence of this duty not having been sufficiently attended to, that so many of the leading doctrines of popular Christianity are full of perplexities. Take, for example, the general proposition that there is a Divine Trinity in God: this, as a general proposition, presents no difficulties; but the moment we begin to inquire into the particular notions, of which that Trinity is popularly said to consist, the subject becomes dark, and its advocates are compelled to wrap it up in the cloak of wonderment and mystery! The same may be said of the doctrines of the atonement, mediation, the resurrection, and several other tenets, as they are commonly understood. We refer to these subjects merely to illustrate the distinction which may exist between the general and particular ideas of a subject, and to suggest that all general ideas, to be salutary and useful, must take their rise from such as are clear and sensible in particulars. It is only when this is the case that the mass of truth is made up of coherent parts, and each contributes its light and strength to increase the power and brilliancy of the whole.

The corruptions of the antediluvian Church, viewed under a general idea, were similar to those which have taken place with the churches of after times. It rejected the goods of charity and perverted the truths of faith, as was done by the Jewish Church before the coming of the Lord; also, as he predicted would be the case, by that which he came to establish.* But there was a peculiarity about the genius and character of the antediluvian people which has not prevailed in after times, and this gave to their corruptions a peculiar enormity. In the possession of Eden they enjoyed a state of *perception:* by this they intuitively, and from an impulsive love of goodness, were immediately enabled to comprehend the ideas and purposes of faith. In consequence of their internal eminence, they could acquire the knowledges and delights of religious principles by

* See Matt. xxiv. throughout.

an influx from the Lord: whereas the people of after times have had to procure those things by external teachings, the difficulties of receiving which have been increased by the evil inclinations transmitted to them by the transgressions of their progenitors. Those who, by actual evils, render them infixed principles of their nature, must needs transmit the seeds thereof to their immediate descendants. The parent can only communicate to his offspring that which he himself possesses. Posterity is affected with his vices or benefited by his virtues, so far as he makes them his own by actual life. Revelation declares the action of this law, and experience proves the truth of it.* With the early posterity of the Adamic people, evils were not so deeply rooted as they afterwards became; and therefore, those internal influences from the Lord, by which their ancestors had been raised to the summit of religious intelligence and enjoyment, were not suddenly destroyed: that was a progressive work, and it was eventually effected. Now, as no other than an internal way had yet been opened out in man for the Lord's approach to him, it is plain that whenever that channel should be closed, mankind would be left without a guide, and that, consequently, they would rush without a check into every enormity, and guilt would necessarily bring about their destruction. But here we are anticipating an argument we shall have again to raise. The circumstances of the Adamic Church having been once distinguished by the most exalted purity, and that in successive generations the people fell from their elevated condition into the fiercest wickedness, show that their state was essentially different from that of any other church which has since been planted. Every other has had its commencement with mankind in a state of evil: this was not the condition of the primeval people of the Adamic Church; consequently, when they fell, it was from a greater height than it has been possible for any dispensation since to do, and therefore it was that they entailed, in that descent, so disastrous a calamity. It is a law that "unto whomsoever much is given, of him shall be much required." There are a propriety and reasonableness about this Scriptural enactment which every one may see. It is also a law, that the "servant which knew his Lord's will,

* Exod. xx. 5, 6.

and prepared not *himself*, neither did according to his will, shall be beaten with many stripes,"* which plainly means, that if those fall who have had superior advantages, they will sink into deeper degradation than those who may not have been so favourably circumstanced. The opposite of the highest good is the deepest evil: the higher the summit is from which a man falls, the more certain—the more terrible—becomes his destruction. Hence the fall of the Adamic Church was so dreadful in its results! It was effected by the successive shutting out of good and truth from their affections and thoughts, until at last both their wills and understandings were closed against their admission. Hereupon they became infested with all sorts of abominable persuasions, from which they were not afterwards willing to recede. "The wickedness of man was great in the earth, and every imagination of the thoughts of his heart was only evil continually:"† therefore, whatever fell into their ideas was, by the cupidity of their self-love, converted into a means of lust, and, finally, they supposed themselves to be as gods. This was the state indicated by the delusion of the serpent, who, in effecting his seductions, is reported to have said, "Your eyes shall be opened, and ye shall be as gods."‡ Evil loves and false persuasions took possession of their minds, and became the sole influence in their conduct. "The earth was corrupt before God, and the earth was filled with violence. And God looked upon the earth, and, behold, it was corrupt; for all flesh had corrupted his way upon the earth."§ While this account at first sight furnishes us with a general idea of the enormity of those times, the considerations adduced present us with a more particular idea concerning the nature and extent of it. The genius of the people being peculiar, arising from the intimate association of their wills and understandings, became admissive of states of evil, against the entrance of which posterity was to be secured. With the people called Noah, it was provided by the Lord that there should be some few remains of innocence and knowledge stored up in the interiors of their minds, as planes upon which the Divine influence might operate for the production of another church, to effect the

* Luke xii. 47, 48.   † Gen. vi. 5.
‡ Gen. iii. 5.   § Gen. vi. 11, 12.

restoration of those who fall, and so to become the groundwork of their regeneration: this we believe to be signified by the promise, "Yet his days shall be a hundred and twenty years." It was seen in a preceding chapter,* that this statement had no reference to the age of man: and we here observe that it expresses the state of *remains* concerning faith, which should be provided for in subsequent generations of men. Remains are all those true ideas and good impressions which are derived from the Lord's Word, and introduced into a man's memory during the periods of his infancy and childhood, also of those states which are derived therefrom; such as the states of innocence from infancy; states of love towards parents, relations, instructors, and friends; states of kindness towards one's neighbour, and of tenderness towards the poor and needy. These states, with the sentiments and feelings connected with them, are now preserved in the internal man by the Lord, and carefully separated from all that is evil and false. Every one is aware that such things *remain* with him, notwithstanding the evils into which he may have fallen; and in that circumstance he has what is promised by his "days being a hundred and twenty years." For by these *remains* man has the orderly groundwork for reflecting upon what is good and true, and so to think and reason upon religious things; for they are among the first receptacles of celestial and spiritual life in fallen man.

The reason why a hundred and twenty denote *remains*, may be seen by referring to the signification of twelve and ten, by the multiplication of which that number is obtained. Those two numbers very frequently occur in the Scriptures, and they are connected with some of the most conspicuous circumstances mentioned therein. It will be sufficient for our purpose to notice, in respect to the number twelve, a few instances in which it occurs; and, in reference to the number ten, the Decalogue, and tithings. It must be plain to every one who will carefully study the use of those numbers in the Word, that they involve a meaning different from what they literally express. Nor need we be surprised at this, for it is no uncommon thing in our own day to hear persons, in certain kinds of conversation, speak of *dozens* and *tens*, without intending thereby to express what is

* See page 241.

numerically correct, but chiefly to indicate some general idea. The numbers mentioned in the Scriptures were selected for the sake of the representation they were intended to sustain, and in no case are they to be considered accidental or indifferent.

By *twelve* are signified all things belonging to love, and faith grounded therein. It was on this account that Aaron's breastplate had *twelve* precious stones,* and the genuine Church has *twelve* foundations and *twelve* gates.† It was for the same reason that there were *twelve* tribes of Israel, and *twelve* apostles; also, that Jesus, when *twelve* years old, went up to Jerusalem, sat with the doctors in the temple, and aroused their astonishment at his understanding and answers.‡

But by ten are denoted *remains*. The Decalogue is so named because the commandments of the moral law are called the "ten words."§ The sentiments therein contained were not promulgated for the first time when revealed to Moses; they were the holy truths which *remained* of a more ancient dispen-

---

* Exod. xxviii. 21. † Rev. xxi. 14–21.

‡ Luke ii. 42–47. A more enlarged view of the ground on which numbers have a spiritual signification, with ample illustrations, is furnished in an interesting little work, "*A Key to the Spiritual Signification of Numbers, Weights, and Measures,*" *by the late Rev. Hindmarsh.*

§ Exod. xxxiv. 28, marginal reading. These "words" or commandments are not numerically divided in the Scriptures; nor are they called ten for a numerical purpose; if so, it would have been indicated in the letter; whereas no one can say, on such authority, which is the *first*, *second*, and so on. They have been divided, so as to make that number, by Biblical critics; and the convenience thus afforded has led to the reception of such a division by the Church from a very early period. But the mode of division has not been uniform. Most of "the fathers" have written upon this subject: while they all admit that there should be *ten*, differences of opinion exist as to where the separations should be made, particularly concerning those which are recorded from the first to the twelfth verse, and at the seventeenth verse, of the twentieth chapter of Exodus. The division adopted by the Greek, Reformed, and Anglican Churches is that of *Origen*, which places five upon each table, making the fifth upon the first table to be, "Honour thy father and mother," &c. Of course, there is no Divine authority for such an arrangement, and some have doubted whether calling them first, second, and so on, is not an addition to the Word, which ought not to be made. PHILO JUDÆUS, in his "*De Decalogo*," supposes that they were called the Decalogue to denote their perfection, *ten* being considered the most perfect number. The true reason is indicated above.

sation: for every one may see that the evils therein forbidden were known to be such, by the Israelites and other nations, before they were delivered upon Mount Sinai. But as such knowledges *remained* without the source of them being acknowledged, they were re-enacted in a miraculous manner, before the sons of Jacob, in order to signify their Divine origination. Hence it is plain that *ten* denote remains in general. This idea explains why Abram is said to have given Melchizedek "tithes of all";* and why it was directed that a *tenth* part of the fruits of the earth should be offered to the Lord, and by Him was given to Aaron and the Levites.† These tenths represented what remained of truth and good among the Israelitish Church, and consequently that they belonged to the Lord, therefore it is written, "The tenth shall be holy unto the Lord."‡

From these significations of *twelve* and *ten*, we may perceive that the number, "a hundred and twenty," which results from their multiplication, and is said to be the day of the years of man, denotes the remains of truth and good, for the security of which the Lord would provide in the future generations of our race. From these considerations we learn that numbers in the Word are to be understood altogether abstractedly from the sense of the letter, they being inserted mainly to carry on the historical series, which appears in the literal sense.

The corruptions of the people, up to the period of this announcement, were of a kind that never existed before or since. That a provision was to be made against their recurrence, by means of a change about to be induced upon the subsequent condition of mankind, is declared by the Lord, where he said to Noah, "Behold, I establish my covenant with you, and with your seed after you;—neither shall all flesh be cut off any more by the waters of a flood; neither shall there any more be a flood to destroy the earth."§ The *covenant* thus declared to have been made plainly shows that a new state must have been induced upon the minds of those who received it. A covenant is an agreement between two, with the conditions of which they are mutually satisfied. It is true that in the covenants

---

* Gen. xiv. 20. † Numb. xviii. 24–28 ; Deut. xiv. 22.
‡ Lev. xxvii. 32. § Gen. ix. 9–11.

which the Lord effects with men, he alone offers the conditions; the reason is, because he can present nothing but what is right and just: those who accept the Divine propositions are favourably disposed to what is good. His covenants therefore relate to internal and spiritual things, and consequently to human regeneration; and for this, it is obvious, in the case before us, that a new mental state must have been provided. The *promise* that there should not any more be a flood to destroy the earth, certainly indicates that this new state was ever afterwards to exist and to prevent the return of such a calamity.

But this leads us to ask what it was which constituted this peculiar mental characteristic of the antediluvians; because, without some idea of that peculiarity, we must be at a loss to account for the circumstance of their *remains* having perished in their corruptions, with the exception of those which were preserved with Noah, to become the groundwork of another dispensation. In reference to this point, it was shown in a preceding chapter, treating of the occupation and enjoyments of Eden, that love was the reigning principle of their character, and that all their wisdom arose therefrom; *their wills and understandings acted, not as two, but as one faculty;* so that in whatever direction their affections were placed, their intellect took the same course; their thoughts and affections acted in unity. That was their genus: each part of their minds cohered with the other, and they formed one. This mental characteristic, when employed in the service of God, led to the highest results in religious attainment; but when they fell, they also carried this genus with them into their corruptions. When they began to love what was evil, they also began to think what was false, and this distinguished every act. This state may be compared to a glutinous substance, so that when any goods or truths came into contact with it they were ensnared, and could not be separated: consequently *remains*, with the antediluvians, instead of being stored up and preserved as the plane for subsequent regeneration, were profaned, their *profanation* consisting in this, that they had received truth and good in faith and heart, and had afterwards in faith and heart denied them. Hence, in their last posterity, it produced those dire persuasions by which all spiritual goodness and truth was overwhelmed, and through which they became extinct: for a man, when his *remains* are destroyed, has nothing left through which the Lord can reach and save him.

Such was the mental constitution or genus of those ancient people, yet it perished with them; for the Lord said, "All flesh shall not be cut off any more by the waters of a flood." But why? Clearly because a new state was to be provided, through which it would be prevented. In what was this new state to consist? There can be little doubt that it was to consist in the separation of the intellectual principle from the will; so that man might, by the intellectual principle, be enabled to know what is true and good, notwithstanding the entire corruption of his will; and thereby to provide for the safe custody of his "remains." Every one's experience proves to him that this is now the condition of man: every branch of the authentic history of our race, from the period of the flood, contributes proofs of this fact. If a man love an evil, and pursue it, his understanding tells him of the iniquity. The will may, nay, it does, strive to induce the understanding to favour its impurities, and to some extent it may succeed; but there are certain states implanted during the innocence of youth which cannot be obliterated. The greatest criminals are not found insensible to every virtue; they are known to feel acutely, on being reminded of the better states of their early days. The idea that such states are favourable to good, cannot perish. In separating the intellectual faculty from the will, the Lord has provided a means for the access of himself to the human race, which cannot be entirely closed by man during his residence below; and thus He has mercifully erected a barrier against the recurrence of such an inundation of false persuasions, grounded in evil loves, as prevailed in the last days of the antediluvian world, and which led to the destruction of its inhabitants.

The narrative of Moses furnishes us with two particulars concerning the enormities in religion that prevailed in those times. The first, with the consideration of which we shall close this chapter, is thus related: "It came to pass, when men began to multiply on the face of the earth, and daughters were born unto them, that the sons of God saw the daughters of men that they *were* fair; and they took them wives of all which they chose."* This is certainly intended to express some atrocity, which assisted in bringing about the catastrophe of the flood. But what was the nature of it? Daughters were born to men long before the chronological era which the narrative is supposed to contemplate. Adam and Seth, Enos and Cainan, with several others, are stated to have begotten sons and daughters many hundreds of years before this period.† The birth of daughters, therefore, was no new thing when men began to multiply. But why not sons as well as daughters? Is it not plain that this cannot have been recorded to indicate what the letter seems to express? On such a supposition the narrative will present no ordinary difficulties. These daughters are said to have been fair; ‡ but surely there was nothing very sinful in such a circumstance. It is not very reasonable to identify crime with beauty. We can conceive how beauty may lead to vanity and evil in a certain class of characters, but not how it can be an evil in itself; and the statement before us merely announces what is conceded to be the natural inheritance of the sex, namely, that they were at least physically adapted to become objects of affection. They were so considered by the "sons of God"; and whatever popular idea may be attached to this phrase, there is no ground for denying that they might have been tolerable judges of such a matter. If the daughters of men were fair in their eyes, that is good reason to presume that they really were so.

But what idea is the phrase "sons of God" intended to express? The literal sense has furnished, among others, the following opinions on the subject: first, that they were *angels*. Now, if we so consider them, then the circumstance of their having taken to themselves wives of the daughters of men is not very easily comprehended. We do not see how purely spiritual beings could fall in love with really natural women, so long as they existed in the material world; neither do we perceive how women could reciprocate an affection for husbands who, for the want of corporeity, could not be seen or touched. But as this idea of "the sons of God" is not generally insisted on, we need not dwell upon its consequences. Another idea which the

---

* Gen. vi. 1, 2. † Gen. v. 4-10. ‡ Heb., *good*.

phrase has been thought to signify is, that they were *good men.**
The faithful and obedient are sometimes so called in the Scriptures. Of the Lord it is said, to "as many as received him, to them gave he power to become the sons of God, *even* to them that believe on his name."† But if this be the meaning of the phrase, of what enormity were they guilty? Surely it is difficult to perceive any evil in the circumstance of a good man choosing a fair woman for his wife. Marriage is one of the institutions of God himself, and human choice in such a matter is one of the ingredients requisite to contribute to the happiness of which it is productive. A good man is not forbidden to marry, or deprived of choice in such an affair; and yet the narrative before us presents the circumstance as having been one of the proximate causes which hurried on the disaster of the flood! But where shall we find those good men of whom the phrase "sons of God" is considered to be descriptive? It is true, indeed, that "Noah found grace in the eyes of the Lord": that "he was a just man and perfect in his generations."‡ Nevertheless, this is not the character which the "sons of God" are contemplated to have sustained: they were guilty of some enormity, therefore a "good man" cannot be the right signification of the phrase; and the notion commonly attached to the fairness of the women excludes from it such an idea. It has been supposed that those fair daughters were merely beautiful as to their persons, and that they were taken as wives from their physical aspect, irrespective of any sound consideration of character.§ Of course, this can only be a conjecture; yet if it is conceded as probable, what is to become of the above idea of the *sons of God?* they cannot be good men who sacrifice principle to appearance in so serious a matter. They cannot be the sons of God in such a sense, who prefer appetite to virtue. If the sons of God were good men, they must have made a prudent choice of wives, and in that case there seems

---

* This is the opinion of Dr. A. Clarke, who says, "They were such as were, according to our Lord's doctrine, *born again* from above, and made children of God by the influence of the Holy Spirit."

† John i. 12. ‡ Gen. vi. 8, 9.

§ See Commentary of Henry and Scott, published for the Religious Tract Society.

no ground for the calamity towards which their choice is said to have contributed. If they did not make such a choice, then the title "sons of God" cannot mean what it has been supposed to mean. Indeed, the general scope of the history, as well as the particular declarations of it, show "that the wickedness of man *was* great in the earth, and *that* every imagination of the thoughts of his heart *was* only evil continually." * What, then, is to be done with this passage of our history? The more it is viewed in the light of a literal narrative, the more dense becomes the fog by which it is surrounded.† The word of the Lord is spirit; and it is to this that we must go, to be delivered from the embarrassments of the letter. Let us try the effect of such a course.

It came to pass, when men began to multiply on the face of the earth, that daughters were born unto them. By men are plainly meant mankind who lived in those times of the declining Church. The spiritual quality of this people, in respect to the things of love and faith, was exceedingly corrupt. The wickedness of men was great in the earth; and they are here called men, not because they possessed the principles of religious manhood, but chiefly because they were responsible for their perversities. The multiplication of such men denoted the increase of those corruptions into which the race at that time fell; and they are said to have multiplied on the face of the earth (properly *ground*), to signify that the increase of their

---

* Gen. vi. 5.

† Three other views have been taken of this passage, which it may be useful to notice. One is, that the phrase "sons of God" ought not to be understood in a strict sense, but as denoting that men distinguished for their position in society were, with a profane use of language, called sons of God by the servile portion of the community; and, consequently, that Moses adopted their expression in his history. But of this the text affords no evidence; nor do the Scriptures present an instance of wicked men being so denominated. Another idea is, that the term translated *god* ought to have been given as "princes," "great men," "rulers," or some equivalent word. To this it may be sufficient to observe, that the original word is Elohim. The third opinion is, that the "sons of God" were the sons of Seth, Orientally expressed, and that their sin consisted in marrying with the daughters of Cain, which is considered to have been prohibited. These, however, are mere conjectures, for which there is no evidence in the letter of the history.

wickedness spread itself abroad upon the visible Church at that period. The face of the ground is the visible character of the Church, and this is presented in the lives of its professors. If their lives be wise and virtuous, the face of the ground is bright and lovely; but if their lives be ignorant and vicious, then the face of the ground is benighted and defiled. This latter was the condition of the visible Church now treated of. The people had successively abandoned the ways of God, and pursued the criminal indulgence of their own follies; and in this perverted state, daughters are said to have been born unto them—not sons, but daughters only—because by the daughters of the wicked are spiritually denoted the lusts which they originate. The wicked, as is well known, are continually engendering some new *lusts*, and these, in the figurative style of antiquity, are here represented by daughters. The good also are never unmindful of genuine usefulness, and they are always giving origination to some new *love*, which, upon the same principle, where good is the subject treated of, is likewise spoken of as a daughter. The precise signification is determined by the quality of the things which are predicated. Thus when the affections of goodness and truth are spoken of as existing in the Church, they are called the daughters of Zion, the daughters of Judah, and the daughters of Jerusalem.* But when the lusts of evil and falsehood are treated of, they are called the daughters of Babylon, the daughters of the Philistines, the daughters of Moab,† and in the instance specially before us, the daughters of men. The ground of these significations is, that woman is affection by nature. The affection of good is soft, delicate, and persevering,—thus, as a female; while the understanding of truth is discriminating, robust, and powerful,—and thus, as a male. On whatever woman sets her heart she is extreme: when she directs her affections to what is good, she is inexpressibly loving; when she dedicates herself to vice, she is horribly revolting. A woman in the search of excellence is sweet and prudent; but in the pursuit of wickedness she is coarse and disgusting. A virtuous woman is a ruby, a vicious woman is a

---

* Zech. ii. 10; Psa. xlviii. 11, &c., &c.; Lam. ii. 13.
† Psa. cxxxvii. 8; 2 Sam. i. 20; Numb. xxv. 1.

viper; and from these circumstances we may readily see that what is *love* with the good, is converted into *lust* with the wicked. Wickedness was the characteristic of the men under consideration, consequently the daughters said to have been born unto them were *lusts*, manifesting a distinctiveness in the evil conduct of the times.

It is in consequence of the will having sunk into mere evil, while the understanding, by having been separated from it, was preserved in a state capable of having something that is intellectual and rational formed within it, that there were so many laws enacted under the Jewish dispensation, pointing out the prerogatives of man; that is, of the faculty of the understanding, and of the obedience due from the woman, which is the submission of the will. Those laws and statements are not to be understood to mean that there is any natural superiority or mastery belonging to the one sex, and some inferiority or subordination proper to the other. The distinction is not of such a kind, but it consists in the circumstance, that with the woman, the *will* is her extreme characteristic; and with the man, the *understanding* is his extreme characteristic. On these grounds, therefore, it is that the two sexes represent their most visible characteristics,—the woman, *will* and its affections, and the man, *understanding* and its thoughts. If the will, in consequence of its fallen quality, do not submit to the government of the rational thoughts of the understanding, it goes astray from every good, and thereupon all those lusts are engendered which contribute so largely to bring about the moral desolation of the Church.

Seeing, then, that by the daughters of men, in the case before us, are spiritually denoted those lusts of evil which were brought forth by the wickedness of those early inhabitants of our earth, let us in the next place endeavour to ascertain what is meant by "the sons of God." Now, as by daughters in general are signified the things of affection in the will, so by sons are spiritually represented the things of thought in the understanding. While affection, as the offspring of the will, is as a daughter, thought, as the offspring of the understanding, is as a son. Hence *sons*, apart from the mere letter of the expression, represent the thoughts of the understanding, and therefore the phrase "sons of God" denotes all those thoughts which proceed from God; consequently, Divine truths.

The Lord Jesus Christ is called the *Son of God* in a pre-eminent sense, because that name expresses the Divine truth which he manifested and sustained. "I am," said he, "the truth."* Again, it is written of him that he was "the Word,"† which is the truth. He was the living impersonation and embodiment of the Word; he likewise declared that those "were called gods to whom the word of God came"; ‡ but it is evident that it was the reception of the Divine truth which conferred this remarkable distinction. Judges are called gods,§ because the judgment they were required to exercise was to be formed according to truth and equity. Moses is said to have been a god to Pharaoh,|| because he was the messenger by whom Divine truth was to be communicated to that obstinate monarch. In these cases Divine truth is called God, and particular truths derived therefrom are called "the sons of God." Hence those who believe in God are said to be his sons,¶ because such belief is founded on the reception and acknowledgment of the Divine truth from him. The power which is given to men to become the sons of God results from their knowing Divine truth, and applying it to the formation of their character. Hence the Apostle says, "As many as are led by the Spirit of God, they are the sons of God." ** The Spirit of God is the influence of Divine truth proceeding from him.

The sons of God, then, in the remarkable passage we are considering, is a phrase intended to express those doctrinal truths which yet remained among the people. They had been handed down to them from a remote and superior ancestry, and had not yet been dissipated by the corruptions of the people: that was an enormity they were now about to perpetrate. They are said to have seen the daughters of men that they were fair, to inform us that they were about to favour and subserve the lusts of evil; and the consummation of this iniquity is thus described: "They took to them wives of all which they chose."

This is a peculiar circumstance, which takes place in the human mind as the things of the Church are departing out of it;

* John xiv. 6. † John i. 1–14. ‡ John x. 35. § Exod. xxii. 28.
|| Exod. vii. 1. ¶ John i. 12. ** Rom. viii. 14.

and therefore it may be useful to elucidate it by an additional remark. When a man turns himself away from goodness, and goes in an opposite direction, a change takes place both as to the objects of his love and the subjects of his thinking. That also which he loves pre-eminently he thinks continually, and so all the knowledges of his mind are brought into requisition, to serve and favour the objects of his love. If there be any powerful truth which cannot be easily made to bend in such a direction, it is rejected and ultimately forgotten; but all other truths are induced to favour the *lusts* desired, and so to look upon them as "fair." By this means men confirm themselves in their impurities, and thereby they are not unfrequently led into the delusion of believing their evil to be good. This state is spoken of in the Scriptures as putting bitter for sweet, and sweet for bitter;* and it may readily be conceived by any one who will attentively observe what passes in himself and others. Every one who loves an evil will endeavour to invent arguments to persuade himself that it is allowable, as well as agreeable. Men are exceedingly expert in reasoning favourably for the things they love. The materials for such reasonings they will draw from any and every source at their command: nor will the Word of the Lord itself be left untouched in such a course. Approximations to this are occasionally observable in quoting the Scriptures upon light and frivolous occasions; and particularly when its passages are cited as the authority or excuse for any questionable conduct. As, for instance, when the wars to which the Israelites were directed are referred to as a sanction for the prosecution of wars in general; or when the conduct of David is cited to justify the indulgence of some criminal propensity. But whenever any of the statements of Divine truth are employed to favour and forward the pursuits of a selfish love, then the sons of God are in the act of seeing the daughters of men to be fair—the Divine truths are employed to subserve the purposes of human lusts. Those who are in evil will excuse the outbreaks of their anger by adducing passages expressive of the Divine wrath;† and they will defend the hatred of their

---

* Isa. v. 20.

† It is reported that the Pope, Julius III., had been greatly enraged at the Bishop of Rimini, his major-domo, about a peacock; that his Holiness

enemies by citing the laws of retaliation: in short, evil men, like devils, can quote Scripture for their purpose, pervert its design, and thus bring its truth into contact with impurity.* All such cases may be taken as illustrations of those dark scenes of moral turpitude which transpired in the latter days of the antediluvian world, expressed in the remarkable yet powerfully significant sentence, "The sons of God saw the daughters of men that they were fair."

Those abandoned people, having perverted the truth to subserve an evil purpose, must needs have profaned it; and thereby they deprived themselves not only of every spiritual good, but even of those remains which might have conduced to its attainment. All such profanation of the Word closes the interiors of the mind against the influence of heavenly graces, and prepares it for the inundation and overflow of those infernal principles in which they perish.

It was to describe that desperate condition, in which the mind would no longer be led by the spiritual things of heaven, that the Lord is stated to have said, "My spirit shall not always strive with man." The Spirit of the Lord consists in those holy influences which proceed from him to operate on men the graces of salvation, through the teaching of his Word; and the strivings of this Spirit consisted in its efforts to rescue men from evil, and better their condition in respect to heavenly things. When this effort ceased to be effective, in consequence of its being resisted on the part of man, then this Spirit is said to strive no longer; not that the mercy of the Lord was withdrawn, but that it had ceased to be perceived or acknowledged by

twice blasphemed; and that when one of the cardinals told him that he ought not to be so angry upon so small a matter, the Pope answered, "If God was so much disturbed, and filled with such anger and fury, and did such a quantity of evil to the whole human race about an apple, why may not I, who am his vicar upon earth, be angry with my major-domo about a peacock?"—*Examiner of May* 18, 1817, *as cited by the Rev. R. Hindmarsh.*

* I remember reading some few years ago, in a police report, of a man who had neglected and run away from his family defending himself with the following passage of the Word: "Every one that hath forsaken houses, or brethren, or sisters, or father, or mother, or wife, or children, or lands, for my sake, shall receive an hundredfold, and shall inherit everlasting life."—Matt. xix. 29.

mankind. Nevertheless, the design of perpetuating the human race was not to be abandoned, though new ground was to be provided for the reception of the means. It was pronounced that there "should not be any more a flood to destroy the earth";* because means for its prevention had been adopted in the new arrangement of the human mind before referred to. The *remains*, which were to be inseminated into the intellectual faculty, and there preserved by the Lord, were no more to be destroyed, as they had been by the last posterity of the most ancient people.

* Gen. ix. 11.

CHAPTER XX.

THE GIANTS THAT WERE IN THE ANTEDILUVIAN WORLD,— AND THE REPENTANCE OF THE LORD THAT HE HAD MADE MAN.

"It is not necessary to understand any particular race of men, of higher stature than usual, as many ancient interpreters have done; for since *nephil* means, to fall or rush on any one, *nephilim* will mean those who rush or fall on others, *i. e.*, robbers, banditti,—the centaurs of the Greeks were the same kind of people."— ROSENMÜLLER.

It is a remarkable circumstance that, towards the closing of the antediluvian period, we should be informed that "there were giants in the earth in those days; and also after that, when the sons of God came in unto the daughters of men, and they bare *children* to them, the same *became* mighty men which *were* of old, men of renown." * The most accomplished scholars admit that the original term, here translated giants, does not necessarily mean men of extraordinary stature, and that it may be very fairly construed to signify persons with remarkable minds.† Taking this view of the subject, we at once perceive a reason for the statement, which otherwise seems disconnected. It comports with the circumstance of their origin being traced to a connection of the sons of God with the daughters of men; and doubtless it is designed to point out one of the mental phenomena developed by an expiring church, and it must be understood to indicate some enormity, which the idea of gigantic bodies does not furnish.

There might have been individuals in those times, as there have been in all subsequent ages and nations, whose physical

---

* Gen. vi. 4.

† Some derive the original from a Hebrew root which denotes *to fall*, and render it *apostates*, *i. e.*, men who *fell off* from the faith of God; others render it oppressors, *i. e.*, men who *fell upon* or assaulted their fellow-men. Others, deriving the original from another root, render it *men of distinction*. This they certainly were; but for what were they distinguished?

stature exceeded the average size of men. Several instances are mentioned in the really historical portions of the Scriptures. Og, the king of Bashan;* Goliath, of Gath;† the fathers of Ishbibenob and Saph,‡ may be cited as examples; and even Saul, the king of Israel, "from his shoulders and upward was higher than any of the people."§ Indeed, it appears that there were some families or tribes who attained an uncommon height: the sons of Anak are so described; || so also are "many" of those whom the Moabites called Emims, and the Ammonites, Zamzummims.¶ The Rephaims likewise, from the name, are considered such a race. Now there cannot be any moral wrong in the circumstance of the body being developed into extraordinary magnitude: it is a consequence of the action of some natural law, over which men have but very little control. But it is remarkable that in every case where such persons are treated of in the Scriptures, they are contemplated as being at enmity with God and religion!

This circumstance forcibly suggests that such cases are recorded, not so much to supply us with historical information, as to afford the means of a spiritual representation. We do not obtain much religious knowledge from being told that certain men or classes of persons attained to an unusual height. Such a fact may be interesting to science, but it conveys no information about the characteristics of the mind, heart, or religion: these, after all, are the great topics upon which the Scriptures treat in every part; and the machinery of eloquence, poetry, history, and figure in a variety of forms, is employed to subserve this momentous purpose.

---

*Deut. iii. 11. He is said to have been a remnant of giants; most probably to intimate that he was the last of a family possessing unusual stature. His real height is not recorded; his *bed* (Michaelis and Dathe translate it his *coffin*) is said to have been nine cubits long, which are fifteen feet four inches and a half.

† 1 Sam. xvii. 4. He was six cubits and a span in height; that is, ten feet seven inches. The skeleton of O'Brien, preserved in the Museum of the Royal College of Surgeons, in London, measures seven feet eleven inches in height.

‡ 2 Sam. xxi. 16, 18.   § 1 Sam. ix. 2. || Numb. xiii. 33.

¶ Deut. ii. 10, 11, 20.

Although, then, there might have been exceedingly tall men in the antediluvian world, we conceive that by the giants of whom Moses speaks, as existing in the earth in those days, were represented some enormous condition of mind rather than of body; and that it was produced, as intimated, by that profane commerce which existed between the sons of God and the daughters of men. It is easy to see that such a result must have taken place when the doctrines of truth were prostituted so as to favour the lusts of men. Under such a circumstance they forgot the greatness of God, and strove to increase the proportions of themselves. They grew big in their own eyes, and their phantasies caused them to suppose that they possessed a large mental stature. The mind has its dimensions as well as the body; and hence we sometimes speak of great and little minds, of giant thoughts and dwarfish notions. The term giant is derived from words which express the idea of earth-born; and those of whom Moses treats, in the case before us, were so because they possessed an enlarged condition of selfish love, which "is of the earth, earthy." By a great opinion of their own height and pre-eminence, they set aside whatever was humble, contrite, and holy, and blew themselves into unseemly proportions. "Charity," says the Apostle, "vaunteth not itself, is not puffed up, doth not behave itself unseemly";* but self-love and its persuasions, which are the opposites to this heavenly grace, do all these things. The wicked who have knowledge, make it bend to favour their criminal pursuits, and so their vices become gigantic. It is the obvious result of such a course. This idea is such as most persons can appreciate; for every one has met with men who were more or less great in their own estimation,—who considered themselves somewhat above the ordinary dimensions of the mental standard. Such phantasies swell out their imaginary importance, and, in the absence of the only correctives,—religious influences and truths,—they are sure to become great in their own eyes. Now this condition, which has been more or less realized in every age of the world, was, at the period of which we are treating, developed in great enormity; hence it became one of the effective causes which hastened on the inundation of the world.

* 1 Cor. xiii. 4, 5.

This posterity of the dying Church were called in Hebrew, Nephilim, which Aquila translates, Ἐπίπτωντες (Epipiptontes), men who attack; and Symmachus, Βίαιοι (Biaioi), violent men, those whose rule of action is by force of arms; these interpretations agree with the idea above expressed. There are, however, several words in the Hebrew Scriptures signifying giants, which are not distinguished in the English version. They are used merely as names, and the ordinary reader only learns that they have such a meaning by collateral circumstances. Among these are Emim, Anakim, and Rephaim;* each of them is expressive of some bad quality, which had become conspicuous by the rejection of some particular good of religion and the Church. But the Nephilim, which our version calls giants, were of the most atrocious kind; and hence the best scholars have considered the word to express the idea of men whose minds had become somewhat enormous, in consequence of the guilt and profanation into which they had plunged themselves.†

These mental enormities were produced, as before observed, in those who perverted the doctrines of faith to favour the filthy loves, signified by the sons of God going in unto the daughters of men, and their bearing to them.‡ The result of such a froward course must obviously have been the profanation of the holy things of the Church, and thus to hasten on its desolation and produce its end.

Profanation consists in first knowing what interior truth and goodness are, then in perverting them to selfish purposes, and finally making them favour things impure and wicked: this, for example, is the case with those who have once acknowledged the sanctity of conjugal love, but on hearing anything about the heavenly origin of marriage and the holiness of that estate, turn

---

* The Septuagint sometimes translates the Hebrew word Gibbor, γίγαντες, gigantes. For instance, it says that Nimrod was a γίγας, i. e., a giant, before the Lord (Gen. x. 8, 9). Our version says he was a "mighty one,"—"a mighty hunter before the Lord." The idea intended to be expressed by this passage is that Nimrod was powerful in persuasion.

† Dr. A. Clarke says, "Fallen, earth-born men, with the animal and devilish mind, were the Nephilim."

‡ It is not said in the original that they bare *children;* and the word *children* is italicized in our version to point out that fact.

it into ideas of lasciviousness and lust; or, to take another instance, namely, those who have once been made acquainted with the sacred things of religion, and thence acknowledged them; afterwards come to regard them only as means by which to impose upon mankind, to acquire dominion in the circle wherein they move, and so procure gratification for their loves of self and of the world. Those who possess within themselves any knowledges of Divine truth, and at the same time do not acknowledge the Lord and his authority therein, are obviously guilty of this profanation. There are various degrees of this enormity, some more interior than others; some affecting goodness, and some affecting truth, each genus having many species; so that it behoves men to be watchful over every sentiment or emotion that would lead them to employ Divine things to other than heavenly uses. Whenever such profanation takes place, then "the sons of God have gone in unto the daughters of men," and Nephilim are born,—enormities of spiritual state and life come forth.

But they are also called "mighty men which were of old, men of renown." They are thus denominated to signify the power which selfish love had developed among them. It is well known that self-love is mighty in all its endeavours to secure the ends which it proposes. The desires of reputation, wealth, honours, place, distinction, or any other worldly eminence, when uninfluenced by the principles of religion, are so many varying forms of self-love, in which may be seen its might in setting aside obstacles, surmounting difficulties, and successfully securing the objects at which it aims. It is against the might of this nefarious principle that the graces and teachings of religion have to contend. So long as self-love reigns and sways its iron sceptre over the human character, so long love to God and charity to man are excluded from exercising their beneficent influences upon the heart, and it is exposed to the inflowings of every impurity. Self-love is a principle that is mighty for evil; and it is in the continual effort to render all persons subservient to its purposes, and all things contributory to its designs. It was the influence of this unhallowed might that brought the world into that condition which rendered redemption necessary for man's safety and continuance. It was spiritual wickedness in high places, so induced, with which the Lord wrestled in order to accomplish that work; therefore it is written, "A sword is upon her mighty men; and they shall be dismayed";* where by a sword is not meant the weapon of the soldier, but the Lord's Divine truth; for, when judgment comes, that truth resists and inflicts dismay upon all who derive their might from selfish love. It is to the same purpose that Amos declares, "The strong shall not strengthen his force, neither shall the mighty deliver himself"; † where by the mighty are denoted those who from self-love are powerful to do evil. Again, Isaiah says, "Woe unto them *that are* mighty to drink wine, and men of strength to mingle strong drink: which justify the wicked for reward, and take away the righteousness of the righteous from him!" ‡ where the "mighty," and the "men of strength," denote self-love and the love of the world. These considerations sufficiently show that the Nephilim or giants are called "mighty men" in reference to the powerful nature of that self-love in which they were principled; and which resisted, in pursuing its delights, all those orderly influences of truth and heaven which the Divine Providence had brought to bear upon their condition.

But it is said of such mighty ones that they "were of old, men of renown." Hence we learn that this very ancient narration refers to a period which then belonged to a remote antiquity, and to a description of character which existed at that time,—to persons who had the genus of the Nephilim, but who had not reached so great a depth in degradation. Those of old "were men of renown," or of a name, who had acquired a quality and distinction from the influences of self-love, but with whom it had not attained so atrocious a development as with those Nephilim, who are now called "mighty men."

All these circumstances, showing the depraved condition into which the people of those times were sinking, are fully corroborated by the declarations which immediately follow, namely, "And God saw that the wickedness of man *was* great in the earth, and *that* every imagination of the thoughts of his

* Jer. l. 36. † Amos ii. 14. ‡ Isa. v. 22, 23.

heart *was* only evil continually."* This, indeed, is a forcible description of their moral profligacy, and we at once grasp the general idea of it. But it also announces some particulars, and points out the peculiar quality of their state.

By the wickedness of man being great, with the statement that it proceeded from the heart, are plainly denoted that there began to be no will for anything that is good. The will of man is a principle peculiar to his nature; but it is truly human only so far as it is directed to the love and pursuit of intelligence and virtue. This is the interesting use for which it was given, and it is preserved by being dedicated to it. When men reject goodness, the will, as a human principle, perishes, and instead thereof lusts take place: this was the perilous condition of the people at the time now treated of. Their will was averted from the purposes of good, and converted into a means of evil. Its primitive condition may be compared to a beautiful palace, erected for the residence of a king, but which was subsequently turned into a dwelling-place for robbers and desperadoes of every grade. It consequently ceased to be the habitation of the king, and became the abode of the lawless. So the will of this ancient people was no longer a will, but a lust of the heart, out of which, the Lord says, "proceed evil thoughts, murders, adulteries, fornications, thefts, false witness, and blasphemies."† Nor was the will alone depraved; the understanding became equally corrupt. While the love of good passed away from the former, the perception of truth perished in the latter. Men's thoughts were conjoined with the evils of their heart; the imagination of the one favoured the lusts of the other: for the function of willing, and the power of thinking, were yet as one; so that every imagination of their thought was from the heart, consequently, in conformity with its desires, and this being evil continually, must have induced corresponding falsehoods perpetually. What a state of horrible corruption had thus fastened itself upon the human character! and how dreadfully abandoned must have been the people thus treated of! Evils had driven out goodness, and, seizing upon the will, directed it to lust; they also destroyed the perceptions of truth, and, per-

* Gen. vi. 5. † Matt. xv. 19.

verting the understanding by falsehood, infused into it those dreadful persuasions and deadly phantasies, which finally brought on their extinction, as by the suffocation of a flood. This condition, produced by the voluntary action of the people themselves, in opposition to all those orderly influences of the Divine purposes and principles, which are exerted to impress and maintain the excellence of religion, led to these remarkable expressions: "And it repented the Lord that he had made man upon the earth, and it grieved him at his heart." *

It must be evident that this description of the Divine sentiments is given in accommodation to the appearance which arises before man's perverted imagination. The sun, when seen through a fog, is red and dusky: that is not his genuine aspect. To the froward the Lord appears froward, but to the upright in heart he appears upright; he is good to all, and, therefore, the language expressing his *repentance* and *grief* must be understood to signify the yearnings of the Divine mercy and compassion, in reference to a people who had brought themselves into such a degraded condition.

Repentance is an affection of the mind which results from a consciousness of having done something that is wrong, and *grief* is a feeling produced either by a sense of our own transgression or by the vices of others. In any case, they imply a violation of the laws of virtue and the discipline of intelligence; therefore it is evident that the Lord cannot be said to repent and grieve in this sense of the terms. He cannot do anything that is wrong; whatever he does is wise and good: therefore it is written, "God *is* not a man, that he should lie; neither the son of man, that he should repent: hath he said, and shall he not do *it?* or hath he spoken, and shall he not make it good?"† Again, "The Strength of Israel will not lie nor repent: for he is not a man, that he should repent."‡ It therefore follows that the repentance and grief which are attributed to him must be understood to mean his Divine mercy; that which was about to become manifest in the establishment of a new covenant with Noah; and which was to provide against the recurrence of such a calamity as that which was about to be produced. Men, by a misdirection of their voluntary powers, bring evil upon them-

* Gen. vi. 6.   † Numb. xxiii. 19.   ‡ 1 Sam. xv. 29.

selves, and this insinuates falsehood into their understanding; from this falsehood they think God brings calamity upon them; and, consequently, when they experience any abatement of punishment which evil inflicts, they also begin to suppose that God is repenting; but even in this mistaken view of the subject there is included an idea of the Lord's mercy. The Scriptures frequently represent the goodness of God to us under this peculiar aspect; and, indeed, it is founded in the very nature of the circumstance. When the Jews, by their abandonment of the Lord, and their following of other gods, brought themselves into distresses, they commonly attributed those evils to the angry visitations of the Almighty; and when they returned to him by a penitent observance of his precepts, and thereby came into the enjoyment of his blessings, they considered that he was repenting of the evil which they erroneously believed that he had brought upon them.

Nor has this mistaken notion of God's procedure been confined to the Jewish nation only. Similar ideas form a part of the religious history of most people in times of calamity. Famines and pestilences, which have not unfrequently been produced by avarice, ignorance, idleness, filth, and "man's inhumanity to man," have been very commonly ascribed to the vengeance of God; and upon this principle he has been prayed to, to remove the afflictions. But in the midst of such distresses, sensible men have found it necessary to bestir themselves, and look, with scrutinizing eyes, for the natural causes of such results. Hence the land has been cultivated more scientifically and to a greater extent, nuisances have been removed, restrictive laws have been repealed, and superior attention given to personal and residentiary cleanliness; the consequences of which have been, that the famine has been stayed, the pestilence abated, and God supposed to have repented; that is, to have turned away the fierceness of his wrath. But whoever will venture to look beneath the surface of such appearances, must see that God cannot have undergone any change of disposition in all these painful vicissitudes of men. If they neglect or transgress his laws, they bring calamity thereby upon themselves. If they obey his laws, they open the channel for the incoming of his blessings. He is the same yesterday, to-day, and for ever.* He is essential love and goodness, and never brings affliction upon men. They are the authors of their own distresses, either by an ignorance of God's laws, or by the wilful transgression of them: in either case, the consequence in this life will be the same,—in the life to come, the ignorant neglecter may be excused, but the wilful transgressor will be condemned. Fury is not in God, and he changeth not.† He is ever waiting to be gracious: but men must comply with the laws and conditions for receiving grace, or it cannot be communicated. Therefore, any improvements in our condition are not to be attributed to the Lord having turned away from his anger and repented, but to the circumstance of man having changed, and become more favourably disposed towards him. It is upon this principle that the Lord has declared by the prophets, "If that nation, against whom I have pronounced, turn from their evil, I will repent of the evil that I thought to do unto them"; ‡ which plainly means, that if the people improve their states by a renunciation of their evil ways, they will then become recipients of the Divine mercy: and therefore the Psalmist, when treating of the bountiful goodness of the Lord, says, "He remembered for them his covenant, and repented according to the multitude of his mercies."§ Whence it is evident, that the communication of mercy is that which is meant by the Lord's repentance.

But let us endeavour to penetrate a little farther into the mental philosophy of this fact. It is quite clear that the mercy of God is exercised with a view to produce graces in men. How then are those graces to be implanted, so long as evils and errors maintain an uppermost position in their character? We answer that they must become known to their possessor, and be repented of by him. The light by which a man is enabled to see his sins is a communication from the Divine mercy; and the power whereby he is enabled to repent of them is from the same source; so that this Divine principle is present in all the phases of human repentance. Repentance cannot take place in a man without the presence of the Divine mercy; and it is

---

* Heb. xiii. 8. † Isa. xxvii. 4 ; Mal. iii. 6.
‡ Jer. xviii. 8. § Psa. cvi. 45.

on this account that this holy principle is sometimes so denominated in the Word. The Divine mercy produces human repentance; this is a good which leads to the establishment of good in man, hence it is a most appropriate expression, under such a circumstance, to signify that mercy. Moreover, as it has been intimated, that disorderly state of a man which needs repentance, causes an appearance in him, when it takes place, as though the Lord were becoming more favourably disposed towards him; whereas the real truth is, that man is becoming more favourably disposed towards the Lord. The change is in the man, and not in God.

The mercy of the Lord consists in everything which he does for mankind to relieve them from darkness and distress. When they fall into disorders and transgression, he does not withdraw his tenderness, but he pities and regards them with mercy. The punishment which the wickedness of the wicked brings upon themselves, is permitted by the Divine mercy, because thereby evil is to be checked and removed, and good developed and promoted. The happiness, also, which is enjoyed by the faithful and obedient is the result of the Divine mercy, because the Lord is present with his own principles in them. It was to such that he said, "The Spirit of truth dwelleth with you, and shall be in you." *

The mercy of the Lord is essential, infinite, and active goodness. But all human ideas of this mercy are formed from what we know of this principle and its operations among mankind. If men did not form their ideas of the Divine principles according to their own apprehensions of them, it is plain that no conception at all could be obtained concerning them, and in that case they would be left without instruction. It is in consequence of man's ideas of the Lord's infinite principles being formed on finite notions of them, that merely human and finite actions are, in the Scriptures, so frequently attributed to the Lord. He, however, is not a man, that he should repent; nevertheless, he is the God that will be merciful, and when he is said to repent, it is a declaration that his mercy is about to be displayed.

The same general remarks apply to the sentence, "and it

* John xiv. 17.

grieved him at his heart." The Lord cannot grieve on account of anything that he may have done. On the completion of his works, it is written, that he beheld them all, and pronounced them to be very good. The grief, therefore, which is predicated of him, must be intended to express the interposition of his mercy, at a time when its blessedness was about to be rejected by the perversities of men; and thus it is similar to his repentance; for repentance includes grief, and grief indicates repentance, so that both terms are significant of the Divine mercy, yet with a distinction which it may be useful to explain.

Although the Divine mercy is ever active for the benefit of men, and is unfolding itself in a thousand forms of beneficence and use, yet upon examination it will be found to operate in a twofold manner, including the intelligence of wisdom as well as the clemency of love. Mercy, without the intelligence of wisdom, would be blind; and without the clemency of love it would be cold. Now it is this twofold or distinctive action of the Divine mercy which is intended to be expressed by the repentance and grief at heart which are predicated of the Lord. By repentance is denoted that activity of the Divine mercy in which wisdom is the most conspicuous; and by grief at heart, that in which love is the most distinguished. The Divine mercy, indeed, always includes the activity of these principles in their utmost fulness; but then both of them are not at the same time equally prominent with their recipients. Sometimes one and sometimes the other is most easily observed. For instance, in the blessings of peace, which may have been promoted by a succession of wars, we at once recognize the love of the Divine mercy; but the wisdom of Divine mercy is not so very conspicuous in the wars by which that peace may have been secured. So we can see the love of the Divine mercy in creation and redemption; but the wisdom of the Divine mercy in the means is not so evident. We perceive that there is love in the Divine mercy which has provided and declared that there is a heaven for the good of the human race; but we do not so clearly see the wisdom by which it has become necessary to surround the nature of that kingdom with some obscurity. Persons who are rescued from dangers, or the perils of death, are said to be providentially saved. The love of the Divine mercy, in such cases, is very evident; but the wisdom involved in it is surrounded with haze and mist, particularly when others are known to have perished in the same calamity. These cases show very satisfactorily that the wisdom and love included in the Divine mercy are variously manifested, according to the varying circumstances in which they operate; and consequently we learn that those two terms, repentance and grief at heart, are significant of the wisdom and love which are always included in the activities of the Divine mercy, and these, in the circumstance before us, are very evident.

That to repent has respect to the wisdom of mercy, and that grief at heart has reference to the love of mercy, may also in some measure appear to those who will venture to reflect a little beneath the surface of the expressions. In that case repentance will be found to be an affection of the understanding, produced therein by the implantation of truth when errors prevail; and grief at heart will be seen to be a sensation of the will, induced therein by the insemination of good when evils are urgent. Those who receive truth into their understandings, and by the light thereof are led to examine and acknowledge the disorders of their life, are in a condition of *repentance;* while those who receive good into their wills, and by the influences thereof are made to experience the impurities which prevail, are in a condition of *grief*. Both conditions are from the activity of the Divine mercy, though there is an evident distinction between them; the former arising from the reception of truth, and the latter from the reception of goodness. So that the mercy of the Lord, signified by the statement of his repentance, consisted in the manifestation of his wisdom; and that which is denoted by his grief at heart, consisted in the display of his love. Hence, for the Lord to repent and to grieve that he had made man, are forms of expression which mean that the Divine mercy, under both aspects, was now about to become conspicuous.

Was it not so? Did not the Lord interpose for the preservation of our race? Although men had abandoned themselves to the most wicked persuasions, and had destroyed within them the faculty of perceiving what was good and true; notwithstanding they had voluntarily brought themselves into excesses of iniquity, and were upon the point of bringing down everlasting destruction upon the human race, yet the Divine mercy of the Lord interposed to hinder the catastrophe. The threatened calamity was prevented, and mankind have been preserved. This could not have been the case if the Lord's repentance and grief that he had made man, meant what a superficial understanding of the terms seems to imply. He surely would not have perpetuated the existence of that which had afflicted him with regret and sorrow. Man remains, and it is true that he has continued to live in evils, but then the evils are not of God's origination, nor are they perpetuated by Him; therefore, he can have nothing to repent of: but man, having both produced the evils and continued them, has become a perpetual subject of God's mercy; hence this is plainly what is meant by those penitential expressions. The interposition of God for the purpose of continuing our species at a period when mankind had sunk so deeply into spiritual wickedness, evinces most conspicuously the mercy of the Lord, in regard to his wisdom and his love. Man was preserved, not to perpetuate the evil, but that he might have the opportunity of attaining good by the rejection of evil, and so become the recipient of God's mercy.

But while it is evident that the interposition of God, for the perpetuation of man upon the earth, was an act of Divine mercy, in what did that interposition consist? It could not have been an act independently of the state of man. God does not operate among his people like a tyrant; he acts like a father, and pitieth those who fear him: and we find that there yet remained, among the last posterity of this profligate people, some who did so. "Noah found grace in the eyes of the Lord"; and the Lord said unto him, "Thee have I seen righteous before me in this generation." * These statements disclose to us the existence of a qualification for the reception of the Divine favours. This qualification consisted in a capacity for the understanding of truth, when presented in a form suitable to man's state. He could no longer be approached by an internal way: he had closed the interiors of his mind against those celestial influences which had originally reached him from within, and, therefore, a medium for approaching him by instruction from without was promised, and provided in the covenant that

* Gen. vi. 8 ; vii. 1.

was about to be established with Noah. This, as a new covenant, consisted in a new method of communication from God to man; in the adaptation of Divine truth to that external capacity for its comprehension, which appears to have been retained among the people called Noah and his family, and signified by the statement that he found grace in the eyes of the Lord.

The human race have since that period been instructed in the things of faith, charity, and religion, by an external revelation; that is, a revelation partaking of a documentary character, and adapted to their external capacities for appreciation. Thus, at the time of Noah, the mental constitutions of the people were different from what they had been in preceding ages. The people in the better times of those ages enjoyed perception; that is, an internal impression and discernment concerning holy and heavenly things: they felt, from an internal dictate, what were right and excellent; and this, to them, was instead of a documentary revelation. But in the days of Noah this state perished, and then that new method of communication with man, of which we have spoken, was begun. Thus the knowledges of religion have been preserved, and man's acquaintance with them has been also maintained; hence we see the mercy of the Lord as manifested in the provisions of that new covenant,—that new characteristic of revelation, and consequent church, by which so important a result has been accomplished. Unless there be a communication kept up between the Lord and man, man must perish. It may vary in its form,—it may be by an internal dictate and impression, as was the case with Adam and his immediate posterity; or it may be by documentary declarations, as it has been in subsequent ages. Nevertheless its existence, in some form, is indispensable to the perpetuation of man. It was because this communication had ceased with the principal part of the people of the later antediluvian periods, that they perished in the catastrophe called the flood.

Here we close this chapter. We have endeavoured to rescue the points that have been handled from the marvellous and incomprehensible character which they present in their merely literal structure; and we have shown, that in their esoteric sense, they present a reasonable view of human nature, and of God's dealings with men, and so commend themselves to our faith in them, as portions of God's Holy Word.

CHAPTER XXI.

THE ARK—NOAH AND HIS FAMILY ENTERING INTO IT—THE BEASTS PRESERVED THEREIN.

> "Those who have written professedly and largely on the subject, have been at great pains to provide for all the existing species of animals in the ark of Noah, showing how they might be distributed, fed, and otherwise provided for. But they are very far from having cleared it of all its difficulties, which are much greater than they, in their general ignorance of natural history, were aware of."—Kitto's "*Cyclopædia of Bib. Lit.,*" Art. Ark, Noah.

To provide for the continuation of mankind, by saving some from the flood that was about to overwhelm the general population of the antediluvian world, Noah was directed to make an ark of certain dimensions, having three stories, with one door in the side and one window above, for the whole; and having finished what was thus commanded him, "the Lord said unto him, Come thou and all thy house into the ark; for thee have I seen righteous before me in this generation. Of every clean beast thou shalt take to thee by sevens, the male and his female: of beasts that are not clean by two, the male and his female: of fowls also of the air by sevens, the male and the female; to keep seed alive upon the earth. For yet seven days, and I will cause it to rain upon the earth forty days and forty nights; and every living substance that I have made will I destroy from off the face of the earth."* The subjects announced in the literal sense of this history have always been considered exceedingly difficult to comprehend. To science they appear inexplicable; to religion they seem miraculous. For ages they have been placed in the niches of a misty faith; and the effort to understand them has not unfrequently been denounced as infidel and presumptuous. Ecclesiastical authorities of a bygone period, having committed themselves to a certain course of thinking upon these subjects, have succeeded in fastening their notions

---

* Gen. vii. 1-4.

of them upon the minds of the multitude; and their descendants in later times have found it more convenient to stigmatize the doubter of their views with an odious name, than to remove his scruples or satisfy his inquiries with information. The few who have thought upon the popular views of those matters, and ventured to question their accuracy, have been treated as unfriendly to revelation by the many who have not thought at all upon the subjects. The populace are led more by passion than by reason, and they are too frequently influenced more by those who hold offices of authority, than by the dignity of their own thinking. If men would receive religious knowledge, and improve their own intellectual condition, they must reflect for themselves. It is that which they make their own, by an effort of their own mind, which remains and endures with them. They take nothing with them into the other life which has not been incorporated into their affections and thoughts during their abode below. The profession to believe the dogmata of faith, upon the authority of others, is not a belief in the thing proposed, but in the persons proposing; and such a belief is rather a reliance upon man than a faith in God. It is of importance that this circumstance should be reflected on: those who desire wisdom will do so; those who prefer to remain without it will culpably neglect this duty. But wisdom is not to be moved from her pedestal by the clamour of ignorance. She looks with pity upon the crowd who receive a certain opinion for no other reason than because authority has propounded it, or that their fathers believed it; and she is ever ready to afford assistance to all who wish to form their faith upon a holier and a sounder basis.

There is a great distinction between believing the Scriptures, and believing what men have said to be contained in them. It is well known that some authorities have declared the Word to present a variety of dogmata for the faith of men, which other tribunals, of equal character and intellect, have not been able to discover. But it does not follow, because one man cannot find another man's conceit in the Bible, that therefore he does not believe in the Bible itself. This, however, is what prejudice and clamour would lead the multitude to think. The Scriptures may be fully believed to be the Word of God, although certain views which men have taken of its statements may be intelligently and conscientiously rejected. The Bible, and men's interpretation of it, are very frequently two different things. In many points they have been so for several ages. Conjectures and ingenious speculations are among the chief sources through which the difficult narratives of revelation are commonly explained. This is the origin of those various opinions concerning them which the differing sections of Christianity prove to exist. For a long period men have not suspected that the Scriptures are written according to a fixed law. It seems to have been overlooked that the Word of God was a work of God, and that, therefore, like all his other works, it must have been constructed on some fixed principles. This, however, is the case, and it must be so if it be the Word of God: and it can no more be accurately interpreted without a knowledge of the laws and principles of its composition, than the works of God in the stellar universe can be explained without an acquaintance with the laws and mathematics of gravitation.

The nature, objects, and phenomena mentioned in the Scriptures are the appropriate symbols of spiritual thoughts and affections pertaining to man; and those spiritual things are what the natural descriptions are intended to reveal. The world of matter is an emblem of the world of mind, and God has chosen the former as the means for disclosing the facts and circumstances relating to the latter. Some portion of the letter of the Scriptures consists of national history, as is the case with what is said of the Jewish nation; but there are cases of merely emblematical history, the chief of which is that portion of the Word which precedes the time of Eber, mentioned in the eleventh chapter of Genesis. We discriminate between the actual and the emblematical history, but regard both to be of equal weight and authority, as to their Divine origination and spiritual purpose. The narrative of the flood, and all the particulars that are grouped therewith, we look upon as factitious history only, embodying indeed a revelation from God, and intended to make known certain moral and spiritual events connected with the corruption of an ancient people. We receive the narrative as one which has been produced under the Divine superintendence and direction. We cherish it as a portion of

God's revelation to man. But we do not believe that literal interpretation which has long prevailed concerning it. We do not mistake, as is the common and popular course, the figurative terms for the real meaning. We discriminate between the figure and the thing which is signified. It is admitted, by all candid minds, that the subject of the ark, with its remarkable contents, presents very embarrassing ideas to a rational understanding. Much labour and some ingenuity have been employed in the attempt to explain the arrangements of the ark, so as to adapt it for the reception of seven pairs of clean animals, and two of the unclean, of all the earth, besides the room necessary for eight human beings, and stowage for food requisite for upwards of twelve months' sustenance.* The success has not been equal to the exertions. Nor has it ever been shown how eight persons could keep in order, feed, and water such an immense number of inmates. Moreover, if the ark had been a natural ship, the closing of the window and the door (there was but one of each) for so many months must have effectually prevented the admission of air, which is now known to be so essentially necessary for the preservation of health and life; and the respiration of the multitude of inmates must have completely vitiated that which was within. How, then, did they survive? Upwards of a hundred men have been known to perish in a few hours, in consequence of being confined in a small building, to which a sufficient quantity of wholesome air could not gain access.† It was only the other day that a similar calamity occurred to a number of passengers in a ship, from the like cause. How was it, then, that Noah, his family, and

* Bishop Wilkins: "Essay towards a Philosophical Character and Language."

† When Calcutta was attacked by Suraja ud Dowlah, the viceroy of Bengal, in 1756, the English factory, which had been removed from Hooghly, and established there, was deserted by the governor, the commandant, and many other European functionaries and residents. On the capture of the place, the English who had remained to defend the factory were thrust into a small unwholesome dungeon, called the Black Hole, and of 146 individuals who were thus shut up at night, only 23 were found alive in the morning. The cause of this frightful circumstance was the presence of carbonic acid gas, produced by respiration and other means, for which there was no escape, nor any sufficient aperture for the admission of fresh air.

the numerous beasts, were enabled to live under such unfavourable circumstances? We do not read of any provision having been made for ventilation, which must have been absolutely necessary to preserve the lives of those within. Thus sanitary science suggests new difficulties in the inquiry.

However, the dimensions of the ark do not afford sufficient room for the accommodation of all the animals of the earth. Those who have supposed there was space enough, have considerably underrated the number of the species to be provided for:* they have also overlooked many other circumstances, which a true solution of the problem requires to be carefully remembered. Three or four hundred species is the most that have ever been calculated for; whereas, of mammalia alone, there are more than a thousand species; of birds, fully five thousand; besides reptiles, of which there are upwards of two thousand species that cannot live in water, and at least a hundred thousand insects, besides millions of animalcula. The size of the ark was evidently inadequate to stable them: nor is it easy to see how eight persons could have attended to them. The difficulties attending the collection of the mammalia and birds alone from the various regions of the earth, and introducing them into the ark, with their necessary provision, are quite sufficient to suggest that there is some very considerable error in the current belief upon this subject. The best writers have been led to abandon the idea that species of animals of all the earth were collected in the ark, and to suppose that they were only such as inhabited the regions where man was located.† These, indeed, are concessions to science and enlightened inquiry; and farther investigation will show it to be requisite to take an entirely different view of the whole subject.

Those who receive the literal sense merely, have an easy method for removing objections. They say that God, who can do everything, could have had no difficulty in providing against those things which may seem obstacles to science, reason, or

---

* Le Pelletier, a merchant of Rouen, proposed towards the close of the last century a plan for building a vessel in which all kinds of animals might be included and maintained for a year.

† Dr. Pye Smith, Bishop Stillingfleet, Matt. Poole, Le Clerc, Rosenmüller, &c., &c.

philosophy. They assert that the whole affair must have been easy to Him to whom all things are possible. Of course this silences inquiry; and there is no arguing with those who will not reason. We do not address ourselves to such. Those who admit these principles, deprive themselves of all ground for resisting the belief of any physical extravagance that may be propounded to them. Such principles are favourable neither to sound piety nor to intelligence. They close the mind against a candid investigation of that which God has said in his Word. This is contrary to the benevolent design of Him who said, "Come, let us reason together."*

To avoid those difficulties, and to obtain a clearer insight into the meaning of this remarkable history, we must remember a point which has been attempted to be set forth in a preceding chapter, namely, that with the Noachic people the understanding was separated from the will, by which means they became admissive of external instruction concerning spiritual and religious things, hence they found grace in the eyes of the Lord, and became the subjects of His covenant. The internal channels of immediate communication from the Lord had been closed by the corruption of the will. When this took place, the understanding was mercifully separated from the will, in order to provide a medium of access to the interiors of the mind, through instruction presented from without. This was a new condition in man's mental structure, which has ever since been faithfully preserved in him. Hence a new form of Divine communication was adopted, and spoken of as the covenant that was to be established with Noah and his seed after him, also with every living creature that was with him.†

Remembering this point, we shall at once be prepared to enter into the meaning of the command, "Make thee an ark of gopher wood; rooms shalt thou make in the ark, and shalt pitch it within and without with pitch."‡ We consider this direction to refer to the construction of a certain state of the human mind, and the orderly arrangement of its internal principles, through which a church might exist, and by which preservation from evil and the reception of good were to be provided for; and not to the building of a wooden vessel. If that had been the case,

---

* Isa. i. 18. † Gen. ix. 9, 10. ‡ Gen. vi. 14.

the purpose of such an erection could not have been concealed. It was an extraordinary undertaking, requiring for its execution a large number of workmen, and no inconsiderable pecuniary resources to procure the materials and reward the labour; it therefore must have excited curiosity and inquiry. Noah did not receive any instruction to conceal the knowledge of the predicted flood from the people, nor the means which he had been commanded to adopt for his own safety; and, therefore, it is reasonable to suppose that the purpose of the erection must have obtained extensive publicity. How is it, then, that we do not find the slightest intimation of other parties endeavouring to save themselves from the impending catastrophe by building vessels for the purpose? It may be replied, although they might have been made acquainted with the prediction of the approaching flood, that their evil lives prevented them from having any faith in its realization; and the Lord's observation, "They knew not, until the flood came, and took them all away," may be adduced as the evidence of such unbelief; and this, it may be argued, was the reason why they did not make any provision for their safety. Be it so; and one objection is removed. The love of life, however, is very ardent, even among the most abandoned; and if it were known to them (and this can hardly be doubted) that a vessel had been built to save a certain family from an approaching flood, it is reasonable to suppose that upon the rising of the waters they would have become alarmed, and instantly have betaken themselves to the ark for safety. Under such circumstances, they would not have been deterred by any delicacy about entering another man's property; and if room were wanted for their accommodation, it is not likely that they would have hesitated to make it, by removing some of the animals and their provender. Human life is more precious than the beasts, and its preservation would be chiefly aimed at: nor would the owner of such a vessel have thrust them away in such an effort, if he had been a good man. This we say is a highly reasonable view of the case, supposing the ark to have been a natural vessel. The dismay which must have overtaken the inhabitants it is not easy to imagine: the horror which must have distressed the living, and the agonizing shrieks that would have proceeded from the dying, must have been exquisitely frightful: surely such circumstances must have constituted the very terror of the story, if it had been a physical occurrence; yet there is not the slightest intimation concerning them. It is not easy to conceive a reason for omitting such descriptions, nor do we think they would have been left out, if the event had been such as it is currently supposed.

Doubtless the Lord said, "As the days of Noe *were*, so shall also the coming of the Son of man be. For as in the days that were before the flood they were eating and drinking, marrying and giving in marriage, until the day that Noe entered into the ark, and knew not until the flood came, and took them all away; so shall also the coming of the Son of man be."* But the "ark" and "flood" mentioned in this passage are no proofs that they were natural things. To regard them as representing certain spiritual things, pertaining to the mind, answers all the purposes of the argument they are introduced in the gospel to sustain. To say that they were spiritual things, is not to say that they were less real. The mere circumstance of mentioning "Noe," the "flood," and the "ark," offers no explanation of the subject, and, therefore, the ideas and facts which they were employed to express in the original narrative are precisely those to which the Lord referred. The plain scope of the passage is to show that the state of mankind at the coming of the Son of man would be similar to that which preceded the entrance of Noe into the ark. The comparison instituted is between the two states of mankind; and the revelation made is that the spiritual life of religion always perishes by similar means; namely, by yielding to the love of self and the world, and neglecting God and heaven. The means by which this life perishes with some, and is preserved with others, are spoken of in the Scriptures under a variety of figures. Thus, the means which destroyed the spiritual life of religion with the antediluvians, is described to have been a flood; the means by which it was to be preserved with Noah, is represented by his entering into an ark. That by which it was extinguished with the inhabitants of Sodom and Gomorrah, was "brimstone and fire," but that by which Lot and his family were saved from the conflagration, was the instruction and guidance of

* Matt. xxiv. 37–39.

two angels.* So the means by which it will perish with some, under the Christian dispensation, are described as the darkening of the sun and moon, and the falling of the stars; whereas its preservation with others is to be accomplished by their seeing the Son of man coming in the clouds of heaven with power and great glory. There is, then, nothing in the above passage inimical to the view we are taking of the general subject.

If the ark, and the particulars which are related of it, had no other signification than the letter presents, there would be nothing at all religious or spiritual in the account of them, and consequently they would be of no more value to mankind than a similar history composed by profane writers, in which case it would be a kind of dead letter. But these are ideas which cannot attach to any portion of the Lord's Word; therefore, the ark, with its construction and arrangements, must refer to something that is spiritual and living,—something pertaining to the mind and soul of man, rather than to his body and the world.

The literal sense of the narrative is not sufficiently clear to have led the "orthodox" to any settled opinion concerning the form and materials of the ark. The word here employed for the ark is *tebath*, not *aron*, which is used to express the ark of the covenant; and *tebath* is used only of the Noachic vessel, and of that in which Moses was preserved.† Hence Dr. Geddes ‡ and others have supposed that it was a large coffer formed of twigs, like basket-work! and covered over with bitumen, both within and without, to keep out the water. The Greek speaks of its material as ἐκ ξύλων τετραγώνων (*ek xulon tetragonon*) of square boards: Jerome, in the Vulgate, calls it "planed wood," and "pitched wood," and several other commentators have imagined that it was built of several sorts of wood, though only one is expressly mentioned. Thus, even those who abide in the letter do not seem to know what the letter means. A popular opinion respecting its form, as presented in "orthodox" pictures, is that it was a kind of house erected in a boat; for which idea, however, there is no foundation in the narrative. There is nothing about the description to suggest that it was a regularly

---

* Gen. xix. 15-22.   † Exod. ii. 3, 5.
‡ See his "Critical Remarks," pp. 67, 68.

built vessel, and all that is fairly to be inferred from the evidence of the letter is, that it was a building of a certain wood, in the form of a parallelogram. But what is the meaning of such descriptions?

We conceive them to refer to the establishment of a new Church, for which the people under the name of Noah were instructed to prepare. The Adamic Church, as a celestial dispensation, was about to perish, and now the Noachic Church, as a spiritual dispensation, was to be developed. This new Church, of course, implied a new state of mind on the part of those who were the recipients of its principles. Every one sees that the Church is as an ark, in which men are to be saved from spiritual perils; also that the Church which so saves is a state of the affections and thoughts implanted in the mind. The state of the Church, and the state of the mind, run parallel to each other. As the mind sinks down by corrupting loves, the Church declines; as the mind improves by heavenly delights, the Church advances: so that whether we speak of a new Church, or of a new state of mind, as being represented by the ark, it amounts to the same thing; for a man is a Church, in consequence of his mind being imbued with its principles.

The mind, considered as a faculty, consists of will and understanding: of will, to love what is good; of understanding, to comprehend what is true. These have been the characteristics of mind in all ages posterior to the time of Noah; but it was with that people with whom these two principles first came into distinct activity; and the command given them to make the ark, under the perilous circumstances which surrounded them, has some practical bearing upon a like duty in all subsequent times. The mind of man is a spiritual vessel, created with capacities for the reception and preservation of the spiritual and celestial things of religious life. This capability of the mind, under this new condition of its existence, was now to be tested and developed; but this was no ordinary work. The formation of the mind, considered as a faculty, with the use for which it is designed, is the act by which it becomes properly a mind; and the building up of this ark, so as to render it a safe vessel in times of storm and peril, requires much care, instruction, and devotedness. This is implied in the directions given to Noah, and in the dangers which prevailed before they were completed.

But this ark was to be of certain dimensions, and to be made of gopher wood, pitched within and without. These particulars are stated to represent the means to be adopted, in order to render the mind a safe and effectual medium for the right development of that new covenant which was about to be established.

The kind of wood denominated *gopher* has not been satisfactorily ascertained. It is a problem for the Biblical student. On the assumption of its having been a natural production, the name has been supposed to designate a species of the pine, or perhaps to denote several species of it, which yielded resin and other easily inflammable matter, because it is thought that they were abundantly produced in the locality where the ark is considered to have been erected. Dr. Geddes thought that it must have been the *osier;* * Dr. Mather conjectured that it was the *Juniperus arbor tetragonophyllos*, frequent in the East Indies.† The Chaldee version regards it to have been the *cedar;* the Arabic version translates it *saj*, which is considered to mean the *teak;* and others, as the Vulgate, say it was the *cypress.*‡ Here, then, are plenty of conjectures, and very much learning has been employed for the purpose of upholding them. Still it is an open question; and although the progress of science may conduce to the discovery of something more decided upon the subject than what at present exists, that will not derogate from the fact of its having been mentioned chiefly for a representative purpose. *Gopher* is the original Hebrew word, without any attempt to translate it, and this is the only instance in which it occurs throughout the whole Scriptures; and this wood is here mentioned for the purpose of signifying a mental condition, which now became a specialty among the Noachic people.

It is well known, as a general idea, that the ancients com-

---

* "Critical Remarks," pp. 67, 68.   † Abr. Phil. Trans., vol. vi., p. 86.

‡ Rosenmüller was of this opinion. He considers the wood gopher to have become obsolete and fallen into disuse among the later Hebrews, and shows that the radical consonants in "gopher" and "cypress" are substantially the same: he also thinks it probable that the words signify, etymologically, "a resinous wood."—"*Mineralogy and Botany of the Bible*," *Art. Gopher.*

pared the internal things of orderly men to *gold, silver, brass, iron, wood,* and *stone;* but it has not been so frequently observed that such comparisons were adapted to signify different states of the mind: thus, that the good things of the will were likened to *gold, brass,* and *wood;* and the true things of the understanding to *silver, iron,* and *stone.* Of this the prophet furnishes us with a remarkable example. "For *brass* I will bring *gold,* and for *iron* I will bring *silver,* and for *wood brass,* and for *stones iron.*"* Here, to bring gold for brass, and brass for wood, plainly denotes, to supply the will of those who are being "born again," with superior good for the inferior; and to bring silver for iron, and iron for stone, signifies, to supply the understanding of those who are regenerating, with superior truths for such as are inferior. Thus, *wood* in general, denotes the lowest degree of good pertaining to the will which may be called corporeal: precious woods, as the cedar and the like, signify woods of a higher quality; the cedar used in the temple † had this signification, so also had that which was employed in cleansing the leprosy; ‡ also that wood by which the bitter waters of Marah were sweetened.§ But woods which were not precious, those which were made into images,|| and applied to the making of funeral piles,¶ signify cupidities, and among these are to be classed the wood of gopher.

This wood, then, is named to signify that peculiar concupiscence by which the Noachic people were distinguished, and from which they were directed to construct the ark; or, what amounts to the same idea, to build up their mind, so that it should be as a vessel fitted for the reception and preservation of spiritual things.

If it be asked, How can concupiscence afford the materials for such a result? we answer, that it does so much in the same way that men who are altogether evil can become regenerate.

---

* Isa. lx. 17. † 1 Kings v. 8.
‡ Lev. xiv. 4, 6, 7. § Exod. xv. 25.

|| "Among the trees, of whose timber idols were formed, mention is made, in Isa. xliv. 14, of the *Oren,* by which both the oldest Greek and the oldest Latin translators understood the pine tree."—*Rosenmüller,* "*Botany of the Bible,*" Art. Pine Trel.

¶ Isa. xxx. 33.

They possess remains, and the capability to evolve them. Men, at the commencement of their regeneration, do not listen to spiritual instruction and religious duties for the sake of their intrinsic excellence; but because they either afford gratification to the intellect, or because they furnish information by which to avoid something that may be dangerous to self: in either case some advantage will be gained; and all the early states of man's religious improvement are more or less built up from some personal and selfish consideration, and so from his concupiscence. He wishes to avoid some danger or procure some blessing; but the early efforts to secure these things will, upon examination, be found to arise from something that is low and selfish. As, then, the Noachians were a fallen people who were about to be regenerated, we may readily see why they were directed to make an ark of gopher wood. Concupiscence was the readiest and most abundant material of which they could command the use; but, being directed to religious inquiries and purposes, it, under the Divine Providence, resulted in safety. It was making friends of the mammon of unrighteousness, in order to be received into everlasting habitations.* But the state of mind so produced admitted both the clean and the unclean beasts and fowl: it was also liable to grievous temptation; consequently, when these were experienced and overcome, the ark which had been constructed of such materials was abandoned, and we read no more about it!

It was commanded that the ark should be pitched within and without, to point out the care that was to be exercised in preventing falsehood from entering into the mind, either by impure excitement from without, or by seducing impulses from within. The original text does not say that it should be pitched with pitch, but an expression is employed which denotes preservation,† and it has only been so translated in consequence of its supposed relation to a natural ark. The pitching is representative of preservation, on the ground of its natural use being to exclude both the entrance and emission of all such waters as

---

* Luke xvi. 9.

† "It is derived from the verb to expiate, or propitiate, wherefore the same sense is implied; the Lord's expiation, or propitiation, is protection from the overflowing of evil."—*Arcana Cœlestia*, n. 645.

would endanger personal safety. It thus denotes that means were to be employed by which the mind was to be preserved from the inflowings of those false persuasions, which would cause it to sink and perish.

The various measurements of the ark were intended to denote the several qualities which were to distinguish the mind in the progress of its erection or development into a saving condition. These are similar in import to the dimensions which are given of the tabernacle, the temple, the mercy-seat, the altar, and, especially, the new Jerusalem, which is said to be the measure of a man; whence it is evident that such measurements denote the extent of mental condition in reference to the things of the Church. Thus, the *length* of the ark had reference to the quality of good which should exist in the will; the *breadth* of it, to the extent of truth in the understanding; and the *height* of it, to the elevated origin of these good things, which is the Lord. Every one may see that such particulars concerning the ark are given with a view to their spiritual import, because they have no natural or scientific value; also, because without such a signification they would be of no religious use to mankind. But by drawing aside the curtain of the letter, and looking into the spiritual sense, we at once discover the presence of a Divine principle, and recognize its instructive purpose. The spiritual sense raises us into the intellectual world: the letter perplexes and produces doubts, which vanish on the approach of spiritual light. How beautifully true is the apostolic declaration, "The letter killeth, but the spirit giveth life"!*

While all the details respecting the construction of the ark signify particular circumstances connected with the human mind, during the process of its reformation and preparation for the reception of spiritual and heavenly things, yet the popular view we are solicitous of presenting requires that we should dwell mostly on the more general description. For instance, the ark was to have "rooms," "a window above," "a door in the side, with lower, second, and third stories." †

Inasmuch as the ark is mentioned to represent a certain state of the human mind which was to be built up as a means of deliverance from the ills which threatened desolation to sur-

* 2 Cor. iii. 6. † Gen. vi. 14, 16.

rounding society, it will follow that the rooms in that ark denote the two faculties of will and understanding. These, however, are very general distinctions, each of which is arranged into a variety of others. The division of the intellectual sentiments, which belong to the understanding, and the distinction of moral affections, which pertain to the will, are very numerous. Thus, the *rooms* in the ark denote all that variety of intellectual and moral principles which are built up in man during the progress of his regeneration; the numerous species of goodness and truth occupy their respective positions in the mind, each of which is as a room for their reception, and all are arranged according to their relation to heaven or the world. The inferior goods take up their residence in those lower rooms of the mind, which are formed by information and sciences: the superior goods enter into those higher capabilities, which are formed by affection and intellect. The regenerate man—he with whom the Lord enters into conjunction—has all the things of intelligence and duty arranged in his mind with the most distinctive order. The things of science, rationality, pure intellect, and affection, have each their respective mansions in the human mind. They have their appropriate rooms in the ark. It is in consequence of the minds of the regenerate having this orderly arrangement, that the Lord said of them, " Behold, the kingdom of God is within you"; * also pronounced that kingdom to be a house with many mansions.† It is easy to perceive that the regenerated mind is as a house in which the Lord dwelleth with its possessor, and that this dwelling-place must have many mansions, each of which is intended for the reception of some of the distinctive varieties of truth and goodness. The Lord also recognized this signification of rooms when he commanded the prophet to enter into his chambers, and there remain till the indignation was overpast: ‡ likewise where he directs that when we pray we should enter into our closets; § for by chambers and closets are evidently meant interior but different principles of the mind, from which those distinctive duties are to be performed. Seeing, then, what is

* Luke xvii. 21. † John xiv. 2.
‡ Isa. xxvi. 20. § Matt. vi. 6.

spiritually meant by the rooms of the ark, let us next consider what is signified by the window above.

By this, we at once perceive, is denoted the intellectual principle which acknowledges the Lord to be the source of light. The intellectual principle is compared to a window, because it is that by which the light of truth enters in to illuminate the whole mind, and through which man, as it were, looks out to view religion and contemplate his God: and, in the instance before us, it is said to have been above, plainly to express the idea of its elevation towards the Lord, who is the "true Light which lighteth every man who cometh into the world."* Daniel is said to have prayed to the Lord with his windows open,† to represent the expansion of the intellectual principle during his solicitation of the Divine graces. So, likewise, Jeremiah speaks of death having come up into our windows,‡ to signify the darkening of our intellect through the approach of some evil influence. The analogy existing between the window in the ark above, and the intellectual principle of the mind acknowledging the Lord as the source of all spiritual light, is very remarkable and singularly striking.

But there was also to be a door in the side, because by this is denoted the inlet of hearing, by which faith enters. Seeing and hearing are two common entrances into the mind; the former admits ideas through an intellectual perception, the latter permits them to enter by means of external teaching. It is on these grounds that the eye is sometimes spoken of as a window, and the ear as a door. Hearing is as a door through which oral instruction passes into the mind, and from mind to mind. Every one is aware that hearing implies the entrance of something into the memory, and instruction thence; likewise reception into the understanding, and the formation of belief accordingly: also, to receive in obedience and to do,—for all the teachings of religion have relation to the duties of life. The reason why hearing involves these things is, because speech, which enters into the mind by means of hearing, presents itself to the intellect, and there, according to the efficacy of reason, of the power of persuasion from some other source, it is retained,

* John i. 9. † Dan. vi. 10. ‡ Jer. ix. 21.

believed, and obeyed. Hence it is that hearing, as the medium through which instruction, the knowledges of faith, and the precepts of obedience, enter into the mind, is compared to a door. So that hearing is as a door in the side of the ark, or human mind, in respect to the window that is above. The window that is above admits of illumination from the Lord, thus of internal instruction; but the door which is on the side is the common entrance for things from this world, thus for external instruction. These two inlets of knowledge, one from above and the other from the side, are indispensable to the existence of the mental ark,—that condition of mind in which we are to be preserved in good and saved from evil.

But it was farther directed that this ark should consist of lowest, second, and third stories, to inform us that there are three different degrees belonging to the orderly existence of a regenerated mind. Every one's experience sufficiently proves that there are different degrees in the mind; nor can it require any very interior reflection to discover that they must consist of the lowest, the middle, and the highest. This, indeed, as a general truth, is perfectly intelligible; and a little consideration will show that these three degrees are the natural, the spiritual, and the celestial; also that each of them has its own continuous elevation, but is distinct from the others.

For instance, when a man is first born he comes merely into the natural degree of his mind, and this, by means of instruction and the sciences, is successively developed and increased. By these means it may attain to a considerable elevation; still, whatever may be its height, it will always be a natural degree, or the lowest story of the ark, remaining distinct from the spiritual, which is immediately above it. No expansion of the natural degree will ever open out the spiritual; that is effected by another process. Hence it is that we sometimes meet with persons who are exceedingly well informed in most things pertaining to the world and nature, but who, nevertheless, have not a spiritual idea opened in their mind,—who treat the existence of such ideas as the chimera of enthusiasts, and who, in consequence, think nothing of religion or its teachings. Hence we see that the natural degree of the mind is that which is meant by the lowest story of the ark.

The middle compartment consists of the spiritual degree, and this is begun to be developed, or built up, as a man begins to reverence the truths of religion, to love his neighbour, and to do good to society, from a religious principle of intelligence and use. The love of our neighbour is the spiritual principle of religion; consequently, when a man does this, the spiritual degree of his mind is unfolded: and this may go on increasing in its elevation, through the accumulation of appropriate knowledge and the application of it to use; still it is a degree which must always be distinct from that which is immediately above, and thus it is the second story in the ark.

The third story is the celestial degree, in which resides the love to God above all things. This is the highest degree of the human mind, wherein the highest things of religion take up their abode, and which in itself is nearest heaven; those who have had this degree opened have had built up in their minds the third story of the ark. How beautifully, and at the same time how satisfactorily, do these facts, relating to the structure of the mind, coincide with the description of the ark! When thus built up, it becomes the distinguished means for safety and the reception of blessings, which are the obvious purposes for which it was commanded to be raised.

Let us, then, in the next place, inquire what is meant by entering into it. There are two reasons, both of which have respect to the necessary qualification, why this privilege was granted to Noah. *First*, he found grace in the sight of the Lord;* and *second*, the Lord saw him righteous before him in that generation.† The *grace* is said to have been found in him before the building of the ark, because it denoted the remains of some *truth* by which it was to be accomplished: but the *righteousness* is ascribed to him after the work was completed, because that expressed a state of *good* which resulted from obedience to the command for building it: "Noah did according to all that the Lord commanded him." ‡ These are additional particulars which show the ark to have been significant of that new development of mind, which was necessary for the appreciation of that new Church or covenant then about to be formed. The Church in after times has not unfrequently been called the

* Gen. vi. 8.   † Gen. vii. 1.   ‡ Gen. vi. 22.

ark of God. The ark of the covenant, in which was deposited the law delivered to Moses, was carried by the sons of Israel in their travels in the wilderness, and it operated with them as a protection from danger and a source of blessing. The reason was because it represented the Church. It shadowed forth what ought to be the mind of the people of this pasture, and what would be its results when properly developed; namely, that it ought to contain the commandments of God, because these preserve from evil and bless with good, whenever they are cherished as the inner principles of religious life and moral guidance. It was also for this reason that John said, "The temple of God was opened in heaven, and there was seen in his temple the ark of his testament";* because by the temple in heaven is meant the universal worship and acknowledgment of the Lord which prevail in that kingdom, and the ark in the temple plainly denotes that state of mind in which has been deposited the Divine commandments, and from which all genuine acknowledgment and worship arise. The human mind is still a human mind, though it may exist in heaven! God's regard is not directed to a senseless ark of wood, but to those living mental principles which he has designed for the reception of his precepts, and which are built up as their teachings are loved and practised. It is the ark thus constituted, of which the Lord makes use to save mankind from the influences of evil; and which, when so built up, causes the builder to be found righteous in the sight of the Lord.†

The directions, then, which were given to Noah and his house for going into the ark, are to be understood as instructions for entering into the interior things of the Church. Men are said to enter into that which they understand and love: hence, upon the same principle, the Lord, who knows and regards the good of the human race, is said to enter into them, and abide with

---

* Rev. xi. 19.

† Moses is said to have been placed for safety in an ark of bulrushes, Exod. ii. 3, because he represented the Divine law in its origin ; but by the ark of bulrushes, in which he was preserved, is signified that literal form, for the embodiment of the Divine law, which is respectively external and worldly, and which a low and degraded condition of mankind had rendered necessary—necessary for bringing some knowledge of that law down to man's perverted apprehension, and at the same time to protect it from profanation.

them.* "Behold," said he, "I stand at the door and knock: if any man hear my voice, and open the door, I will come in to him, and sup with him, and he with me."† If men love what is good and true, they enter into the virtues and intelligences which are required, and these will preserve them from dangers and promote their welfare. The spiritual and intellectual things which constitute the mind of the Church can only be entered into from a love of what is good and true. Hence Jesus said to the faithful servant, "Enter thou into the joy of thy Lord"; ‡ where by entering is plainly meant the experience of delight from a principle of love. The Lord said unto Noah, "Come thou and all thy house into the ark," when he had "seen him righteous before him in that generation." That was the qualification by which those people were enabled to comply with the gracious invitation, and so to be protected from surrounding peril. When a man is taught what are the interior arrangements of an orderly mind, and, by things intellectual, is convinced of their use, he may be said to have built the ark: but he can enter into it only from an activity of love; that is the principle by which he is seen to be righteous before the Lord, and he is then invited to enter, because he is inclined to do so, and can be saved thereby.

But it was not only Noah and his house who were to enter into the ark: he was told to take with him "every clean beast by sevens, the male and his female: and of beasts that were not clean by twos, the male and his female. Of fowls also of the air by sevens, the male and his female: to keep seed alive upon the face of the earth."§ What can be the meaning of this?

It was an observation of the ancients, that a man is a microcosm or little world; by which they meant that all things in the world of nature have a sort of antitype in the world of mind,— mind being the specific inheritance of man. On this ground, beasts among the ancients were named to signify certain living affections in man; the clean beasts the good affections, and unclean beasts the evil affections pertaining to his nature. The reason why man's affections are so signified is, because in his

---

* John xv. 4.   † Rev. iii. 20.

‡ Matt. xxv. 21.   § Gen. vii. 2, 3.

fallen condition he has had induced upon his senses, appetites, and feelings, sensations similar to those which are common to the beasts. The only ground or cause of his excellence or superiority is his interior life, which the beasts have not, nor are they capable of having it. This interior life is man's spiritual nature, and God's special gift to him. It is maintained by means of the knowledges of truth and the love of goodness communicated to him from the Lord. There is a living and enduring principle in all the virtues which he communicates to forms created for their reception. All truth and goodness are His, and He is in them; and man, their created recipient, derives his immortality from them. It is the life inherent in truth which influences his understanding, and the life inherent in goodness which influences his will: these distinguish him from the brute, and without which he would in no respect be man.

It was because the ancients knew, and when they were in humility acknowledged, that they had, by the fall, partaken of a low and bestial nature, that they compared their affections to beasts, and their thoughts to fowls, distinguishing the good from the evil. The good affections they compared to lambs, sheep, goats, and oxen, because they were harmless and gentle; also because of their usefulness in respect to human convenience and life: whereas the evil affections were compared to unclean beasts, such as foxes, wolves, and serpents. This also is the reason why the Lord afterwards spoke of the members of his Church as sheep and lambs, as in the case where he directed Peter to feed his lambs and sheep; also why he spoke of the wicked as wolves, foxes, serpents, and a generation of vipers, as in the case of the Pharisees and Herod.

Again, under the representative economy, clean beasts, without spot or blemish, were directed to be offered in sacrificial worship, because they were designed to represent the pure affections by and with which the Lord can alone be worshipped. Unclean beasts were most scrupulously excluded, because the Lord cannot be worshipped acceptably from the impure affections which they signify. Fowls, also, such as doves and pigeons, were portions of the sacrificial ritual, because they represented true ideas pertaining to the thought. This ceremonial worship was performed by means of beasts and birds, to represent that the true worship of the Lord is offered up by means of pure affections of love and correct ideas of thought. The two faculties of man, and the internal things belonging to them, when in a state of order, are to be brought into activity in the performance of this high and important duty.

Much perplexity has been experienced at the mention of clean and unclean beasts, before the institution of the Levitical law, by which that distinction is declared; and to account for this circumstance, it has been supposed that Moses spoke by way of anticipation in reference to those animals which the Jews so denominated at the time of his writing. This, however, is not the correct reason. Although the law announces the distinctions, the principles upon which they are founded are those different classes of affections and thoughts, which a more ancient and better informed people than the Jews knew to have their representations in different classes of animated nature; and consequently they spoke of them as such. This is the ground of those distinctions being mentioned in the case before us; and those of the Levitical law arose therefrom. Under this view the whole perplexity disappears, and the facts are highly suggestive. They show that the beasts and fowl, which Noah was directed to take with him into the ark, are mentioned merely to represent that great variety of affection and thought which distinguished the people who were entering into the Church then in the process of being established.

Man, on entering into the Church, necessarily took with him all his affections, both good and bad: the good affections were the clean beasts; and these were to be taken in by sevens, to denote that there is a holiness about all good, of which that number is significant.* The fowls also were to be taken in by sevens, to denote holiness which pertains to the knowledges of truth, of which the fowls were the types. The unclean beasts represented the impure affections which had fixed themselves on man; and these were to be taken in by twos or pairs,† to indi-

---

* For illustration, see pp. 57, 62.

† At verses 19 and 20 of the preceding chapter, Noah was directed to take into the ark "*two of every sort,*—of fowls after their kind, and of cattle after their kind, and of every creeping thing;" nothing is said about taking any

cate the profane conjunction which they had formed with his nature. The number two denotes conjunction: in the case of what is clean, the conjunction of what is true and good; but in the case of what is not clean, as in the instance before us, the conjunction of what is false and evil. Hence by the unclean beasts, or man's evil affections, are not to be understood that they were so few in comparison with the clean beasts, or good affections, as to be only in the proportion of *two* to *seven;* for the evils in man are more numerous than his goods. But *seven* are predicated of what is clean, to indicate the sanctity of all that is good; and *two* are predicated of what is unclean, to express in this case the profane conjunction which exists between what is false and evil.

Two signifies conjunction, because all things in creation have reference to the two principles of goodness and truth: to good, as to what is agent and influent; and to truth, as to what is patient and recipient. From this ground there is something resembling a marriage in all things of the three kingdoms of nature, and, indeed, without it nothing at all could exist: for in order that anything may exist in nature there must be heat and light, and these two must act in unity if anything be produced; and if they do not act in unity, as is in some measure the case in winter, nothing is effected. This also is the case, spiritually, with man. There are two faculties appertaining to him, namely, the will and the understanding: the will is formed to receive the good of love, which corresponds to heat, and the understanding to receive the truths of faith, which correspond to light. Unless, therefore, the good of love and the truth of faith make a one in man, nothing is produced; for the good of

in by *sevens;* nor is there any distinction made between the clean and unclean. This appears like a discrepancy, yet it is not so; the reason for the various statements is the different aspects of the general subject treated of in each case. The statements at chap. vi., ver. 19, 20, are made in connection with the directions for *building the ark*, and thus refer to things intellectual, and the regeneration of all the things of faith, by means of all the goods of charity, and so by pairs. But the invitation for *entering into the ark*, after it was built, refers to the things of the will, for the reasons stated above. Hence also it is, that in chap. vi., from the 9th verse to the end, the Supreme Being is not called Jehovah, but God; though in chap. vii. he is spoken of as Jehovah. Notice is taken of a similar circumstance at page 59.

love, without the truth of faith, does not determine or qualify anything; and the truth of faith, without the good of love, does not effect anything: wherefore, to the intent that there may be in man a heavenly marriage, those two principles must make a one with him, and become conjoined.* It is hence, then, that *two* signifies conjunction: in the case before us, the conjunction of what is evil and false, because these are represented by the unclean beasts.

It is farther said of each class, that they were to be taken in, "male and his female," to denote that all things of thought were united to some affection. Indeed, no thought can exist in the understanding which is not, at the same time, conjoined, as in a kind of marriage, with some affection in the will: hence male and female are mentioned to represent this marriage,—the male referring more to the things of intellect and understanding, the female more to the things of affection and the will. So that the very *minutiæ* of the narrative are found to disclose remarkable particulars concerning the metaphysical constitution of mankind. The Word of God is the only book on true metaphysics. It was written by God's direction; He knows what is in man, and it is a revelation to him of all the characteristics of his mental condition. For a man to know himself he must study the Word of God.

Beasts, the clean and unclean, with fowls, were to be taken into the ark, because the man of the Church was then, as he is now, of a mixed character, as to his intellect and will. He has affection for goodness, and thoughts towards truth; he has propensities to evil, and inclinations to falsehood; (God has mercifully provided for the former by the preservation of remains): and these are the clean and unclean beasts and fowls. By Noah taking them with him into the ark, was represented man's entering into the Church with these opposite characteristics in his nature: and the reason assigned for so doing was, "to keep seed alive upon the earth"; that is, to perpetuate truth in the world. The *seed* is the truth of the Church, of which the Lord is the sower. Some of this seed remained with Noah, hence it was that he found grace in the sight of the Lord. All the rest of the posterity of Adam had destroyed this

* Arcana Cœlestia, n. 5194.

seed in themselves, and were in consequence about to perish: the seed of truth is kept alive by use in goodness. Truth lives when it is employed in promoting the works of virtue.

It may appear from the circumstance of taking in the unclean beasts by pairs, as if the Lord arranged for the perpetuation of what is evil and false, as well as what is good and true; still, every one must see that this was not intended, because it is contrary to His nature and His providence. It was only SEED that was to be kept alive, and this is predicated of TRUTH as the vessel for the reception of good. It is no part of God's designs to perpetuate man's disorders; but they being inrooted in his nature, he is invited by the Lord to enter with them into the ark, that there they may be weakened and moderated by holy influences, and so be prevented from manifesting themselves, or becoming hurtful to society.

The circumstance of the diversified beasts and fowls which Noah took with him into the ark, denoting the various affections and thoughts which men take with them on entering into the Church of God, is not without a parallel, in predictions which are delivered concerning the Christian Church. It is written, that "the wolf shall dwell with the lamb, and the leopard shall lie down with the kid; and the calf and the young lion and the fatling together; and a little child shall lead them. And the cow and the bear shall feed; their young ones shall lie down together: and the lion shall eat straw like the ox. And the sucking child shall play on the hole of the asp, and the weaned child shall put his hand on the cockatrice's den. They shall not hurt nor destroy in all my holy mountain."* This is universally allowed to be a representation of the peaceable character, which, at some period, is to distinguish the true Church. That Church is called the Lord's "Holy Mountain"; therein are to be assembled the wolf and the lamb, the leopard and the kid, the calf and the lion, the fatling and the child, the cow and the bear, the asp and the cockatrice. Thus the clean and the unclean beasts are to be assembled in the holy mountain, and dwell together in peace. There is, then, an obvious parallelism between the clean and the unclean beasts to be gathered on the holy mountain, and those which were collected

* Isa. xi. 6, 9.

in the saving ark; but as the prediction of the prophet is not intended to express a physical occurrence, so neither is the narrative of Moses. They both refer to spiritual and intellectual phenomena, which take place with man during the process of his regeneration; though this description in one case is written in the shape of a figurative history, yet, in the other, it is put forth in the form of a symbolical prediction. The clean beasts and fowls enter into the Church to have their condition preserved and elevated: the unclean are permitted to enter in order that they may be restrained, and have their ferocity extracted, which purposes are accomplished by those salutary influences which the Lord supplies through the instrumentality of His Word.

CHAPTER XXII.

THE DELUGE AND THE DEATH OF ALL FLESH BUT THOSE WHO ENTERED INTO THE ARK.

"The idea of a universal deluge, Mosaic or historical, is not sustainable. Such is the opinion of most of the geologists on the Continent. The proofs of its absurdity are so evident, that for a long time the Lutheran clergy have given it up. At length the English clergy, the most tenacious of all, have surrendered their arms. They have at last acknowledged, by the organ of Mr. Sedgwick and Mr. Conybear, that if there have been deluges, they have not been general; and that the Mosaic deluge, if it ever took place as it is related, could in no case produce the ancient alluvions, or the pretended diluvium."—A. Bone, "*Mem. Geol.*" v. i., p. 149. Paris, 1832.

We now enter upon the consideration of one of the most remarkable events mentioned in the Sacred Scriptures. A belief in the literal sense of the Mosaic history of the deluge has so long and so extensively prevailed, that to question its accuracy may produce some anxiety and alarm. This, however, must be done, in order to arrive at a correct view of the subject; and the theological prejudices thereon formed by a misrepresentation of the narrative, must give way to the truths established by sober criticism and the discoveries of science. The evidences favourable to this conclusion are so strong, that Dr. Pye Smith candidly says, "We must admit the probability that we have not rightly interpreted those portions of the Scriptures."[*] Other writers of ecclesiastical distinction and scientific celebrity have arrived at the same conclusion.[†] The question does not affect the authenticity or the divinity of the narrative; it is one of interpretation only. The ancient notions upon the subject are thoroughly disturbed,—and disturbed by testimonies of so irresistible a nature, as to compel their relinquishment by all who have the courage to open their eyes to evidence, and then to think. It may be useful to advert to a few of the circumstances which have conduced to this result.

[*] "Geol. and Scriptures," p. 295. Sec. Ed.
[†] Professors Baden Powell and Adam Sedgwick.

What the populace, from the teachings they have received, regard as the *orthodox belief* is, that the flood was an overflow of water, by which the whole surface of the earth was submerged, and produced by a breaking up of the fountains of the great deep, and forty days of incessant rain.* The evidences on which these views rest are supposed to be furnished by the letter of the narrative; and it is considered that the fact itself is also corroborated by very numerous traditions, and substantiated by geological phenomena.

The facts presented in the Mosaic narrative are these: The Lord said, " I will cause it to rain upon the earth forty days and forty nights. The fountains of the great deep were broken up, and the windows of heaven were opened. And the rain was upon the earth forty days and forty nights. And the waters prevailed exceedingly upon the earth; and all the high hills that were under the whole heaven, were covered fifteen cubits."† It is plain from these statements, whatever may be the sense attached to the deluge, that an idea of some universal destruction in reference to man is intended to be expressed; but whether it was produced by an overflow of water is another question. It is true that the narrative so represents it; yet it is equally true that the Scriptures frequently employ the terms, water and floods, in a purely figurative sense, and this we think is the way in which they are used in the instance before us. All who have examined the narrative in its literal sense merely, have been compelled to acknowledge the great difficulties by which it is beset, and to relinquish many notions which were formerly attached to it. It has not been unusual to regard the catastrophe as having been a tumultuous movement of the agitated waves sweeping along the valleys with destructive violence,‡ and majestically rising up the mountain sides, with furious uproar, to overwhelm the wretched beings who might have fled for safety to their summits. But it must

---

* This view is set forth and defended, in some instances very absurdly, in " An Enquiry into the Truth and Certainty of the Mosaic Deluge." *By Patrick Cockburn, M.A., Vicar of Long Horsley, in Northumberland.*

† Gen. vii. 4, 11, 12, 19, 20.

‡ Dr. Buckland sets forth this view in his " Reliquiæ Diluvianæ," though he has candidly abandoned it in a note in his " Bridgewater Treatise."

be plain to all who will calmly examine the subject, that these are exaggerations of the imagination, having no foundation in the description itself. It does not represent the circumstance, either at its commencement or termination, to have been of so disrupting and earth-disturbing a character as was once vulgarly supposed.* The rise and subsidence are spoken of as having been gradual and quiet: so much so, that the vegetation at the earth's surface, in some districts, was not destroyed by it; at least an olive leaf is described to have been plucked off after the tree had been submerged in exceedingly deep waters for nearly three hundred days! The ark experienced no storm, sustained no injury, but rode with gentleness upon the waters. These circumstances seem to render it unnecessary to appeal to geological phenomena in proof of the deluge. For why refer to a science which proves such extraordinary convulsions to have taken place with the earth's crust, when the clear inference from the Mosaic narrative is that the earth's surface was very little disturbed? Those who appeal to geology to prove the deluge, concede these facts: they even suppose what they understand to be the geography of the antediluvian world to have been so little disarranged by the flood, that it is admissive of identification in our own day. They even think that some of the rivers of Eden may still be pointed out.† While such a view can require no aid for its support from geological science, it need not fear any difficulties arising from its discoveries. It may be said to be unique, but it is hardly satisfactory.

The prosecution of geological studies has shown with the utmost clearness, that what was once understood to have been diluvial action, is not the result of one universal or simultaneous submergence of the earth, but the consequences of many distinct local watery forces; and produced not by a gradual inundation of only three hundred and sixty days' duration, but by the continued action of aqueous forces for periods of incalculable extent. Moreover, a recent overflow of water, simultaneously covering the earth and rising above the summits of the

---

* See Rev. Dr. Fleming, on the Geological Deluge. *Edin. Phil. Journ.*, vol. xiv., p. 205; also a paper in the *Quarterly Review*, Oct., 1827, No. lxxii., p. 481.

† See page 89, note.

highest mountains, must have left peculiar evidences of such circumstances; such, however, are not to be found, but instead thereof, there are positive facts standing out against it.

Of course, efforts have not been wanting to make the discoveries of science harmonize with the pre-conceived notions of the narrative; but then those notions have themselves given way! They have acquired an elasticity, in which their original character has entirely disappeared. There is no uniform opinion upon the subject now extant. The populace, indeed, retain the notion concerning it which has been taught them in preceding ages; but the learned are not yet sufficiently agreed upon any new explanation to enter upon the work of rectification. The whole matter is now in a transition state; and we have no doubt that a time will come when the narrative will no longer be considered as the literal history of natural phenomena, but a figurative description of the mental condition of mankind, and of God's merciful interposition to preserve the human race from perishing by a wicked influence. This we conceive to be the only view in which the history can be presented in a rational and satisfactory light. If it were not written to describe an event in outward nature, we need not be surprised at its want of agreement with the discoveries and demands of science.

Although the rising and falling of the waters seem to have been too tranquil to allow geological phenomena to be referred to their action, still it may be asked, whether the *breaking up of the fountains of the great deep* may not have occasioned those irregularities and divergences of the strata from that horizontal position which they must have originally possessed, and which are now observable? Before such a question can be properly replied to, it will be requisite to define what the fountains of the great deep are. It has been conjectured that the antediluvian world contained, within its centre, immense reservoirs of water; and the surrounding strata, having been made to give way, sunk into it, and so occasioned its elevation; this, it has been supposed, was the breaking up of the fountains of the great deep, and the occasion of those irregularities of strata observable. But it is an hypothesis without sufficient data; it is not recognized by the scientific inquirer, nor does it agree with the facts which geology discloses. It is one of those ingenious conceptions of the earlier cosmogonists, which have been abandoned as impossible by all who are in possession of later and riper information.

Still the inquiry whence the water was to be obtained, by which all the high hills were to be covered fifteen cubits, naturally suggests itself.* Here other difficulties arise; for when we know that it would require for the supply an amount equal to five miles above the ordinary level of the sea,—that it would increase the equatorial diameter of the earth eleven or twelve miles,—that the earth's gravity would be increased, and the causes of its previous precession and nutation disarranged,— and that these circumstances must needs have propagated their effects throughout the whole solar system;—we say, when these astounding facts are known to be the consequences of water having covered all the high hills of the earth fifteen cubits, the theological view popularly received must needs give way to some more reasonable and modified interpretation of the narrative.

The most plausible geological facts on which the evidences of the deluge have most recently been thought to rest, are those which are presented in what has been generally included in the common name, *diluvium*. This is considered to describe superficial accumulation, such as sand, soil, gravel, and those loose aggregations of larger stones and blocks which are to be found throughout the whole surface of the earth. But the examination of their contents, and an inquiry into the direction of the currents by which those fragments must have been driven, and afterwards deposited in their present situations, have proved most conclusively, to all competent judges of the subject, that they were the results of *different* diluvial actions, that they must have taken place in *different ages*, and that all of them are of *local extent*, though the locality of some may have been very

---

* Isaac Vossius on this subject observes, "that the waters of the whole globe would not suffice to overflow the earth to such a height as is mentioned, although all the seas were drained: more waters must either have been created for that purpose, or we must say with some, that that vast quantity of water fell down from some other of the celestial orbs, and that the deluge ended, the water returned to its former place. But these are only pious fooleries. God works no miracles in vain."—*Treatise of the True Age of the World*.

large. Instances are known in which one stratum crosses another and overlies it. From these circumstances, scientific men —men influenced by piety and a belief in revelation—have concluded that these phenomena could not have been produced by such an event as the terms of the Noachic deluge seem to require.*

Another class of evidences leading to the same result is furnished by volcanoes. In the south and towards the centre of France, there are several hundred conical hills, having the forms of modern volcanoes, with craters more or less perfect on many of their summits. None of these have been in action within the period of history or tradition. Some have had channels cut in them by ancient rivers, through masses of solid lava, a hundred feet in thickness; and these channels have since been choked up by streams of lava.† The time required for the production of these phenomena is incalculable; still it is evident that they cannot have transpired since the period which chronology assigns to the Noachic deluge: and the circumstance of there being present, on the sides of these volcanoes, loose scoriæ, pumice, and cinders, proves that they have not been submerged, and, consequently, that they were not inundated by "Noah's flood."‡

---

* "That a transient deluge, like that described in the Scriptures, could have produced and brought into its present situation all the diluvium which is now spread over this continent [America] will not (it seems to me) be admitted for a moment by any impartial observer."—*Prof. Hitchcock's* "*Geology of Massachusetts,*" p. 148.

† Lyell's "Elements of Geology," Sec. Ed., vol. i., p. 11 ; vol. ii., p. 190. See also his "Principles of Geology." Sir H. De la Beche's "Geological Manual" may also be consulted, 3rd Ed., p. 172. Dr. Colenso urges these facts against the literal history of the deluge, and says: "I now know for certain, on geological grounds, a fact of which I had only misgivings before I left England, viz., that a universal deluge, such as the Bible manifestly speaks of, could not possibly have taken place in the way described in the Book of Genesis."—"*The Pentateuch and Book of Joshua Critically Examined,*" Preface, p. vii.

‡ "When did these fires burn? When took place this amazing combination of volcanic eruptions and their terrible accompaniments? How long ago was the last of them? And by what intervals of time could we ascend from that last to the earlier eruption, and to the earliest of the astounding number? These questions cannot be answered by any assigning of our

The idea of its universality had been relinquished by many distinguished Biblical scholars before geology became a science. Among others may be named Bishop Stillingfleet, the learned Vossius, and Matthew Poole; the former observes, "I cannot see any urgent necessity from the Scriptures to assert that the flood did spread itself over all the surface of the earth;"* and the latter observes, "It is not to be supposed that the entire globe of earth was covered with water."† Rosenmüller has given a summary of the arguments which modern critics have advanced to prove that the deluge was not universal.‡ Dr. Pye Smith, one of the most recent and accomplished writers on this subject, contends that the expressions which have been so interpreted are mere orientalisms, and that they mean no more than a large extent. He thinks it was only great enough to overwhelm the whole of the human race, that being the principal object of it; and considers that, at the time of its occurrence, men had not emigrated beyond a comparatively small district in the East; and he finally fixes the scene of the inundation described by Moses in and about that portion of Western Asia where there is a large district now considerably depressed below the level of the sea.§ That there might have been a local deluge in the district named, as doubtless there has been in many other portions of the East and elsewhere, need not be questioned. But was it the Noachic flood? There is not sufficient evidence to

measures of time,—years and centuries. Such analogies as may be inferred by comparative examination of the condition of Etna, Vesuvius, and other active volcanoes, carry us to the contemplation of a period which runs back, not to the age of Noah, but immeasurably beyond the date of the creation of man and his contemporary plants and animals."—*Dr. Pye Smith,* "*Scrip. Geo.*," Sec. Ed., p. 146.

* "Origines Sacræ," Book III., chap. iv.   † "Synopsis," Gen. vii. 19.

‡ "Schol. in Gen.," vol. i., pp. 92-94. See also King's "Morsels of Criticism," vol. iii., pp. 103-108.

§ Mesopotamia and Persia, part of Afghanistan and Turkistan, taken generally. Vossius also contends that mankind had not then extended themselves beyond the borders of Syria and Mesopotamia, and says, "No reason obliges us to extend the inundation of the deluge beyond those bounds which were inhabited."—*Treatise of the True Age of the World.*

Coetlogon places mankind at this period at the confluence of the two great rivers, the Euphrates and Tigris, and supposes the deluge to have been occasioned by their overflow.—*His* "*Universal History of Arts and Sciences,*" Art. *Antediluvians.*

affirm it, and there is some amount of negative evidence against it. By defining the locality, and concentrating the race to be destroyed, the probability is increased of finding *human remains* for the proof of it. But what is the fact? It is notorious that no bed produced by diluvial action has ever been discovered, which contained a single bone or tooth of the human species.*

---

* This question has been investigated with much scientific care by competent observers in various parts of Europe and elsewhere; and the results have been recently published by Sir Charles Lyell, F.R.S., in his "Geological Evidences of the Antiquity of Man," 1863. The reader who wishes for farther information on this point is referred to that work. It may, however, be useful to notice two or three facts brought out with considerable prominence. Fragments of human bones have been found in the caverns of Bize, in the department of Aude, and in Pondres, near Nismes (both in France), embedded with the bones of extinct mammalia, and others of recent species; but it is the concurrent opinion of scientific inquirers, that they cannot be referred to a "diluvial catastrophe," and that they did not belong to antediluvian periods, but to a people in a state of similar civilization to those who constructed the tumuli and altars (pp. 60, 61). Other fragments have been found in other places, but under circumstances which leave no doubt in the minds of scientific geologists, that man was not only contemporary with the extinct animals with which his remains have been found mingled, but that they could not have been left in the places where they have been discovered; the geological formation of these places plainly showing that the antiquity of those remains is much greater than that which is commonly supposed to have been the date of that catastrophe. In the delta of the Mississippi, for the formation of which the lowest estimate of time is calculated to be 100,000 years, there have been found four forests, one superimposed upon the other, some charcoal, and a human skeleton. To this skeleton Dr. Dowler ascribes an antiquity of 50,000 years (p. 44). The flint implements which have been discovered in several parts of Europe, and which are evidently of human workmanship, show, from their geological situation, that they must have been made prior to the date claimed for the deluge, and that such an event could not have been the cause of such a deposit. Although Sir Charles Lyell is very exact about his facts, he is exceedingly careful to avoid Biblical interpretations. Professor Sedgwick, of Cambridge, who at one time referred all secondary formation of geology to Noah's flood, on quitting the chair publicly read his recantation, and said we ought to have paused before we adopted the diluvian theory; "for of man, and the works of his hands, we have not found a single trace among the remnants of a former world entombed in these ancient deposits." The learned Bunsen observes, "We have no hesitation in asserting at once that there exist Egyptian monuments, the date of which can be accurately fixed, of a higher antiquity than those of any other nation known in history, viz., about 5000 years." This is nearly a thousand years before the date assigned for the deluge.— "Egypt's Place in Universal History," p. 23.

Dr. A. Clarke calculates, that within the first 128 years of the world, there were upwards of half a million of inhabitants: taking the same data on which he computed, and carrying it down to 1656 A.M., the year of the flood, according to Archbishop Usher, there must have been a population of many millions. Is it not remarkable, then, if such an immense number of persons perished in the way supposed, and within the limited district pointed out, that there should not be discovered any remains to prove it? It is by no means unreasonable to expect that such a proof might be produced, if the event happened in the way it is interpreted. How, then, have the traces and marks of the catastrophe been so completely effaced and destroyed in reference to humanity, when we find a great variety of remains belonging to other different departments of animated nature, which have been submerged for incalculable periods, and by the action of water embedded in numerous rocks and strata of the earth? We cannot answer this question. It is for those to do so who have adopted the hypothesis which has suggested it.

The phenomena, then, to which the theologians of the last century appealed, as proofs that the Mosaic description of the deluge referred to an overflow of the earth by water, about four thousand years ago, upon the fullest inquiry, made by competent authorities, prove no such thing! The whole of such phenomena are demonstrated to have resulted from a long-sustained action of aqueous currents and local submergence, and not from a universal and steady overflow of only one year's duration, as expressed in the narrative. The phenomena previously resorted to by theologians as proofs are abandoned by many, whose bias would have kept them to their former system with the utmost pertinacity, if it could have been done with any consistency, after the production of such incontestable physical evidence to the contrary.

The modern interpretation of the narrative is not much better substantiated. It is said to have been universal in respect to man only, but limited to some geographical district. Thus the idea of its having been a physical occurrence is still maintained, though not a single physical proof of it can be produced! Men have been so long accustomed to view it in that light, that notwithstanding the difficulties by which it is surrounded, they are reluctant to behold it in any other. We, however, as before observed, have no doubt that time and farther inquiry will lead to the establishment of an entirely different opinion. By relinquishing the literal interpretation, the authority of the narrative is not renounced; it is only a giving up of the ideas which men have attached to it, from a want of acquaintance with this ancient and Divine style of composition. Its religious value and sacred importance will remain in all their integrity if we consider it to be a figurative description of spiritual phenomena only;—a figure nevertheless provided, in all probability, by the occurrence of some local flood which had happened, and in which many members of society had disastrously perished.

We may be reminded that the event is alluded to in other parts of the Scriptures. So it is. Ezekiel mentions Noah's name twice,[*] and Isaiah speaks of the waters of Noah.[†] The Lord Jesus Christ referred to it as a general calamity;[‡] so also do his Apostles Paul[§] and Peter:[||] but the object of those references is not to set forth the physical nature of the circumstance. None of those parties speak of it in that light at all; nor is there any precise allusion made to the catastrophe. It is mentioned incidentally, and with the view of supporting some other truth; it is contemplated merely as a calamity, but whether it was of a natural or spiritual kind is not declared. It is reasonable to suppose, if it had been a natural event, that it would have been referred to with great frequency and force in other portions of the Word. This is the case with many other circumstances of actual history: it is very conspicuous in the case of the liberation of the sons of Israel from Egyptian bondage. Their unhappy condition in that country, and the advantages of their having been delivered therefrom, are alluded to with more or less emphasis in almost all the books of the Hebrew Scriptures; whereas the flood is only once hinted at, and that in the way of figure! Surely there must have been some cause for this; and may not that cause have been its spiritual character, and thus its unsuitableness for being appre-

---

[*] Ezek. xiv. 14, 20.   [†] Isa. liv. 9.
[‡] Matt. xxiv. 37–39 ; Luke xvii. 26, 27.
[§] Heb. xi. 7.   [||] 1 Pet. iii. 20 ; 2 Pet. iii. 6.

ciated by so sensual a people as the Jews most unquestionably were? But without insisting upon these points, we think that a legitimate argument could be drawn from the connection in which the above passages occur, to show that the writers and the Divine speaker regarded it as a spiritual transaction: but of this again.

Our attention may be directed to the traditions of such an event, which are found to prevail in almost every part of the world. To what we have already said upon this subject we have but little to add.* Details of those traditions have been learnedly collected by Mr. Bryant, and preserved in his *"Ancient Mythology."* Other writers have usefully and learnedly pursued a similar study. Mr. Sharon Turner, in his *"Sacred History of the World,"* has referred to such traditions somewhat extensively, and attempted an elaborate argument to prove from them the certainty of the deluge. It would have been a more satisfactory effort if he had shown the *kind of deluge* referred to by them. This point is assumed to have been a natural phenomenon;—it was prejudged to be so, but it is not proved. It must be confessed that some of those traditions are exceedingly remote, obscure, and rude, and that much scope has to be given to the imagination, in order to establish any identity between them and that of the Mosaic record.† But although we may admit

---

* See pp. 21, 22. It is highly probable that many of the traditions referred to did not arise from the event spoken of in the Hebrew Scriptures, but from some destructive local inundations by which the nations had been visited; for there is scarcely a country to be mentioned that has not experienced some extensive disaster of the kind, and of which there are either historical or traditional reminiscences. It is proper to distinguish, in an inquiry of this sort, between the traditions of *a* deluge and *the* deluge spoken of by Moses. It is plain that many which are mentioned by writers on this subject have not the slightest allusion to it.

† For instance, the EGYPTIAN TRADITION, as related by Diodorus Siculus, when speaking of their persuasion that they were the first of mankind, is this : "They say, on the whole, that either in the flood which occurred in the time of Deucalion, the greatest part of living things perished ; but that it was likely that those who inhabited Egypt so much to the south, and so free from rain, were mostly preserved ; or, as some declare, that all that were alive being destroyed, the earth again brought forth new natures of animals from their beginning."—*Diod. Sic.*, l. i., p. 10.

The GREEK TRADITION is given by Apollodorus thus: "When Jupiter

that there is a number of them sufficiently plain to show that they do refer to some circumstance denominated the flood, still this does not concede them to mean an overflow of natural water. Some *spiritual* calamity, which had befallen a people among whom figurative language was in high repute, might have been spoken of in such terms; but as the right signification of them was lost in after ages, mankind would then very naturally regard them to express a physical event. That tradition may arise from such a source is very evident; and that the views which they were originally intended to express may, by the diversity of national genius, prejudices, vanity, or ambition, have their signification entirely changed, will scarcely be doubted. It is plain that this has been the case. The generality of the traditions which have been collected upon this subject, and which are found to prevail in those countries where the Christian Scriptures are not known, show most conclusively how the original idea, whatever it was, has been mixed up with some national circumstance. We therefore hold that it is not enough for the point in hand to show that there are such traditions, or that they have been for many generations understood to refer to a deluge of natural waters; and we contend that, to make out such an understanding of those traditions to be correct, it is first requisite to define the true meaning of what is thought to be the historical source of them. This source must

determined to destroy the brazen race, Deucalion, by the advice of Prometheus, made a great ark, λαρνακα, and put into it all necessary things, and entered it with Pyrrha. Jupiter then pouring down heavy rains from heaven, overwhelmed the greatest part of Greece, so that all men perished except a few who fled to the highest mountains. He floated nine days and nights on the sea of waters, and at last stopped on Mount Parnassus. Then Jupiter sent Mercury to ask him what he wished; and he solicited that mankind might be made again. Jupiter bade him throw stones over his head, from which men should come; and that those cast by Pyrrha should be turned into women."—*Apoll.*, l. i., p. 23.

The CHINESE TRADITION is the following statement by Confucius: "Alas! the deluging states are spreading destruction. They surround the mountains. They overtop the hills. They rise high and extend wide as the spacious vault of heaven."—*Dr. Morrison*, in his Preface to the Chinese Dictionary.

These citations are as they are given by Sharon Turner, in his "Sacred History of the World," vol. ii., pp. 313, 314, 324.

have been some *description* derived from the Noachic people, and that description must have partaken of the same character and genius as those which are found in the Scripture narrative. The whole inquiry therefore resolves itself back to the Mosaic record. It is the meaning of that document, and not the ideas which tradition may be supposed to speak, which has to be determined.

Most persons are aware that tradition presents a variety of subjects with which it has dealt in a light very different from that in which they originally transpired. A sensible writer observes, "Those who know how, even in our own days, reports are changed and embellished, how some features are omitted and others added, during the process of passing from mouth to mouth, and how in the end they frequently assume a totally different aspect from that which they originally had, will readily admit that such traditions cannot be received with the same faith as contemporary history. We may add, that the more important the occurrence handed down by tradition is, and the more it affects the feelings and passions of man, the greater will be the changes and corruptions which it will experience in its progress. The desire of seeing things clear and complete is inherent in the human mind; and hence we find, that in innumerable instances, when a tradition, or a series of traditions, was deficient, unclear, or incomplete, man's imagination and ingenuity have been at work to make up an apparently complete account, either by filling up the gaps in the original account with pure fictions, or by transferring and combining events which belong to different times and countries. Specimens of traditions of this kind may be found in great numbers in the early history of every nation."* Hence it is evident that the prevalence of traditions concerning the deluge having been an inundation of waters, is no proof that such was the idea attached to the original description. They must have sprung from a *description*, whatever view may be taken of the circumstance; and the Noachic people, as the only recorded survivors of it, must have been its authors, and the first communicators of it to their descendants. That the sense of the original information concerning it has been essentially altered, in consequence of passing through such a diversified

* "Penny Cyclopædia," Art. Tradition.

series of sensual and perverting channels, may be reasonably supposed. What is more likely to have transpired with a narrative of spiritual things couched in the form of factitious history, than that it would come to be understood in a literal sense, as men sunk more and more deeply into naturalism? Does not the supposition of its having been a figurative narrative better account for those great differences which tradition presents, than the popular idea can possibly do? Surely such a view is more likely to have been spread into a greater variety of modes of thinking and speaking about it, than the record of a purely physical transaction would admit. At all events, the utmost that can be said of those traditions is, that they speak of a deluge which is *now* considered to have been an inundation of waters, but that they do not contain any evidence to show that such was the meaning of the description from which they originally sprung, or that such is the sense in which the Scripture narrative ought to be understood.

Hence, neither science nor tradition contributes any information capable of unfolding the meaning of this remarkable point in the Mosaic records. Indeed, it has been felt by some of the most able literal critics, that although science might, if rightly interrogated, afford some collateral testimony to the idea of Moses having recorded a physical circumstance, still it is found to be perplexed with so many difficulties, that in order to relieve the embarrassment, they assert it to have been a miracle.*
Of course this view of the subject overcomes the difficulty; still, it creates others of no inconsiderable weight. Science, so far as it investigates the usual laws and general phenomena of nature, can have nothing to do with a transaction brought about by a supernatural means and fiat, of which it can know nothing. Reason must be silent where a miracle is declared. But if the flood were miraculously produced, it must have been supernaturally sustained and terminated, and all its evidences miraculously effaced: as such, it has no analogy to any of those events which the Scriptures distinctly inform us to have been the result of special Divine interference. Upon what evidence is it said to

---

* "As there was a peculiar exercise of the almighty power of God in effecting the deluge, it is vain and presumptuous to attempt explaining the method of it on the principles of philosophy."—*Comment. Henry and Scott.*

have been a miracle? It is not so stated in the narrative itself, and the idea has originated wholly in the discovered impossibility of reconciling such a phenomenon with the known laws and developments of nature. In short, it has been invented to get rid of difficulties, which otherwise would ere long lead men to abandon the idea of the history referring to a natural circumstance at all, as they have already contributed to destroy the once orthodox notion of its universality.

Moreover, the idea of its having been a miracle is not common to every critic. The very great amount of supernatural agency that must have been called into action, and the gigantic scale over which it must be supposed to have operated, have led many judicious inquirers to hesitate and doubt the propriety of adopting such an idea. It may be said, that to Him who can perform them, all miracles are alike,—that the greatest can present no more obstacles to Omnipotence than the smallest.* But however plausible this may seem, it overlooks one great principle, which is that Omnipotence, because it is an attribute of the God of order, must be regulated by the laws of order. Neither God nor any of his attributes acts independently of laws. From inattention to this fact, innumerable things have been thought possible to Omnipotence,† which a judicious consideration must show to be otherwise. It is most true that "with God all things are possible";‡ that is, all things consistent with his wisdom and his goodness. Those who overlook this fact sometimes run into great extravagance of opinion. They are deterred by no difficulty, nor awed by any improbability. They omit the word impossible from their theological vocabulary, and find in the term Omnipotence all that any difficult hypothesis could wish for, or any pressing exigence desire. But surely there is some

---

* "There is no difficulty with God to perform anything,—no greater endeavour or activity to produce the greatest than the least of creatures; but an equal facility in reference to all things, which cannot be imagined but by an infinite excess of power above and beyond all resistance."—*Bishop Pearson on the Creed*, p. 287.

† "Is it not possible for God to change an ox or a stone into a rational philosopher or a child of Abraham ?—to change a man or a woman into an angel of heaven? Poor Omnipotence which cannot do this!"—*Rev. J. Wesley, A.M., Letter to the Rev. Mr. Law, in Wesley's Works*, p. 356.

‡ Matt. xix. 26.

mistake, not to say irreverence, in making thus free with a Divine attribute to unfasten the knot which, after all, human ignorance or perversity may have tied. There are some things which we believe Omnipotence cannot do,—not that God wants the power, but because they would be contrary to his purity and character. Indeed, it may be doubted whether he has the power to make another equal to himself: if he have, no idea of it is conceivable by man. We do not think it irreverent to say that God could not have created a better universe than he has; nor could we think so without impeaching both his knowledge and his goodness. We see Omnipotence displayed in nature, and also that it operates according to some orderly laws. There are several instances mentioned in the Scriptures, in which it was specially displayed; yet there are none wherein it was lavishly exhibited, or extended beyond the immediate occasion for it: hence it must have operated in them all according to some orderly law. Whatever God does must be regulated and influenced by his wisdom and benevolence. There can be no exceptions. Every effect in nature is the result of some law peculiar to itself; and the miracles, so far as they were effects in nature, must also have originated in laws peculiar to themselves. The planets revolve, trees grow, animals live, and men exist; but each department of nature stands by its own respective laws. The laws that result in the production of an oak are different from those which conduce to the existence of a man. The Lord, in guiding the laws which produce vegetation, does not interfere with those which contribute to humanity. They are distinct productions growing out of the activity of different laws. Thus every effect in nature comes into existence by the operation of its own orderly laws; and we cannot view the miracles recorded in the Word in any other light. It does not appear to us to have been any more requisite to interfere with the common laws of nature in order to produce a miracle, than it is requisite to suspend the laws of vegetation in order to produce a man. Miracles, as specific productions, must have been the result of specific laws, operating in harmony with the designs of infinite beneficence. A miracle may be called a new temporary creation, mercifully adapted to the wants of a low and depressed condition of the human character. They have been performed only in times of darkness and distress, and have ceased as virtue and intelligence have been enabled to fix themselves with men. In the Jewish Church, external miracles stood in the place of internal intelligence; in the Christian Church, spiritual intelligence supplies the place of outward miracles: and as the Christian dispensation is more excellent than the Jewish, so intelligence is superior to a miracle as a means of forwarding the designs of God for leading men to heaven.*

Those who make so free with Omnipotence as to suppose that it can do anything which their imaginations may suggest, have not been rightly informed concerning it. "God is not the author of confusion." † He acts omnipotently when he acts according to order; and a true idea of this Divine attribute can be formed only by connecting its operations with the laws of order. God is essential order, because he is love itself and wisdom itself. The universe and all its parts were created in order and with order. The order of creation and its laws are physical evidences showing that God operates in these things according to fixed principles. Omnipotence was necessary to produce creation; Omnipotence is requisite to preserve it. These results are effected by Omnipotence through the laws of order, whence it is plain that God acts omnipotently by those means.

Everything is what it is by means of the order, and consequently of the laws, of its existence. Man is distinguished from the animal, the fowl from the fish, and the tree from the stone, by the laws of order which are proper to their being. This is a universal truth. To change the laws of existence would be to change the things themselves. This fact being disclosed in every department of nature, is a plain revelation that God is God by virtue of the laws which are appropriate to his being, and, consequently, that he can no more depart from the laws of his own nature and remain God, than a man, if deprived of the laws of manhood, could remain a man. Hence it is easy to see that the order appropriate to the Divine Being can only render itself manifest by the invariable observance of his own laws,—

---

* See these views more extensively treated in a discourse by the author, on the Revealed Nature and Orderly Operations of Omnipotence; also a chapter on Miracles, in his "Peculiarities of the Bible."

† 1 Cor. xiv. 33.

laws which have been provided by his own infinite understanding.

The Omnipotence which the miracles display is to be considered as special instances for special purposes; but that in no case was there any interference with the established laws and orderly operations of the universe. The wisdom of God would not have fixed certain laws of action at one time, which that same wisdom must have foreseen would afterwards have to be disrupted to bring about some other end. This, however, must have been the case, if the flood were a miracle of the kind supposed. If that event took place according to the popular apprehension, then it was a miracle which has no analogy with any other that is recorded in the Scriptures, for it would not only have inverted the whole order of the earth's condition, but also have disturbed its orbicular and other motions, and so have interfered with all the laws of physical action throughout the universe. These consequences show that it ought not to be considered a miracle of such a kind. But where is it said to have been a miracle at all? It is not so spoken of in the history itself, nor is it ever alluded to as such throughout the whole Scriptures. So far as the narrative is viewed in a literal sense, the occurrence is represented to have resulted from two natural causes, namely, "rain," and the rising of water from some other source called the "great deep." The idea of its having been a miracle of so stupendous a kind, and requiring supernatural agency upon so extensive a scale, springs wholly out of the literal interpretation: it is this, and not the history itself, which demands it. Commentators have taken a view of the subject which more matured inquiries prove to involve a great number of insuperable difficulties, and then, to help themselves out of these embarrassments, they assert it to have been a miracle, and plead the ability of Omnipotence to perform it. The idea of its having been a miracle in any ordinary sense of the term has been engendered by, as we think, a total misapprehension of the subject; and the appeal to Omnipotence for its execution is resorted to in complete forgetfulness of its order and its laws.

But upon these points we cannot longer dwell. What has been said concerning them is very general, and partakes in some measure of the character of a digression. However, we have seen from them that neither science nor tradition contributes any facts to prove that the deluge of the Scriptures was that natural event commonly supposed; also that the resort to miracle and Omnipotence, though it may silence inquiry, overlooks their laws, and does not bring any satisfactory light to explain the subject. Let us then endeavour to examine it upon the same principles that we have adopted for the deciphering of the preceding histories.*

In closing the last chapter, it was shown that the clean and unclean beasts which Noah took with him into the ark were very similar to the tame and ferocious animals that are predicated to be in the Lord's holy mountain, and that the significations of the two circumstances closely resemble each other. It is easy to see that painful trials must have been among the first consequences of clearly discovering that antagonistic affections and thoughts existed in the same mind or Church: "for what fellowship hath righteousness with unrighteousness? What communion hath light with darkness?" † Opposing sentiments and loves will not harmonize: the unclean may be brought into a state of quiescence and subjection to the clean, but the process for effecting it is one of great anxiety and temptation. Temptations, then, are the subjects which we believe to be treated of under the figure of a flood. These, with the Noachic people, were the means of purification and safety, because they provided for the emergency, and were enabled to overcome it; while all those who yielded to their influence necessarily perished. This is the spiritual philosophy of the circumstance, and the general instruction it was intended to communicate: as such it harmonizes with the whole scope of revelation, which is to warn us against evil and teach us the way

---

* "Was it a flood of water or of wickedness? Those who have not reflected much on spiritual things are startled even at the mention of a spiritual flood, although the thing itself is not at all unknown or unfamiliar. They have been so long accustomed to the vulgar idea, and are habitually so persuaded of the value of natural life, that, although the destruction of virtue and truth by torrents of iniquity is far more appalling to the wise, to the heedless it seems of little moment."—*Dr. Bayley's* "*Divine Word Opened,*" p. 597.

† 2 Cor. vi. 14.

to good. Temptation is one of those means by which the regeneration of the well-disposed is promoted; it also brings about the desolation and consequent destruction of all those in whom evil obliterates the capacity of salvation. But to understand this matter it will be necessary to make ourselves acquainted with its nature.

Temptations consist in all those things by which men are influenced to think, and so to believe, what is false; and to love, and so to do, what is evil. The internal straits, mental sufferings, and distress, which are experienced during their operation, arise from the efforts which they make to destroy something that is good and true in the internal man. The experience of temptations may be taken as a proof that man is inclined towards the evils which they suggest. But for this tendency he could not be tempted. When a man is tempted, it is a sort of revelation to him that he has a bias in that direction, and of this fact it is important that he should be aware, if he would successfully resist and overcome it. It is also true that the experience of temptation proves that there have been present in its subject some degree of charity and faith, since without these he would not be qualified to see its danger or feel its pain.

Whence, then, do these temptations originate, and by what are they resisted? To answer these questions satisfactorily, we must go one degree farther back in the inquiry than is usually contemplated. It is a doctrine of the Sacred Scriptures, frequently expressed with much clearness, that man is, by virtue of his spiritual nature, in association with certain inhabitants of the spiritual world; that, so far as he is possessed of anything that is good and true, he is the companion of some of those happy beings whom the Lord sends forth to minister to those who shall be heirs of salvation: and that, so far as he is principled in anything that is evil and false, so far he is the confederate of some of those spirits of darkness who are called the devil and Satan: but that, because man is more or less of a mixed character, there are attendant upon him during his lifetime in the world spiritual beings of each class; evil spirits who excite man's fallen propensities, and good spirits who defend him by means of any intelligence or virtue he may have cherished. The pains of temptation arise from the combats of these principles, and their resistance of each other.

That some may doubt the circumstance of good and evil spirits attendant upon the human race is to be expected. The world is not yet cleared of sceptics in spiritual things; mere naturalism may have its advocates for a long time yet, but this is no evidence against the fact that invisible spiritual beings do exercise an influence over men's sentiments and conduct. The sensualist may say this opinion is superstition; but the Scriptures set it forth as a fact, and there are phenomena to prove that it is so. All persons who have attended to what frequently takes place in their own minds possess the evidence. How suddenly do thoughts and feelings sometimes arise in the mind, even when it is directed some other way, and to the production of which neither premeditation nor desire has contributed. They spring up spontaneously: sometimes they are of a favourable and encouraging description, and at others they are of a most fearful and diabolical character. Whence do they come? We are not sensible of having made any effort to produce them, yet there they are. These experiences, when connected with the assertion of the Scriptures that good and evil spirits are present with the human race,* enable us to conclude very reasonably concerning their origin.

But whatever hesitation there may be to accept this view of the source of temptations, there can be no doubt as to their existence. In general they are of two kinds,—those which affect the understanding and any truths it may possess, and those that act upon the will and any goodness it may have acquired.

---

* Psa. xxxiv. 7: "The angel of the Lord encampeth round about them that fear him." Psa. xci. 11: "He shall give his angels charge over thee, to keep thee in all thy ways." 1 Pet. v. 8: "Your adversary the devil, as a roaring lion, walketh about, seeking whom he may devour."

Dr. S. Johnson, in his philosophical tale of "Rasselas," has made Imlac, in speaking of a kindred subject, say, "This opinion, which perhaps prevails as far as human nature is diffused, could become universal only by its truth: those that never heard of one another would not have agreed in a tale which nothing but experience can make credible. That it is doubted by single cavillers can very little weaken the general evidence; and some who deny it with their tongues confess it by their fears."

When men are tempted to doubt, and so to reject the truths in which they have been educated, and with the value of which they have been favourably impressed, they will find, if they be attentive to what is taking place within them, that there is at the same time excited the remembrance of many evil actions of which they have been guilty. These will be attended with numerous anxieties, and they will produce much perturbation and painful disquiet; still these temptations are somewhat mild when compared with those that assail the will, or any of the good things which affection and habit have fixed upon it. If those who suffer from these temptations will carefully observe what is transpiring in their minds, they will find that they are not so much distressed by the recollection of the misconduct into which they may have fallen, as by some powerful influence urging them on to gratify some cupidity or to indulge some lust; they will also find that a restlessness of feeling and moral agony, attended by an obscurity concerning truth, will prevail, according to the depth and severity of the temptation endured.

These temptations are productive of two different consequences, according to the manner in which they are received by the subject of them. It must needs be that temptations will come, and woe is the unavoidable result of their activity. But those who resist them increase their virtues, and so are saved; while those who yield to them enlarge their vices, and so must perish. Hence, the antediluvians whose wickedness was great were destroyed; while those whose obedience gave them grace in the eyes of the Lord were saved. The wicked take in the evils of temptation like sponges imbibing water: the good repel them, and by that resistance they increase the sources and energies of virtue, till at last their characters are raised above them. Noah is called righteous because of his resistance, and he was saved in consequence. The grace and righteousness said to have been found in him were the qualification by which, as it is written, he did according to all that God commanded him.

As man in his fallen state is inclined to what is evil and false, and as the Lord is solicitous to raise him out of that degradation, he must, in order to effect it, experience temptation. His affections cannot be changed from iniquity to holiness without the endurance of a struggle. The impression which earthly and sensual delights have made upon his character, renders it difficult to lift him out of it, and the act of so doing will be attended with resistance. He is closely attached to worldly things; and it requires more effort to produce the separation than it does to continue it when it is accomplished. Like the severance of iron, when in contact with the magnet, the effort to sustain the connection is great so long as they touch each other; but effect their separation, and it is easily maintained. But the difficulty of separating man from his evil influences will be increased if he lean towards them; and if he entirely refrain from co-operating in the means of rescue, his deliverance is impossible. The obstacle, however, is lessened in proportion to the force with which he inclines to what is good. These things may be compared to a man who has fallen into bad society, and whom his friend endeavours to lead away from them. Such society is urgent that he should remain, participate in their coarse enjoyments, and treat his friend with indifference and disdain. If he incline to their solicitation, the greater is the difficulty which his friend will have to promote his rescue, because his wicked associates are encouraged by his inclination, and they become more importunate; but if he lean towards the advice of his friend they are discouraged, and he is finally induced to leave them, though in the process much coarse and ribald treatment may be displayed. Such wicked society is man's evil influence, and his friend is the Lord, who is wishful to deliver him. Although, then, temptations are inseparable from man's present condition, the good or evil which results is largely dependent on the way in which he employs his freedom. Those who use it to resist impurity are preserved; but those who do not will obviously perish. Now these temptations are, in the Scriptures, represented by a flood, and their different effects upon different classes are described by the Noachic people having risen above them, and the residue having sunk beneath them.

Thus, while the popular view of the subject regards it to have been a catastrophe relating to the bodies and the natural lives of men, we look upon it to have been a calamity affecting the souls and spiritual lives of men, and thereby to the injury and destruction of their physical existence. It is written, that "evil shall slay the wicked." * Experience proves that this is true of natural things, and reason shows that it must be so of spiritual. The event called the flood is not to be considered less real to that ancient community, and all that vitally concerned them, because it is not regarded to have taken place in the way commonly supposed. We believe spiritual things to be as real as any natural things can possibly be. Indeed, the reality of things natural is contingent upon the reality of things spiritual, more or less remotely. The flood, considered as a spiritual phenomenon, was equally, nay, more afflicting and disastrous to society, than any notion which can be associated with the circumstance, considered as a physical occurrence. Look for a moment at the terrible idea of mankind having been so powerfully inflamed by filthy lusts of every description, that they were not only immersed therein, and so profaned all they knew of spiritual and religious truth, but that they also closed up every avenue in their minds by which heavenly influences could reach and operate upon their *remains.* A reflection upon these melancholy circumstances cannot fail to show that it must have brought in upon them destructive influences as a flood, and have overwhelmed in eternal ruin all who fell therein. This view of the deluge is eminently calculated to strike the reflecting with dismay. It is consistent with the spiritual design of revelation, to disclose to posterity spiritual information concerning the moral turpitude of their predecessors, and the influences which their conduct and condition have had upon the world. It makes known to us that it was not merely a scene in the natural world, by which the civilizing influences of religion were destroyed, but that it was a spiritual circumstance which afflicted and destroyed society; and that, upon the principle, "where the tree falleth, there it shall be," † it must have induced some inordinate condition even in the infernal world.

But, as it was said, the Scriptures speak of temptations as a *flood.* For instance, the Psalmist says, "Save me, O God; for the waters are come in unto my soul. I sink in deep mire, where there is no standing: I am come into deep waters, where the *floods* overflow me.—Let not the *waterflood* overflow me,

---

* Psa. xxxiv. 21. † Eccles. xi. 3.

neither let the deep swallow me up." * Here it is plain that the waters which were come into his soul, and the waterfloods from which he was so earnestly wishful to be delivered, were not floods of natural water, but the infestations of false principles, by which he was so severely tempted and distressed. Again, speaking of the Lord's protection in times of such spiritual danger, it is said, "For this shall every one that is godly pray unto thee in the time when thou mayest be found; but in the *floods of great waters* they shall not reach him." † To the same purpose it is written, "He bindeth the *floods* from overflowing." ‡ So, also, in the prophet, it is declared, "When the enemy shall come in like a *flood*, the Spirit of the Lord shall lift up a standard against him." § Jeremiah, likewise, treating of the temptations which arise from false principles, signified by Egypt and the army of Pharaoh, inquires, "Who is this that cometh up as a *flood*, whose *waters* are moved as the rivers? Egypt riseth up like a *flood*, and his *waters* are moved like the rivers." ‖ Daniel, when predicting that the Messiah should be cut off, and that the city and sanctuary would be destroyed, says, "And the end thereof shall be with a *flood*"; ¶ which plainly means, that those evils which attend the rejection of the Messiah, his doctrine and worship, will terminate in the production of the most dangerous temptations. Amos, announcing the perversities of the Jewish Church, describes the Lord as saying, "Shall not the land tremble for this, and every one mourn that dwelleth therein? and it shall rise up wholly as a *flood;* and it shall be cast out and drowned, as by the *flood of Egypt*." ** Where, by the land rising up as a *flood*, is denoted the Church, inflated by its false persuasions; and by its being cast out and drowned as by a *flood*, is signified the desolation which their temptations would induce. Many other illustrations of this idea could be produced from the Scriptures; we will, however, just advert to another. The Apocalypse, treating of the Man-Child, born of the woman, clothed with the sun, by which was represented the birth of genuine truth in

* Psa. lxix. 1, 2, 15. † Psa. xxxii. 6, amended translation.
‡ Job xxviii. 11. § Isa. lix. 19.
‖ Jer. xlvi. 7, 8. ¶ Dan. ix. 26. ** Amos viii. 8.

the Church from heavenly affection, says, "And the serpent cast out of his mouth *water* as a *flood* after the woman, that he might cause her to be carried away of the *flood*. And the earth helped the woman, and the earth opened her mouth, and swallowed up the flood which the dragon cast out of his mouth."* Here, by the serpent, which is also called a dragon, is represented the sensual condition of a perishing church; by the waters, which issued out of its mouth as a flood, are denoted the abundance of false reasonings and persuasions which it produces, especially with the view of overwhelming the good and the truth by which it is about to be exposed. By the earth, which helped the woman, is denoted the new Church, which receives and cherishes heavenly affections; the earth opening its mouth, and swallowing up the flood which the dragon cast forth, denoted that the understanding of the people of this new Church will be so enlightened by truth that they will be capable of resisting and dissipating all the temptations which sensual reasonings may produce. It is, then, very evident that the Scriptures employ the idea of a flood to represent the infestation of false principles, with their evil consequences, and that those who resist them will be enlightened and saved, while those who yield to them are benighted, and must perish.

It was a flood of this description in which the antediluvians perished. The mere circumstance of being drowned as to the body is no corresponding consequence for the sins of the soul. Many good men have so died: many wicked men have not so suffered. There is no connection between such a natural catastrophe and the spiritual state of the people. It is the soul, and its condition, of which the Scriptures treat. The principles which give it everlasting life, and the perversities which produce its eternal death, are the things which God has condescended to reveal, and which men should strive to know.

But these conclusions will have their certainty brought out with greater clearness if we inquire into the meaning of what are described to have been the sources of this catastrophe. These sources are two,—the breaking up of the fountains of the great deep, and the opening of the windows of heaven.† Surely,

* Rev. xii. 15, 16. † Gen. vii. 11.

every one whose mind is not entirely pre-occupied with the idea of a physical occurrence being intended, must see that these sentences were not constructed with a view to express it. The style is highly figurative, and resembles very closely that employed by the prophets, of which one instance will suffice: "He who fleeth from the noise of the fear shall fall into the pit; and he that cometh out of the midst of the pit shall be taken in the snare: *for the windows from on high are open, and the foundations of the earth do shake.*"* Neither the Mosaic terrors nor those of the prophet refer to any natural phenomena. "*Foundations of the great deep!*" What is there, in mundane things, answering to these expressions? Conjectures on this subject were abundant a century or less ago, † but they have vanished before the progress of philosophy, and now, nothing that can with any reasonableness be said to answer the description is known to science. "*Windows of heaven!*" What are they?‡ Surely the phrase

---

* Isa. xxiv. 18.

† It was long thought to be a vast abyss of water in the centre of the earth. Many speculations upon the matter may be seen in King's "Morsels of Criticism," vol. ii., pp. 355, 417. Englefield, with a view to find a sufficient quantity of water to cover the whole earth fifteen cubits, supposed the globe of earth to consist of a crust of solid matter one thousand miles thick, enclosing a sea or body of water two thousand miles deep, within which was a central nucleus of two thousand miles in diameter; and then concluded that he had found about one hundred and thirty-seven times more water than would have been required for the submergence of the earth. Other philosophers think that *fire*, and not *water*, is in the centre of the earth. We have nothing to say about these speculations and calculations: it is requisite, in the first place, to inquire for the facts. The conclusion about the water is arrived at on supposititious grounds only, for which there are no philosophical data. Dr. P. Smith considers the phrase to mean merely the general collection of oceanic waters.

‡ This is thought to be a Hebrew phrase for the sky. It is interesting to observe the frequency with which modern critics endeavour to remove the difficulties of expression with which the Scriptures are considered to abound, by referring them to oriental genius. It is found to be exceedingly convenient so to do; but it does not explain the matter. We have still to ask, Why was that mode of expression so peculiar to Eastern genius? and, Whence did it arise? That there are both propriety and good judgment in ascribing many expressions to that source, may be readily admitted; nevertheless, their figurative character remains; nor is the circumstance of their having been originally employed, representatively, to denote spiritual things at all

ought not to be understood to mean the clouds of the earth, whence it is known the showers descend: to open these, when they prevail, is to disperse them, and so let in the sunshine, and not pour down their rain. Moreover, the clouds are watery vapours originally derived from the earth, and the densest of them will not contain more water than would cover very slightly the locality in which it may be discharged. If the whole atmosphere surrounding the earth were saturated with water to its fullest capacity, and then precipitated, the result, according to Mr. Rhind,* would not deluge the earth more than seven inches. Rain can only contribute to the production of a flood in a comparatively small district. Numerous destructive instances of this kind are well known; they were occasioned by continued evaporation from the ocean, with successive and long-sustained discharges of rain. But this could not be universal. The laws of evaporation, and the capacity of the atmosphere for holding water, render it impossible except by a miracle; and that we have no right to invent, in the absence of all proper authority for so doing. But as the earth supplies the clouds with all the rain that ever descends from them, they, as *the windows of heaven*, cannot be considered as any source separate from the *fountains of the great deep*, supposing them to mean the oceanic waters; nevertheless the different sentences must be intended to express some distinction. If the phrase, "windows of heaven," be regarded merely as an orientalism, denoting the clouds and their rain, and if it be remembered that those clouds can have no water to precipitate but what is first raised by evaporation from the earth, then we are compelled to say the flood was produced by the breaking up of the fountains of the great deep *only;* because *the deep* was the *only* source whence the water was supplied, the rain being merely a means for its distribution: but this, we hold, is not in agreement with the design

---

disturbed by it. Therefore, in referring peculiarities of expression to be found in the Scriptures to the genius of the people, or to the idiomatic character of the language spoken by them, and from which such expressions are derived ; and considering them to mean certain natural things, poetically expressed, their spiritual, which is their chief design, must not be overlooked.

* Rhind's " Age of the Earth," p. 100.

of the narrative, which plainly presents *two* distinct *sources* of the catastrophe, and thus shows us that natural things are not intended to be described.

When it is remembered that the flood is significant of temptations in general, and it is known that they arise from two specific causes, which are evil in the will and falsehood in the understanding, it will not be difficult to find the proper relatives for those two phrases, namely,—fountains of the great deep being broken up, and windows of heaven being opened; for by the former, it will be seen, is denoted extreme temptation arising from evil influences upon the will; and by the latter is signified severe temptation operating by falsehood upon the understanding.

The will of man is compared to the *deep*, because it is so in reference to the things of love. In our own language it is employed as a figure with that signification. Those in whom intense affection is excited are said to love *deeply*. It matters little whether the object of it be good or not, it is the *depth* of the love, and not the character of the object, which is spoken of. A like mode of expression is frequently employed in the Scriptures: great sin is called *deep* corruption,* and the rebellion of Israel is said to have been a *deep* revolt.† The will, as a seat and receptacle of affection, is influenced by a variety of conflicting sentiments and feelings, which keep it in continual agitation, and in this respect it is also as the deep, considered as an ocean: sometimes those feelings are more tranquil and subdued, at others they are more tumultuous and fearful; and in this, likewise, it presents an analogy to the deep. It is in consequence of this signification, that the prophet, speaking of the Assyrian, says, "The waters made him great, the deep set him up on high;" ‡ because by the Assyrian is denoted the rational principle. The waters are declared to make him great, because truths regenerate and make it good; and the *deep* is declared to set him up on high, to signify the elevation which is attained by the activity of the *will*. The deep before us is called *great*, to denote that it had been *good*, for greatness is goodness in a spiritual sense; and the fountains thereof refer to and signify all those affections by

* Hos. ix. 9.   † Isa. xxxi. 6.   ‡ Ezek. xxxi. 4.

which that characteristic had been procured. Every one sees that affection is a spiritual fountain, through which arise innumerable joys. But we are informed that all these were broken up: the will, as a will for good, was now disrupted, and had become a lust; and the affections, as the fountain through which had arisen orderly delight and blessedness, were now entirely destroyed. Therefore it is evident that the breaking up of the fountains of the great deep denotes extreme temptations, arising from evil influences upon the will.

But while the fountains of the great deep signify the affections of the will, the windows of heaven denote the perceptions of the understanding. It is by those perceptions that we are enabled to behold anything of spiritual truth, and the understanding, when enlightened thereby, is as heaven, by virtue of the wisdom that is present. They are the windows through which the mind derives all its illustrations; and they are the windows of heaven when they are turned to heavenly things, and admit the light of heavenly truth to illustrate the understanding. This had been the case with them in previous and better times, though it was not so at the period which is before us. The will, having become a lust, would needs corrupt the understanding also. It is a law that where the deeds are evil, darkness will be preferred to light.* Those windows are said to have been opened, yet not for a good, but for a destructive purpose. This opening implies an unguarded exposure, and so a carelessness as to what may enter, in which case falsehood is sure to find its way. Though they were open, it was not to receive heavenly light, but to admit some destructive influence: this is plain from the whole tenor of the narrative. The nature of that influence must have been false reasonings and persuasions, and these produced extreme temptations and delusions in the understanding.

It was when the things of the will and understanding were so entirely disarranged and perverted, that the rain is said to have been upon the earth forty days; because by the rain is here not meant rain, but the influx of evil and false principles into these two faculties of the human mind. This must be evident to all who can see the flood to have been an inundation

---

* John iii. 19.

of wicked persuasions and delights, which the Psalmist calls the floods of ungodly men which made him afraid.

Rain, when mentioned in a good sense in the Scriptures, denotes the influence of holy enjoyments from the Lord: hence they are called "showers of blessing";* and among many features of his Divine care for the Church is that of "making it soft with showers";† and he himself is said to "come down like rain upon the mown grass." ‡ These blessings are compared to rain because there is an analogy between the natural effects of gentle and seasonable showers, and the spiritual results of orderly and refreshing influx. In a literal sense it irrigates the soil, increases its fertility, and renders it capable of producing the food which is requisite for our physical sustenance; in a spiritual sense it softens the asperity of man, improves his docility, and enlarges his power of bringing forth the meat necessary for promoting life eternal.

But when rain is spoken of in an opposite sense, and from which disastrous consequences ensue, as in the case of the subject before us, then it denotes the influx of impurity from the infernal world. The context will always determine which is the character of the influx treated of. § While some rains are gentle and eminently useful, others are violent and lamentably destructive; and the latter are frequently employed in the Scriptures as the emblems of spiritual desolation. As for instance, it is written, "The tabernacle shall be for a covert from storm and from rain"; ‖ where the tabernacle is mentioned for the Church; and this, considered in reference to its wisdom and virtue, was to be a protection from the *storm*, because by that, in respect to wind, is denoted a tumultuous influx of false persuasions: it was also to be a shelter from the *rain*, because by that is represented a destructive influx of evil loves. Ezekiel, speaking of those who daub the wall with untempered mortar,— by which is to be understood all such as confirm themselves in

---

* Ezek. xxxiv. 26. † Psa. lxv. 10. ‡ Psa. lxxii. 6.

§ *Influx* is a flowing down or into a subject, and is distinguished from *influence*, which simply means acting upon a subject. In the above case it denotes the inflowing of wicked spirits into the minds of men with a view to their destruction.

‖ Isa. iv. 6.

false ideas of religion by the fallacies of appearances,—represents the Lord as saying, "There shall be an overflowing shower in mine anger, and great hailstones in my fury to consume it";* where by an overwhelming shower is denoted a destructive influence. So also, in his prophecy against Gog, it is declared, "I will rain upon him, and upon his bands, and upon the many people that are with him, an overflowing rain";† where, again, by an overflowing rain is plainly meant an inundation of pernicious influences, by which they would be destroyed. The Lord said, "Every one that heareth these sayings of mine, and doeth them not, shall be likened unto a foolish man, which built his house upon the sand: and the rain descended, and the floods came, and the winds blew, and beat upon that house; and it fell: and great was the fall of it."‡ Here the building of the house is another form under which the development of the Church with man is represented. When this is grounded on genuine truth, represented by the permanent *rock*, it is capable of resisting and outliving any storm of temptation by which it may be assailed; but when it has its foundation in shifting falsehood, denoted by the unsteady sand, then, when storms of temptation arise, it is eminently unsafe, and it will be sure to perish when the rains thereof descend, the floods come, and the winds blow.

Other passages could easily be produced to show that rain, when spoken of in a destructive sense, is significant of those dangerous influences which overwhelm those in whom the will for good has been destroyed and the understanding of truth uncared for: but these are sufficient. They will convince the reflecting that temptations, and their desolating consequences on the souls of men, and so the complete destruction of the most ancient Church, are the subjects treated of under the figure of the deluge. This, indeed, is still farther evinced by the circumstance of its being said that "rain was upon the earth forty days and forty nights"; for that number, in the Scriptures, is continually associated with subjects in which temptations are conspicuous. Of Scripture numbers, considered in the abstract, we have already spoken;§ and many instances might be ad-

---

* Ezek. xiii. 13. † Ezek. xxxviii. 22.
‡ Matt. vii. 26, 27. § See pp. 242, 259.

duced, in which it is evident that natural computations are referred to merely for the sake of their spiritual sense. The "Molten Sea" is said to have been "ten cubits from the one brim to the other; and a line of thirty cubits did compass it round about";* but the number of the circumference does not geometrically answer to that of the diameter. So also it is written that "the sojourning of the children of Israel, who dwelt in Egypt, was four hundred and thirty years"; † but this period does not agree with the Scripture chronology, and it is mentioned only because it was requisite to the correct expression of the spiritual sense; ‡ and the forty days' and nights' continuance of the rain is intended to denote the severity of the temptation, rather than the time of its duration. That the Scriptures employ the number *forty* in connection with the subjects of temptation is remarkably evident. Of the children of Israel it is said that they should "wander in the wilderness *forty* years, until the carcases of their fathers were wasted. After the number of the days in which ye searched the land, even *forty* days, each day for a year, shall ye bear your iniquities, even *forty* years." § The Lord is said to have been grieved *forty* years with that generation.|| It is written of Egypt that it should be "utterly waste and desolate, from the tower of Syene even unto the border of Ethiopia. No foot of man shall pass through it, nor foot of beast shall pass through it, neither shall it be inhabited *forty* years." ¶ Jonah cried, and said unto the Ninevites, "Yet *forty* days, and Nineveh shall be overthrown."** The prophet was directed to lie upon his right

---

* 1 Kings vii. 23. † Exod. xii. 40.

‡ This is shown by the Rev. R. Hindmarsh, as follows: "Moses sprang from Amram, Amram from Kohath, and Kohath from Levi, and Kohath went with his father Levi into Egypt (Gen. xlvi. 11). Now the age of Kohath was a hundred and thirty-three years (Exod. vi. 18); the age of Amram one hundred and thirty-seven years (verse 20); and the age of Moses, when he stood before Pharaoh, eighty years (Exod. vii. 7). All these years added together make only three hundred and fifty, which are considerably short of four hundred and thirty, and therefore it is impossible the children of Israel could have been four hundred and thirty years in Egypt."—*Letters to Dr. Priestley*, Second Edit., p. 160.

§ Numb. xiv. 33, 34. || Psa. xcv. 10   ¶ Ezek xxix. 10, 11.
** Jonah iii. 4.

side, and bear the iniquity of the house of Judah *forty* days. *
Moses "abode in the mount *forty* days and *forty* nights, neither
did he eat bread nor drink water," † praying for the people
lest they should be destroyed. It is said that the people "were
led forty years in the wilderness, to humble them, and to prove
them." ‡ In all these instances we find that the number *forty*
is associated with some afflicting circumstance; and when it is
farther remembered that the Lord Jesus Christ "was in the wilderness
forty days, tempted of Satan; and was with the wild
beasts,"§ men can no longer have any scepticism about the
number *forty* denoting the severity of temptation; and, consequently,
that the rain for forty days and forty nights in the case
of the deluge represented the painful sufferings of temptation
in every state, whether of light or darkness. This was the
circumstance in which we conceive the wicked antediluvians to
have perished: they yielded to its urgency, and so were finally
overwhelmed: while the people called Noah were saved, because
they resisted and overcame it.

These different effects of temptation, which may be easily conceived,
are represented to us by other circumstances recorded in
the Scriptures. Those which attended the journeyings of the
children of Israel in the wilderness toward the land of Canaan
afford a remarkable example. Their looking back to Egypt,
and murmuring for its fleshpots; their idolatry and backslidings;
their vicissitudes and disasters; their plagues and desolations,
are all plain evidences of their having sustained temptations.
But the history of those events, viewed in its complex,
is intended to show forth the two different and general effects
of temptations upon distinct classes of mind and character,
namely, the exaltation of some and the destruction of others.
The salutary effects of temptations are exhibited to us in those
who, having endured and overcome the hardships of the desert,
were finally introduced into the promised land; and their destructive
consequences are disclosed in the distresses which befell
those who perished in the wilderness. All who were above
twenty years old on their departure out of Egypt died in the
wilderness, with the exception of Caleb and Joshua. Those

---

* Ezek. iv. 6.   † Deut. ix. 9.
‡ Deut. viii. 2.   § Mark i. 13.

who entered into Canaan were either a new or more obedient race. The extinction of the former represented the destructive effects of temptations on those who yield to them; the preservation of the latter, and their introduction into the land of promise, exhibit the salutary results of temptations on those who resist and overcome them. They produce death on those who follow their own heart's lusts, but they induce a superior degree of spiritual life in all who endure and conquer them. One class perished in the disasters of the wilderness, another class were rescued from them, and entered into Canaan. There are, then, several parallelisms between the circumstances which attended the formation of the Israelitish Church in Canaan, and the establishment of the ancient Church with Noah. The difference is more in outward form than in essential things. Thus the land of Canaan was to the Israelites who were saved from the dangers of the wilderness what the ark was to Noah, who was preserved from the inundation of the flood. The death of those who died in the desert was to the formation of the Church in Canaan what the destruction of the antediluvians was to the establishment of the Church with Noah. Caleb and Joshua, being the only surviving adults who were delivered from the bondage of the Egyptians and the trials of the wilderness, were, to the planting of the Israelitish Church, what Noah and his house, as the only parties who escaped from the rains and the flood of the ancient world, were to the covenant then established. These parallelisms arise, as we have said, from the similarity of essential ideas intended to be included in both narrations, though the outward structure of the one is a real, and that of the other only a figurative history.

Concerning the deluge, as a temptation from which the Noachic people were delivered, Peter says, "The long-suffering of God waited in the days of Noah, while the ark was a preparing, wherein few, that is, eight souls were saved by water. The like figure* whereunto even baptism doth also now save

---

* 1 Pet. iii. 20, 21. The original word here used is ἀντίτυπον, antitype. The theological meaning of the terms type and antitype is, that the *type* is an impression, image, or representation of some model, which is termed the *antitype*. But there is some reason to ask whether this is not an inversion of the true scriptural sense? If the water by which Noah was saved were

us." Here the Apostle calls the circumstance of being saved by water a figure of baptism, because by the waters of baptism are signified purification, effected by means of temptations sustained and conquered. Calling the deluge a figure affords no evidence as to the real character of the event. Things purely spiritual can be types, equally with things natural. Moses was shown the pattern of the tabernacle in a vision on the mount. * As, then, the Apostle affirms that the waters of Noah were a figure of the waters of baptism, and as the waters of baptism are a symbol of purification acquired by overcoming temptation, it follows, upon his evidence also, that such was the signification of the deluge from which Noah was saved. Those who perished in it were those who yielded to the abominations to which they were incited. The death which they suffered, as being that which is primarily treated of, was of a spiritual kind, being induced by the love and life of evil. This is the death of which the Scriptures speak as the event to be avoided: "Be not afraid of them that kill the body, and after that have no more that they can do. But I will forewarn you whom ye shall fear: Fear him, which after he hath killed hath power to cast into hell; yea, I say unto you, Fear him." † He who killeth and casteth into hell is the devil, that is, evil; for this, in its complex, is so personified: to fear him is to oppose evil influences; wherefore it is written, "Resist the devil, and he will flee from you." ‡ The antediluvians did not so fear and resist: their wickedness was great in the earth, and every thought of the imagination of their heart was evil continually; hence they perished.

It is to be observed that it was every *living substance which the Lord had made* that was about to be destroyed. That it is important to remark. It is, indeed, said that the Lord would do it, because it appears to the wicked, when, by ignorance and misdoing, they bring calamity upon themselves, that the Lord is its author. Of this mode of speaking of the Divine character

the *antitype* of that by which baptism saves us, then the waters of baptism were the *type*. Thus, that which succeeds an impression and proceeds from a model is really the type. In John xx. 25, it is said, τὸν τύπον τῶν ἥλων, which literally means, the type of the nails.

* Exod. xxv. 40; Heb. viii. 5. † Luke xii. 4, 5. ‡ Jas. iv. 7.

we have already treated. All that the Lord made was pronounced to have been very good: there is no intimation of the animal or vegetable world having departed from its original excellence; nor is there any reasonable ground to suppose that any such things which may have survived the flood could have regarded the extermination of their predecessors as a calamity. It was man alone who had strayed from the ways of purity and knowledge, and he alone could contemplate death as a terrible catastrophe. The destruction of the insentient and irresponsible objects of nature cannot be reasonably attributed to God, from whose wisdom and goodness they have proceeded. As the Creator of all that is good, he cannot also be the destroyer! His continual efforts are, according to the Scriptures, to preserve and bless, to remove the evil and increase the good. He, therefore, cannot destroy what he has really made; such an act would imply a condemnation of his own wisdom. It is evil which the Lord is solicitous to remove, so far as it can be done consistently with man's freedom and responsibility. This evil he did not make, although there have been men who have so believed and taught.* Wicked persons, so far as they acknowledge God, believe him to be the author of the calamities they bring upon themselves. Such a false position is a consequence of the inverted state of their mental character. Job's wife so regarded the affliction of her husband, and bade him "curse God, and die"; † but she talked as one of the foolish women. Nevertheless, the providences by which the Lord hinders the manifestation of particular evils, and so causes their cessation and removal, are, by such persons, considered as the destruction, by God, of what he himself has made. The passage, then, which represents the Lord as saying, "Every living sub-

---

* " If God foresaw that Judas would be a traitor, Judas *necessarily* became a traitor, nor was it in his power to be otherwise."—*Martin Luther.* See *De Servo Arbitrio,* fol. 460.

"God not only foresaw that Adam would fall, but ordained that he should."—*Calvin. Inst.,* b. 3, chap. xxiii., sec. 7.

"God is the author of every action which is sinful, by his irresistible will."—*Dr. Twiss,* part iii., p. 21.

What shocking and detestable sentiments!

† Job ii. 9.

stance that I have made will I destroy," refers to the dissipation of those evil principles which had gained a fierce ascendency over society, and, so far as this could not be effected without it, the permission of means by which society itself was to be dissolved. It was not the things of orderly nature, but the principles which had disordered humanity, that had to be destroyed. These had become living substances with men; and men, in the midst of their wickedness, regarded them as God's creation: and this is the reason why he is said to have made them. They were opposed to his merciful design in our creation, and, therefore, the permission of means for the removal of obstacles which stood in the way of manifesting his good providence is perfectly consistent with that clemency and wisdom which regard eternal ends in all they do.

But what were the means so permitted? They were the waters of temptation. Evil, having become an infixed principle in man, attracted corresponding influences from the infernal world. Those influences destroy all who give themselves up to their impulses and suggestions; though, when they are resisted and conquered, good enters into man, and he becomes exalted. For, by temptation, man is brought acquainted with his evils, since he cannot be tempted to anything unless he is in some measure previously inclined to it: thus, temptations act as a sort of revelation to man, as before observed, informing him of the evils which he loves. If he do not resist them, then of course they triumph, and he falls: this was the case with the antediluvians who perished; but if he repulse them and conquer, then his evils are so dispersed that goodness and truth from the Lord can flow into his affection and thought, and so produce salvation. This was the case with Noah, and it became the ground on which the Lord could establish a covenant with him. When "*the waters increased,*" "the ark went up"; that is, when temptations were urgent, the men of the Church acquired, by their resistance, a spiritual elevation: but when "the waters prevailed," "the high hills were covered"; by which we are informed that, when temptation conquered, good was overwhelmed. The inundation of every good from the Lord is represented by "the covering of all the high hills that were under the whole heaven." Hills denote elevated principles: hence we

read of the hill of the Lord, and the mountain of his holiness; *
and that to cover them signifies to overwhelm them, is evident
without farther explanation. How fearful was this state of
temptation! yea, how awfully destructive was its character!
For in obtaining an ascendency over the moral sentiments and
spiritual hopes of men, we are informed that "all flesh died
that moved upon the earth, both of fowls,. and of cattle, and of
beasts, and of every creeping thing that creepeth upon the earth,
and every man." † This serial statement of the death of all
animated nature is intended to express the extinction of all those
spiritual principles of evil and falsehood which had become
living things with the antediluvian people, and which gave to
them a peculiar malignity of character.

It is exceedingly difficult to conceive how the death of all
natural creatures should have been involved in the transgression
of man! What had the irresponsible beasts done that they
must perish? It does not remove the difficulty to say that God
willed it so: he could not have willed it without a sufficient
reason; for all he does proceeds from intelligence, and regards a
moral. The narrative gives no reason; and reason finds it difficult to see what moral could be inculcated by such a course.
Some may say it was to display the terribleness of God's anger!
We have no sympathy with such a notion. He creates to sustain by laws of preservation and perpetuation, and in no case to
destroy. The change and dissolution to which material things
are subject arise from the action of laws peculiar to their existence, and they do not properly come within the meaning of the
word *destroy* as it is here employed. There is no perceptible
connection between the infliction of death upon the beasts of
the earth, and the punishment of man's iniquity, unless, perhaps, in cases where they are viewed as property, which will
hardly be contended for in the present case. But why should
this infliction have been upon the terrestrial creatures only?
Why were the marine animals to escape? as they must have
done, because the means adopted for the supposed destruction
of others could not have exterminated them. If terrestrial
beasts must die in consequence of man's transgression, why
were the fishes spared? It is said that all the fowls perished;

---

* Psa. xxiv. 3; xlviii. 1; Isa. ii. 3.   † Gen. vii. 21.

but as there is a great variety of aquatic birds, which would scarcely have been destroyed by the rising of the waters, is it not highly probable that they escaped the danger? Interrogatories of this nature might be indefinitely extended, because they are founded on the idea of the narrative describing a physical circumstance, which we think these investigations show to be a mistaken view of it. The fact that it is not a literal history, but the description of spiritual phenomena, at once disarms science and philosophy of all their difficulties, and enables us to think of it on spiritual, which are its proper, grounds.

It has been shown on several occasions during the progress of this work that various orders of animated nature are mentioned in the Scriptures as types or symbols of certain moral sentiments and intellectual principles of man. It was adverted to when speaking of the fourth and fifth days' creation; also when treating of Adam's naming the creatures; and likewise in noticing their introduction into the ark. We therefore need not adduce farther illustrations. The principle involved in those explanations is applicable to the case before us. It leads us at once to see that the animals which are mentioned to have perished at the deluge were significant of certain principles of life, which were extinguished through the inflowing of those false persuasions and evil loves from which the flood resulted.

It is, however, of importance to observe in what those principles of life consisted. The people had been, for many generations, descending deeper and deeper into the mire and filth of their corruptions, and the posterity now treated of had become the sink of all that was vile in perversity and lust: these are the various principles of degenerate life belonging to this abandoned condition, that are specifically referred to by the animals which perished in the flood. All man's noble affections and elevated sentiments had previously passed away in the degeneracy that had set in, and those which now remained were low and sensual merely. The unhallowed nature of these perversities and loves had closed the interiors of that people against the reception of all heavenly influences, so that, in addition to their own vicious inclinations, they were acted upon by urgent impulses from the infernal world, through the inundations of which they finally perished from the earth, carrying with them all the fallen appetites and persuasions *peculiar* to the race. These, we say, were represented by the general description, "All flesh died that creepeth upon the earth, as to fowl, and as to beast, and as to wild beast, and as to every reptile creeping upon the earth, and every man." It is to be remarked that the animals described to have perished are called "creeping things." The fowls, the beasts, and wild beasts, are all included in the general statement that "all flesh died that creepeth upon the earth." This is said of them to indicate the earthly persuasions and delights of men; and in order to represent the dispersion of their peculiar enormities, these creeping things are said to have died. That flesh is mentioned in the Scriptures to denote man in general is well known; and therefore it is easy to see, when he is spoken of as *flesh that creepeth upon the earth*, that his corporeal and earthly condition is described. The *fowls* of this state represented his perverted reasonings and false persuasions; the *beasts* were significant of lusts of various sorts; *wild beasts* denoted the inordinate delights of the sensual man; and *reptiles* meant all those pursuits which are grovelling, earthly, and disgusting. The interior principles of those people had become altogether vile; the life of their understandings was a mere animus of false persuasions; the life of their wills had degenerated into abandoned lusts, and they perished in following the wickedness to which they were impelled.

To show that the peculiar kinds of false and evil principles which had been developed in society were to be extirpated, it is said that "all flesh died that moved upon the earth, both of fowl, and of cattle, and of beasts, and of every creeping thing that creepeth upon the earth," and which, in one complex, are called "every man";* man here denoting the profane character which he had become.

Such we conceive to have been the horrible nature of the flood—that is, of the inundation of false principles and evil loves into the minds and hearts of men—that it not only overwhelmed the spiritual lives of all those who had not prepared to resist their suggestions and impulses, but it also promoted a disastrous termination of their natural existence.

It may not be easy for some to see how those evil influences,

* Gen. vii. 21.

operating upon the mind, were capable of producing such a physical result, because we live under an economy in which the Redeemer has mercifully provided against the return of events which might have afforded illustrative evidence and examples. Yet they are not entirely without a witness, as we shall see presently.

The first means adopted to prevent the recurrence of such a calamity was the reconstruction of the human mind, by the separation of the will from the understanding, and thereby making provision for the security of *remains*. This means, although up to a certain period it realized the promise that "all flesh should not be cut off any more by the waters of a flood," yet it was not a full and complete preventive against its possibility. For we find that evil influences from the infernal world had again obtained an ascendency over at least a certain portion of the human race, at the time of the advent of the Lord Jesus Christ, since it is written, "For this purpose was the Son of God manifested, that he might destroy the works of the devil"; * and he said, "I am come that they might have life, and that they might have it more abundantly."† At this time the Gospels inform us of several instances in which evil spirits had not only taken possession of the minds, but had obsessed the very bodies of mankind, so much so as to endanger their physical existence. We will only advert to two examples. When Jesus went "into the country of the Gergesenes, there met him two possessed with devils, coming out of the tombs, exceeding fierce, so that no man might pass by that way"; these were cast out, and they entered into a herd of swine, which ran "into the sea, and perished in the waters." ‡ Again, one of the multitude brought unto Jesus his son, who had a dumb spirit, "and when he saw him, straightway the spirit tare him, and he fell on the ground, and wallowed foaming;—and ofttimes it cast him into the fire, and into the water, to destroy him."§ These facts, taken in connection with the circumstance that the Lord was manifested to destroy such works—they being phenomena which were peculiar to the time, and of considerable prevalence—(for the Apostles state, as one of the consequences of their ministry, that

---

* 1 John iii. 8. † John x. 10.
‡ Matt. viii. 28-32. § Mark ix. 17-22.

the devils were subject to them through the Lord's name)— afford us historical evidence of an unquestionable kind that infernal influences were capable of compassing even the natural death of society, when it had voluntarily sunk into perversities and lusts. That which can be done to an individual can be done to a multitude. But by the redemption that the Lord effected, and by the glorification of his humanity, which was accomplished in the process of that work, a safe provision and complete barrier have been raised against the return of such a state of things, and therefore it is that they are happily not within the experiences of Christian society. It was, however, in some measure realized by society at the period of the Lord's coming, and we refer to this circumstance merely to illustrate the idea of direful persuasions opening in man channels for the reception of that malignant and suffocating influx, by which we conceive the antediluvians to have perished. Surely every one may see that when men are so separated from the Divine principle that they possess no spiritual life therefrom, but are merely influenced by sensual impulses, similar to those of beasts, no society can be formed and governed by the laws of use and order; because when men are of such a nature, and so without heavenly guidance, they become, as it were, insane, and rush openly into the commission of every evil, one against another, acquiring stimulus thereto from an infernal origin, in which case the human race must perish.

This, indeed, is going directly to the root of the catastrophe; but, upon more general principles, it must be conceded that "evil will slay the wicked," * at least as to all spiritual hopes and happiness; hence it is easy to conceive that this, when manifested in the life with unrestrained malignity, must bring about the physical destruction of the society among whom it prevails. The truth of this idea is known and acknowledged. Most persons are acquainted with cases in which individuals have brought on their own death by the pursuit of criminal indulgences. How many of our race perish annually from drunkenness and other enormities! How much more extensive would this calamity become, if it were not for counteracting influences! That which can sweep away an individual may carry

* Psa. xxxiv. 21.

off a community. Has it not done so? What says authentic history upon the subject? It shows us many cities, yea, whole nations, that have been swept from the map of existence, and of which nothing remains but the scanty vestiges of ruin, to mark their profligacy, or chronicle their end! How many lands have been depopulated through the depravity and ignorance of their inhabitants! How has Nineveh become a waste, and Babylon a desolation! The prophets answer, and say it was through the wickedness of their inhabitants.* The blinding of their eyes, and the hardening of their hearts, having led them to a forgetfulness of God, and a disregard for their neighbour, also opened out innumerable channels for the admission of principles and the performance of acts by which destruction came. While, then, we hold that the flood consisted in the direful influences of evil and false principles, by which the light of religion was extinguished, and the emotions of virtue destroyed; we also conceive that these principles were productive of characteristics and proceedings which were dangerous to personal safety; and consequently, that they were, as external causes, the means of sweeping from natural existence a peculiarly profligate and abandoned race. The manner in which these causes operated to dissolve society and terminate its existence was, doubtless, very various. Evil is diversified in all its kinds; and it displays its malignity in a multitude of ways, all of which are more or less fatal in their results to the people who walk therein. The narrative, however, does not deal with external causes; it treats of those that are primary in such results; consequently, of man having ceased to live according to the order of heaven, and, thereby, of his having become the subject of temptations, in which his moral sentiments and religious life were finally overwhelmed. Hereby "all in whose nostrils was the breath of life, of all that was in the dry land, died." † Those in whose nostrils *was* the breath of life were the people who had constituted the most ancient Church during the time of its integrity. Of them it is written, the Lord God breathed into their nostrils the breath of life"; ‡ which means, the im-

---

* See Jer., chaps. xlix. and l.; and Nahum throughout.

† Gen. vii. 22. ‡ Gen. ii. 7.

plantation of love, and faith originating therein: these principles, as we have seen, were successively abandoned and destroyed, and now the seeds thereof, which had been hereditarily transmitted to the last posterity of the antediluvian community, were by them entirely extinguished. Wherefore it is said, everything died in whose nostrils *was* the breath of lives: and hence it follows, that all who were in the dry land perished, because thereby are represented those who had become, as it were, parched with lusts, and in whom there were none of the remains of celestial and spiritual life. Everything of this character passed away, and thereby the cessation of the people with whom it took place. "Noah only remained *alive*, and they that *were* with him in the ark":* the reason is, as previously intimated, because the Noachic people found grace in the eyes of the Lord, and were righteous in his sight. The *grace* denoted that they retained some truth; their righteousness shows that they possessed some good: and these were the principles which enabled them to erect the ark, collect the fowls and beasts, rise above the waters of temptation, and receive the covenant which God established, for the purpose of commencing an entirely new dispensation of Divine things, as the Adamic or most ancient Church had, after innumerable corruptions, divisions, and perversities, passed away in the manner we have attempted to describe.

Here we terminate our exposition of the most remarkable events recorded in the first seven chapters of Genesis. We have endeavoured to show that they were not written to express that literal sense which they are commonly understood to do. We have regarded the history as purely figurative, not only because such a mode of expressing spiritual and intellectual subjects was common to mankind in the early ages of enlightened society, but also because such a method of indicating internal and spiritual things of the Church is in agreement with the Divine style of communication evinced throughout the whole Word; and likewise because this kind of composition is eminently adapted to portraying the interior principles of men, by means of appropriate representatives and correspondences chosen from

* Gen. vii. 23.

the world of nature—the figures employed not being the analogies of human rhetoric, but types of the Divine selection.

This being the ground we have taken for the explanations, we have not hesitated to produce many of the difficulties which obviously surround the common views of the subjects discussed, because we were desirous of showing to those who hold such views, the inconsistencies they have to encounter, and the contradictions they must believe, if they will retain them.

These difficulties, however, are not to be understood as being urged against the narratives themselves; but only against that which we conceive to be their erroneous interpretation. We repeat this, that the reader, in drawing his conclusions, may discriminate between our belief in the Divine character of the documents themselves, and our disbelief of those opinions which they have been supposed to express. The path we have pursued in this investigation effectually avoids all their difficulties, and maintains throughout a rational consistency and religious character.

We have seen that those early portions of the Word treat of the rise and perfection of the most ancient Church, which was pre-eminently MAN, in the enjoyment of the intelligence of love. We next contemplated the existence of the sensual principle, pointing out the nature of its seduction, and the decline of the people. Then, in the people represented by Cain and Abel, we saw the separation of faith from charity, with their respective characteristics; also the death of charity, by which faith became a fugitive and a vagabond principle in the Church; and that this likewise perished in the time of the first Lamech. Afterwards it was shown that those histories reveal the rise of heresies in a variety of forms, and disclose the enormities of the imagination and heart of which they were productive among mankind; and, finally, that they announce an awful inundation of false persuasions and evil influences, by which all branches of society were overwhelmed, with the exception of the Noachic people, who were saved from the catastrophe, because they resisted and conquered those temptations in which others fell and perished.

The narrative, therefore, is a consecutive history of the states experienced by the most distinguished Church which has ever existed upon this earth, during the process of its rise, fall, and extinction—the extinction of a celestial Church, whose primeval name was Adam, and which was succeeded by another, of a spiritual quality, under the appellation of Noah.

Being deeply impressed with the truth of these views, we venture humbly to urge them upon the serious attention of the reader, and earnestly solicit him to think carefully and religiously upon them, for the purpose of adopting some rational and consistent conclusion; for, most certainly, a period is advancing in which will take place a complete revolution and thorough change of popular opinion concerning the meaning of those early portions of the Lord's most holy Word. May that change be effected under the Divine influence, and mankind have their eyes opened to the enjoyment of a purer light, and thus may they intellectually appreciate the wonderful things contained in His law.

THE END.

APPENDIX.

THE SCIENCE OF CORRESPONDENCES.

It is not known at the present day what correspondence is. That it is not known is from several causes. The primary cause is that man has removed himself from heaven by the love of self and of the world, for he who looks to himself and the world above all things, regards only things which are of the world, because these gratify the external senses and delight the natural inclinations, and pays no regard to spiritual things, which gratify the internal senses and delight the rational mind; wherefore they cast these things from them, saying that they are too high to be objects of thought. The ancients did otherwise; to them the science of correspondences was the chief of all sciences; by that, also, they acquired intelligence and wisdom; and those who were of the church had by it communication with heaven, for the science of correspondences is an angelic science. The most ancient people, who were celestial men, thought from correspondence itself, like the angels; therefore, also, they spoke with angels, and the Lord often appeared to them and instructed them. But at this day that science is so entirely lost that it is not known what correspondence is.

Now, because without a perception of what correspondence is nothing can be known in light concerning the spiritual world, nor concerning its influx into the natural, nor even what the spiritual principle is in respect to the natural; nor can anything be known in light concerning the spirit of man, which is called the soul, and concerning its operation in the body, nor concerning the state of man after death; therefore it is to be told what is correspondence and what is its quality.

The whole natural world corresponds to the spiritual world, not only the natural world in general, but in every particular;

wherefore, whatever exists in the natural world from the spiritual, that is said to be correspondent. It is to be known that the natural world exists from the spiritual world, altogether as an effect from its efficient cause. What is called the natural world is all that extense which is under the sun, and receives from it heat and light, and the things that thence subsist belong to that world; but the spiritual world is heaven, and to that world belong all the things which are in the heavens.

Because man is a heaven and also a world in the least form after the image of the greatest, therefore there is with him a spiritual world and a natural world. The interiors, which are of his mind and which have reference to the understanding and will, constitute his spiritual world; and the exteriors, which are of his body and which bear reference to his senses and actions, constitute his natural world. Whatever, therefore, exists in his natural world,—that is, in his body,—and its senses and actions, from his spiritual world,—that is, from his mind, understanding, and will,—is called correspondent.

What the quality of correspondence is may be seen in man from his face. In the face which has not been taught to dissemble, all the affections of the mind present themselves visibly in a natural form as in their type; hence the face is called the index of the mind. In like manner, the things which are of the understanding are sensibly manifested in the speech, and the things which are of the will in the gestures of the body. Those things, therefore, which are done in the body, whether in the face or in the speech or in the gestures, are called correspondences.

There is also a correspondence of man with heaven, and from that correspondence he subsists; for man does not subsist from any other source than from heaven. Heaven is distinguished into kingdoms, one of which is called the celestial kingdom and the other the spiritual kingdom. The celestial kingdom in general corresponds to the heart and to all things in the body that refer to the heart, and the spiritual kingdom to the lungs and to all things in the body that refer to them. The heart and the lungs also constitute two kingdoms in man: the heart reigns there by the arteries and veins, and the lungs by the nerves and moving fibres, both of them in every force and action.

In every man, in his spiritual world, which is called his spiritual man, there are also two kingdoms: one of the will and the other of the understanding. The will reigns by the affections of good, and the understanding by the affections of truth. These kingdoms also correspond to the kingdoms of the heart and the lungs in the body. The case is similar in the heavens: the celestial kingdom is the will-principle of heaven, in which kingdom the good of love bears rule, and the spiritual kingdom is the intellectual principle of heaven, and in that kingdom truth bears rule; these are what correspond to the functions of the heart and lungs in man. It is from that correspondence that *heart* in the Word signifies the *will*, and also the good of love; and that the breath of the *lungs* signifies the *understanding* and the truth of faith: hence also it is that the affections are ascribed to the heart, although in reality they are not there seated nor thence derived.

It is now to be shown that all things of the earth and of the world are correspondences. All things of the earth are distinguished into three kinds, which are called kingdoms—namely, the animal kingdom, the vegetable kingdom, and the mineral kingdom. Those things which are in the animal kingdom are correspondences in the first degree, because they live; those which are in the vegetable kingdom are correspondences in the second degree, because they only grow; those which are in the mineral kingdom are correspondences in the third degree, because they neither live nor grow. The correspondences in the animal kingdom are living creatures of various kinds, both those which walk and creep upon the earth and those which fly in the air. The correspondences in the vegetable kingdom are all things which grow and bloom in gardens, forests, fields, and plains. The correspondences in the mineral kingdom are the more noble and the baser metals, precious stones and those not precious, the earths of various kinds, and also waters. Besides these things those are also correspondences which by human industry are prepared from them for use, as food of every kind, garments, houses, edifices, and the like.

The things which are above the earth, as the sun, the moon, the stars, and also those which are in the atmosphere, as clouds, mists, rain, lightnings, thunders, are also correspondences.

The things which proceed from the sun and its presence and absence, as light and shade, heat and cold, are also correspondences; and likewise those which, hence, exist in succession, as the seasons of the year, which are called spring, summer, autumn, winter, and the times of the day, as morning, noon, evening, night.

In a word, all things that exist in nature, from the least to the greatest, are correspondences. That they are correspondences is, because the natural world with all things in it exists and subsists from the spiritual world, and both from the Divine Being. All that is correspondent which from nature exists and subsists from Divine order. The Divine good, which proceeds from the Lord, makes Divine order; it begins from Him, proceeds from Him, through the heavens successively into the world, and is there terminated in ultimates. The things which are according to order there are correspondences, and all things are according to order there which are good and perfect for use, for every good is good according to use.

But what the correspondence of spiritual things with natural is, may be illustrated by examples. The animals of the earth correspond to affections; the gentle and useful to good affections, the fierce and useless to evil affections. Specifically cows and oxen correspond to affections of the natural mind; sheep and lambs to the affections of the spiritual mind; but winged animals, according to their species, correspond to the intellectual things of each mind. Hence it is that various animals, as cows, oxen, rams, she-goats, he-goats, he-lambs and she-lambs, and also pigeons and turtle-doves, in the Israelitish Church, which was a representative church, were applied to holy uses, and from them were made sacrifices and burnt-offerings; for they correspond, in that use, to spiritual things, which were understood in heaven according to correspondences. The reason why animals according to their kinds and species are affections is because they live, and everything has life from no other source than from affection and according to it; hence every animal has innate knowledge according to the affection of its life. Man, also, is similar to them as to his natural man, and therefore he is compared to them in common discourse, as, if gentle, he is called a sheep or a lamb; if fierce, he is called a bear or a wolf; if cunning, a fox or a serpent, and so forth.

There is a similar correspondence with the things of the vegetable kingdom. A garden in general corresponds to heaven, in relation to its intelligence and wisdom; wherefore, heaven is called the garden of God and paradise. Trees, according to their species, correspond to the perceptions and knowledges of good and truth, from which are derived intelligence and wisdom. Wherefore, the ancients, who were in the science of correspondences, had their holy worship in groves; and hence, also, it is that, in the Word, trees are so often named, and heaven and the church and man are compared to them, as to the vine, the olive, the cedar, and others, and the good works which they do are compared to fruits. The food, also, which is from them, especially that which is from seed raised in fields, corresponds to the affections of good and truth, because these nourish spiritual life as earthly food nourishes natural life. And hence bread, in general, corresponds to the affections of all good, because that, more than the rest, sustains life, and also because by bread is meant all food. On account of this correspondence, also, the Lord calls Himself the Bread of Life; and, for the same reason, bread was in holy use in the Israelitish Church, for it was set upon the table in the tabernacle and called "the bread of faces," and, also, all Divine worship which was celebrated by sacrifices and burnt-offerings was called bread.

On account of that correspondence, also, the holiest thing of worship in the Christian Church is the Holy Supper, in which there is given bread and wine.

In what manner the conjunction of heaven with the world is effected by correspondence shall be briefly told. The kingdom of the Lord is a kingdom of uses; on this account the universe was so created and formed by the Divine Being that uses may everywhere be clothed with such things as may be instrumental in presenting them, in act or in effect, first in heaven, and next in the world; thus, by degrees and successively, even to the ultimates of nature. Hence it is evident that the correspondence of things natural with things spiritual, or of the world with heaven, is effected by uses, and that uses conjoin them; and that the forms with which uses are clothed are so far correspondences, and so far conjunctions, as they are forms of uses. In the world of nature, in its triple kingdom, all things which there exist according to order are forms of uses, or effects formed from use for use; wherefore, the things that are there, are correspondences. With respect to man,—as far as he lives according to Divine order, thus as far as in love to the Lord and in charity towards the neighbour—so far his acts are uses in form, and are correspondences by which he is conjoined to heaven; to love the Lord and the neighbour is to perform uses. Further, it is to be known that it is man by means of whom the natural world is conjoined with the spiritual, or that he is the medium of conjunction; for in him, as before shown, there is a natural world and there is a spiritual world: wherefore, as far as man is spiritual, so far he is a medium of conjunction, but, so far as he is merely natural and not spiritual, so far he is not a medium of conjunction. Still, there continues, without man as a medium, a Divine influx into the world, and also into those things which are from the world with man, but not into his rational principle.

As all things which are according to Divine order correspond to heaven, so all things which are contrary to Divine order correspond to hell. The things which correspond to heaven have all reference to good and truth; those which correspond to hell, to evil and falsity.

It was said above that the spiritual world, which is heaven, is conjoined to the natural world by correspondences, hence by means of correspondences there is given to man communication with heaven. For the angels of heaven do not think from natural things, as man does; wherefore, when man is in the knowledge of correspondences, he can be together with the angels as to the thoughts of his mind, and thus be conjoined to them as to his spiritual or internal man. In order that there might be conjunction of heaven with man, therefore, the Divine Word was written by pure correspondences; for all and each of the things which are there correspond. Wherefore, if man were acquainted with correspondences, he would understand the Word as to its spiritual sense, and thence it would be given him to know arcana, nothing of which he sees in the sense of the letter. For in the Word there is a literal sense and there is a spiritual sense. The literal sense consists of such things as are in the world, but the spiritual sense of such things as are in the heavens; and, because the conjunction of heaven with the world is by correspondences, therefore such a Word has been given, that everything in it, even to an iota, corresponds.

I have been instructed that the most ancient people on our earth, who were celestial men, thought from correspondences themselves, and the natural things of the world that were before their eyes served them as means of so thinking; and because they were such, they were consociated with the angels of heaven and spake with them, and thus by them heaven was conjoined with the world. On this account that time was called the Golden Age, concerning which it is also said by the ancient writers that the inhabitants of heaven dwelt with men, and had intercourse with them as friends with friends. But after their time there succeeded those who thought not from correspondences themselves, but from the science of correspondences; there was conjunction of heaven also then, but not so intimate. This time was what is called the Silver Age. Afterwards those succeeded who, indeed, knew correspondences, but did not think from the knowledge of them because they were only in natural good, and not, like the former, in spiritual good. The time of these was called the Copper or Brazen Age. After their times man became successively external, and at length merely corporeal, and then the science of correspondences was altogether lost, and with it the knowledge of heaven and of most things relating to heaven. That they named those ages from gold, silver, and copper was also from correspondence, since gold from correspondence signifies celestial goodness, in which the most ancient people were; silver, spiritual good, in which were the ancients that succeeded them; and copper, natural good, in which their next descendants were; but iron, from which the last age was named, signifies hard truth without good.

ORIGIN OF IDOLATRY.

The idolatries of the Gentile nations, in ancient times, had their origin in the science of correspondences. For all things which appear upon the earth correspond, not only trees, but also beasts and birds of every kind, and also fishes and other things. With the ancients there was a knowledge of this science, and it was the chief science among the wise. It was cultivated especially by the Egyptians, and hence their hieroglyphics. From that science they knew what every animal represented and signified, also what was signified by trees of every kind, and what by mountains, hills, rivers, fountains, and what by the sun, moon, and stars. By means of that science they had also the knowledge of spiritual things, since these, which constitute angelic wisdom, were the origin of those representatives in nature. Now, because all their worship was representative, consisting of mere correspondences, therefore they held their worship upon mountains and hills, and likewise in groves and gardens, for gardens and groves signify wisdom and intelligence, and every particular tree something of these, as the olive, the good of love; the vine, truth from that good; the cedar, rational good and truth; mountains and hills signified the heavens. For the same reason they consecrated fountains, and turned their faces to the rising sun in their adorations; moreover, they made sculptured horses, oxen, calves, lambs, and also birds, fishes, and insects, and set them in their houses and elsewhere, in their order, according to their correspondence with the spiritual things of the church which they represented. Like things they also placed in their temples, that they might recall to mind the holy things of worship which they signified. In process of time, when the science of correspondences became obliterated, posterity began to worship the sculptured things themselves as in themselves holy, not knowing that the ancients, their fathers, did not see anything holy in them, but merely viewed them as, by the law of correspondence, representing and signifying holy things. From this origin sprang the idolatries that filled the whole world, not only Asia and the neighboring islands, but Africa and Europe.

THE GRECIAN MYTHOLOGY DERIVED FROM THE SCIENCE OF CORRESPONDENCES.

How much the ancients excelled the moderns in intelligence may be manifest from this, that the former knew to what things in heaven many things in the world correspond, and hence what they signified; and this was known not only to those who were of the church, but also to those who were out of the church, as to the inhabitants of Greece, the most ancient of whom describe things by significatives, which at this day are called fabulous because they are altogether unknown. That the ancient Sophi possessed the knowledge of such things is evident from this, that they described the origin of intelligence and wisdom by a winged horse, which they called Pegasus, and his breaking open with his hoof a fountain, at which were nine virgins, and this upon a hill: for they knew that by a horse was signified the intellectual principle; by his wings the spiritual; by hoofs, truth in the lowest degree, which is the basis of intelligence; by virgins, the sciences; by hill, unanimity and, in the spiritual sense, charity; and so with the rest. But such things at this day are among those that are lost.

THE FOUR CHURCHES.

On this earth there have been many Churches, one after another; for where the human race is given, there a church is given; for heaven, which is the end of the creation, is from the human race, and no one can come into heaven unless he is in the two universals of the Church, which are to acknowledge a God and to live well; hence it follows that there have been Churches on this earth from the most ancient time down to the present. These Churches are described in the Word, but not historically, except the Israelitish and Jewish Church, before which there were yet many; and the latter are only described there by the names of nations and persons, and by a few things concerning them. The Most Ancient Church is described by Adam and his wife, Eve. The following Church, which is to be called the Ancient Church, is described by Noah and his three sons, and by the posterity from them; this was large, and extended through many kingdoms of Asia, which were the Land of Canaan within and beyond the Jordan, Syria, Assyria and Chaldæa, Mesopotamia, Egypt, Arabia, Tyre, and Sidon. That that Church was in these kingdoms is evident from various things that are related concerning them in the prophetical parts of the Word. But that Church was remarkably changed by Heber, from whom arose the Hebrew Church; in this, worship by sacrifices was first instituted. From the Hebrew Church sprang the Israelitish and Jewish Church, which was solemnly instituted for the sake of the Word, which was written out there. These four Churches are understood by the statue seen by Nebuchadnezzar in a dream, the head of which was of pure gold, the breast and arms of silver, the belly and thighs of brass, and the legs and feet of iron and clay. Nor is anything else understood by the golden, silver, brazen, and iron ages mentioned by the ancient writers. That the Christian Church succeeded the Jewish is known.

That all those Churches, in process of time, decreased even to the end, which is called their consummation, may also be seen from the Word. The consummation of the Most Ancient Church, which was caused by eating of the tree of knowledge, by which is signified the pride of one's own intelligence, is described by the deluge. The consummation of the Ancient Church is described by various devastations of the nations treated of in the historical as well as the prophetical Word, especially by the casting out of the nations from the land of Canaan by the children of Israel. The consummation of the Israelitish Church is understood by the destruction of the temple of Jerusalem, and by the carrying away of the Israelitish people into perpetual captivity, and of the Jewish nation into Babylonia; and at length by the second destruction of the temple, and at the same time of Jerusalem, and the dispersion of that nation, which consummation is foretold in many of the prophets.

The fourth Church is the Christian, instituted by the Lord, through the evangelists and the apostles. Of this there have been two epochs—one from the time of the Lord to the Council of Nice, and the other from that Council to the present day. But this, in its progress, has been divided into three parts—the Greek, the Roman Catholic, and the Reformed; but still all these are called Christian. Besides, within each general Church there have been several particular ones, which, although they have receded, have still retained the name from the general one, as the heresies in the Christian. But the successive vastation of the Christian Church, even to its end, is described by the Lord in the twenty-fourth chapter of Matthew, and other places; and the consummation itself is described in the Apocalypse.— *From the Writings of Emanuel Swedenborg.*

INDEX.

ABEL, his mystical character admitted, 176.
Abel represents charity, 176.
Abel, what the firstlings of his flock signified, 185.
Abel, why the Lord had respect to his offering, 187.
Abel, his character and death, and inquiry respecting them, 195, 197, 198.
Adam, book of the generation of, 26.
Adam a community, 65, 66, 67.
Adam naming the creatures, 97, 98.
Adam, a help meet for him, 112.
Adam, the principles by which he was distinguished, 121.
Adam did not fall into every evil by one transgression, 131.
Adam a free people, 127.
Adam's transgression the beginning of the fall, illustrated in a note, 131.
Affections compared to beasts, 308.
Age, spiritual, 245.
Ages, great, not of individual men, 241.
Alone, it not being good for Adam to be, 108.
Animals, difficulty in collecting them into the ark, 291.
Anger no attribute of God, 150, 151.
Animals to be provided for in the ark, 291.
Animals significant, 99, 100.
Animals which Adam did not name, 103.
Appeal, concluding, 359
Antitype and type, 348
Ark, attempts to explain its arrangements, 290.
Ark, dimensions not sufficient for all the animals, 290.
Ark, requirements for the building of it, 292.
Ark and flood represent spiritual things, 294.
Ark, *tebath*, the word only used in reference to the Noachic vessel, 295.
Ark, what it represented, 296.
Ark pitched within and without, 299.
Ark, room, door, window, &c., their significance, 300, 301, 302.
Ark, entering into, by Noah and his house, 306.
Authority, its influence, 288.
Article on faith only, 169.

Beasts representative, 105.
Beasts, clean and unclean, and fowl, their signification, 306, 307, 308, 310.
Beasts which entered into the ark, and those on the holy mountain, compared, 311.
Beasts which perished at the flood, 352.
Beasts, various principles of degenerate life, 353.
Beasts, wild, inordinate delights, 105, 353.
Beginning, no history of, 12.
Beginning, opinions about the meaning of the word, 9.
Beginning, the, 30.
"Bending," the language of God's book, 2.
Belief of Scripture, and belief of men's interpretation, 288.
Bible, what it was before the time of Moses, 25.
Books, ancient, produced under Divine superintendence, 26.
Book of the generation of Adam, 26.
Breath of lives, what it is, 59.
Buckland, Dr., his opinion about the purpose of the first chapter of Genesis, 6.
Building a city illustrated, 234.

Cain denotes the doctrine of faith only, 172.
Cain, his character, and talking with his brother, 195, 196.
Cain's countenance fell, 188.
Cain and Abel two classes of religious communities, &c., 163, 166.
Cain and Abel's occupations, difficulties respecting them, 164, 165.
Cain and Abel, how made acquainted with the results of their respective offerings, 187, 188.
Cain's offering of the fruit of the ground, what this was, 184.
Cain's complaint and apprehension, 205.
Cain, who he was to fear among men, 206.
Cain not to be slain, 212.
City the representative of doctrine, illustrated, 231.
Character springs from love, 58.
Chloroform objected to when first employed, 156.

Church an ark of safety, 296
Church, the state of, and the state of the mind, run parallel to each other, 296.
Church, how it should understand the early documents of Moses, 3.
Churches give birth to the things of charity and faith, 171.
Colenso, Dr., his statements the opinions of many, 4.
Colenso, Dr., cited, 318.
Commandments, ten, not promulgated to Moses for the first time, 259.
Conscience, what it is, 198.
Conception and birth of religious principles, their longevity, 166.
Corruption of the antediluvian world, peculiarity of their nature from the peculiarity of men's passions at that time, 254, 255, 256.
Corruptions, provision to be made against the recurrence of those which prevailed with the antediluvians, 260.
Covenant with Noah, 260.
Creation, Mosaic records of, give way before the discoveries of science, 1.
Creation of male and female, 50.
Crime, how men pass into it, 146.
Curious notions about the phrase, "Male and female created he them," 109.
Cush and Ethiopia, remarks concerning, 91.

Day, opinions concerning the signification of, 8.
Day, first, second, third, fourth, fifth, and sixth, 36, 40, 42, 46, 48.
Daughters, the signification of, both in a good and a bad sense, 266.
Daughters born to the sons of God, 265.
Darkness, ignorance, called Night, 37.
Death induced by criminal indulgences, 355.
Deep, fountains of the great, 340.
De la Beche cited, 318.
Deluge, mistaken opinions respecting it, 313.
Death extant before the creation of man, 8.
Depravity of the antediluvians, 278.
Discrepancies of the literal history, 50, 51.
Discrepancies about taking the beasts into the ark, 309.
Discrepancy noticed and reconciled, 98.
Distinction between the first and second chapters of Genesis, 98.
Difficulties of the literal sense admitted, 4, 5.
Difficulties cut short, how, 6.
Difficulties urged, not against the documents, but their interpretation, 358.
Diluvium, 317.
Diluvial action different in different ages, 317.

Disputes in the Church whether faith or charity is the primary principle, 174.
Divine word for all time, 191.
Document not intended to express physical truths, 5.

East, turning to the, in prayer, 75.
East, children of the, 75.
East, tradition of knowledge therefrom, 74.
Eating interdicted, what this signified; now in force, 140, 142, 144.
Earth supposed to mean only a limited district, 12.
Earth without form and void, the meaning of, 32.
Eden, the use of knowing its geographical situation considered, 68, 69.
Eden an undiscoverable spot, 69.
Eden significant of love, 71.
Eden, why said to have been in the east, 74.
Eden, the river of, without a name, 87.
Eden, to be sent from, 148.
Eden lost to all who transgress the Divine law, 148.
Enochs, two; the heresy of one, 231.
Enoch, the city of, a representation of doctrine, 232.
Enoch denotes instruction, 234.
Enoch from Seth, 250.
Enoch, book of, 251.
Enoch, his translation, 252.
Error of the doctrine of salvation by faith only, 170.
Ethiopia and Cush, remarks concerning, 91.
Eusebius, a statement of his, 6.
Eve, why so called, 170.
Evil attributed to God, why, 348, 349.
Evil influences from the infernal world when God was manifest, 354.
Evil spirits possessed mankind, 354.
Evil slays the wicked, 355.
Explanations, natural, vague, 7.

Fall, the germ of it, 111.
Fall, the Scripture account of it, 119.
Fall, Dr. A. Clarke's view of it, 119.
Fall a gradual event, how effected, 130.
Fall completed when Jesus came, 133.
Faith and charity, their characteristics, 167.
Faith, how it becomes heresy, 202.
Faith endangered when charity is dead, 211.
Faith and charity separated, 167.
Faith, what it is, not acceptable without charity, 173.
Faith essential to charity, 184, 197.
Faith destroyed by Lamech, 227.

INDEX.

Father and mother, leaving them for a wife, 116.
Fathers, the views of some of them concerning the early records of Genesis, 20.
Face the idex of emotion, 222.
Fear the result of wrong-doing, 207.
Female characteristics, 51.
Figurative language natural, 62, 63.
Figurative language did not take its rise with mythology, 2.
Firmament, expanse, why called heaven, 39.
Fishes not named by Adam, 103.
Fishes, their signification, 47.
Fishes, why spared at the time of the flood, 351, 352.
Flood, legends concerning it, 22, 23.
Flood scarcely disturbed the earth's surface, 315.
Flood, the narrative of, factitious history, 289.
Flood could not drown the fish and some fowl, 351, 352.
Flood, supposed locality of it, 319.
Flood a direful temptation, 336.
Flood, the sources of it considered, 338, 339, 340.
Floods alluded to in Scripture, 322.
Flesh, all, &c., died, 351, 352, 353.
Fountains of the great deep broken up, 316.
Fountains of the great deep, the meaning of, 338, 339, 340, 341.
Fowls, their signification in a good and bad sense, 91, 105, 353.
Freedom, its capability, 139.
Fugitive and vagabond, what they are, 203.

Garden of the Divine planting, 61.
Garden eastward in Eden, 75.
Garden in Eden signifies intelligence in love, 72, 73.
Garden, analogy between it and the mind, 85.
Genesis, first chapter of, a history of the rise and attainment of manhood, 14.
Genesis, first and second chapters, opinion as to how they should be considered, 9.
Genesis, chapters i. and ii., the peculiar distinction of the narratives, 58, 59.
Genus of the people among whom mythological history was constructed, 20.
Genus of the people among whom the antediluvian history was written, 26.
Geology, the results of its teachings, 5.
Geology, the demands of it, 8.
Geology proves the earth to have experienced great convulsions, 316.
Giants mentioned in the Scriptures, 273.
Giants as to character, 275.
Gihon, its signification, etc., 91.
God, the Spirit of, moving on the face of the waters, 33.

God operates by laws, 327.
"God said, Let us make man," considered, 50.
God ending his work, and resting, what are these, 56.
God not a destroyer, 349.
God desires that men should understand his word, 218.
God changeth not, 280.
God's providence, mistaken notions respecting it, 280.
God's interposition to preserve man, 284.
Gold, its signification, 90.
Goodness and wisdom essential to innocence, 186.
Gopher wood, opinions about it, and its signification, 297, 298.
Ground the external man, 160.
Ground, the tilling of it, 175.
Grace and righteousness of Noah, 304.
Guilt, its progress illustrated, 147.

Havilah, conjectures respecting, 90.
Help meet for Adam, 113.
Heaven and earth, the meaning of, 31.
Hiddekel, its signification, 92.
Hills, high, covered, 350.
Heresies, prolific, 226.
Heresies, their tendency, 202.
History to be traced to the first Olympiad, 21.
History of mundane things would not advance our spiritual knowledge, 63.
Human remains, 320.
Hypotheses concerning the strata of the earth, 7.
Hypotheses which have been held concerning the initial verses of Genesis, 10.

Ideas, general and particular, 254.
Illustrations from mythology concerning the origin of extraordinary persons, 116.
Immunities of Protestant Christendom, 4.
Influx, the meaning of, 343.
Inequality of the supposed curse on the land, 158.
Ingenuity employed to defend the doctrine of faith alone, 172.
Initial verses of Genesis, opinions about them, 10.
Infernal influences, 206.
Instruction by an internal dictate, and by external documents, 286.
Innocence of two kinds, 186.
Interpretation necessary, 3.
Interpretation, modern, of the flood, 321.
Inventions to remove the difficulties of the letter, 13.
Israelitish history, its commencement and design, 24.

Josephus, his opinion of some of the writings of Moses, 20.
Jesus Christ the son of God in a pre-eminent sense, 268.

Knowledge, the tree of, 77, 82, 83.
Knowledge of spiritual things the result of revelation, 143, 144.

Land, dry, 41.
Lamb, Dr., cited, 25.
Lamb the symbol of innocence, 187.
Lamech, the signification of his speech to his two wives, 227.
Lamechs, two, 230.
Law, the broken, 140.
Lawful to see the forbidden fruit, 145.
Learned criticism, facts established by, 19.
Learned men have abandoned long-standing opinions concerning the early portion of Genesis, 5.
Learned men not agreed about an explanation of the narrative of the flood, 313, 317, 318, 319.
Light before the sun, theories about it, 9.
Light, truth, called day, 37.
Lights, two great, what they are, 42, 43.
Light of stars that have reached our earth prove their great antiquity, 43.
Living things destroyed, 349, 350.
Longevity, theories respecting it, 238, 239.
Longevity of opinions, 248.
Longevity predicated of the line of Seth, 248.
Lord, the, speaks to men by an internal dictate, 198.
Lord speaking to the serpent, 154.
Lyell cited on the antiquity of man, 318, 319.
Lusts, 267, 269.
Luther's statement concerning faith and the commandments, 170.

Male characteristics, 51, 268.
Male and female to be taken into the ark, 310.
Man ignorant and innocent, 31,
Man, what by original creation, 32.
Man, how regenerated, 35.
Man viewed under different aspects, 49.
Man as an image of God, 50.
Man required to think and reason, 292.
Man blessed, 51.
Man, how he becomes spiritual, 55.
Man associated with spiritual beings, 332.
Man, Adam, a community, 65, 66, 67.
Man the author of evil, 131.
Man as man, and as a husband, 158.
Man's prerogative, 52.
Man's lowest nature, its tendency, 128.
Man's days 120 years, 241.

Mark set upon Cain, curious conjectures concerning it, 214.
Mark, Scripture instances of setting a, 215.
Marriage of affection and opinion, 225.
Marriage a Divine institution, 264.
Men called gods, 268.
Men reason in favour of what they love, 269.
Men, of renown, 277.
Men, mighty, 276.
Men, how they pass into crime, 146.
Mental characteristics of the antediluvians, 261.
Mercy of the Lord twofold, of wisdom and of love, 281, 282, 284, 285.
Metals, their signification, 298.
Mind, rise of, out of darkness, 1.
Mind a microcosm, 1.
Miller, Hugh, his theory, 11.
Mind, degrees of, 88.
Mind consists of will and understanding, 296.
Miracle, the flood nowhere so called, 330, 331.
Moral evil induces natural death, 357.
Mythological and traditional intimations of the deluge, 22.

Nakedness without shame, 116.
Name, to call by a, 106.
Names of individuals frequently express the idea of communities, 163.
Names of places significant, 85.
Names of animals founded on some of their characteristics, 103, 104.
Natural and spiritual laws, 201.
Nephilim, 275.
New states induced upon the Noachic people, 261, 262.
Noah, his grace and righteousness, 357.
Nod, the land of, its meaning illustrated, 219, 224.
Night excluded from the meaning of the term day, 38.
Numbers signify spiritual ideas, 243, 247.
Number 666 illustrated, 243.
Numbers 10 and 12, 258, 259.

Objects of Christian faith said to be mysterious, 172.
Objections urged of weight only against men's opinions, not against the documents, 27.
Offerings of Cain and Abel the first intimations of Divine worship; what those offerings were, 179.
Offerings under the ceremonial law, types, 180.
Offerings of Cain and Abel not like those of the Jewish sacrifices, 187.
Omnipotence has its laws, 328, 329.

Old views uprooted, 13.
Origen, his opinion cited, 21.

Parallelism between the flood and other events recorded in Scripture, 347.
Passages from the Word illustrating the signification of numbers, 242, 259.
Passages from the Word in which floods are mentioned which are not floods of water, 337.
Parable of Jotham illustrated, 80.
Peter's reference to the deluge considered, 347.
People of whose origin there is no history, 66.
People, why they did not seek for safety in the ark when the waters rose, 293.
Perception and its use, 250.
Peculiarity in the character of the Adamic people, 255.
Phrat, its signification, 93.
Piety necessary to Scripture interpretation, 3.
Pison, its signification, 89.
Pison and Gihon unknown, 88.
Populace, what they have been taught to believe on the subject of the deluge, 314.
Population, supposed, at the time of the flood, 321.
Pratt (Archdeacon, of Calcutta), his remark on the seventh day, 15.
Pratt's, Archdeacon, view of the designs of Scripture, 6.
Presence of the Lord, going from the, 220.
Predestination and grace, controversies about them, 234.
Predestination, correct ideas about it, 233.
Profane use of the Word, 269.
Profanation, what it is, 275.
Progress of guilt illustrated, 147.

Rain could not produce a universal inundation, 340.
Rain, passages of Scripture illustrated in which the word occurs, 343, 344.
Rain, forty days and forty nights of, 345.
Rain denotes influx, 342, 343.
Rationale of Adam's fall, 146.
Remains, what, and how their safety was provided for, 242, 258, 354.
Records, early, of Genesis cannot be history, 13.
Reasonings of criminals, 199.
Regeneration before and after the fall, 55.
Regeneration, how its early states are built up with something selfish, 299.
Religious dissensions, their origin, 190, 193.
Religion endangered by evil lives, 210.
Religion as the result of perceptions, 218.

Redemption provided against the recurrence of obsessions, 355.
Repentance and grief of man, not of the Lord, 279, 280.
Repentance and grief of the Divine mercy, 281.
Reptiles never endowed with the capability of speech, 118.
Reptiles denote grovelling pursuits, 353.
Rhind, Mr., his opinion as to rain producing the deluge, 340.
Resemblance between some points in mythology and some in the early parts of Genesis, 21.
Revelation makes us acquainted with spiritual things, 54.
Richness of ancient Egyptian soil, 159.
Rival parties in religion, their bitterness illustrated, 190.
Rivers the symbols of wisdom, 86.
Rivers, mythological intimations respecting some, 86.
River of Eden parted into four heads, 95.

Sabbath, a representative institution, 16.
Sacrifice of animals in itself irrational, 99.
Science, the facts of, inconsistent with the Mosaic cosmogony, 6.
Scriptures, two modes of speaking of them, 27, 28.
Senses inlets for certain knowledge, 122.
Senses, their deception, 129.
Sensual principle, its subtlety, 136.
Seed to be kept alive, 310.
Sects in the Adamic Church illustrated, 229.
Sevens and twos, 309.
Seventh day a celestial state with man, 54.
Seventh day cannot mean the seventh day in the ordinary acceptation of the word, 56.
Seventh day called the Sabbath, how it is holy, 15, 57, 58.
Seventh day, why no labour was to be done thereon, 57.
Separation of the will from the understanding, 262.
Serpent, the, and its deceptions, 118, 129.
Serpent which poured out water as a flood, 338.
Serpent, as a symbol, illustrated from history, 123, 124, 125.
Serpent, the sensual principle, illustrated, 126.
Serpents, the power to take them up and to tread upon them, 134.
Serpents which the rod of Aaron and the rods of the magicians became, 134, 135.
Serpent of brass, 135.
Seth instead of Abel, 236.
Seth significant of a new faith, 237.
Shepherd, its signification, 177.

Six days' work, epitome of its meaning, 70.
Six days' creation, what it was, 53.
Simplicity of the Word, 28.
Smith, Dr. Pye, cited, 23, 24, 319.
South, Dr., on man's understanding in paradise, 75.
Spiritual intelligence the main purpose of God's communication to men, 14.
Spirit of Lord striving, 270.
Spiritual sense of the early chapters of Genesis their only sense, 64.
Sons of God, what they are considered to have been, 263.
Sons of God seeing the daughters of men to be fair, 269.
Streams, their signification, 86.
Suffocating influx among the antediluvians, 355.
Summary of histories, 358.

Teachers of truth, builders of the city of God, 235.
Ten commandments, 259.
Temptations, their nature explained and illustrated, 333.
Temptations treated of under the figure of the flood, 332.
Theories about light before the sun, 9.
Theories of interpretation, 10, 11, 12, 13.
Thorns and thistles, what they signify, 160.
Tilling the ground, 175, 201.
Transgression produces doubts, 223.
Traditions of the deluge considered, 323.
Tradition and science do not afford any materials for explaining the flood to have been a natural phenomenon, 326.
Trees of the garden, opinions concerning them, 76.
Trees, the general signification of, 78.
Trees of life and knowledge, 77, 82, 83.
Tree of life still extant, 84.
Type and antitype, 348.

Understanding and will separated, 169.
Universal destruction of some sort intended to be described by the deluge, 314.

Universality of the flood relinquished by scholars before geology became a science, 319.
Use of knowing where Eden was; 68, 69.

Various principles in man, 120.
Vengeance to be taken of those who slew Cain, 211.
Vegetables not named by Adam, why, 104.
Ventilation of the ark, difficulties concerning it, 290.
Vision of dry bones, 115.
Volcanoes extinct, ancient, in the south of France, 318.

Waters gathered together, what, 40.
Waters denote knowledges, 40.
Waters that become seas, 41.
Waters commanded to bring forth creatures that have life, 46.
Wisdom communicated by an internal dictate, 96.
Wiseman, Dr., cited, 23.
Wise and friendly character of revelation, 29.
Wicked, the, can be clever, 209.
Wife of Cain, 225.
Will and understanding separated, 169.
Will, how it became a lust, 278.
Wives, the choice of, 264.
Windows of heaven, 339, 340, 341, 342.
Woman's desire towards her husband, 156.
Woman the type of affection, 225.
Woman the selfhood of the man, 157.
Woman, the multiplication of her sorrows in conception, 150, 155.
Words, their signification, 298.
Word for all time and all men, 219.
Word of God a work of God, 289.
Words in the Bible have a signification frequently different from their grammatical meaning, 2.
Worship, its acceptance and rejection, 189.
Writing, different styles of, 1.

Years and numbers, 246.
Youth, spiritual, 245.

The Church's One Foundation.

By REV. B. F. BARRETT.

Price, 75 cents.

The New York *Independent* says of it:

"These sermons will appeal to a wide company of readers outside of the New Church, to whose ministry the author belonged. They are gentle and catholic in spirit, take a strong hold on the reader's conscience and in his relations to present duty, and are composed in an attractive literary style."

The *Kingdom* says of it:

"This volume of sermons by an eminent minister of the New Church (Swedenborgian) is one of the most spiritually and practically helpful which has come to our table.

"There are many who have an entirely false understanding of the teachings of Emanuel Swedenborg, and think that he was intent mainly on setting forth his ideas concerning the heavenly state. Such persons should read this little volume."

The *New Unity* says of it:

"The dedication of this book expresses the spirit of the man who preached the sermons. It reads: 'To all God's children, of every faith and every creed, and to those also who as yet have found no faith and no creed to satisfy them, this volume is affectionately dedicated.'

"They are simple, direct, and strong expressions of what truths the preacher prepared for his own people when he was in the pastorate. Besides having a value of their own, they are a help to the understanding of the influence of Swedenborg's teachings over a great and free mind. . . ."

The *Church Union* says of it:

"Swedenborg's position is now well established as one who has helped, more than any other man, perhaps, in preparing the world for a rational, as opposed to a scholastic, view of Christianity. The key to his teachings is afforded by this sentence from his pen, which he reiterated and illustrated in a thousand ways: '*All religion has relation to the life, and the life of religion is to do good.*'

"Mr. Barrett's sermons are an unfolding and illustration of the same great truth. . . . His style is earnest, direct, and clear. Among all the volumes of sermons that are now being published, it will be difficult to find any that are more truly edifying—that is, helpful to the spiritual life—than these."

SWEDENBORG PUBLISHING ASSOCIATION,
GERMANTOWN, PA.

The Word and Its Inspiration

Can be procured for $1.00 at the following places (it will be sent by mail for the same price):

SWEDENBORG PUBLISHING ASSOCIATION,
42 West Coulter St., Germantown, Pa.

NEW CHURCH BOOK ROOM,
16 Arlington St., Boston, Mass.

NEW CHURCH BOOK ROOM,
3 West 29th St., New York, N. Y.

NEW CHURCH BOOK ROOM,
2129 Chestnut St., Philadelphia, Pa.

WESTERN NEW CHURCH UNION,
901-902 Steinway Hall, Chicago, Ill.

From Different Points of View.

Price, 50 cents.

An English Reviewer says of this book:

"We heartily and confidently commend this book as containing a forcible and logical presentation of New Church truth; as encouraging independence of thought and action; and as promoting *a bold, comprehensive, affirmative Christianity of a thoroughly practical and social nature.*"

The *Literary News* says of it:

"It presents in an interesting manner the leading features of the New Church teaching as distinguished from that of other churches. The presentation of New Church truths is logical and forcible. It points out the encouragement this church gives to independence of thought and action."

The *New Unity* says of it:

"This little book not only gives a glimpse of a great soul and an interesting life, but helps one to understand more fully the religious movements of our times. No one can fully understand the new orthodoxy without understanding something of the influence of Swedenborg in the modern pulpit; an influence greater and more extended than any man unacquainted with the facts is willing to admit."

The *Church Union* says of it:

"This is at once an interesting sketch of an interesting life, and a partial exposition of the spiritual truths to the elucidation of which the life was ardently consecrated. The Swedenborgian philosophy has had many able exponents, but none more able and useful than Mr. Barrett. Underneath all his writings (which were many and varied) there was one continual purpose—namely, to show that Swedenborg never intended or expected that his philosophy would become the basis of a new sect, but that it would permeate and influence the religious thinking of all classes of Christians. It has done so to an extent that can not be measured or imagined, and Mr. Barrett's untiring labors probably contributed more than those of any other preacher and writer to this result."

The Chicago *Tribune* says of it:

"It will amply repay any reader who desires acquaintance with a beautiful and little understood doctrine, or with a character which is in itself the best exemplar of what this doctrine may result in when carried from precept to practice."

Light on the Problems of Life and Death.

BY

REV. J. M. SHEPHERD.

Price, 25 cents; postage, 3 cents.

A Methodist minister says of it:

"I have read with *intense interest* 'Light on the Problems of Life and Death.' It is characterized by mental and spiritual virility and must impart its life to others."

A Baptist minister says of it:

"To every seeker after truth it will furnish interesting and profitable reading."

SWEDENBORG PUBLISHING ASSOCIATION,
GERMANTOWN, PA.

Kindly Light in Prayer and Praise.

BY

PASTOR QUIET.

Price, 60 cents; 8 cents postage.

WHAT SOME OF ITS READERS SAY OF IT.

FRANCES E. WILLARD said of it:

"If all of us could really hold these thoughts steadily, we should find ourselves so panoplied that no harm could ever reach us. It seems to me one might well afford to sell all and buy this blessed immunity. . . . A sweet hopeful book like this is the best medicine for the spirit in a sorrowful experience."

THEODORE F. SEWARD says of it:

"Verse and prose are full of aspiration and inspiration. Concerning the style, it may be said to have the quaintness of George Herbert and the devotional spirit of Thomas à Kempis, combined with the scientific thought of the Nineteenth Century."

PROFESSOR NATHANIEL SCHMIDT says of it:

"It is like the ebb and flow of the tide, like the song of the bird and its echo. There is so much of deep and genuine religious life in this book that every man who looks to the fostering and sound development of the religious impulse as the chief means of lifting mankind again, will hail it with delight. It is eminently a book for the seeking soul and for the weary heart."

A Presbyterian minister says of it:

"It is a delightful book from the twentieth century's Thomas à Kempis."

The *New Unity* says of it:

"In so effective and winning a manner does the author entice us along the upward path that it is a little hard to follow his advice and lay the book aside after reading one meditation, taking the thought in that single one to ponder upon, and leaving the rest for another quiet time.

"The opening poem and many of the others are simply classics of their kind, worthy of being classed with Faber's Hymns, and fit to be sung in any sanctuary, from that in the humblest human heart to the loftiest cathedral built by man."

The *Outlook* says of it:

"A book of meditation and devotion, written with genuine spiritual insight."

LEAFLETS.

No. 1, Spiritual Recompense; 2, Hell-Fire—What is it? 3, True Charity; 4, Ends and Uses; 5, The Use of Prayer; 6, The Life of Religion; 7, The Higher Life; 8, The New Birth; 9, Children after Death; 10, The New Church; 11, The Divine Trinity; 12, Swedenborg; 13, Swedenborg's Writings; 14, Catholicity; 15, Marriage and the Sexes; 16, Key to the Spiritual Sense; 17, The Church that is to Be; 18, What Can I Do?—I am Poor. Price, 8 cents a set, three sets for twenty cents.

Address THE SWEDENBORG PUBLISHING ASSOCIATION,
Germantown, Philadelphia, Pa.

GOD WINNING US.

BY

REV. CLARENCE LATHBURY.

Price, 40 cents.

A clear and simple statement of Our Father's method of dealing with His children, which, if carefully considered, will prove most helpful in teaching us how to deal with our children and with each other.

Some of its chapters are:

God Accommodating Himself to Us . . . . (Incarnation)
God Winning Us . . . . (Atonement)
God Opening Our Eyes . . . . (Faith)
God Growing in Us . . . . (Regeneration)
God Acting Through Us . . . . (Religion)
God Caring for Us . . . . (Providence)

HELPFUL PAMPHLETS.

"**THE CHURCH THAT IS TO BE.**" A Pastor's plea for a broader religion. Price, 1 cent; 20 copies 10 cents.

"**THE LIBERAL MINISTER'S PLACE.**" Price, 2 cents; 30 cents per 100.

"**A LOVE LETTER.**" A plea for only the Saviour's requirements for full Christian fellowship. Price, 2 cents; 30 cents per 100.

"**CHEERFULNESS A RELIGIOUS DUTY.**" Price, 3 cents.

"**TO MY BISHOP.**" Part of a letter written by a priest of the Protestant Episcopal Church. Price, 3 cents.

"**THE ONLY INTERPRETATION OF THE BIBLE,**" which deprives the Higher Criticism of all power to disturb, and proves the book to be *The Word of God*, consistent in every part and worthy of Divine authorship. Price, 3 cents.

SWEDENBORG, PUBLISHING ASSOCIATION,

GERMANTOWN, PA.

www.ingramcontent.com/pod-product-compliance
Lightning Source LLC
Chambersburg PA
CBHW022116290426
44112CB00008B/698